AUSTRALIA IN THE INTERNATIONAL LEGAL SYSTEM

What impact has Australia had on international law and how significant is that impact for the international legal system? This collection of essays delves into the history of Australia's interactions with international law and considers how its people have shaped the contemporary practice of that law. It explores key issues such as the country's imperial and settler past. It assesses how Australians have contributed to institutions such as the ICJ, the UN and the Commonwealth. It gives a fascinating insight into the impact of international law on a domestic legal system and the complex and multifaceted nature of that relationship. Scholars from across the international spectrum, whether in the field of law, politics or history, will welcome this erudite and engaging work.

Australia in the International Legal System

From Empire to the Contemporary World

Edited by
Madelaine Chiam
and
Alison Duxbury

•HART•
OXFORD • LONDON • NEW YORK • NEW DELHI • SYDNEY

HART PUBLISHING

Bloomsbury Publishing Plc

Kemp House, Chawley Park, Cumnor Hill, Oxford, OX2 9PH, UK

1385 Broadway, New York, NY 10018, USA

Bloomsbury Publishing Ireland Limited, 29 Earlsfort Terrace, Dublin 2, D02 AY28, Ireland

HART PUBLISHING, the Hart/Stag logo, BLOOMSBURY and the Diana logo are trademarks of Bloomsbury Publishing Plc

First published in Great Britain 2025

A catalogue record for this book is available from the British Library.

A catalogue record for this book is available from the Library of Congress.

Library of Congress Control Number: 2025936941

ISBN: HB: 978-1-50994-163-6
ePDF: 978-1-50994-165-0
ePub: 978-1-50994-164-3

Typeset by Compuscript Ltd, Shannon
Printed and bound in Great Britain

For product safety related questions contact productsafety@bloomsbury.com

To find out more about our authors and books visit www.hartpublishing.co.uk. Here you will find extracts, author information, details of forthcoming events and the option to sign up for our newsletters.

Foreword

Australia has a long history of engagement with and contributing to the international rule of law and the rules-based international legal order. This active involvement reflects the view of successive Australian governments that support for the rule of law and the legal order is in Australia's national interests: that it is important for Australia to engage in shaping those rules and that order to protect and further these interests –which include foreign policy, security, economic, trade, environmental, social, human rights – and to reflect our broadly Western-based values.

The international structures of the rules-based order are underpinned and forged essentially through agreements reached between states. Many of these agreements are multilateral, although some are plurilateral, trilateral and bilateral. The structures have, on the whole, been created as a result of negotiations since the end of the Second World War. As the late Allan Gyngell, "the definitive historian of Australian foreign policy",[1] mentions in his *Fear of Abandonment: Australia in the World Since 1942*,[2] which is a comprehensive history of Australia's foreign policy, *that* was the starting point for the new international order, with the negotiation of the United Nations Charter and the establishment of the United Nations. Australia was "present at the creation".[3] H.V. Evatt, as Attorney-General and Minister for External Affairs at the time, played a significant role in the negotiation of the UN Charter. So, too, did Sir Kenneth Bailey, a distinguished lawyer, who as a member of the Australian delegation contributed to the drafting of both the Charter and the Statute of the International Court of Justice.

Since the establishment of the United Nations, Australia has continued that legacy and has been actively involved in building the rules-based order in a wide range of areas, including: international humanitarian law; arms control, disarmament and non-proliferation; the law of the sea and associated agreements; international criminal law; the environment and climate change; Antarctica and the Antarctic Treaty System; and international trade.

Australia has shown over many decades that it fully respects its treaty commitments and obligations. This is demonstrated by its support for the

[1] Senator the Hon Penny Wong, Minister for Foreign Affairs, National Press Club Address, 'Australian interests in a regional balance of power', 17 April 2023.

[2] Allan Gyngell, *Fear of Abandonment: Australia in the World Since 1942* (Carlton, La Trobe University Press, 2017).

[3] To quote the title of Dean Acheson's memoirs, *Present at the Creation: My Years in the State Department* (New York, W.W. Norton and Company, 1969).

dispute resolution mechanisms which have been established by various international agreements and by its engagement with them when required.

In relation to all the agreements that have been concluded since the end of the Second World War, Australian involvement and representation has very much reflected a whole of government approach: delegations have comprised officers from the Department of Foreign Affairs and Trade and the Attorney General's Department (those two Departments, together with the Australian Government Solicitor, having tied responsibility under the Legal Services Directions for the Australian government's international law work), the Departments of Defence, Environment, Climate Change, Energy, Agriculture, Fisheries, Industry, Science, Health and Treasury at times, as well as other agencies linked to the specific subject matter being covered in the negotiations. Academics have also been included in delegations and on occasion there have been representatives from Australian States and from NGOs.

From a practitioner's perspective as someone who has been conscious over many years of the key role that the Department of Foreign Affairs and Trade has had and continues to have as the lead agency in many treaty-related negotiations, I am convinced that it is definitely in Australia's national interests to continue to work assiduously together with the Attorney-General's Department and other agencies as required, to support the rule of law and the rules-based international legal order. The Australian contribution towards this objective, when assessed by what has been achieved since the end of the Second World War, including by individuals such as the late Professor and ICJ Judge James Crawford and by Professor and current ICJ Judge Hilary Charlesworth and by other academics, has been considerable. The chapters in this book attest to this assessment. It is so important that this engagement has been recorded.

Does this contribution over many decades constitute a distinct 'Australian International Law'? I do not think that it does *per se*. However, this view does not in any way detract from the history of Australia's substantial role and input in relation to the progressive development of international law. Looking ahead, it is important, indeed imperative, from a national interests perspective, for Australia to continue to protect the rules and norms that we have been involved in creating while also engaging, as required, in the development of new areas of international law. We must also, consistent with "the Australian tradition" which we have established as a middle power and for which we are respected, continue to advocate for strict adherence to the rule of law. This is vital in these times of geo-political contestability and disregard for the international legal order as evidenced by the Russian Federation's illegal invasion of Ukraine.

Richard Rowe PSM
Former Senior Legal Adviser
Department of Foreign Affairs and Trade
May 2025

Acknowledgements

THIS EDITED COLLECTION arose out of a symposium, hosted by the Faculty of Law, La Trobe University, designed to examine Australia's relationship with international law from three perspectives: history, biography and the study of institutions. The La Trobe symposium brought together scholars and practitioners from the disciplines of international law, history and politics to explore questions of Australia's international legal history and contemporary practice of international law, and to provide accounts of some of the individuals and institutions that have influenced Australia's approaches to international law.

As often happens after symposia where interesting and exciting papers are discussed, in 2019 we reached out to a publisher (Hart) to collect these papers in an edited volume. Authors were contacted and deadlines were set. But, as every reader knows, when the COVID-19 pandemic arrived on our doorsteps people's lives were disrupted in multiple ways. Borders were closed (both international and state, in the case of Australia), cities went into lockdown, people fell ill, and many took on multiple caring responsibilities. There were new modes of working to be mastered – particularly for those involved in teaching. Despite these many challenges, our original authors stuck with this project and new authors came on board. This volume is the result of their endeavours.

Given the difficult circumstances faced by the authors, we would like to thank all for contributing to this volume – we have very much enjoyed working with you. We would also like to thank the Faculty of Law, La Trobe University, for its support of the symposium and Melbourne Law School, University of Melbourne, for providing the funding for research assistance by Ken Kiat, Dannielle Feng (in the Academic Research Service) and Rebecca Bourdreaux. We thank Ken, Danielle and Rebecca for their detailed editorial work. We also thank Ann Mills and Annabelle Burley for granting permission to use 'Black Mountain', a painting by Grace Cossington-Smith on the cover, as well as Dr Ann Stephen, Senior Curator of the University Art Collection at the University of Sydney, for providing the image of the painting. Finally, we thank Sasha Jawed from Hart Publishing for her work on this project.

Contents

Foreword ... *v*
Acknowledgements ... *vii*
Notes on Contributors ... *xi*

1. *Is there an Australian International Law?* ... *1*
   Alison Duxbury and Madelaine Chiam

PART I
AUSTRALIA AS EMPIRE

2. *Participation in the 'Gilded Ball': Australia and the Council of the League of Nations* ... *17*
   Alison Duxbury

3. *The Rise and Fall of 'a Hyphenated Condition': Australia, the British Empire and the Commonwealth* ... *41*
   Frank Bongiorno

4. *'Treat-Them-Gently-at-All-Costs-and-Please-the United Nations': The UN Trusteeship Council and Capital Punishment and Clemency in Papua and New Guinea, 1954–65* ... *59*
   Murry Chisholm

5. *Australia, Timor-Leste and International Law* ... *75*
   Clinton Fernandes

PART II
AUSTRALIA AND INSTITUTIONS

6. *Australia and the United Nations* ... *99*
   Alison Pert

7. *The Increasing Results of Indigenous Peoples' Engagement in International Law and Geopolitics* ... *125*
   Les Malezer

8. *Australia and the International Court of Justice* ... *155*
   Margaret A. Young

9. *International Law in the Attorney-General's Department: 1901–2000* 181
Henry Burmester

10. *Australian Government Practice of International Law in the Twenty-First Century* 211
Bill Campbell

11. *Ad Hoc and Arbitrary: International Criminal Law in Australian Courts* 231
Monique Cormier

PART III
AUSTRALIANS AND INTERNATIONAL LAW

12. *Child Refugees, Child Rights: Sidestepping International Law in Australian Policy-Making* 255
Jordana Silverstein

13. *'This is Our Conference': Elizabeth Reid, Second Wave Feminism and Australia's Performance of International Law in the 1970s* 273
Jon Piccini

14. *The First Australian and New Zealand Society of International Law, 1933–38* 293
Madelaine Chiam

Index 309

Notes on Contributors

Frank Bongiorno is Professor of History at the Australian National University and a Distinguished Fellow of the Whitlam Institute at Western Sydney University. He is a Fellow of the Royal Historical Society, the Academy of the Social Sciences in Australia, and the Australian Academy of the Humanities, and was Smuts Visiting Fellow in Commonwealth Studies at the University of Cambridge from 1997 to 1998. Frank's most recent book was *Dreamers and Schemers: A Political History of Australia* (Black Inc Books, 2022). He has also published articles on Australia's place in the British Empire and Commonwealth in the *Australian Journal of Politics and History*, *Irish Historical Studies* and *Australian Historical Studies*.

Henry Burmester AO KC was an Australian government lawyer from 1972 to 2009, except from 1981 to 1985 when he was at the Australian National University. He was Chief General Counsel in the Australian Government Solicitor from 1995 to 2009 and before that was Head of the Office of International Law in the Australian Attorney-General's Department from 1990 to 1995. Throughout his time as a government lawyer, he was involved particularly in law of the sea issues, International Court of Justice litigation involving Australia and the domestic implementation of international law. His chapter draws on his long personal involvement in many of the issues covered in the chapter.

Bill Campbell AO KC is an Honorary Professor of Law at the Australian National University College of Law. He was formerly General Counsel (International Law) and Head of the Office of International Law in the Australian Attorney-General's Department. In that capacity he advised successive Australian governments on all aspects of international law. He also was responsible for the conduct of Australia's litigation before international courts and tribunals. He appeared as Agent and Counsel for Australia in cases before the International Court of Justice, the International Tribunal for the Law of the Sea and arbitral tribunals. These cases include: *Whaling in the Antarctic*; *Certain Documents and Data*; the *Chagos Archipelago Advisory Opinion*; *Southern Bluefin Tuna*; and *Tobacco Plain Packaging Arbitration*. He was also Head of the Australian delegation to the Commission on the Limits of the Continental Shelf.

Madelaine Chiam is an Associate Professor at La Trobe Law School. Madelaine researches primarily in public and international law, in particular the histories of international law, the relationships between the global and the local, and the role of international law in Australian life. Her work is published in journals including the *European Journal of International Law*, the *London Review of*

International Law and the *Journal of Conflict and Security Law*. Madelaine's monograph, *International Law In Public Debate* (Cambridge University Press) was published in 2021. Madelaine is a member of the Council of the Australian and New Zealand Society of International Law and is faculty at the Harvard Law School Institute for Global Law and Policy Workshops.

Murray Chisholm completed his PhD in history at ANU in 2019 with his thesis 'Clemency and Capital Punishment in Papua New Guinea, 1954 to 1964'. He published a book with ANU Press – *Colonialism, Capital Punishment and Clemency in Papua New Guinea, 1954 to 1965* – based on his doctoral thesis. He is currently a Curriculum Officer at the Australian Capital Territory Board of Senior Secondary Studies. He has been a secondary school teacher since 1997.

Monique Cormier is an Associate Professor at Monash University Faculty of Law where she teaches criminal law and international law. Her primary research interests include jurisdiction and immunities in international criminal law and legal issues relating to nuclear non-proliferation. Her monograph *The Jurisdiction of the International Criminal Court over Nationals of Non-States Parties* was published by Cambridge University Press in 2020. Monique has a PhD from the University of Melbourne, a Master of Laws from Columbia University, and undergraduate degrees from the University of Adelaide. Monique is Treasurer of the Australian and New Zealand Society of International Law, and a member of the Board of Experts for the *Asia Pacific Journal of International Humanitarian Law*.

Alison Duxbury is a Professor at Melbourne Law School, University of Melbourne, and the President of the Australian and New Zealand Society of International Law. Alison's major teaching and research interests are in the fields of international law, international institutional law and human rights law. Her publications include: *The Participation of States in International Organisations: The Role of Human Rights and Democracy* (Cambridge University Press, 2011); a co-edited book, *Military Justice in the Modern Age* (Cambridge University Press, 2016); and a co-authored book, *Can ASEAN Take Human Rights Seriously?* (Cambridge University Press, 2019).

Clinton Fernandes is Professor of International and Political Studies at the University of New South Wales. He has published on the relationship between science, diplomacy and international law, intelligence operations in foreign policy, the political and regulatory implications of new technology and Australia's external relations more generally. His research in the Future Operations Research Group at UNSW analyses the operational environment, and the threats, risks and opportunities that military forces will face, in the 2030–50 time frame.

Les Malezer is descended on his father's side from the Gubbi Gubbi/Butchulla peoples of the Mary River and Fraser Island region of southeast Queensland

and, on his mother's side, from the Gamiliroi peoples of northwest NSW. He has worked in state and federal government departments as well as in community organisations. Les became Secretary General of the National Aboriginal Conference in 1984, joined the Royal Commission into Aboriginal Deaths in Custody in 1989, and was appointed as Executive Assistant to the Chairman of the Aboriginal and Torres Strait Islander Commission (ATSIC) in 2002. In 2010, he was elected Co-Chair of the National Congress of Australia's First Peoples. Les Malezer is well known internationally for his work on human rights and raising the profile of Indigenous Peoples in the United Nations and Commonwealth Heads of Government meetings.

Alison Pert lectures at the University of Sydney Law School in public international law, specialising in the use of force and international humanitarian law. She qualified as a barrister in London after a pupillage with Rosalyn Higgins DBE QC and has practised as a lawyer in government and the private sector in London, Papua New Guinea and Australia. She has represented Australia at international organisations including UNIDROIT and UNCITRAL, and in treaty negotiations. Her interests in the convergence of politics, international law and international relations led to her doctorate and her 2014 monograph, published by Federation Press, *Australia as a Good International Citizen*. She is also the author (with Emily Crawford) of *International Humanitarian Law*, 3rd edn (Cambridge University Press, 2024) and co-editor of the textbook *Public International Law* (Cambridge University Press, 2023).

Jon Piccini is Senior Lecturer in History at the Australian Catholic University. His research focuses on the connections between Australian and global history. Jon is the author of *Human Rights in Twentieth Century Australia* (Cambridge University Press, 2019) and *Transnational Protest, Australia and the 1960s: Global Radicals* (Palgrave Macmillan, 2016). His current projects explore the place of Australia in post-war decolonisation, and American servicepeople who took their 'R&R' leave in Sydney during the Vietnam War.

Jordana Silverstein is a Senior Research Fellow in the Peter McMullin Centre on Statelessness in the Melbourne Law School. She is the author of *Cruel Care: A History of Children at our Borders* (Monash University Publishing, 2023) and *Anxious Histories: Narrating the Holocaust in Jewish Communities at the Beginning of the Twenty-First Century* (Berghahn Books, 2015), and co-editor of *In the Shadows of Memory: The Holocaust and the Third Generation* (Vallentine Mitchell, 2016) and *Refugee Journeys: Histories of Resettlement, Representation and Resistance* (ANU Press, 2021). A cultural historian, she researches histories of statelessness, Australian child refugee policies, and Australian Jewish history, focusing on questions of belonging, nationalism, identity, historiography, emotions, sexuality and memory.

Professor Margaret A. Young FAAL is the Director of the Institute for International Law and the Humanities, Melbourne Law School, and an Australian Research Council (ARC) Future Fellow. She served as Visiting Legal Fellow at the Department of Foreign Affairs and Trade from 2019–2020. In 2016, she was the Director of Studies for public international law at the Hague Academy of International Law. She holds a PhD and LLM (Hons) from the University of Cambridge and a BA/LLB (Hons) from the University of Melbourne. Her chapter forms part of a broader ARC Discovery Project on 'The Potential and Limits of International Adjudication' (DP180101318), which was co-led by Judge Hilary Charlesworth before her election to the International Court of Justice.

1

Is there an Australian International Law?

ALISON DUXBURY AND MADELAINE CHIAM

I. INTRODUCTION

INTERNATIONAL LAW HAS long been embedded in Australian public and legal life. Recent examples from our time of writing include media reports on the 2022 Russian invasion of Ukraine and the continuing crisis in the Middle East, where the applicable treaty and customary law regimes are at the forefront of discussions.[1] Australia's commitments under the Nuclear Non-Proliferation Treaty feature in the media coverage of the Australia, United Kingdom and United States security pact (AUKUS).[2] Australia's domestic policies on climate change and refugees are frequently measured against our commitments in the Paris Agreement and the Convention Relating to the Status of Refugees and its 1967 Protocol.[3] When Australian citizen Julian Assange sought asylum in Ecuador's embassy in London, the law of diplomatic immunity was discussed extensively in reporting in Australia and elsewhere.[4] International legal practice,

[1] See, eg, 'Putin's War Crimes Case to Answer' *The Australian* (3 March 2022) 10; Sherryn Groch and Chris Zappone, 'What are war crimes and could Putin be put on trial? *Sydney Morning Herald* (24 March 2022); Riley Stuart, 'Australia Backs Landmark UN Court Ruling for Israel to Halt Rafah Offensive' (*ABC News*, 24 May 2024); Henry Ergas, 'Barbaric Hamas is No Respecter of Rules of War' *The Australian* (10 November 2023); Matthew Knott, 'Mass Pager Attacks "A Terrifying Violation of International Law"' *The Age* (19 September 2024); Lara Jakes, 'Israel Says it has a Right to Defend itself. But Does it have a Right to Invade Lebanon?' *The Age* (13 October 2024). See also M Chiam, *International Law in Public Debate* (Cambridge, Cambridge University Press, 2021).

[2] See, eg, Phillip Coorey, 'PM Hoses Down Internal Unrest But AUKUS Still Simmers' *The Australian Financial Review* (13 August 2023).

[3] Paris Agreement under the United Nations Framework Convention on Climate Change (adopted 12 December 2015, entered into force 4 November 2016) 3156 UNTS 79; Convention Relating to the Status of Refugees (adopted 28 July 1951, entered into force 22 April 1954) 189 UNTS 137; Protocol Relating to the Status of Refugees (adopted 31 January 1967, entered into force 4 October 1967) 606 UNTS 267.

[4] See, eg, Steven Viney, 'Diplomatic Asylum: How Long Can Assange Stay in the Ecuadorian Embassy, and is His Case Unique?' (*ABC News*, 19 June 2016).

previously largely the preserve of government lawyers in the Attorney-General's Department (AGD) and the Department of Foreign Affairs and Trade, has expanded to include lawyers in private practice working on interstate arbitrations and barristers appearing in the international criminal tribunals in The Hague. Australians play a significant role in many international organisations. Most prominently, Australian Judge Hilary Charlesworth, is a member of the International Court of Justice (ICJ), the first Australian woman and the third Australian (following Sir Percy Spender and James Crawford) to occupy this coveted role.[5]

The purpose of this book is to examine Australia's relationship with international law by examining Australia's legal history, for example, its place as a Dominion, as well as forwards, to Australia's practice of international law and role in the United Nations (UN) this century. The role of international law in Australia has been the subject of extensive debate, underpinned by legal and political dualism. The tensions within Australian government desires to preserve national legal and political structures while enabling interactions with the international legal system have been evident since Prime Minister Billy Hughes fought to prevent the inclusion of the racial equality clause in the Covenant of the League of Nations.[6] Previously, scholars have described Australia's approach to international law as demonstrating 'deep anxieties': that 'it has largely been ignored by the Australian public' and that its reception into Australian law 'suggests a Trojan house importing dangerous foreign values'.[7] Twenty years ago, Australia's relationship with international human rights law was described as 'Janus-faced' – Australia is a party to the major international human rights treaties, but has failed to implement all of these rights in domestic legislation.[8] However, these anxieties about international law do not appear to be felt by students in Australian law schools given the popularity of international law, and associated specialised subjects such as international human rights law, international humanitarian law, international environmental law and refugee law in undergraduate and graduate programmes.[9] A number of law schools include a compulsory unit discussing international law in their Bachelor of Laws and Juris Doctor courses, thus suggesting its relevance and importance to legal education

[5] See M Young, 'Australia and the International Court of Justice', ch 8 in this volume.

[6] See A Duxbury, 'Participation in the "Gilded Ball": Australia and the Council of the League of Nations', ch 2 in this volume.

[7] H Charlesworth et al, *No Country is an Island: Australia and International Law* (Sydney, UNSW Press, 2006) 4.

[8] H Charlesworth, *Writing in Rights: Australia and the Protection of Human Rights* (Sydney, UNSW Press, 2002) 56.

[9] I Baghoomians, E Crawford and J Mowbray, 'The Teaching of Public International Law in Australian Law Schools: 2021 and Beyond' (2022) 43 *Adelaide Law Review* 8. In 1995 Harry Reicher wrote that 'the pleasant and heartening reality is that students are enrolling in international law courses in unprecedented numbers': H Reicher (ed), *Australian International Law: Cases and Materials* (Sydney, Law Book Company Information Services, 1995) Preface, ix.

in this country.[10] Certainly, as the editors of this collection, we understand the pull towards these subject areas from our own study of international law in the 1990s.

II. SCHOLARSHIP ON AUSTRALIA AND INTERNATIONAL LAW

Scholarly work about Australia and international law has flourished through some key inflection points. Three editions of the collection *International Law in Australia* – 1966, 1984 and 2017 – punctuate scholarship in this field.[11] The 1966 edition, edited by DP O'Connell, announced the arrival of Australia as a state whose breadth and depth of participation in international law was worthy of analysis. This first edition aligned with Australia's military intervention in Vietnam (1962–76), which had itself signalled a significant shift in Australia's great power alliances from the United Kingdom to the United States. The second edition, edited by KW Ryan, was published in 1984, a year after the decision in *Commonwealth v Tasmania*,[12] which had cleared any remaining constitutional impediments to the domestic implementation of international law. This edition captured the expansion of international law into fields such as human rights and environmental protection. Thirty-three years later, in 2017, the third edition, edited by Donald R Rothwell and Emily Crawford, was published, with chapters on the protection of Indigenous rights and international counter-terrorism law and practice.

The three decades between the second and third editions of *International Law in Australia* were a fertile (and fevered) time for scholarship on international law and Australia. The scholars publishing in the 1990s and 2000s were writing in an atmosphere of optimism for international law that began with the fall of the Berlin Wall in 1989 and ended with the fall of New York's Twin Towers in 2001. There were a number of casebooks on international law published by Australian authors with an Australian focus in the 1990s and 2000s.[13] This was

[10] See Baghoomians, Crawford and Mowbray, above n 9. See also J Crawford, 'Teaching and Researching International Law in Australia' (1981–83) 10 *Australian Yearbook of International Law* 176; D Otto, 'Handmaidens, Hierarchies and Crossing the Public–Private Divide in the Teaching of International Law' (2000) 1 *Melbourne Journal of International Law* 35; A Duxbury, 'International Human Rights Law and the Events of 2001: Has the World Changed Forever?' (2012) 30 *Australian Yearbook of International Law* 13, 40–43.

[11] DP O'Connell (ed), *International Law in Australia* (Sydney, Law Book Co, 1966); KW Ryan (ed), *International Law in Australia*, 2nd edn (Sydney, Law Book Co, 1984); D Rothwell and E Crawford (eds), *International Law in Australia*, 3rd edn (Sydney, Law Book Co, 2017).

[12] *Commonwealth v Tasmania* (1983) 158 CLR 1. See, M Chiam, 'Tasmanian Dams and Australia's Relationship with International Law' (2015) 24 *Griffith Law Review* 89.

[13] eg, H Reicher, *Australian International Law: Cases and Materials* (North Ryde, LBC Information Services, 1995); DK Anton et al, *International Law: Cases and Materials* (Melbourne, Oxford University Press, 2005); DR Rothwell et al, *International Law: Cases and Materials with Australian Perspectives* (Cambridge, Cambridge University Press, 2011) (with two further editions in 2014 and 2018).

the period when Gareth Evans aimed to construct Australia as a 'good international citizen', when the major political parties had frenzied responses to the UN Human Rights Committee finding in *Toonen* and the High Court decision in *Teoh*, and when the Government of Prime Minister John Howard withdrew from interacting with the human rights treaty bodies because they had 'criticized [Australia] … for its human rights record'.[14] It is not surprising that many key works on Australia's participation in the international legal system were published during, or shortly after, this decade.

If the third edition of *International Law in Australia* came after the most productive period for scholarship in the field, it also stands as a lonely flag-bearer for ongoing interest in Australia's relationship with international law. After the high points of the 1990s and early 2000s, scholarly interest in Australia's interactions with international law as a discipline, as distinct from individual areas of international law, has waned and is sustained by a smaller group of committed academics and practitioners. It was within this context that we conceived of the project that has produced this book.

This volume examines Australia's membership of international organisations both past and present, Australia's practice of international law at the domestic and international level, and the contributions of Australians to the development and implementation of international law. This is not the first volume that examines Australia's place in the international legal system or that integrates the perspectives of both legal scholars and practitioners.[15] What distinguishes this volume is the inclusion of a range of disciplinary perspectives, including historians and political scientists, as well as lawyers. This book not only focuses on Australia's recent practice of international law, but also contains chapters exploring Australia's international legal history, including its position as a sub-imperial power in the Pacific,[16] the work of the first Australian and New Zealand Society of International Law in the 1930s, and Australia's role in the League of Nations and the Commonwealth. In this way, this volume may be seen as part of the trend to what has been termed a 'turn to the history of international law'.[17] It also analyses more recent debates, such as the application of international law in Australian courts (through cases considering international criminal law concepts) and the implementation of its international commitments under instruments such as the UN Declaration on the Rights of Indigenous Peoples (UNDRIP) and the Convention on the Rights of the Child (CRC).

[14] Attorney-General, D Williams, *CERD Report Unbalanced* (Media Release, 26 March 2000).

[15] eg, O'Connell, above n 11; S Blay, R Piotrowicz and M Tsamenyi (eds), *Public International Law: An Australian Perspective* (Melbourne, Oxford University Press, 1997); JP Fonteyne, A McNaughton and J Stellios, *Harris: Cases and Materials on International Law – An Australian Supplement* (2003); Rothwell et al, above n 13; Rothwell and Crawford, above n 11.

[16] For a discussion of the use of the term 'sub-imperial power', see A Anghie, 'Race, Self-Determination and Australian Empire' (2018) 19 *Melbourne Journal of International Law* 423, 451.

[17] I Rasilla, *International Law and History: Modern Interfaces* (Cambridge, Cambridge University Press, 2018) 11.

III. SCOPE AND STRUCTURE

Like all volumes on such a broad theme, this book cannot, and does not purport to be, comprehensive of Australia's engagement with the international legal framework. Instead, as detailed in part IV, the contributions highlight several themes in Australia's relationship with the international legal system and practice of international law at the domestic and international levels. One strength of this collection is that not all authors 'sing from the same songbook'. While some writers see Australia's role in a largely positive light, others are more critical of Australia's place in the international legal system and sceptical of the adoption and implementation of international law at the domestic level.

This book is divided into three parts: part I examines Australia's relationship with Empire – both as a part of the British Empire and as a sub-imperial power in the region. Chapters explore Australia's place in the Empire, including its role as a Dominion member of the Council of the League (by Alison Duxbury) and, later, as a member of the Commonwealth (by Frank Bongiorno). Two other chapters in this part, by Clinton Fernandes and Murray Chisholm respectively, consider Australia's troubled relationship with East Timor/Timor Leste, and its colonial role in the administration of Papua and New Guinea through the lens of grants of clemency for capital cases.

Part II of this book turns to 'Australia and Institutions', including external organisations, for example, the United Nations and associated organs, and internal institutions, for example, the Office of International Law in the AGD and Australian courts. Alison Pert considers Australia's relationship with the United Nations since its creation, highlighting the work of HV Evatt (Doc Evatt) at the San Francisco Conference on the Security Council's veto power and the role of the General Assembly. She then explores Australia's role as a UN member through the lens of successive Australian governments, including its contribution as a member of various UN organs and its ratification of UN treaties. Les Malezer's chapter considers a key aspects of Australia's (and Indigenous Australians') relationship with the United Nations: the establishment of institutions and the adoption of international instruments (notably UNDRIP) designed to engage with the concerns of Indigenous Peoples around the world. Malezer's chapter highlights the difficulties faced by Indigenous Peoples in interacting with UN bodies and the importance of creating separate organs focused on Indigenous issues. Margaret Young turns to Australia's relationship with the UN's judicial organ, the ICJ, including Australia's support for the system of international dispute resolution and the ICJ's role in delivering advisory opinions. Young examines Australia's changing optional clause declaration as well as its roles as an applicant and defendant before the Court and its interventions in requests for advisory opinions. These chapters demonstrate that Australia's relationship with international organisations has fluctuated depending on the outlook of the government of the day and the issue under consideration, and that these differences have not always fallen along predictable political lines.

In part II, authors also examine the practice of international law in Australian institutions. Henry Burmester and Bill Campbell analyse the practice of international law in the AGD in two key periods: 1901–2000 and the twenty-first century. Both writers highlight the contribution of key individuals, many of whom worked comfortably across both constitutional law and international law issues. The matters dealt with by the Department have covered a wide range of issues, including human rights, law of the sea, international trade, as well as participation in international litigation. The Department has been involved in both the representation of Australia's interests in international fora, as well as the domestic implementation of international law back home. It is clear from these two chapters that the role of a government legal adviser requires an individual to be creative and proactive as well as have a broad understanding of different areas of international law. The final chapter in part II, by Monique Cormier, examines the ad hoc way in which domestic courts in Australia have approached international crimes through cases covering such diverse areas as defamation, extradition and genocide. In Cormier's view, the courts' haphazard approach to dealing with international criminal law reflects Australian governments' varying attitudes to the international criminal justice project.

Part III turns to the role of 'Australians in international law'. In a sense, the entire book is concerned with Australians' engagement with the international legal system since Australia's place in the international community and its understanding of international law can only take place through the agency of individuals, whether they be prime ministers, foreign ministers, Indigenous Australians engaging with UN institutions, judges, government lawyers or civil society advocates. The chapters in this part take a different approach – examining Australia's engagement at home (Jordana Silverstein on the construction of Australia's international legal obligations towards child refugees by various individuals) and abroad (Jon Piccini on Elizabeth Reid's role at the World Conference for International Women's Year). Finally, Madelaine Chiam completes this part by exploring the role of Australians, in particular, Queensland lawyer Thomas Fry, in the foundation of the first Australian and New Zealand Society of International Law in 1933. These three chapters highlight the way in which key individuals have played a role in the implementation (or non-implementation) of international law in Australia, as well as the adaptation and pursuit of Australia's policies internationally.

IV. THEMES IN AUSTRALIA'S PRACTICE OF INTERNATIONAL LAW

The idea that there may be distinct national or regional approaches to international law has been discussed previously and in relation to other states. Such studies have frequently coalesced around the question of whether there are unique national approaches to international law, which in turn leads to consideration of the broader question, epitomised in the title of Anthea Roberts' book-length study, *Is International Law International?*[18] For example, Juan Scarfi in *The Hidden History of International Law in the Americas: Empire and Legal Networks* has written that '[t]he history of international law is in part the history of both the attempt to legitimize imperial or hegemonic projects and provincialize and adapt international law for continental or regional purposes'.[19] In *Dugard's International Law: A South African Perspective*, the introduction contextualises the development of international law in South Africa in light of its history of colonialism and apartheid.[20] Dugard's historical overview of international law in South Africa begins with European settlement, acknowledging that '[t]his is an unashamedly Eurocentric view, but international law, until the last century, was unashamedly Eurocentric'.[21] Closer to home, in another former Dominion, Anna Hood and An Hertogen engage with the question of whether there is a particular approach to international law in Aotearoa New Zealand.[22] Together with other authors in their edited collection, Hood and Hertogen raise questions as to the dominant view, both at the international and domestic level, that Aotearoa New Zealand is a 'good international citizen'.[23]

The place of international law in Australia must be situated in relation to Australia's place as a settler-colonial state – as a land that was originally regarded as *terra nullius*.[24] Unlike other settler states, for example New Zealand and Canada, there was no treaty (or treaties) negotiated between Aboriginal and Torres Strait Islander peoples and the Australian colonies or the Commonwealth of Australia after Federation. As Sophie Rigney writes, 'Australian international law is European in origin and settler-colonial in application'.[25] In contrast to this Eurocentric vision of international law, Wiradjuri scholar Mark McMillan describes an 'Indigenous international', a space that allows 'the historic and contemporary experiences of Indigenous peoples to found … a gathering point … and then simultaneously position those experiences against the nation states … capturing a place within the "international" without falling into the "domestic"'.[26] The call

[18] See the detailed discussion of this question in A Roberts, *Is International Law International?* (Oxford, Oxford University Press, 2017).

[19] JP Scarfi, *The Hidden History of International Law in the Americas: Empire and Legal Networks* (Oxford University Press, 2017) xvii.

[20] J Dugard, 'South Africa and International Law: A Historical Introduction' in J Dugard, M Plessis and T Maluwa, *Dugard's International Law: A South African Perspective* (Cape Town, Juta, 2018) 18.

[21] ibid.

[22] A Hood and A Hertogen, 'Introduction: International Law as Seen from Aotearoa New Zealand' in A Hertogen and A Hood (eds), *International Law in Aotearoa New Zealand* (Wellington, Thomson Reuters, 2022).

[23] ibid 7.

[24] This legal fiction was overturned by the High Court in *Mabo v Queensland (No 2)* (1992) 175 CLR 1.

[25] S Rigney, 'On Hearing Well and Being Heard Well: Indigenous International Law at the United Nations' (2021) 2 *TWAIL Review* 122, 124.

[26] M McMillan, '*Koowarta* and the rival Indigenous international: our place as Indigenous peoples in the international' (2014) 23 *Griffith Law Review* 110, 110.

in the Uluru Statement from the Heart for an agreement between Aboriginal and Torres Strait Islander tribes as the 'first sovereign Nations of the Australian continent and its adjacent islands' and governments[27] is one manifestation of the desire to acknowledge and formalise the relationship between Indigenous and non-Indigenous Peoples in Australia. The push for a treaty as a method of reaching a settlement between Indigenous Peoples and non-Indigenous Peoples, as well as constitutional change to reflect Australia's commitments pursuant to UNDRIP, were both discussed in the *Final Report of the Referendum Council* in 2017.[28]

In addition, any discussion of international law in Australia must be viewed in light of Australia's sense of geographic isolation. Sir Garfield Barwick, in his foreword to the first edition of O'Connell's, *International Law in Australia*, pointed to Australia's '[g]eograhical isolation and remoteness from what has heretofore been the centre of international activity and the sense of security derived from the protection of British naval strength'.[29] This feeling of isolation is apparent in successive statements made by Australian representatives in the Council of the League of Nations when debating the international issues of the day.[30] It is also linked to Australia's languid approach to embracing full international legal personality. Several authors in this volume point to Australia's indifferent attitude to the adoption of the Statute of Westminster after it was passed by the British Parliament in 1931. The Statute, which repealed the automatic extension of Acts of the British Parliament to the Dominions, was not implemented domestically in Australia until 1942. The multiple appearances of the Statute of Westminster in these chapters speaks not only to the legal significance of its adoption, but also to the place of the Statute in the ways that Australians perceived their connections with the world in the inter-war period.[31]

The centrality of the distinction between what is 'inside' and 'outside' Australia is also evident throughout this book. There is, of course, a legal explanation for this attitude. Australia's legal system is classified as 'dualist' in that international law has no domestic application until it is transformed into domestic legislation. In his chapter, Bill Campbell, a former head of the Office of International Law in the AGD, describes his role as one of 'reminding successive governments that they must have regard to, and abide by, two bodies of law – domestic and international law'.[32] The impact of Australia's borders is also evident in successive governments' attitudes towards refugees who arrive by boat on Australia's north

[27] Referendum Council, 'Uluru Statement from the Heart' (Statement of the First Nations National Constitutional Convention, 26 May 2017): ulurustatement.org/the-statement/.

[28] P Anderson and M Leibler, *Final Report of the Referendum Council* (Australia Referendum Council Report, 30 June 2017).

[29] G Barwick, 'Foreword' in O'Connell (ed), above n 11, v.

[30] Duxbury, ch 2 in this volume.

[31] M Chiam, 'The First Australian and New Zealand Society of International Law, 1933–38', ch 14 in this volume.

[32] B Campbell, 'Australian Government Practice of International Law in the Twenty-First Century', ch 10 in this volume.

coast – as illustrated by Jordana Silverstein's chapter on Australia's policies towards its international obligations and the detention of child refugees. It is also apparent in discussions on the approach of Australian courts towards international law: long have writers debated monism versus dualism; transformation versus incorporation and the legitimacy of these distinctions.[33] Monique Cormier's chapter demonstrates that these (sometimes circular) debates appear to be refreshingly absent from recent Australian case law examining issues of international criminal law. However, this does not mean that Australian courts have taken a robust approach to analysing international law and its relevance to Australian common law or statute. Instead, Cormier concludes that '[i]ndividual judicial predilections towards the role of sovereignty' means that 'ad hoc and arbitrary'[34] are the most apt descriptors of Australian courts' attitudes to international criminal law, despite Australia's diplomatic support for the international criminal justice project.

The political character of Australian governments and their foreign policy goals clearly have an influence on Australia's relationship with international law. Alison Pert writes that Labor governments have 'generally been more multilateralist in outlook' than Coalition (Liberal/National Party) governments and her chapter outlines how this difference has influenced Australia's engagement with the United Nations.[35] Pert highlights that, for a brief time under Labor governments, Australia focused on being a 'good international citizen'. This framing did not last, however, with subsequent Coalition governments rejecting international scrutiny of Australia's human rights practices and, as we write, both Coalition and Labor parties preferring to uphold a 'rules-based international order',[36] with all the ambiguities that this phrase allows.[37] But it is not the case that the Australian international legal landscape can be divided into those 'for' (Labor) and 'against' (Coalition) international law. Margaret Young's chapter on Australia and the ICJ illustrates commonalities in the approaches of multiple Australian governments to the Court, with the major political parties sharing an openness to the contentious jurisdiction of the Court, which contrasts with their reticence to its advisory jurisdiction.[38]

[33] See, eg, S Donaghue, 'Balancing Sovereignty and International Law: The Domestic Impact of International Law in Australia' (1995) 17 *Adelaide Law Review* 213; K Walker, 'Treaties and the Internationalisation of Australian Law' in C Saunders (ed), *Courts of Final Jurisdiction: The Mason Court in Australia* (Sydney, Federation Press, 1996); E Crawford, 'Monism and Dualism: An Australian Perspective' in M Novakovic (ed), *Basic Concepts of Public International Law: Monism and Dualism* (Faculty of Law, University of Belgrade, Institute of Comparative Law, Institute of International Politics and Economics, Belgrade, 2013).

[34] M Cormier, 'Ad Hoc and Arbitrary: International Criminal Law in Australian Courts', ch 11 in this volume.

[35] A Pert, 'Australia and the United Nations', ch 6 in this volume.

[36] N Bisley, 'Australia's Rules-Based International Order' *Australian Institute of International Affairs: Australian Outlook* (27 July 2018): www.internationalaffairs.org.au/australianoutlook/australias-rules-based-international-order/.

[37] J Dugard, 'The Choice Before Us: International Law or a "Rules-Based International Order"?' (2023) 36 *Leiden Journal of International Law* 223.

[38] Young, ch 8 in this volume.

A sense that governments in Australia have been more alike than different in their approaches to international law also emerges from the chapters that consider Australia's role as a sub-imperial power. Murray Chisholm's chapter on clemency and capital punishment in Papua and New Guinea in the late 1950s and early 1960s reveals that, when Australia exercised its trusteeship powers under the Charter of the United Nations, it did so mainly for pragmatic rather than principled reasons.[39] While this is not the first time that Australia's role in the Pacific has been critiqued,[40] Chisholm's archival research demonstrates the degree to which decisions on clemency were designed to avoid the attention of the UN Trusteeship Council about Australia's colonial project.[41] The collision of Australia's sub-imperialism with its prioritisation of extraction is apparent in Australia's relationship with Timor-Leste, as Clinton Fernandes' chapter outlines.[42]

Domestically, the similarities between Coalition and Labor government approaches to international law are sometimes more apparent than the differences. Both Coalition and Labor governments, for example, reacted strongly against the High Court's decision in *Minister for Immigration and Ethnic Affairs v Teoh*, which had the potential to give direct effect to international human rights treaties.[43] Similarly, while Gough Whitlam can be hailed as the Prime Minister who deepened Australia's engagement with the UN system, his government was also in favour of East Timor's incorporation into Indonesia rather than the exercise of the right of self-determination.[44] As Jon Piccini argues in his chapter, Whitlam concealed a strong commitment to an American alliance beneath his government's open multilateralism.[45] Prime Minister John Howard's Coalition Government was hostile to human rights treaty bodies and voted against UNDRIP in the UN General Assembly. However, it led a multinational peacekeeping force in East Timor after the referendum for independence

[39] M Chisholm, '"Treat-Them-Gently-at-All-Costs-and-Please-the-United-Nations": The UN Trusteeship Council and Capital Punishment and Clemency in Papua and New Guinea, 1954–65', ch 4 in this volume.

[40] eg, C Storr, '"Imperium in Imperio": Sub-Imperialism and the Formation of Australia as a Subject of International Law' (2018) 19 *Melbourne Journal of International Law* 335.

[41] Chisholm, above n 39.

[42] C Fernandes, 'Australia, Timor-Leste and International Law', ch 5 in this volume.

[43] *Minister for Immigration and Ethnic Affairs v Teoh* (1995) 183 CLR 273. In this case, the High Court ruled that Australia's ratification of the Convention on the Rights of the Child created a legitimate expectation that decision-makers would abide by the Convention in decisions which affect children, 'absent statutory or executive indications to the contrary': 291–92 (Mason CJ and Deane J). Both Labor and, after an election, Coalition governments issued statements repudiating the decision: Minister for Foreign Affairs and the Attorney-General, 'Joint Statement on International Treaties and the High Court Decision in Teoh' (Media Release, 10 May 1995); Minister for Foreign Affairs, the Attorney-General and the Minister for Justice, 'The Effect of Treaties in Administrative Decision-Making' (Media Release, 25 February 1997). See H Burmester, 'International Law in the Attorney-General's Department: 1901–2000', ch 9 in this volume.

[44] See Fernandes, ch 5 in this volume.

[45] J Piccini, '"This is Our Conference", Elizabeth Reid, Second Wave Feminism and Australia's Performance of International Law in the 1970s', ch 13 in this volume.

in 1999[46] and, after some urging, ratified the Rome Statute for the International Criminal Court in 2002.[47]

Australia's engagement with the international legal system might be framed by the policies of successive governments, but it is also the result of the views and vigour of individual Australians – as evidenced by Prime Minister Billy Hughes at the Paris Peace Conference, Evatt at the San Francisco Conference and Foreign Minister Gareth Evans' role in the Cambodia peace plan.[48] Immi Tallgren has highlighted the importance of individuals to a discipline that 'at its best is imagined as gathering all humans together to care for humanity, led by the international lawyer as the mediating figure'.[49] The role of individual Australians – in both Australia's engagement with the international legal framework as well as the practice of international law at the domestic level – is apparent throughout this volume. The chapters by Henry Burmester and Bill Campbell illustrate how government and non-government Australian representatives have contributed to the drafting of treaties and other instruments of international law and have been regular participants in Australia's appearances before international dispute resolution processes. Some figures in Australia's international legal history, much discussed in other literature, such as HV Evatt, Kenneth Bailey and Robert Garran, receive attention in this volume, but perhaps not the significance accorded elsewhere.[50] Instead, the role of Stanley Bruce in the League of Nations, John Latham and his involvement in multiple Australian societies devoted to international relations, and Elizabeth Reid at the World Conference for International Women's Year, are brought to the fore in these pages. When it comes to the development of the government practice of international law at home in the AGD, the dominance of men in Australia's legal history is apparent in these chapters. However, one of the best-known critics of Australian practice on international law and child refugees, the former President of the Australian Human Rights Commission Gillian Triggs, is also prominent in Jordana Silverstein's chapter.

There is no doubt that the 'images of the history of international law are gendered',[51] but as students of Charlesworth, a co-author of the ground-breaking

[46] Pert, ch 6 in this volume.

[47] ibid; Charlesworth et al, above n 7.

[48] Pert, ch 6 in this volume.

[49] I Tallgren, 'Re-curating the Portrait Gallery of International Law: The Objectives, Process and Floorplan of the Exhibition' in I Tallgren (ed), *Portraits of Women in International Law*, Online edn (Oxford, Oxford Academic, 18 May 2023) 5.

[50] Evatt's role is discussed in Pert, ch 6 in this volume. A more detailed discussion of the role of these lawyers can be found in TLH McCormack, 'H.V. Evatt at San Francisco: A Lasting Contribution to International Law' (1992) 13 *Australian Yearbook of International Law* 89; K Sellars, 'Rules or Law? Kenneth Bailey and the Law of the Sea' *Australian Institute of International Affairs: Australian Outlook* (26 July 2018): www.internationalaffairs.org.au/australianoutlook/rules-or-law-kenneth-bailey-and-the-law-of-the-sea/; and C Milner, 'An Empire Man on the Road to Dominion Independence: Robert Randolph Garran and the "Armistice Blunder"' in MJK Walsh and A Varnava (eds), *After the Armistice: Empire, Endgame and Aftermath* (New York, Routledge, 2021).

[51] Tallgren, above n 49, 7.

article 'Feminist Approaches to International Law',[52] we hope that other portraits will adorn the wall of Australia's gallery of international lawyers in future analyses of the field.[53] Indeed, on the international stage, chapters in this volume point to Charlesworth's election to the ICJ and Elizabeth Reid's role at the World Conference in Mexico. Three of the last four presidents of the Australian and New Zealand Society of International Law (ANZSIL) have been women. This is very different from the situation in 1933, discussed by Chiam, when the first ANZSIL was created by a group of prominent men. Future contributions to be examined may include those of Rosalie Balkin (former Director of Legal Affairs and External Relations and Assistant Secretary-General of the International Maritime Organization), Megan Davis (the first Indigenous person from Australia elected to the UN Permanent Forum on Indigenous Issues) and Helen Durham (the first woman Director of International Law and Policy at the International Committee of the Red Cross). All of this points to rapid changes in 'who' practices international law at the end of the twentieth century and the beginning of the twenty-first century in, and for, Australia.[54]

V. CONCLUSION

There are certain dates that stand out in this volume: 1933 is the year that Australia attained the presidency of the Council of the League of Nations and the year that the first Australian and New Zealand Society of International Law was established; 1942 is significant as the date when Australia finally adopted the Statute of Westminster; and 1972, with the election of the Whitlam Labor Government and the accompanying flurry of ratifications of human rights and other international treaties. Perhaps we can add to this list, 2009 – the date when Australia endorsed UNDRIP – an instrument of international law discussed in Malezer's chapter that can be used to 'measure state and domestic behaviour in relation to Indigenous peoples'.[55] Bongiorno observes in his chapter on Australia and the Commonwealth that the upheavals of the post-war world ushered a time when Australians 'could no longer look to the UK as the ultimate authority on wisdom and standards'.[56] Before then, the intimate connections between Dominion Australia and Great Britain, and the Imperial governance structures

[52] H Charlesworth, C Chinkin and S Wright, 'Feminist Approaches to International Law' (1991) 85 *American Journal of International Law* 613.

[53] On the idea of a gallery, see Tallgren, above n 49.

[54] As evidenced in the chapters by Burmester and Campbell, there have also been changes in the range of matters included in the practice of international law. See Burmester, ch 9 in this volume; Campbell, ch 10 in this volume.

[55] M McMillan and S Rigney, 'The Place of First Peoples in the International Sphere: A Logical Starting Point for the Demand for Justice by Indigenous Peoples' (2016) 39 *Melbourne University Law Review* 981, 1001.

[56] F Bongiorno, 'The Rise and Fall of "a Hyphenated Condition": Australia, British Empire and the Commonwealth', ch 3 in this volume; Burmester, ch 9 in this volume.

on which they were built, embodied a monist spirit. The colonies that became the Dominion of Australia sought a measure of independence from Britain, but, as Bongiorno argues, its people also had an internalised 'Britishness' that held together a conception of Australia as both independent and as part of an external polity that was larger than itself.

Throughout the eras discussed in this book, there is a legal and political diversity that characterises Australia's relationship with international law. Interspersed with evidence of Australia's anxiety towards international law and international institutions, is a spirit that sees international law as an enabler of communities (for example, our respective chapters on the Council of the League of Nations and the first ANZSIL), and as a resource for creative law and policymaking (for example, Burmester and Campbell on the AGD, Piccini on Elizabeth Reid, Pert and Young on the UN and ICJ respectively). James Crawford concluded his article on teaching and research in international law in Australia, published in the early 1980s by noting his view that as Australia lacks a 'distinctive national tradition' in international law, there is an opportunity for Australian international lawyers to contribute to crucial issues in the future.[57] He predicted the emphases in the next 10 years to be on the relationship between international and domestic law, international economic law, and international peace and security (including nuclear disarmament).[58] The list of fundamental issues in the twenty-first century may be similar (eg, AUKUS) or have radically changed (the acknowledgement of the consequences of colonialism and the impact of climate change on the discipline, particularly in Australia).

We conclude with the question that opens this chapter: is there an Australian international law? In our view, the chapters in this book show how the international law practised in and by Australia and Australians has been characterised by anxiety and engagement, creativity and retreat. Are these characteristics distinctively Australian? Or can they form a cohesive whole that could be called 'Australian international law'? For both questions, we suspect the answer is 'no'. But we also think that it is not the answer that matters. In posing the question of a potential 'Australian' international law, this book brings to light new accounts of Australian engagements with international law, captures the reflections of significant individuals in Australia's interactions with international law and, we hope, helps to restore Australian approaches to international law to the foreground of academic and public conversation.

[57] Crawford, 'Teaching and Researching International Law in Australia', above n 10, 196.
[58] ibid.

Part I

Australia as Empire

2

Participation in the 'Gilded Ball': Australia and the Council of the League of Nations

ALISON DUXBURY

I. INTRODUCTION

AUSTRALIA'S RELATIONSHIP WITH the League of Nations – the first international organisation with a broad mandate to prevent war and to preserve the peace – was fraught with tensions before it had been established. At the end of the First World War, Prime Minister William (Billy) Hughes regarded proposals to create the new organisation with suspicion due to his belief that the main business of the Paris Peace Conference should be reparations for losses suffered during the war and the disposition of Germany's territories.[1] In accordance with this understanding, Hughes described the proposed League at a meeting of the Imperial War Cabinet in December 1918 as the 'the gilded ball on the dome of the cathedral, and not the foundation-stone'[2] of the Conference. Australia's early interactions with the body tasked with creating the League in 1919 – the Commission on the League of Nations – were no more promising. Hughes' determination to prevent the inclusion of a racial equality clause in the Covenant and to preserve Australia's control over New Guinea are well documented.[3] Despite these unpromising beginnings, Australia obtained separate membership of the League and on return home, Hughes described the organisation as '[lighting] the way to a better road' – although

[1] Imperial War Cabinet, 'Imperial War Cabinet 47: Minutes of a Meeting of the Imperial War Cabinet, Held at 10, Downing St, SW, on Monday, December 30, 1918, at 3.30 pm' in Imperial War Cabinet, *Minutes of Meetings, 30–48* (1918) 7 (December 30, 1918). See also DL George, *The Truth about the Peace Treaties, Vol I* (London, Gollancz, 1938) 196–97.

[2] Imperial War Cabinet, 'December 30, 1918', above n 1, 7.

[3] See, eg, LF Fitzhardinge, *The Little Digger: 1914–1952* (Melbourne, Angus and Robertson Publishers, 1979) vol ii, 387–410.

this was tempered by his remark that the League 'does not make the road, nor does it carry us along it'.[4]

This chapter will examine Australia's view of the role of the League of Nations and Australia's perception of its place as a member. The focus will be on one period of Australia's involvement with the organisation: its non-permanent membership of the Council from 1933 to 1936. Section II will explore Prime Minister Hughes' view of the plan to establish the League, specifically the functions and powers of the Council. Section III will turn to the question of Dominion representation on the Council and section IV will examine Australia's place as a non-permanent member. This period has been chosen for three reasons: first, because Australia's membership of the Council has not received much separate scholarly attention;[5] second, because Australia's membership coincided with three momentous international events: Germany's rearmament, the breach of the Locarno Pact and the Abyssinia/Italy crisis; and third, because it provides an insight into the way in which Australia perceived the League's main objective of international peace and security.

This chapter falls within a tradition of renewed emphasis in scholarship on the League. As Susan Pedersen has noted, for many years after the establishment of the United Nations (UN), the League was not a favoured topic of academic commentary or discussion – '[f]or thirty years, the archives of the League's own Geneva Secretariat were very little disturbed'.[6] From the Australian perspective, commentary on the League has often been concerned with the 'C' Class mandates – this is unsurprising given Hughes' desire to annex New Guinea at the 1919 Conference and the subsequent Reports on the Administration of the Territory submitted to the Council in compliance with Australia's obligations under the Covenant.[7] Early scholarship about the League appears to have viewed the League as either sad (because the major and minor powers did not join or left too early);[8] mad (the idea of establishing a universal peace organisation at the end of the First World War was a utopian vision that – for some – came

[4] 'Treaty with Germany: Explained by Prime Minister' *The Australasian* (Melbourne, 13 September 1919) 37.

[5] The most comprehensive account of Australia's membership of the League is WJ Hudson's, *Australia and the League of Nations* (Sydney, Sydney University Press, 1980). Hudson includes chapters on Australia's interactions with the League, including Australia's attitude to events that occurred while it was on the Council; however, he does not deal with the Council as a separate aspect of Australia's membership.

[6] S Pedersen, 'Back to the League of Nations' (2007) 112 *American Historical Review* 1091, 1091.

[7] Australia was granted a C Class Mandate over New Guinea and administered Nauru on behalf of three mandatory powers (Australia, New Zealand and Great Britain) pursuant to another C Class Mandate. For recent scholarship on Australia's territorial ambitions at the Paris Conference, see C Storr, '"*Imperium in Imperio*": Sub-Imperialism and the Formation of Australia as a Subject of International Law' (2018) 19 *Melbourne Journal of International Law* 335.

[8] For commentary on what 'might have been' if the US had joined the League, see G Scott, *The Rise and Fall of the League of Nations* (London, Hutchinson, 1973) 38–39.

perilously close to world government);[9] or even bad (the presence of the League lulled states into a false sense of security).[10] At various points Australia's politicians and representatives to the League voiced all three points of view.[11] However, since the 1990s new historical research has examined the role of the League in a variety of contexts. Much of this work focuses on the question of what the League meant over its 25 years of existence, rather than asking 'why the League failed'.[12] This is the point of departure for this chapter.

II. PRIME MINISTER HUGHES AT THE PARIS PEACE CONFERENCE

When Prime Minister Hughes travelled to Paris for the Peace Conference he had three main aims: to ensure Australia's control over New Guinea; to confirm that Germany would pay reparations for losses suffered during the war; and to uphold the White Australia policy by opposing Japan's racial equality amendment in the Covenant.[13] It was well known that Hughes was sceptical of the League and hostile to Woodrow Wilson's proposals.[14] Prior to the Paris Conference, Hughes' lack of support for a strong League was apparent at meetings of the Imperial War Cabinet. At one such meeting on 26 November 1918, Hughes described Wilson's plans for a League as potentially leading to a 'world-State and the surrender of the Great Powers of their self-governing rights'.[15] At a further meeting on 30 December 1918, Hughes labelled Wilson's proposal

[9] Leonard Woolf, an advocate for the League, was disparaging of those who labelled the scheme for the League as 'Utopian': LS Woolf (ed), *The Framework of a Lasting Peace* (London, Allen & Unwin, 1917) 57.

[10] Even before the League was created, Randall warned of the dangers of an organisation that 'might engender a false sense of security, and give a great opportunity to a robber state to essay the domination of the world': see HL Randall, 'The Legal Antecedents of a League of Nations' (1919) 28 *Yale Law Journal* 301, 307.

[11] eg, in a statement written by Stanley Bruce and read by Frank McDougall at the Second Committee in 1938, he referred to 'the absence of certain great nations from our counsels' as a 'serious handicap to our work'. However, Bruce was of the view that this absence would not prevent progress in the economic field: 'Records of the Nineteenth Ordinary Session of the Assembly: Minutes of the Second Committee (Economic, Financial and Transit Questions)' (1938) (Special Supp 185) *League of Nations Official Journal* 1, 26 (Fifth Meeting). One of Hughes' criticisms of the proposed League was that it was an idea for a 'world-State': see below n 15 and accompanying text; and Hughes' 'Notes on the Draft Covenant' dated 21 March 1919, reproduced in DH Miller, *The Drafting of the Covenant, Vol I* (New York, GP Putman's Sons, 1928) 363–64. For an Australian perspective on the view that the League lulled states into a false sense of security, see below nn 146, 174 and accompanying text.

[12] Pedersen, above n 6, 1092.

[13] Hughes articulated these views at the Imperial War Cabinet on 30 December 1918: see Imperial War Cabinet, 'December 30, 1918', above n 1, 6–7.

[14] See Hudson, above n 5, 22–23.

[15] Imperial War Cabinet, 'Minutes of a Meeting of the Imperial War Cabinet, Held at 10, Downing St, S.W., on Tuesday, November 26, 1918, at 12 Noon' in Imperial War Cabinet, *Minutes of Meetings, 30–48* (1918) 5 (November 26, 1918). See also DH Miller, *The Drafting of the Covenant*, above n 11, 363–64.

as 'no practical scheme at all ... the League of Nations was to [Wilson] what a toy was to a child – he would not be happy till he got it'.[16] For Hughes, the League had to be properly constituted – this meant that the British Empire must occupy 'a place corresponding to its sacrifices in the war and its place in the world'.[17] In any event, Hughes clearly thought that starting with the League was putting the cart before the horse: the League should be the 'shadow' and not the 'substance' of Versailles.[18] According to Prime Minister Lloyd George, the 'Cabinet were much impressed by the critical power of the Hughes speech'. Lloyd George wrote that:

> It was their first explanation of the reason why this man of frail physique, defective hearing and eccentric gesticulations had attained such a position of dominant influence in the Australian Commonwealth ... I wish there had been a verbatim report which would reproduce the stabbing sentences in the form in which they were delivered.[19]

Although the Dominions, including Australia, achieved separate representation at the Paris Peace Conference, they were not members of the Commission on the League of Nations – British Empire representation was left to Sir Robert Cecil and Jan Smuts. Neither Sir Robert Garran, Hughes' principal adviser on the League, nor Hughes saw the League as having a strong role to play in maintaining international peace and security. In two separate memoranda Garran wrote that the appropriate functions of a League were investigation and education and that the draft Covenant did not provide 'any real security against the horrors of the past few years'.[20] Hughes' memorandum of 21 March 1919 on the draft Covenant was described by Wilson's lawyer at the Paris Peace Conference, David Hunter Miller, as being 'written from a rather hostile point of view'.[21] Hughes' main objection was that the draft hovered between 'two inconsistent principles of international co-operation and supra-national government'.[22]

In relation to the Council, Hughes was concerned that the use of the term 'Executive Council' in one of the early drafts of the Covenant suggested a 'false

[16] Imperial War Cabinet, 'December 30, 1918', above n 1, 6.

[17] ibid.

[18] ibid 7.

[19] George, above n 1, 201–02. In Paris, not all of the British delegation were so enamoured with Hughes – Cecil labelled him as 'that shrimp' and Balfour remarked to Clemenceau when Hughes rose to speak at the plenary, 'Que Je le déteste': DH Miller, *My Diary: At the Conference of Paris, Vol I* (New York, Appeal Printing Co, 1924) 178 (Cecil), 369 (Balfour).

[20] See Hudson, above n 5, 23; RR Garran, 'Commentaries on the Nature and Role of the League of Nations, 1919' (Papers of Sir Robert Garran Relating to the Peace Conference of 1918, to the Imperial Economic Conference of 1923 and to the Commonwealth Oil Refineries Ltd, NAA, CP351/1, 2/2, 1919) 10. Hudson notes that Garran approached the question 'as a conservative lawyer inclined towards anomalous comparisons between, on the one hand, international law and on the other, bankruptcy and commercial law and industrial relations': see Hudson, above n 5, 23.

[21] DH Miller, *The Drafting of the Covenant*, above n 11, 363.

[22] See ibid 368.

analogy' with a national government.[23] Hughes was at pains to emphasise that the Council and the Body of Delegates (later the Assembly) were organs of 'international consultations' rather than an executive and legislature.[24] Hughes also emphasised that meetings of the Body of Delegates or the Council (an '*advisory*' body) should have the power to make recommendations but not binding decisions.[25] In terms of the League's role in relation to matters of peace and security, Hughes was disturbed by an Article – later to become Article 16 – providing that a state in breach of the Covenant would '*ipso facto* be deemed to have committed an act of war against all the other members of the League'.[26] For Hughes, such a 'pledge' was a mistake.[27] Instead, Hughes believed that the Article should be limited so that a state had the '*right* to make war against a covenant-breaking State' rather than a duty.[28] But Hughes reserved his most damning critique for a draft provision dealing with the Council's powers in relation to mandated territories. The Council had the power of 'executive *action* … to define … the degree of authority, control, or administration to be exercised by a mandatory State' over a territory in the event that this had not previously been agreed upon by the High Contracting Parties.[29] Hughes – keen to ensure Australia's control (preferably in the form of annexation) over New Guinea – described this Article as 'something of an excrescence upon what is otherwise purely a consultative body'.[30] Collectively, Hughes' notes emphasised the need to limit the functions and powers of the League's organs, including the Council. While Miller described most of Hughes' criticisms as 'unimportant', they both agreed that the League would be a standing international conference rather than a super-state.[31]

Australia was granted original membership of the League, as were the other British Dominions, a state of affairs which Miller described as 'perfectly illogical from the point of view of legal precedent, just as it was perfectly inevitable from the point of view of common sense'.[32] This issue was the focus of a memorandum of September 1919, 'The Six Votes', prepared by Miller for Senator Hitchcock, Chairman of the United States (US) Senate Foreign Relations Committee. In the memorandum Miller dampened any suggestion that, as a result of the Dominions' separate membership, the British had six votes in the

[23] ibid 364.
[24] ibid.
[25] ibid 364–65.
[26] ibid 366–67.
[27] ibid 367.
[28] ibid.
[29] ibid.
[30] ibid.
[31] DH Miller, *The Drafting of the Covenant*, above n 11, 363. Miller's description of Hughes' notes can be compared to the combined 'learning, political wisdom and common sense' he attributed to the comments on the draft of the US Ambassador to the UK, John W Davis: ibid 368. Likewise, Miller described the memorandum from Canada's Prime Minister, Sir Robert Borden, on the same draft as written in a 'spirit of helpfulness': ibid 354.
[32] ibid 490–91.

League whereas the United States only had one, describing this suggestion as a 'bogey' or a 'myth'.[33] In Miller's view, the presence of Dominion representatives in Paris was evidence that the 'unity of the British Empire has become a thing of the past and is hardly more than a technical expression of jurists, if, indeed, it is now even that'.[34] Miller's comments in 1919 capture Australia's uncertain status in international law as a result of its separate representation at the Paris Conference. As Hudson writes, 'Australia for the first time moved into international politics outside the confines of the British Empire, but to the eyes of the world and to a degree even in her own she remained a colony'.[35]

The Dominions' separate membership in the League gave rise to a related question: whether they could obtain individual representation on the Council. Hughes did not believe that Australia would ever be a Council member – in February 1919 he sent a telegram to Australia's Acting Prime Minister bemoaning the fact that Australia would only have a 'voice' on the Assembly, which would be controlled by the Executive.[36] However, according to Miller, subsequent to the final meeting of the Commission in April 1919, the question of Dominion representation on the Council caused 'a great deal of difficulty'.[37] Article 4 of the Covenant provided that the Council would comprise the permanent members and 'four other States which are Members of the League' as non-permanent members.[38] Such language excluded the Dominions on the basis that they were not states as a matter of international law.[39] After the English text of the Covenant had been printed, the British suggested a number of amendments, including that the word 'State' or 'States' be substituted for 'Member (or Members) of the League'.[40] This would enable a Dominion to be represented on the Council as a non-permanent member in the future.[41] Miller regarded these changes as more than merely textual and asserted that it was not the intention of the Commission that the Dominions and colonies could be Council members.[42] However, following discussions involving the Americans, the British and the French, Wilson yielded to the British suggestion.[43] As the result of a question from the Canadian Prime Minister, Sir Robert Borden, the notes of a meeting between Clemenceau, Wilson and Lloyd George dated 6 May 1919 record their

[33] DH Miller, 'Six Votes' (13 September 1919) in DH Miller, *My Diary at the Conference of Paris, with Documents, Vol XX* (New York, Appeal Printing Co, 1924) 544.

[34] ibid.

[35] Hudson, above n 5, 3.

[36] Telegram from B Hughes to W Watt (13 February 1919) in 'Copies of Cables sent and received by the Rt Hon William Morris (Billy) Hughes during His Visit to Europe' (National Archives of Australia, NAA, Series CP290/3, Control Symbol 1, Item ID 9579964) 1.

[37] DH Miller, *The Drafting of the Covenant*, above n 11, 477.

[38] ibid 477–78.

[39] ibid 478, 489.

[40] ibid 478–79.

[41] ibid 479–81, 489.

[42] ibid 480.

[43] ibid 489.

agreement that 'representatives of the self-governing Dominions of the British Empire may be selected or named as members of the Council'.[44] Consequently, not only did Australia secure separate membership of the League at Paris, but also obtained the possibility of representation on the peak body dealing with international peace and security in the future.

III. A SEAT ON THE COUNCIL?

The relationship between the United Kingdom (UK) and the Dominions at the League was a topic which exercised the minds of Australia's representatives at various points in subsequent years. At least twice Australia's liaison officer in London, Richard Casey, highlighted to Prime Minister Stanley Bruce in the mid-1920s the disadvantages faced by Dominion delegations in Geneva given their lack of resources and knowledge of the topics under discussion at the League.[45] As a practical matter, Casey was concerned that communication was difficult when Dominion representatives did not stay at the same hotel as the British during League meetings in Geneva.[46] In a letter dated 1926, Casey described discussions between the Dominions and the United Kingdom on the question whether the delegate of the British Empire on the Council (at that time Sir Austen Chamberlain) represented the Dominions.[47] From the UK's perspective, both Chamberlain and Cecil appeared to accept that separate Dominion representation on the Council was possible.[48] Sir Joseph Cook, then Australia's High Commissioner in London, believed that representation of the British Empire on the Council included the Dominions.[49] Casey's own view was that Chamberlain only represented Great Britain on the Council unless authorised by the Dominions to speak on their behalf as well.[50] However, at a 1927 Council meeting Chamberlain stated that the Dominions sat in the Assembly 'in their own names', potentially implying that the seat occupied by the British Empire in the Council encompassed all the Dominions.[51]

[44] ibid.

[45] Casey was also of the opinion that there was 'not nearly enough collaboration between the British and the Dominion Delegations': Letter from RG Casey to SM Bruce (8 October 1925) in 'Personal Papers of Prime Minister Bruce' (National Archives of Australia, NAA, Series A1420, Control Symbol 2, Item ID 202607) 4–5. See also Letter from RG Casey to SM Bruce (25 March 1926) in 'Personal Papers of Prime Minister Bruce' (National Archives of Australia, NAA, Series A1420, Control Symbol 3, Item ID 202608) 1–3.

[46] Letter from RG Casey to SM Bruce (18 February 1926) in 'Personal Papers of Prime Minister Bruce' (National Archives of Australia, NAA, Series A1420, Control Symbol 3, Item ID 202608) 2–3.

[47] Letter from RG Casey to SM Bruce (25 March 1926), above n 45, 4.

[48] ibid.

[49] ibid.

[50] ibid.

[51] 'Fourth Meeting (Public, Then Private): Forty-Fourth Session of the Council' (1927) 8 *League of Nations Official Journal* 377, 377. See M Kennedy, 'The Irish Free State and the League of Nations, 1922–32: The Wider Implications' (1992) 4 *Irish Studies in International Affairs* 9, 18.

The prospect of Australia gaining Council membership was raised in 1929 with Casey proposing William Harrison Moore – a constitutional lawyer on Australia's delegation in Geneva – as Australia's representative.[52] Instead another Dominion, the Irish Free State, obtained a non-permanent seat for a three-year term.[53] In March 1933, Bruce – now a Member of Parliament (MP) rather than the Prime Minister – wrote to Australian Prime Minister Lyons that Riddell (Canada) was of the strong view that there should be continued Dominion representation on the Council – if it was not Australia then it would be South Africa.[54] Bruce was keen that it not be South Africa and Australia subsequently became a member of the Council in October 1933.[55] For the next three years Australia was represented by Bruce, Australia's Resident Minister and then High Commissioner in London, with Keith Officer, John McLaren and Frank McDougall acting as alternatives. Hudson describes Bruce as a 'man of experience, knowledge and reputation' – not least given his position as a former prime minister of Australia.[56] His connections in London and Geneva enhanced his contribution to the Council.[57] The role of these men was particularly important given that Australia's Department of External Affairs, 'revived' by Hughes in 1921, had limited resources and operated as part of the Department of the Prime Minister until 1935.[58] The importance of Australian representatives at the League was later emphasised by a question in the Parliament of Australia in the midst of the Abyssinia crisis when Beasley (MP) asked whether the government gave 'specific directions to its [League] representative, or does it permit him to vote as he pleases, thus committing the Government of Australia without its having any say in the matter?'[59] Casey's response (then Treasurer) is worth repeating in full:

> When questions of very considerable importance, or questions directly affecting Australia's interests, are under consideration instructions are sent to Australia's representative, but in regard to the many other questions arising at the League Assembly, and at Council meetings, he is not given any specific instructions.[60]

Bruce's involvement with the Council was not his first encounter with the organisation – as a young MP he was Australia's delegate to the Second Assembly in 1921, although his appointment was somewhat 'accidental'. The

[52] Letter from RG Casey to SM Bruce (12 September 1929) in 'Personal Papers of Prime Minister Bruce' (National Archives of Australia, NAA, Series A1420, Control Symbol 8, Item ID 202613) 2.

[53] For a discussion of the Irish Free State's candidature for the Council, see Kennedy, above n 51, 15–20.

[54] Letter from SM Bruce to JA Lyons (30 March 1933) in 'Personal Papers of Prime Minister Bruce' (National Archives of Australia, NAA, Series AA1970/559, Control Symbol 7, Item ID 248745) 1.

[55] 'Resolutions Adopted by the Assembly during Its Fourteenth Ordinary Session (September 25th to October 11th, 1933)' (1933) (Special Supp 114) *League of Nations Official Journal* 1, 26.

[56] Hudson, above n 5, 7.

[57] ibid.

[58] ibid 4.

[59] Commonwealth, *Parliamentary Debates*, House of Representatives, 25 September 1936, 564.

[60] ibid.

Bruces were on holiday playing golf in France at the time, which enabled him to travel to Geneva via London quickly.[61] At the Second Assembly, Bruce emphasised two concerns: the need to consider, and possibly criticise, the Council's actions; and the promotion of international justice over war.[62] He supported the League with the following flourish: '[i]f the League goes, the hope of mankind goes also'.[63] In an account of this Assembly, the historian Harold Temperley regarded 'Captain Bruce' positively, describing him as speaking 'seldom, but always with weight and force'.[64] This was no mean feat given that Bruce subsequently conceded that he had little idea of the League at the time and 'not the remotest idea of what it was supposed to be doing'.[65] However, this ignorance did not last long: Bruce's interventions over the years were profound, culminating in the Bruce Report of 1939, which argued the case for the reorganisation of the League's work on economic and social matters.[66] This report was based on two ideas close to Bruce's heart. First, that the phrase 'technical problems' was inadequate to describe the array of economic and social issues discussed at the League. These matters, which included a range of 'commercial, industrial and agricultural questions', could not be sharply divided from 'problems of political relations between states'.[67] Second, Bruce believed that there was an 'intimate relationship between widespread and progressive poverty and world peace'.[68] As such, economic and social welfare were important not only in their own right, but because they would assist in achieving peace.[69]

IV. AUSTRALIA AT THE COUNCIL

Although the Covenant acknowledges the League's work in several fields, including trafficking in people and drugs and the prevention and control of diseases,[70] most of its substantive provisions concern breaches of the peace. Members

[61] C Edwards, *Bruce of Melbourne* (London, Heinemann, 1965) 53–55.

[62] Quoted in HWV Temperley, *The Second Year of the League: A Study of the Second Assembly of the League of Nations* (London, Hutchinson & Co, 1922) 167.

[63] ibid.

[64] ibid 18. Walters also regarded Bruce's speech at the Second Assembly positively: see FP Walters, *A History of the League of Nations* (Oxford, Oxford University Press, 1960) 151.

[65] Edwards, above n 61, 54.

[66] 'The Development of International Cooperation in Economic and Social Affairs' (22 August 1939, LNA A.23.1939) (Bruce Report). For a discussion of the Bruce Report, see MD Dubin, 'Toward the Bruce Report: The Economic and Social Programs of the League of Nations in the Avenol Era' in L'Institut universitaire de hautes études internationales (Geneva), *The League of Nations in Retrospect: Proceedings of the Symposium Organized by the United Nations Library and the Graduate Institute of International Studies, Geneva, 6–9 November 1980* (Berlin, Walter de Gruyter, 1983) 42.

[67] Bruce Report, above n 66, 6.

[68] ibid 10.

[69] ibid.

[70] Covenant of the League of Nations, Art 23(c), (f).

agreed that 'any dispute likely to lead to a rupture, which is not submitted to arbitration or judicial settlement' would be sent to the Council.[71] In such circumstances, the Council could settle the dispute, or if that was not possible, make and publish a report with recommendations.[72] Article 12 provided that if the Council was undertaking an enquiry, members would not 'resort to war until three months after the award by the arbitrators or the judicial decision, or the report by the Council'. In the event that a member resorted to war in violation of the Covenant, sanctions, including trade and financial measures, could be instigated.[73] The Council also had a 'duty' to recommend the use of members' military forces against a Covenant-breaking state to contribute to protecting 'the covenants of the League'.[74] The ultimate sanction against a member was expulsion.[75]

Despite the emphasis in the Covenant on the League's role in response to threats to the peace, in practice the organisation's functions covered an enormous range of subject areas. The titles of some of the Assembly's committees demonstrate the breadth and division of this work: 'Reduction of Armaments' (Third Committee); 'Financial Matters' (Fourth Committee); 'Social and General Questions' (Fifth Committee); and 'Political Questions' (Sixth Committee). This leaves aside the functions undertaken by a plethora of other bodies, including the Permanent Mandates Commission, the Administrative Commissions and Minorities Section (later the Political Section), and the Health Section. It is in the economic and social field that the League is recognised as having the most lasting impact: it was on these matters that the United States participated in the League's work and it was the report of the Bruce Committee that paved the way for the continuation of these functions in the United Nations.[76] This work was seen as 'not merely desirable in itself, but [as contributing] to a peaceful world'.[77] Australia's representatives on the Council supported this link between the functions of maintaining the peace and ensuring social and economic security.

McDougall and Bruce were particularly active in the Assembly and other League bodies with respect to economic and social matters, including nutrition and raising standards of living. For example, when introducing the topic of nutrition to the Assembly in September 1935, in a speech that was scheduled between the distress of Ethiopia's representative at the impending war in his country and Hungary's concern over disarmament and the protection of minorities, Bruce stated that:

[71] ibid Art 15(1).
[72] ibid Art 15(1)–(3).
[73] ibid Art 16(1).
[74] ibid Art 16(2).
[75] ibid Art 16(4).
[76] See FS Northedge, *The League of Nations: Its Life and Times* (Leicester, Leicester University Press, 1986) 190–91.
[77] ibid 166.

> It is important … that we should remember that the League is not concerned solely with political questions but is active also in relation to financial, economic, humanitarian and social issues of most vital concern to all nations.[78]

An Australian initiative in this field led to the Nutrition Report, described as 'the best seller among League publications'.[79] The significance of this work – and McDougall's role – and its place in leading to the establishment of the Food and Agricultural Organization after the Second World War, has been considered elsewhere.[80] The emphasis in this part is on Australia's view of the Council and its representatives' view of Australia's position as a Council member. Two traits stand out: first, Australia's representatives keenly felt, and emphasised, Australia's geographical isolation from the international disputes and other matters being considered by the Council.[81] Second, they used their position on the Council to advocate for the League's role in economic and social matters, cautioning against a focus on political disputes at the expense of these questions. This section will analyse a selection of issues considered by the Council to understand the approach Australia's representatives took to its functions and powers.

A. 'Political Questions'

In the first two years of Australia's Council membership, its representatives remained largely silent when various disputes were discussed. This mimicked Australia's role in the League in the 1920s as a 'conscientious, responsible but distant member … taking no initiatives herself and opposing the more radical initiatives of others'.[82] At the Council, Officer had nothing to say when a report of a committee tasked with dealing with a request from Liberia, which included assistance to stamp out slavery, was presented in October 1933.[83] When the complaints of Assyrian minorities against Iraq (an ex-mandatory of Great Britain) were raised at the same meeting, Officer again remained mute.[84]

[78] 'Fourth Plenary Meeting' (1935) (Special Supp 138) *League of Nations Official Journal* 1, 49, 51.
[79] Walters, above n 64, 755.
[80] For a discussion of this work, see W Way, 'The Marriage of Health and Agriculture' in W Way, *A New Idea Each Morning: How Food and Agriculture Came Together in One Organisation* (Canberra, ANU E Press, 2013) 153.
[81] An early example is Officer's comment during discussions on the appointment of the High Commissioner to the Free City of Danzig that a delay in the appointment would be viewed negatively in 'the more distant countries such as Australia': 'Fourth Meeting (Private, Then Public): Seventy-Seventh Session of the Council' (1933) 14 *League of Nations Official Journal* 1630, 1631 (Fourth Meeting, 1933).
[82] Hudson, above n 5, 6.
[83] 'Fourth Meeting, 1933', above n 81, 1636–41. When Liberia was again discussed in 1934, Australia did not comment: see 'Fourth Meeting (Private, Then Public): Seventy-Eighth Session' (1934) 15 *League of Nations Official Journal* 142, 153–56. For a discussion of the complex background to Liberia's request see Walters, above n 64, 568–71.
[84] 'Fourth Meeting, 1933', above n 81, 1636–41 (Liberia), 1643–49 (Iraq).

In both cases, it appeared that Officer preferred to leave any interventions to the UK's representatives. Similarly, when two territorial disputes involving South American states came before the Council, Australia stood on the sidelines.[85] In terms of the conflict between Paraguay and Bolivia, which led to the report of the Chaco Commission, McLaren expressly declined to make any substantive comment about the report and instead limited himself to supporting the UK's proposals.[86] When the settlement of the dispute between Peru and Colombia over Leticia was discussed two days later, McLaren emphasised Australia's remoteness from the conflict and merely stated that Australia was 'as profoundly interested in the cause of international goodwill as any other country'.[87]

Australia was more vocal when Switzerland and Finland brought claims for reparations from the belligerents in the war, including the United Kingdom, before the Council. In 1934 the Council considered a request from Switzerland for an advisory opinion from the Permanent Court of International Justice (PCIJ) in relation to its claim for war damage and reparations against the United Kingdom, France, Germany and Italy.[88] The Swiss representative (Motta) emphasised that the claim had been brought to the Council because diplomatic channels had failed.[89] There was some doubt as to which provision of the Covenant the Swiss had invoked, with Eden highlighting that Article 13, setting out the members' agreement to submit disputes to arbitration or judicial settlement, was voluntary.[90] Another option was Article 11(2), which provided that:

> It is also declared to be the friendly right of each Member of the League to bring to the attention of the Assembly or of the Council any circumstance whatever affecting international relations which threatens to disturb international peace or the good understanding between nations upon which peace depends.

Eden viewed Switzerland's push for an advisory opinion as an attempt to circumvent the UK's reservation to its acceptance of the Optional Clause of the Statute of the PCIJ, which prevented claims arising from matters that occurred prior to the entry into force of the Statute, such as claims arising from the war. This point was emphasised by both Eden (for the UK) and McDougall (for Australia).[91] Both representatives argued for a restrictive interpretation of Article 11(2), which in Eden's words should only be used 'in serious cases

[85] For a discussion of these two conflicts, see Walters, above n 64, 524–40.

[86] 'Third Meeting (Private, Then Public): Seventy-Ninth Session of the Council' (1934) 15 *League of Nations Official Journal* 748, 758.

[87] 'Fifth Meeting (Private, Then Public): Seventy-Ninth Session of the Council' (1934) 15 *League of Nations Official Journal* 874, 878.

[88] See 'Second Meeting (Private, Then Public): Eighty-Second Session of the Council' (1934) 15 *League of Nations Official Journal* 1433, 1436, 1439 (Second Meeting, 1934).

[89] ibid 1437.

[90] ibid 1439.

[91] 'Second Meeting, 1934', above n 88, 1439 (Eden), 1446 (McDougall). Australia had a similar reservation to its acceptance of the PCIJ's jurisdiction.

involving political issues or affecting questions of policy endangering peace'.[92] This interpretation was supported by McDougall who believed that to describe the Swiss claim as likely 'to disturb international peace or the good understanding between nations' would be 'an undue straining' of the Covenant.[93] When the report on the Finnish claim for reparations from the United Kingdom came before the Council two days later, McDougall repeated his restrictive interpretation of Article 11(2).[94]

Australia maintained this position in 1935 when the Finnish and Swiss claims were again considered by the Council. Officer prefaced his remarks on the Finnish claim by stating that he should like 'to express the opinion of the Government of a small State, a State, too, at a considerable distance from Geneva'.[95] Officer argued against the Council's involvement in too many disputes, invoking 'a considerable body of opinion' which would be frightened, if not terrified, by '[p]recipite action' from the League.[96] He went further, stating that the Council would lose its prestige if it 'took upon itself to consider a great number of questions which to most people would appear to have only minor importance'.[97] For Officer, Finland's claim would appear to have fallen into that category. When a committee's report on the question whether the Council should proceed with the Swiss application was discussed,[98] Bruce reinforced the Council's limited powers. The committee's report recommended that the matter be removed from the Council's agenda as there was no immediate danger to peace or a conflict of political interests, but only a pecuniary claim.[99] Despite the fact that the recommendation effectively ended the Council's role, Bruce stated that he could not accept the report if it implied that the Council had the competence to deal with the matter under Article 11(2).[100] Questions of law arising from the war were off-limits as far as Australia was concerned, particularly when they raised requests for reparations from the Allied powers.

B. Economic and Financial Questions

While Australia's representatives argued for restricting the Council's role when dealing with political disputes that did not disturb the peace, they had

92 ibid 1439.
93 ibid 1446.
94 'Third Meeting (Public): Eighty-Second Session of the Council' (1934) 15 *League of Nations Official Journal* 1449, 1454.
95 'Eighth Meeting (Private, Then Public): Eighty-Fourth Session of the Council' (1935) 16 *League of Nations Official Journal* 161, 173.
96 ibid.
97 ibid 174.
98 'Third Meeting: (Private, Then Public): Eighty-Sixth Session of the Council' (1935) 16 *League of Nations Official Journal* 615, 621.
99 ibid.
100 ibid 624.

a more expansive view of the League – and the Council's – role in economic and financial matters. At Bruce's first Council meeting on 4 October 1933 he was appointed as the rapporteur on financial questions.[101] Consequently, in late 1933 and 1934 Bruce's comments, and the interventions of Australia's other Council representatives, mostly concerned reports relating to the Financial and Fiscal Committees,[102] the Economic Committee,[103] and the Committee of Statistical Experts.[104] Such matters, while seemingly technical, could cause disputes as to the extent of the relevant committee's powers. For example, when the Economic Committee's study of agricultural protectionism was presented in May 1935, Aloisi (Italy) believed that the Committee had gone beyond its remit.[105] Aloisi was concerned that the technical committees were overstepping their powers and that only the Assembly or the Council could initiate studies on specific problems.[106] Responding in part to Aloisi's concerns, Bruce defended the study's scope, describing agricultural protectionism in industrial countries as an 'extraordinarily important question'.[107] Such language can be compared with Officer's earlier comment at the time of the Finnish claim for reparations (of 'minor importance'). When the report of the Economic Committee was again discussed at the Council four days later, Bruce argued that agricultural protectionism (the 'root of the world's economic troubles') had been 'considered a little too much from the European standpoint and not sufficiently from that of the new countries of the world'.[108] Thus, Australia not only regarded economic issues as matters for the Council's agenda, but their consideration also had the advantage of expanding the geographical reach of the League to encompass the concerns of non-European members.

Australia's representatives on the Council were also animated ('intensely interested')[109] in the imposition of barriers to world trade. At a Council meeting in September 1934, McDougall stated that since the Depression 'new barriers to

[101] 'Second Meeting: (Public, Then Private): Seventy-Seventh Session of the Council' (1933) 14 *League of Nations Official Journal* 1604. Lee writes that Bruce's appointment as rapporteur 'set him on a path to becoming an acknowledged authority not only on strictly financial matters but later on the broad social, economic and technical aspects of the league [sic]': D Lee, *Stanley Bruce: Australian Internationalist* (London, Bloomsbury, 2010) 109.

[102] 'Third Meeting (Public, Then Private): Seventy-Seventh Session of the Council' (1933) 14 *League of Nations Official Journal* 1610, 1610–16, 1627–28; 'Fourth Meeting (Private, Then Public): Seventy-Eighth Session of the Council' (1934) 15 *League of Nations Official Journal* 142, 142–46.

[103] 'Second Meeting (Public): Eighty-First Session of the Council' (1934) 15 *League of Nations Official Journal* 1386, 1389–90.

[104] 'First Meeting (Private, Then Public): Seventh-Ninth Session of the Council' (1934) 15 *League of Nations Official Journal* 492, 503.

[105] 'First Meeting (Private, Then Public): Eighty-Sixth Session of the Council' (1935) 16 *League of Nations Official Journal* 592, 598.

[106] ibid.

[107] ibid.

[108] 'Fourth Meeting (Private, Then Public): Eighty-Sixth Session of the Council' (1935) 16 *League of Nations Official Journal* 628, 631.

[109] 'Fifth Meeting (Private, Then Public): Eighty-Second Session of the Council' (1934) 15 *League of Nations Official Journal* 1464, 1472.

trade … constituted one of the gravest problems at present facing the world'.[110] McDougall was keen to expand the League's work in this area – foregrounding Bruce's comments on agricultural protectionism in 1935 – and stated that the League's work on commercial policy should 'arouse the interests' of countries outside Europe.[111] He believed that a proposed enquiry into compensation and clearing agreements by a joint committee of the Economic Committee and the Financial Committee should not take a 'narrow interpretation'[112] of its terms of reference and should include a range of countries. As an aside, he reminded representatives of an earlier League panel of agricultural experts which included 16 experts from European countries and only four from the rest of the world.[113] When the Joint Committee reported to the Council in 1935 Bruce once more highlighted the 'importance of the question' and emphasised that the Council resolution adopting the report should include language 'emphasising the desirability of the fullest consideration being given to the report' by governments.[114]

Australia's advocacy for the League's role in economic and social matters extended well beyond its position on the Council – as demonstrated by Bruce's Assembly speech on nutrition in 1935 and his later work leading to the 1939 Bruce Report.[115] Of course, the push for these issues to be included on the League's agenda accorded with Australia's self-interest as an exporter of primary produce and its goal of economic development.[116] But what is significant is the view that these issues were intimately connected to the League's function of promoting peace. On that basis, economic matters were appropriate for discussion in the Council as well as the Assembly and other technical committees. As Larry Neal has remarked in an article on bilateral clearing agreements in the 1930s, 'decisions about mundane matters of trade and finance were made in a much broader political and strategic context which eventually ended in World War II'.[117] At the Council, Australia argued for a restrictive reading of the League's powers over political disputes, but advocated for a much broader interpretation when discussing economic and social problems. In that sense, Australia's support for the League's role in economic issues could be cast in terms of Australia's desire to see the League limit its sphere to technical questions. However, it can also be viewed as a positive affirmation of the need for the League to expand its functions to

[110] ibid.
[111] ibid 1473.
[112] ibid.
[113] ibid.
[114] 'First Meeting (Private, Then Public): Eighty-Sixth Session of the Council' (1935) 16 *League of Nations Official Journal* 592, 597.
[115] See above nn 66, 78 and accompanying text.
[116] Walters, above n 64, 754; Hudson, above n 5, 4, 7; N Brown, '"Far More than Anyone Could Dream Of": The League of Nations in Australian Economic Analysis of the Nation, the Region and the World' in J Damousi and P O'Brien (eds), *League of Nations: Histories, Legacies and Impact* (Melbourne, Melbourne University Press, 2018).
[117] L Neal, 'The Economics and Finance of Bilateral Clearing Agreements: Germany, 1934–8' (1979) 32 *Economic History Review* 391, 391.

forge links between political and economic issues. Whichever way it is presented, for Bruce and McDougall economic security was international peace and security.

C. Australia and the International Crises of 1935–36

Leaving aside these economic and financial matters, Australia remained largely on the sidelines of Council debates in 1933 and 1934. However, this was not possible in the face of three international crises in the mid-1930s: Germany's rearmament, the breach of the Locarno Pact and Italy's invasion of Abyssinia. Bruce's early attitude towards the League's role with respect to acts of aggression can be gleaned from his remarks to the Assembly in December 1932 in response to the Japanese invasion of Manchuria. In this speech, Bruce stated that the authority of the League lay in moral rather than physical force.[118] On that basis he counselled against a resolution that would censure Japan.[119] Bruce's speech reflected Australia's approach: to concur with the UK government and not to undertake any unilateral act that would limit Australia's trade interests.[120] But, were Bruce, and his alternates in the Council, able to maintain this stance when 'perched in Geneva with both Italo–Abyssinia and the brawl over the German breach of Locarno raging'?[121]

i. Germany's Rearmament

Following the reintroduction of compulsory military service in Germany, the reorganisation of its army and its decision to reconstitute its air force, in March 1935 France appealed to the Council pursuant to Article 11(2) of the Covenant.[122] France argued that Germany's actions amounted to a breach of the Treaty of Versailles and a repudiation of its obligations under the Preamble to the Covenant to maintain 'scrupulous respect for all treaty obligations'.[123] Prior to the Council meeting, Italy, the United Kingdom and France met at Stresa to discuss the situation. At the subsequent Council meeting, Australia supported the resolution sponsored by the three 'Stresa powers', which described Germany's actions as a threat to European security and condemned 'any

[118] 'Thirteenth Plenary Meeting of the Assembly' (1932) (Special Supp 111) *League of Nations Official Journal* 55, 62.

[119] ibid.

[120] See comments of John Greig Latham in Commonwealth, *Parliamentary Debates*, House of Representatives, 9 November 1932; Commonwealth, *Parliamentary Debates*, House of Representatives, 9 March 1933.

[121] Letter from SM Bruce to RG Casey (9 April 1936) in 'Personal Papers of Prime Minister Bruce' (National Archives of Australia, NAA, Series A1421, Control Symbol 3, Item ID 202616).

[122] 'Annex 1536, Request by the French Government under Article 11, Paragraph 2, of the Covenant of the League of Nations, in View of the Decisions of the German Government Relating to Armaments' (1935) 16 *League of Nations Official Journal* 569.

[123] ibid.

unilateral repudiation of international obligations'.[124] However, the resolution did not recommend substantive action. Instead, it called for the establishment of a committee to propose measures to

> render the Covenant more effective in the organisation of collective security and to define ... the economic and financial measures which might be applied, should in the future a State ... endanger peace by the unilateral repudiation of its international obligations.[125]

The circumstances surrounding the adoption of this resolution and the 'summary methods adopted by the Stresa group'[126] have been much criticised. The failure of the Stresa powers to agree to any of the amendments suggested by Council members or to answer questions at the meeting 'mocked all the League had aspired to be and the traditions of open consultation it had laboured to build up'.[127] Effectively, the smaller powers were merely a 'rubber stamp' for the agreement reached by three powers.[128] However, Bruce was in favour of the resolution – Walters describes him as one of only two representatives who gave 'unqualified support'.[129] The language of the resolution, described by Bruce as avoiding 'self-righteousness' and recommending 'no more than is essential if the League of Nations is to become an effective instrument for deterring the aggressor and maintaining the peace of the world',[130] was in line with Bruce's early view of the League's role in response to aggression. It also accorded with the UK's stance on the issue. Bruce described the resolution as dealing with a 'European situation' and opined that although Australia 'is far distant from the centre of these fears, she cannot be indifferent to the situation that is developing'.[131] Australia was interested, but not involved.

ii. Breach of the Locarno Pact

One year later, the Council's resolve was again tested when the French and Belgian governments brought Germany's unilateral repudiation of the Treaty of Mutual Guarantee between Germany, France, Great Britain and Italy (the Locarno Pact) to the League's attention. Importantly, the Locarno Pact mandated the demilitarisation of the Rhineland and provided that it was the Council's role to

[124] 'Second Meeting (Public): Eighty-Fifth (Extraordinary) Session of the Council' (1935) 16 *League of Nations Official Journal* 550, 551.
[125] ibid 551–52.
[126] Walters, above n 64, 610.
[127] Scott, above n 8, 307.
[128] ibid.
[129] Walters, above n 64, 611.
[130] 'Third Meeting (Private, Then Public): Eighty-Fifth (Extraordinary) Session of the Council' (1935) 16 *League of Nations Official Journal* 555, 558.
[131] ibid.

determine if there had been a violation.[132] Article 7 of the Pact gave the Council broad powers, stating that the treaty should not be 'interpreted as restricting the duty of the League to take whatever action may be deemed wise and effectual to safeguard the peace of the world'. Although Australia was not a party to the Locarno Pact, the question whether Australia should become a party had been discussed in a letter from Casey to Bruce (as Prime Minister) in 1926.[133] Casey's view demonstrated Australia's dual status in international law at the time. He opined that the more Dominions adhered to the Pact the 'stronger in the eyes of the world is the British position as a guarantor'.[134] However, 'as a practical matter' Casey felt that British adherence through the King would bind 'all units of the Empire', although only a Dominion Parliament could decide whether it would commit troops in the event of war.[135]

In 1936 Bruce was President of the Council and the meeting to discuss Germany's breach was held in London.[136] The text of the draft resolution presented by Belgium and France called on the Council to find that the German government had committed a breach of the Treaty of Versailles by entering and establishing itself in the demilitarised zone and instructed the Secretary-General to notify the Council's finding to the Pact's signatories.[137] Germany's defence to this allegation, presented by Ambassador von Ribbentrop, was centred on the existence of the Franco–Soviet military alliance.[138] Bruce, in a memorandum in his papers, dismissed this argument and another potential German claim that the Treaty of Versailles had not been signed by the current German government.[139] Bruce was concerned that if this second argument was to be accepted 'it would mean that every Government could repudiate agreements entered into by its predecessor'.[140] Bruce's interjections on the issue were largely as Council President. However, at the sixth meeting where the situation was discussed, he expressed his views as Australia's representative.[141] Bruce stated that, like other non-signatories to the Locarno Pact on the Council, Australia had 'a very great

[132] Treaty of Mutual Guarantee, done at Locarno, October 16, 1925, Final Protocol of the Locarno Conference of the Same Date and Collective Note to Germany Dated London, December 1, 1925, regarding Article 16 of the Covenant of the League of Nations (adopted 16 October 1925, entered into force 14 September 1926) 54 LNTS 289 Art 4(2).

[133] Letter from RG Casey to SM Bruce (12 February 1926) in 'Personal Papers of Prime Minister Bruce' (National Archives of Australia, NAA, Series A1420, Control Symbol 3, Item ID 202608) 2.

[134] ibid.

[135] ibid.

[136] 'First Meeting (Private, Then Public): Ninety-First (Extraordinary) Session of the Council' (1936) 17 *League of Nations Official Journal* 310.

[137] 'Second Meeting (Private Then Public): Ninety-First (Extraordinary) Session of the Council' (1936) 17 *League of Nations Official Journal* 315, 317.

[138] 'Fifth Meeting (Private, Then Public): Ninety-First (Extraordinary) Session of the Council' (1936) 17 *League of Nations Official Journal* 333, 335.

[139] Memorandum dated 13 March 1938 in 'Personal Papers of Prime Minister Bruce' (National Archives of Australia, NAA, Series AA1970/559, Control Symbol 23, Item ID 214407).

[140] ibid.

[141] 'Sixth Meeting, Ninety-First (Extraordinary) Session, Part I' (1936) 17 *League of Nations Official Journal* 339.

interest and a very great responsibility in regard to the situation'.[142] He believed that the Council's duties did not conclude with the pronouncement of a breach and referred to Article 7 of the Pact, which enabled the League to take action to ensure peace.[143] This suggests that Bruce was advocating for an active role for the Council; however, that was not his intention. In fact, Bruce believed the relevant states should resolve the situation through negotiation.[144] Bruce used the dispute to push for a review of the 'whole system of co-operation and common action' for the maintenance of international peace and security,[145] claiming that otherwise it presented 'an ideal' which engendered 'a false sense of security'.[146]

One day later the United Kingdom presented proposals drawn up by the Locarno Powers, together with another draft resolution for the Council.[147] When these proposals were discussed, Bruce suggested that the Council, having already passed a resolution stating that Germany had breached the Treaty of Versailles,[148] had fulfilled its responsibilities with respect to the matter. He believed that the best way to promote peace was for the Council to play a non-role: that is, to adjourn the matter and meet again 'as soon as there was any useful part it could play'.[149] The Council passed Bruce's draft resolution, with some amendments, to that effect.[150] Bruce's stance was in line with the UK's lack of desire to support any form of military measures as a result of Germany's action.[151] But it also accorded with his early views of the League, recorded in a letter to Casey in 1925: '[t]he League of Nations fills a very useful place in the world, but will inevitably come to grief if the extremists in it try to make it go too far and too fast'.[152]

iii. Abyssinia Crisis

Bruce's cautious approach to the Council's role when dealing with breaches of the peace was evident throughout the League's deliberations concerning the crisis in

[142] ibid.
[143] ibid.
[144] ibid.
[145] ibid.
[146] ibid.
[147] 'Annex 1591: Text of Proposals Drawn up by the Representatives of Belgium, France, the United Kingdom of Great Britain and Northern Ireland, and Italy, London, March 19th, 1936' (1936) 17 *League of Nations Official Journal* 348.
[148] 'Sixth Meeting (Private, Then Public): Ninety-First (Extraordinary) Session of the Council' (1936) 17 *League of Nations Official Journal* 338, 340.
[149] 'Eighth Meeting (Private): Ninety-First (Extraordinary) Session of the Council' (1936) 17 *League of Nations Official Journal* 346.
[150] ibid 347.
[151] See R Miller, 'Britain and the Rhineland Crisis, 7 March 1936: Retreat from Responsibility or Accepting the Inevitable' (1987) 33 *Australian Journal of Politics & History* 60, 66–67. In his notes on the breach of the Locarno Pact, Bruce recognised that war 'is the last thing that British Public opinion wants': 'Note on German entry into the demilitarised zone (13 March 1938)' in 'Personal Papers of Prime Minister Bruce' (National Archives of Australia, NAA, Series AA1970/559, Control Symbol 23, Item ID 214407) 11.
[152] Letter from SM Bruce to RG Casey (17 June 1925) in 'Personal Papers of Prime Minister Bruce' (National Archives of Australia, NAA, Series A1420, Control Symbol 2, Item ID 202607).

Abyssinia. While the Council was discussing Germany's breaches of the Treaty of Versailles, it was also debating whether to take action in response to Italy's acts of aggression in Abyssinia.[153] Australia's early views of Abyssinia can be found in the 1923 debates of the Sixth Committee when Abyssinia's application for League membership was considered. Australia's representative, Cook, stated that he favoured admission as it would enable Abyssinia to 'rise gradually to the level of other Members'.[154] However, he was also concerned that membership should not enable Abyssinia to 'criticise those countries, such as New Guinea, where the conditions of life were much more favourable'.[155] Membership was one thing, equality was another, particularly if it gave Abyssinia the ability to criticise a territory under Australia's control. In 1926 Casey expressed similar sentiments when, in a letter to Prime Minister Bruce, he described Abyssinia as 'a State that is a thousand years behind the times' and suggested that the 'machinations of great Powers in Abyssinia' were an 'inevitable manoeuvre'.[156] When the dispute between Italy and Abyssinia was being discussed at a meeting of the Dominions' High Commissioners eight years later, Bruce endorsed a proposal 'on general lines' from Te Water (South Africa) that the League should acknowledge it had made a 'mistake' in admitting Abyssinia.[157] He agreed with Te Water that perhaps an international 'tutelage', such as a mandate, could be imposed.[158] Such ideas did not augur well for Australia's approach to Abyssinia's appeal to the Council.

After attempts at negotiation, conciliation and arbitration had failed to achieve a resolution of the dispute between Italy and Abyssinia, in September 1935 the Council appointed a committee (the 'Committee of Thirteen') pursuant to Article 15(4) of the Covenant.[159] This provision enabled the Council to 'make and publish a report containing a statement of the facts of the dispute' together with recommendations in the event that attempts to settle the dispute had failed. On 7 October the Council accepted

[153] Abyssinia sent early notice of Italian aggression in December 1934 and subsequently followed up with a formal request pursuant to Art 11(2): see 'Appendix 28: Radiotelegram to the Secretary-General of the League of the Nations' (1935) 16 *League of Nations Official Records* 193, 274; 'Telegram, Dated January 3rd, 1935, from the Abyssinian Government to the Secretary-General' (1935) 16 *League of Nations Official Records* 193, 252.

[154] 'Fourth Meeting' (1923) (Special Supp 18) *League of National Official Journal* 14, 15.

[155] ibid 15.

[156] Letter from RG Casey to SM Bruce (4 March 1926) in 'Personal Papers of Prime Minister Bruce' (National Archives of Australia, NAA, Series A1420, Control Symbol 3, Item ID 202608).

[157] 'Note of a Meeting at Geneva on 9th September, 1936': 'Dispute between Italy and Abyssinia: Notes of Discussions with Dominion Representatives' (Dominions No 160, Part I, 1935, UK National Archives, DO114/66) (Dispute between Italy and Abyssinia Part I).

[158] ibid.

[159] The background to the dispute and the Council's involvement is provided in the Committee's report: 'Dispute between Ethiopia and Italy: Report of the Council of the League of Nations' (1936) 30 (Supp) *American Journal of International Law* 1, 1–12. The decision to appoint the Committee was taken on 26 September 1935: 'Third Meeting (Private, Then Public): Eighty-Ninth Session of the Council' (1935) 16 *League of Nations Official Journal* 1198, 1201–02.

the Committee's report, which stated that 'any violation of the Covenant should immediately be brought to an end'.[160] On the same day it also accepted the report of another Council committee – appointed on 5 October – which stated that Italy had resorted to war in violation of Article 12.[161] Following the adoption of the Council's resolution, the Assembly debated the matter and established two further committees to consider the League's response, including the imposition of sanctions.[162]

While Australia's representatives were silent during the early debates in the Council and the Assembly, Bruce had much to say at contemporaneous meetings of Dominion representatives about the League's capacity to deal with the dispute.[163] Bruce was doubtful that the League could play an active role, suggesting that the United Kingdom and Dominions should 'refrain from bluffing ourselves any longer about the real strength of the League'.[164] He was in favour of fact-finding and investigation by the Council,[165] but repeatedly stated his view that economic sanctions would only be a 'gesture' and an 'ineffective', or even 'dangerous' one.[166] He thought that if Article 16 of the Covenant – the provision which Hughes had earlier described as a 'mistake' – was to be applied 'literally' it could mean that the British fleet would have to blockade Italian ports to prevent goods entering from the United States. This was an 'inconceivable position',[167] which would amount to 'a declaration of war'.[168] For Bruce there was little difference between economic sanctions and other hostile acts.[169] Even after the Assembly imposed sanctions in the form of an arms embargo, a ban on all imports and certain exports to Italy and financial measures,[170] Bruce maintained his opposition to sanctions at meetings of the Dominions.[171] While the League's failure to take a more coercive approach and impose an oil embargo

[160] 'Dispute between Ethiopia and Italy', above n 159, 26.

[161] 'Seventh Meeting (Public): Eighty-Ninth Session of the Council' (1935) 16 *League of Nations Official Journal* 1217, 1225.

[162] The Committee of Coordination and the Committee of Eighteen: see 'Seventeenth Plenary Meeting' (1935) (Special Supp 138) *League of Nations Official Journal* 114, 115.

[163] Notes of the discussions of these meetings are found in 'Dispute between Italy and Abyssinia Part I', above n 157.

[164] 'Note of a Meeting at Foreign Office on 29th July, 1935': ibid 4.

[165] 'Note of a Meeting at the Foreign Office on 21st August, 1935': ibid 9.

[166] ibid 10, 11. See also, 'Note of a Meeting at Geneva on 17th September, 1935': ibid 15.

[167] 'Note of a Meeting at the Foreign Office on 21st August, 1935': ibid 10.

[168] Note of Bruce prior to Council Meeting on 4 September 1935 in 'Personal Papers of Prime Minister Bruce' (National Archives of Australia, NAA, Series M104, Control Symbol 3, Item ID 242496) 3.

[169] ibid.

[170] The proposals for the sanctions imposed on Italy are found in the minutes of the first session of the Coordination Committee in 'Dispute between Ethiopia and Italy: Co-ordination of Measures under Article 18 of the Covenant' (1935) (Special Supp 145) *League of Nations Official Journal* 1.

[171] There are a number of accounts of the behind the scenes interactions between Eden and Hoare in the UK, between France and the UK, and between the UK and the Dominions: see, eg, D Carlton, 'The Dominions and British Policy in the Abyssinian Crisis' (1972) 1 *Journal of Imperial and Commonwealth History* 59. This has included analyses of the extent to which Australia was deceived about the UK's apparent embrace of sanctions: see Hudson, above n 5, 79–87.

has been much criticised by commentators, Bruce was apprehensive that such an action could lead Mussolini into a 'mad-dog act'.[172]

As Italian troops bore down on Addis Ababa, the Council met in April 1936, less than one month after it had discussed Germany's breach of the Locarno Pact, to again deliberate on the Abyssinia crisis. Bruce expressed Australia's view that the Council should continue 'along the line of action which [it] had been pursuing, sincerely hoping that an opportunity will present itself in the future for a new effort at conciliation which will meet with success'.[173] Once again, he used the occasion to call for the re-examination of 'the whole system of collective security that has been built up', repeating his concern that the system had 'lulled states into a false belief of security'.[174] Not only was the system weak, Bruce perceived that it was potentially a 'menace' to peace.[175] Bruce's statements accorded with the twin suggestions he made at the Council during debates over Germany's breaches of the Treaty of Versailles: a nominal role for the Council and a review of the League's approach to international disputes. The resolution adopted by the Council took this minimalist line, merely calling on Italy to settle the dispute.[176] Once Italian troops had entered Addis Ababa, Bruce opined at a meeting of Dominions that the 'League had never been conceived as an instrument of punishment … it was better to say that sanctions had failed and try to reform the League for the future'.[177] Two days later at a meeting at the Foreign Office, Bruce repeated his view that sanctions could not be maintained indefinitely. On the one hand, Bruce was terrified of the idea that sanctions should be used as a 'bargaining factor'; on the other hand he was concerned that if sanctions were lifted immediately they would face strong criticism.[178] Bruce continued to advocate for the removal of sanctions at meetings of the High Commissioners[179] until the Assembly voted in July 1936 to recommend that the Article 16 measures cease.[180] Within two weeks Australia's

[172] 'Note of a Meeting at the Foreign Office on 21st February 1936': 'Dispute between Italy and Abyssinia: Notes of Discussions with Dominion Representatives' (Dominions No 160, Part III, 1936, UK National Archives DO114/68) 11 (Dispute between Italy and Abyssinia Part III). See also Hudson, above n 5, 84.

[173] 'Tenth Meeting (Private and Public): Ninety-First (Extraordinary) Session of the Council' (1936) 17 *League of Nations Official Journal* 376, 385.

[174] ibid 386.

[175] ibid.

[176] The resolution also reminded both states that they were bound by the 1925 protocol on asphyxiating and poisonous gases (in response to allegations that Italy had used this weapon): 'Eleventh Meeting (Private, Then Public): Ninety-First (Extraordinary) Session of the Council' (1936) 17 *League of Nations Official* Journal 391, 392–93.

[177] 'Note of a Meeting at the House of Commons on 6th May 1936': 'Dispute between Italy and Abyssinia Part III', above n 172, 21.

[178] 'Note of a Meeting at the Foreign Office on the 8th May, 1936': ibid 25.

[179] See 'Note of a Meeting held on the 22nd May, 1936' and 'Note of a Meeting held on the 8th June, 1936': ibid 26–28.

[180] 'Twenty-Sixth Plenary Meeting' (1936) (Special Supp 151) *League of Nations Official Journal* 66.

Prime Minister had informed the relevant League committee that Australia had terminated sanctions.[181]

V. CONCLUSION

Hudson writes that 'Australia came of age in the League of Nations'.[182] To use the words of Desmond Fitzgerald (Irish Free State), when discussing the evolution of the Dominions in 1926, 'every kitten one day becomes a cat'.[183] This is one account of the League from the Australian perspective – as a vehicle through which Australia increased its international status and 'learned to deal with the world outside the British Empire'.[184] Australia's membership of the Council certainly plays a role in this story. Hughes' initial fears that Australia would be cut out of the peak body for security were unfounded: Australia not only obtained separate representation on the Council, but it held that position, including the presidency, during three of the most tumultuous years of the League's existence. Bruce's role as Australia's delegate on the Council assists in this story: Casey described Bruce's presidency of the Council in 1936 in a letter to Bruce as 'all round, the most fortunate thing that could have happened, both in your own interests – and in the general interest'.[185]

Another account of Australia's membership of the League emphasises that while Australia participated in the organisation, its representatives retained some of Hughes' initial scepticism of the League and fondness for Empire. Australia did not believe that the League would be able to enforce international security, nor that it would be able to guarantee Australia's own security. Australia's representatives were conscious that their country was far 'from the centre of the world's problems'.[186] Reflecting this view, in 1930, John Curtin, as a relatively new MP, queried the expense of Australia's delegation to the League in the Parliament of Australia, suggesting that '[n]o Australian delegate at the Assemblies of the League has yet found it necessary to adopt an attitude distinct from that of the British delegation'.[187] On that basis, Curtin proposed that Australia should merely attach a representative to the British delegation.[188] In this story, Australia, with its small Department of External Relations, still relied upon the United Kingdom for foreign policy advice, consistently followed the UK's approach in Council

[181] See 'Telegram, Dated July 15th, 1936, from Prime Minister of the Commonwealth of Australia to the Secretary-General' (1936) (Special Supp 150) *League of Nations Official Journal* 338, 342.

[182] Hudson, above n 5, 3.

[183] Letter from RG Casey to SM Bruce (25 March 1926), above n 45, 5.

[184] Hudson, above n 5, 7.

[185] Letter from RG Casey to SM Bruce (28 April 1936) in 'Personal Papers of Prime Minister Bruce' (National Archives of Australia, NAA, Series A1421, Control Symbol 3, Item ID 202616).

[186] 'Third Meeting (Private, Then Public): Ninety-Third Session of the Council' (1936) 17 *League of Nations Official Journal* 1154, 1172.

[187] Commonwealth, *Parliamentary Debates*, House of Representatives, 4 August 1930, 5192.

[188] ibid.

meetings, and looked to the British Empire for its security. Thus, on matters of peace and security Australia's representatives followed the UK's approach in the Council, even when they voiced their concern in Dominion meetings.

Yet, another telling of Australia's participation in the League explores the positive contributions of Bruce, and McDougall ('perhaps the most underestimated man in twentieth-century Australian history')[189] to the League's role on economic and social issues. The work on nutrition and League reform are two examples of the work of Australians, demonstrating a preference for boosting the League's role on these 'technical' questions where it was thought that the organisation could add value. Australia's representatives viewed these matters as those where all League members – European and non-European – had an interest. Although Australia took a narrow view of the Council's powers in international disputes and warned against the Council taking too proactive a role in political matters, the reverse was true when discussing economic issues. This does necessarily demonstrate a tension between Australia's perception of the League's role in achieving international peace and security on the one hand, and economic security on the other. Instead, this chapter highlights that Australia's representatives supported the connection between these functions.

In October 1936, having concluded his term as President of the Council, Bruce reaffirmed his view that 'the economic and financial questions which confronted the world were the basis of practically all the troubles with which the world was faced'[190] – a view also articulated in the 1939 Bruce Report. Although this report came too late for the League, Bruce's views found expression in the establishment of a separate organ in the United Nations: the Economic and Social Council.[191] However, Bruce's understanding that economic and social issues were matters of international peace and security has not found favour in all aspects of the UN's division of responsibilities. While the UN Security Council is more powerful than its predecessor, its mandate 'to determine the existence of any threat to the peace, breach of the peace, or act of aggression'[192] has been largely limited to armed conflict and associated issues.[193] Notwithstanding this practice, there have been flashes of Bruce in the last 75 years, for example in the recognition that the 'inter-connected' challenges in Haiti were a threat to international peace and security,[194] and more recently, the description of the COVID-19 pandemic as 'likely to endanger the maintenance of international peace and security'.[195] Such links demonstrate a broader understanding of the way economic and social challenges impact on international peace and security – an understanding promoted by Australia at the League over half a century earlier.

[189] Hudson, above n 5, 7.
[190] 'Eighth Meeting' (1936) (Special Supp 157) *League of Nations Official Journal* 55, 60.
[191] Dubin, above n 66, 42.
[192] Charter of the United Nations, Art 39.
[193] See A Hood, 'Ebola? A Threat to the Parameters of a Threat to the Peace' (2015) 16 *Melbourne Journal of International Law* 1.
[194] UNSC Res 1840 (14 October 2008) UN Doc S/RES/1840 (2008), preamble.
[195] UNSC Res 2532 (14 July 2020) UN Doc S/RES/2534 (2020), preamble.

3

The Rise and Fall of 'a Hyphenated Condition': Australia, the British Empire and the Commonwealth[1]

FRANK BONGIORNO

I. INTRODUCTION

IN HIS AUTOBIOGRAPHY *A Führer for a Father*, the cultural historian and biographer, Jim Davidson, calls himself 'one of the last of the British-Australians – as a hyphenated condition'. 'I was born a few months after the fall of Singapore in 1942', he continues:

> In retrospect, this became the most crucial British defeat of the twentieth century. But in Australia British Australia kept on keeping on, running on empty … It is not surprising, then, that many of us were still educated on outdated assumptions.[2]

Davidson's book centres on his own troubled relationship with his father – a man of the Empire in a boy's own adventure kind of way – and the book weaves an account of the relationship between the brutal patriarchy exercised by a man inside a family with the wider imperial dominance of which it was both a microcosm and buttress.[3] That world came to an end – arguably in the 1960s – but its legacies remain. The novelist David Malouf has pointed to the continuation of subtle connections of a shared language – English – as well as 'a particular habit of mind and all that goes with it'. While this is no longer a feast where Britain 'sits at the head of the table', the networks survive, as do many of the Empire's cultural and psychological traces.[4]

[1] My thanks to Colin Milner for his helpful comments on the draft of this chapter.
[2] J Davidson, *A Führer for a Father: The Domestic Face of Colonialism* (Sydney, NewSouth Publishing, 2017) 248.
[3] ibid 250.
[4] D Malouf, *Made in England: Australia's British Inheritance*, 12th edn (Melbourne, Black Inc, 2003) 3, 62.

The Brexit phenomenon has also, in its own way, generated a good deal of discussion about Empire and Commonwealth. Remainers accuse Brexiteers of the nostalgic fantasy that the United Kingdom (UK) could pick up where it left off when it made its ill-fated detour into the European Union.[5] According to one version of the Brexit fantasy, Britain will turn to the successor states of its old Empire – or at least the white-dominated ones such as Canada, Australia and New Zealand (now dubbed CANZUK) – as part of its revival as 'Global Britain'. Yet just how widely such views are held among Brexiteers is debatable. The historian Robert Saunders argues that one can discern the legacies of Empire on both sides of the debate, not only among advocates of Leave. There was, among Brexiteers, more amnesia about Empire than evocation of it, he suggests. They envisaged not a post-Brexit Empire so much as a buccaneering, enterprising people from a small island, punching above their weight in the wider world.[6]

The Commonwealth featured in the Brexit debate as a convenient alternative to a future in the European Union for Leavers, although it was sometimes pared back to CANZUK, a concept with roots in old imperial ideas of 'Greater Britain'.[7] The Commonwealth itself continues to sustain a civil society of some richness – its website boasts some 80 organisations extending across fields including education, health, law, literature and sport – even while its political significance has long waned.[8] 'What is surely beyond doubt', the historian Philip Murphy argues, 'is that the Commonwealth cannot rescue the UK from the grievous, self-inflicted wound of Brexit'.[9] There has certainly been very little Australian interest in the Commonwealth in recent years; and, notwithstanding the signing of AUKUS (Australia, the United Kingdom and the United States (US)) security agreement in September 2021, there is no sign that Australia considers it time to return to 'mother'. Indeed, within Australia, the new pact was viewed almost exclusively in terms of its effect in binding Australia more tightly to the United States. In 2017 the Australian government's Foreign Policy White Paper contained just two passing references to the Commonwealth, in relation to human rights and sports diplomacy.[10]

The Commonwealth has also largely disappeared from Australian historiography. A telling example of its marginal status is provided by James Curran and Stuart Ward's ground-breaking study, *The Unknown Nation: Australia After*

[5] S Ward, 'The Empire's New Clothes: Come to Britain and See the Crisis' (2018) 59 *Griffith Review* 125, 130.

[6] R Saunders, 'Brexit and Empire: "Global Britain" and the Myth of Imperial Nostalgia' (2020) 48 *Journal of Imperial and Commonwealth History* 1140.

[7] D Bell and S Vucetic, 'Brexit, CANZUK, and the Legacy of Empire' (2019) 21 *British Journal of Politics and International Relations* 367.

[8] The Commonwealth, 'Directory of Accredited Organisations': thecommonwealth.org/organisation-directory.

[9] Philip Murphy, 'Sorry, Brexiters. Banking on the Commonwealth is a Joke' *Guardian* (10 April 2018).

[10] Australian Government, *2017 Foreign Policy White Paper: Opportunity Security Strength* (Canberra, Commonwealth of Australia, 2017) 89, 114.

Empire (2010).[11] It is concerned with how Australia adapted its civic culture and identity to the end of the British Empire. What were Australians when they were no longer permitted to be British, as Britain itself turned to Europe in the 1960s and 1970s? What kinds of ideas, rituals and symbols did they embrace to express their sense of being Australian? Curran and Ward discuss such matters as the debate over a new national anthem to replace 'God Save the Queen'; a new honours system, when a substitute for imperial honours was deemed necessary; even what to call the new currency when Australia decided in the 1960s to abandon the 'Pound' (Prime Minister Menzies wanted to call it the Royal). It is a process that Davidson has called de-dominionisation; the implication of the concept was that Australia, like Canada and New Zealand, but unlike many republics that had emerged from the colonial Empire, had made no definite break with the mother country.[12] *The Unknown Nation* does discuss the Commonwealth occasionally, but unlike the 'British Empire', neither 'Commonwealth' nor 'British Commonwealth' appear in the book's index. Nor is there any suggestion that the Commonwealth might have played any part worth noticing in Australia's transition to a post-imperial nation.

This chapter will briefly re-examine the idea of the Commonwealth in Australian law, politics, diplomacy and culture. It argues that the Commonwealth – a recasting of the idea of Empire – was treated by Australian elites as a serious project throughout much of the twentieth century, surviving even Britain's turn to Europe in the 1960s, a period that several scholars regard as critical in forging a post-imperial Australia.[13] The idea of Commonwealth, which was closely aligned with the notion of a bond between English-speaking peoples that included the United States, eased Australia's passage away from the United Kingdom and an imperial way of life in the 1960s and 1970s.[14] As the hold of the imperial imagination broke – in Britain as well as old Dominions such as Australia – these ideas of a continuing affiliation with Britain provided a narrative of continuity, however tenuous that might now seem in retrospect. The monarchy was also relevant in this context. Certainly the major royal tours, while never as popular as the first by a reigning monarch in 1954, continued to attract massive interest and remained one of the ways that Australia's bonds with the United Kingdom and connections to its history were enacted through ritual performance.[15]

[11] J Curran and S Ward, *The Unknown Nation: Australia After Empire* (Carlton, Melbourne University Publishing, 2010).

[12] J Davidson, 'The De-Dominionisation of Australia' (1979) 38 *Meanjin* 139.

[13] N Meaney, 'Britishness and Australian Identity: The Problem of Nationalism in Australian History and Historiography' (2001) 32 *Australian Historical Studies* 76; S Ward, *Australia and the British Embrace: The Demise of the Imperial Ideal* (Carlton South, Melbourne University Press, 2001); D Goldsworthy, *Losing the Blanket: Australia and the End of Britain's Empire* (Carlton, Melbourne University Press, 2002).

[14] C Waters, *The Empire Fractures: Anglo-Australian Conflict in the 1940s* (Collingwood, Australian Scholarly Publishing, 1995) 6–7.

[15] J Connors, *Royal Visits to Australia* (Canberra, National Library of Australia, 2015) 85–139, 154–83.

II. EMPIRE TO COMMONWEALTH

Recent scholarship has emphasised the richness of debate on the government and organisation of the nineteenth-century British Empire. Duncan Bell has revealed the multiplicity of visions that, in the late nineteenth century, were marshalled under the banner of 'Greater Britain', including but not confined to elaborate schemes for imperial federation that owed much to the example of the United States. The idea gained currency that the United Kingdom could be joined with Canada, Australia, New Zealand and parts of South Africa to create a techno-utopian political entity that would allow an increasingly vulnerable Britain to compete successfully in a globalising order.[16] Such visions gained adherents in Australia, such as with members of the Imperial Federation League in the old century, and the Round Table movement in the new one, but they did not stir sustained enthusiasm.[17] The English author, Richard Jebb, writing in *Studies in Colonial Nationalism* (1905), argued that imperial federation was 'not justified by the tendency either of instinctive sentiment or of actual developments in Canada and Australia'. Rather, as they moved from 'Colonial loyalty' to 'national patriotism', the self-governing Dominions valued the Empire 'less for its own sake, and more in proportion as it subserves the interests and ideals of separate nationalism'. Australian patriots were only 'predisposed to imperialism' to the extent that that it meant cooperation among white nations against a perceived threat from Asia.[18]

The Dominion contributions to the Great War strengthened their sense of national distinctiveness at the same time as the war, very much the British Empire's effort rather than merely that of an *Entente Cordiale* (and then the US), reinforced the sense of imperial 'family'.[19] The war witnessed some experimentation in relations between Britain and the self-governing Empire, notably an Imperial War Cabinet that included Dominion representatives but which was really an extension of the Colonial/Imperial Conference that had brought Dominion premiers together periodically since 1887.[20] The decades that followed saw a substantial recasting of the international standing of the settler Empire and the evolution of Dominion status. For good or ill, Prime Minister Billy Hughes significantly raised Australia's status at the Paris Peace Conference of 1919, opposing recognition of racial equality, insisting on a class of mandate

[16] D Bell, *The Idea of Greater Britain: Empire and the Future of World Order, 1860–1900* (Princeton, NJ, Princeton University Press, 2007).

[17] L Foster, *High Hopes: The Men and Motives of the Australian Round Table* (Melbourne, Melbourne University Press in association with the Australian Institute of International Affairs, 1986); D McKay, 'Imperial Pink: Australia, the Idea of Greater Britain and the Imperial Federation Movement, 1868–1919' (BA (Hons) Thesis, School of History, Australian National University, 2015).

[18] R Jebb, *Studies in Colonial Nationalism* (London, Edward Arnold, 1905) viii–ix, 1–2, 84–85.

[19] J Connor, *Someone Else's War: Fighting for the British Empire in World War I* (London, IB Tauris, 2019).

[20] EM Andrews, *The Anzac Illusion: Anglo-Australian Relations During World War I* (Cambridge, Cambridge University Press, 1993) 132–33.

that would allow Australia control over former German Pacific territories, and pushing for harsh economic treatment of the vanquished. Hughes signed the Peace Treaty on Australia's behalf, although as part of a group of British Empire nations, and Australia joined the new League of Nations in its own right.[21]

In response to these developments, there was a growing recognition among Australian politicians, public servants, lawyers and commentators that the war had changed the British Empire – indeed, the growing use of the term 'British Commonwealth' in public commentary and political discourse registered this change – and grappling with the paradox of Dominion self-government within a united Empire was considered a matter worthy of intellectual and political endeavour. H Duncan Hall, an Australian Fabian socialist and historian studying at Oxford during and immediately after the Great War, was deeply influential as both an analyst of, and contributor to, these changes. James Cotton has argued that Hall's contribution, which had some influence on the Balfour Declaration of 1926 through the South African statesman Jan Smuts, was to grapple with the 'conundrum' of 'a group of more-or-less separate political entities that exhibited extraordinary capacities for cooperation but lacked sufficiently powerful formal machinery to effect this result'. Hall's project was a conception of international relations that would find a place for the 'Empire-Commonwealth in the world of states'. As a free association of nations based on the principle of internationalism and committed to the 'ideal of a good life', the Commonwealth would contribute to the success of the League of Nations – for which Hall himself would work for much of the interwar period.[22]

Writing in 1920 on *The British Commonwealth of Nations: A Study of its Past and Future Development*, Hall thought that the British Commonwealth had reached the third great 'turning-point in its development'. The first two were the American Revolution of the 1770s and the Durham Report of the 1830s, which had resulted in limited self-government for Canada. The third was 'the problem created by the transformation of this limited responsible government into the unlimited responsible government, the equality of nationhood and of statehood, now claimed and practically secured by the Dominions'. Hall distinguished between 'legal power' and 'constitutional right'. For Hall, the Empire's 'formal unity' depended on 'the legal authority possessed by the Imperial Crown and by the Imperial Parliament in every portion of the Empire'. According to

[21] LF Fitzhardinge, 'WM Hughes and the Treaty of Versailles, 1919' (1967) 5 *Journal of Commonwealth Political Studies* 130; WJ Hudson, *Billy Hughes in Paris: The Birth of Australian Diplomacy* (West Melbourne, Thomas Nelson Australia and the Australian Institute of International Affairs, 1978); PJ Spartalis, *The Diplomatic Battles of Billy Hughes* (Sydney, Hale & Iremonger, 1983) chs 5–9; A Duxbury, 'Participation in the "Gilded Ball": Australia and the Council of the League of Nations', ch 2 in this volume.

[22] J Cotton, *The Australian School of International Relations* (New York, Palgrave Macmillan, 2013) 95, 100. See also B Fletcher, 'H Duncan Hall and the British Commonwealth of Nations' (1997–98) 16 *Intellect and Emotion: Essays in Honour of Michael Roe, Australian Cultural History* 210.

this theory, the bonds between, say, the United Kingdom, Australia and Canada depended on their sovereignty having ultimately derived from the prerogative of the same Crown. Dominion independence, practically secured in Hall's view, had no effect on this legal unity, for greater Dominion autonomy had rested on the gradual chipping away of the 'constitutional right' of the United Kingdom over the Dominions, via convention and sometimes Imperial legislation. The self-governing colonies, for instance, gained the option of whether or not to adhere to a new commercial treaty from the late 1870s, and the right to withdraw from the late 1890s. Legislation such as the Australian Colonies Government Act of 1850, and the various Constitution Acts passed in the decade that followed to establish the machinery of colonial self-government, are examples of the legislative 'chipping away' that Hall referred to.

Self-government soon brought with it colonies' rights to impose tariffs and immigration controls; the events associated with the Peace Conference of 1919, Hall thought, had built on these foundations, securing the Dominions' 'constitutional right to control their foreign relations', even while this still lacked 'authoritative confirmation'. Hall therefore advocated 'a general declaration of constitutional right', to be made by the Imperial Conference (1921), which would give full effect to this executive, legislative and judicial independence and yet without disrupting the legal unity of the Empire. Hall saw these adaptations as similar to those that had limited the power of the Crown in the United Kingdom itself. Just as there was no serious danger of the legal authority of the Crown being used to overthrow the constitution in Britain, there was similarly no danger of the Westminster Parliament retaining formal sovereignty in relation to the Dominions. In each case, the flexibility of the British constitution and the operation of convention would forestall any danger.[23]

The young Australian lawyer Herbert Vere Evatt, influenced by Hall's recent writings on the subject, also grappled with these matters in his legal writing of the 1920s, suggesting that Australia's participation in the Great War had raised its status within the Empire and in the wider international sphere. In his 1924 thesis on the Royal Prerogative, Evatt argued that

> the outbreak of the Great War and the despatch of Dominion forces overseas, together with the important relationship which was subsequently created by the Treaty of Versailles and the constitution of the League of Nations, all marked a distinct recognition on all sides that Dominion self-government, legislative as well as executive, must soon be recognised as complete.[24]

Hall's idea of a 'declaration of constitutional right' did not come to fruition at the Imperial Conference of 1921. At a time when Prime Minister Billy Hughes was pursuing greater autonomy within the Empire, he preferred to maintain

[23] HD Hall, *The British Commonwealth of Nations: A Study of Its Past and Future Development* (London, Methuen, 1920) vii–viii, 229–32.

[24] HV Evatt, *The Royal Prerogative* (Sydney, Law Book Company, 1987) 75.

flexibility in such matters rather then seeking to codify them. Nevertheless, the Balfour Declaration of 1926, while rejecting the need for a formal constitution, recognised that the self-governing Dominions were

> autonomous Communities within the British Empire, equal in status, in no way subordinate one to another in any aspect of their domestic or external affairs, though united by a common allegiance to the Crown, and freely associated as members of the British Commonwealth of Nations.[25]

Balfour was a political rather than a legal declaration, but it had implications for Dominions' status to the extent that it gave rise to new legislative and administrative actions that reflected this reimagining of the relationship between Britain and the Dominions. The Australian Nationalist-Country Party government of the day, however, had little interest in Dominion self-assertion. The impulse towards greater recognition of the independence of the Dominions came from South Africa, Canada and the Irish Free State, not from Australia and New Zealand, who looked warily at Japan and hopefully to the naval base that the British government was building in Singapore. There was little popular demand for greater independence in Australia itself, which was connected to Empire by multiple threads: trade, investment, migration, defence, culture and sentiment.[26] Among left-leaning intellectuals, there was some interest in the more independent status within the Empire that was increasingly favoured in the more assertive Dominions. John Curtin, for instance, as Curran has shown, while invariably supportive of Australia's membership of the Empire, would in the 1920s have had Australia follow a path closer to Canada's and South Africa's.[27]

When the British Parliament passed the Statute of Westminster in 1931, which provided for the more or less full legislative independence of the Dominions from the British Parliament, it included a provision that Australia would not be affected until it legislated to adopt the Statute.[28] The federal Parliament would not do so until the Curtin Labor Government, with Evatt as Attorney-General piloting the Bill through the House of Representatives, moved in 1942. When the Bill was introduced, Evatt – in this matter supported by Robert Menzies on the other side of the House – went out of his way to present its import as technically legal, rather than as signifying any wider recalibration of Australia's relationship with Britain and the Empire:

> The question of status has been determined once and for all. Australia's status as a nation was made clear in 1926 in the Balfour declaration. Many people disliked that declaration and many welcomed it. This bill is not concerned with the status of the

[25] Inter-Imperial Relations Committee, *Imperial Conference 1926* (Report No E (IR/26), 1926) 2 in Museum of Australian Democracy, 'Documenting a Democracy': www.foundingdocs.gov.au/item-sdid-95.html.

[26] D Lee, 'Australia and the British Empire between the Wars' (Trevor Reese Memorial Lecture at King's College London, 2004).

[27] J Curran, *Curtin's Empire* (Cambridge, Cambridge University Press, 2011) 48–53.

[28] Statute of Westminster 1931 (22 & 23 Geo 5 c 4) s 10.

> Commonwealth as a part of the Empire. It does not involve the general relations of Australia with Great Britain or with the other self-governing dominions in one iota.[29]

Historians have normally understood the earlier hesitations about the Statute of Westminster as arising from a conservative preference for colonial-style dependence on Britain, combined with a desire for partisan political advantage. But more recent research has suggested that the situation was not quite so simple. Senior members of the conservative Lyons Government, such as John Latham and Robert Menzies, did flirt with activating the Statute, but there had been concerns that its enhancement of federal power – even if not ostensibly at the expense of the states – might further stimulate Western Australian separatism. A majority in that State had voted at a referendum in 1933 to leave the Commonwealth of Australia.[30]

There is some disagreement among historians about whether the Second World War represented rupture, continuity, or a little of both, in Australia's relationship with the British Empire. Neville Meaney argues that Australian nationalism represented a 'British race patriotism' until Britain turned decisively to Europe in the early 1960s with its first, and unsuccessful, bid to enter the European Economic Community. Australian self-assertion was really just an expression of Australia's strategic interests, not of its national identity, for Meaney argues that Australia had no identity that was not just a species of British race patriotism.[31] Australian claims to distinctiveness were essentially 'provincial distinctions, comparable to those of Cornwall and Yorkshire'.[32]

Whatever application these might have to earlier periods, Meaney misjudges the nature and temper of Australian nationalism in the 1940s.[33] Claims to Australian distinctiveness are not comparable with British provincial differences, as Meaney suggests, because by the twentieth century they were underpinned by a democratic sovereign state that was itself an expression of Australians' quest to become something other than mere colonials.[34] It is true that the main thrust of white Australian anti-colonialism had never been anti-British, anti-imperial or anti-monarchical, and it was thoroughly imbued with racial chauvinism – that is, it assumed that white Australians, as the best kind of Britons, should exercise power over supposedly inferior peoples. But Dominion nationalism continued a long-running anti-colonial project in its rejection of the idea of white Australian inferiority and deference, and in its expectation that Australia should be treated respectfully as an autonomous state and a self-governing democracy in control

[29] Commonwealth, *Parliamentary Debates*, House of Representatives, 1 October 1942, 1334.

[30] D Lee, 'States Rights and Australia's Adoption of the Statute of Westminster, 1931–42' (2016) 13 *History Australia* 258.

[31] Meaney, above n 13, 84.

[32] ibid.

[33] C Waters, 'Nationalism, Britishness and Australian History: The Meaney Thesis Revisited' (2013) 10 *History Australia* 12; C Waters, 'A Reply to Neville Meaney' (2015) 12 *History Australia* 232.

[34] J Hirst, *A Sentimental Nation: The Making of the Australian Commonwealth* (Oxford, Oxford University Press, 2001) ch 2.

of its own laws. The Labor government of the 1940s moved quickly to assert these claims, by insisting on separate Australian declarations of war against Japan (1941), and later Thailand (1942), as well as European nations such as Finland, Romania, Hungary (1941) and Bulgaria (1942). By way of contrast, Menzies had treated Britain's declaration of war on Germany in September 1939 as necessarily committing Australia, much as Joseph Cook had done in 1914.

The rapid and dramatic shifts in power politics – and notably the collapse of the British Empire in the 'Far East' in the early 1940s – gave ideas of Australian independence an enormous boost and new political and cultural meanings. Christopher Waters astutely calls these changes a fracturing of Empire; not a complete break, but a fracture.[35] Australia's politicians, bureaucrats and generals had now grasped more firmly what is arguably the primary responsibility of an independent state: to protect its people from coming under the rule of another state. This was a decolonising moment for white Australians – one that prompted urgent reflection among the more thoughtful on what it meant to be Australian – although not an exit from the British World.[36] The Australian nationalism that was increasingly apparent was created in large part out of British materials but it included a more powerful sense of Australia as a distinctive 'imagined community'[37] – one that resembled contemporary European nationalisms while also diverging from them in its entanglement in a wider 'British' transnational community.

The continuities were there: this was fundamentally and explicitly a white nationalism, and it remained 'British' in a cultural, economic and strategic sense. The day after the fall of Singapore, the *Canberra Times* had looked forward, after the war, to a refashioning of the British Commonwealth whose strength would 'be exerted and directed from the Dominions where it belongs'.[38] This vision of a decentralised British Commonwealth reinvigorated by its far-flung and self-governing Dominions gained currency during the war and persisted as an ideal into the 1950s. Australian governments, both Labor and Liberal, made a fair job of carrying on as if the old white men's club were still intact, although Labor in government (1941–49) proved more flexible in accommodating a renovated Commonwealth. Ben Chifley, the Labor Prime Minister, was influenced by a liberal internationalism, but he managed to combine it with a cynically nostalgic view of the old white-dominated Empire, remarking in the late 1940s: 'It used to be a great distinction to be a Prime Minister but now they are two a penny'.[39]

[35] Waters, *The Empire Fractures*, above n 14.

[36] See also K Tsokhas, 'Dedominionization: The Anglo-Australian Experience, 1939–1945' (1994) 37 *Historical Journal* 861; R Waterhouse, 'Empire and Nation: Australian Popular Ideology and the Outbreak of the Pacific War' (2015) 12 *History Australia* 30.

[37] B Anderson, *Imagined Communities: Reflections on the Origin and Spread of Nationalism* (London, Verso, 1983).

[38] *Canberra Times* (Canberra, 16 February 1942) 2.

[39] 'Price to Machtig', 7 June 1948, PREM 8/712E, Records of the Prime Minister's Office, The National Archives, Kew (TNA).

Still, the idea that the Commonwealth could be rebuilt and maintained as an independently influential British force in world affairs was widely shared among Australia's elites, whether they leaned Left or Right. Frederic Eggleston, a veteran lawyer, politician and diplomat, and consultant to the Labor government, asserted in 1947 that

> the old line of communications may have been impaired and the structure of the pre-war Empire may have been broken down, but all the materials exist for a changed orientation to the problem; if this is accepted, an edifice stronger than ever can be built up.[40]

Australia, with Evatt as its external affairs minister at the helm, embraced a regionalised understanding of the Commonwealth in which Australia, as the preponderant power in its part of the world – usually defined as the Pacific – would act as an agent of British Commonwealth influence. Australia would be an independent representative of a renovated and reconstructed Greater Britain – becoming something like the 'new Britannia in another world' that William Wentworth had anticipated in his poem of 1823.[41] Here was a decentralised understanding of Empire that sought to confound older understandings of London as metropole, and Canberra, Ottawa, Wellington, Pretoria and Delhi, as comprising a periphery.

Australia revealed its commitment to a reinvigorated British World as well as a measure of flexibility when it endorsed the London Declaration of 1949. That agreement allowed a republican India to remain a member of the Commonwealth and recognised the King as Head of the Commonwealth – terminology favoured by Evatt – and so valiantly sought to salvage something of the idea of the Commonwealth as 'family' in avoiding the older, more impersonal and essentially constitutional language of 'Crown'.[42] But Australian accommodation of a republican India was largely Chifley's doing, for Evatt – rather like Liberal Party leader Robert Menzies – did not believe a republic should be permitted full British Commonwealth membership.[43] Chifley, by way of contrast, 'was never much concerned with formalities'.[44]

[40] FW Eggleston, 'Australia's Role in the British Commonwealth: A Bastion in the Far East' (1947) 81 *Commonwealth and Empire Review* 29.

[41] WC Wentworth, *Australasia: A Poem Written for the Chancellor's Medal at the Cambridge Commencement, July, 1823* (London, Whittaker & Co, 1873).

[42] 'Crown without Sceptre: A Republic within the Commonwealth' (1948) 39 *Round Table* 203, 207; HD Hall, *Commonwealth: A History of the British Commonwealth of Nations* (London, Van Nostrand Reinhold, 1971) 833, 852; P Murphy, *Monarchy and the End of Empire: The House of Windsor, the British Government and the Post-War Commonwealth* (Oxford, Oxford University Press, 2013) 3.

[43] F Bongiorno, '"British to the Bootstraps?": HV Evatt, JB Chifley and Australian Policy on Indian Membership of the Commonwealth, 1947–49' (2005) 37 *Australian Historical Studies* 18; RJ Moore, *Making the New Commonwealth* (Oxford, Clarendon Press, 1987) 178; Murphy, *Monarchy and the End of Empire*, above n 42, ch 3.

[44] Hall, *Commonwealth*, above n 42, 843.

Menzies argued that allowing republics to remain in the British Commonwealth would transform it into a mini-United Nations. He did not intend this remark to be a compliment. As he put the matter in *Foreign Affairs* in January 1949,

> we must now, once and for all, decide whether the British Commonwealth is to remain as an organic structure in which there must be some permanent binding element which preserves unity, or whether it is to broaden out into a merely functional association, an alliance between otherwise separate and independent nations.

Menzies believed the Balfour formula had recognised 'full legal power of self-government', but that self-government should be exercised within a framework of 'common Kingship and allegiance' that involved the coordination of policies throughout the British Empire.[45] For Menzies, the organic relationship was akin to a familial one, under the headship of the King and with a shared British identity. In this context at least, Menzies called for an end to 'the doctrine of undiluted national sovereignty': 'There will be no real international law, and no real international security, until the sovereignties of nations are abated (not destroyed; that is an unreal conception) in favour of a world sovereignty'. The British peoples of the world, he thought, could lead the way not by emphasising the goal of autonomy but rather by concentrating on their reintegration in the interests of 'cohesion and unity'. By making 'the British Empire one Great Power', not only would its own position be improved, but it would act as an example to the world at large. It was a vision not unlike Duncan Hall's between the wars.[46]

The Menzies Government was elected in December 1949 and in the 1950s, by combining a closer relationship with the United States through the ANZUS Treaty (1951) and a robust defence of Australia's Britishness, Menzies was able to ignore, for a time at least, many of the implications of Asian decolonisation. The old Australian version of 'British race patriotism' continued to thrive, but conservative leaders also thought in terms of an alliance of the English-speaking peoples; a formulation that allowed them to reconcile their new stress on alliance with the United States with their continuing allegiance to a British world.[47] But this balancing act began to falter from the mid-1950s. When 'the English-speaking peoples' found themselves in disagreement in 1956 over Suez, Menzies supported old family rather than new friends, Britain rather than the United States.[48] There was perhaps also, after the joyful royal tour of Australia

[45] RG Menzies, 'The Commonwealth Problem: Union or Alliance?' (1949) 27 *Foreign Affairs* 263, 264–65.

[46] RG Menzies, 'Empire Unity and European Union' *Listener* (12 August 1948) 225.

[47] D Lowe, 'Australia's Cold War: Britishness and English-Speaking Worlds Challenged Anew' in P Buckner and RD Francis (eds), *Rediscovering the British World* (Calgary, University of Calgary Press, 2006).

[48] WJ Hudson, *Blind Loyalty: Australia and the Suez Crisis, 1956* (Carlton, Melbourne University Press, 1989); AW Martin, 'RG Menzies and the Suez Crisis' (1989) 23 *Australian Historical*

by the young Queen and Duke in 1954 – which British officials saw as a way of reminding Australians and especially non-British migrants of the importance of the Commonwealth connection – a flagging of popular enthusiasm.[49] Curran and Ward point out that Empire Day, 24 May, was renamed Commonwealth Day in 1958, but that it failed to capture the public imagination. But then neither, for a long time, did Australia Day on 26 January.[50]

Australia was drawn reluctantly into the 'New Commonwealth' of the 1950s and 1960s, whether one wishes to date its birth from the London Declaration of 1949 or from 1961, when a South African republic committed to white minority rule was effectively ejected from an increasingly multiracial association. Australian governments – whether Labor or Coalition – did not embrace the transformation of the Commonwealth with any real enthusiasm. Yet South Africa's departure dramatised the shift from the Commonwealth as a kind of white man's club.[51] The 1965 Agreed Memorandum on the Commonwealth Secretariat which, although based in London, was to be the 'servant' of the Commonwealth's independent member governments, was another significant stage in this transformation.[52]

Menzies' response to many of these changes was especially disgruntled, for he felt that an organisation lacking the old loyalties and intimacies was no longer worth the candle. He was also disturbed at the unseemly haste with which Britain seemed to be relinquishing its imperial responsibilities under the Macmillan Conservative Government. These changes were reflected in jurisprudence as well as in Australian politics, diplomacy and cultural life. His own friend and former colleague Chief Justice Owen Dixon's effective declaration of independence from British precedent in *Parker v The Queen*, delivered shortly before his retirement from the High Court bench in May 1963, belongs to this moment:

> Hitherto I have thought that we ought to follow decisions of the House of Lords, at the expense of our own opinions and cases decided here, but having carefully studied Smith's Case [1961] AC 290 I think that we cannot adhere to that view or policy. There are propositions laid down in the judgment which I believe to be misconceived and wrong. They are fundamental and they are propositions which I could never bring myself to accept.[53]

Studies 163; R Bowker, *Australia, Menzies and Suez: Australian Policymaking on the Middle East Before, During and After the Suez Crisis* (Canberra, Historical Research Section, Department of Foreign Affairs and Trade, 2019).

[49] Murphy, *Monarchy and the End of Empire*, above n 42, 62.

[50] Curran and Ward, above n 11, ch 6.

[51] Goldsworthy, above n 13, ch 5; Bongiorno, 'British to the Bootstraps?', above n 43; F Bongiorno, 'The Price of Nostalgia: Menzies, the "Liberal" Tradition and Australian Foreign Policy' (2005) 51 *Australian Journal of Politics & History* 400.

[52] 'Commonwealth of Nations: Agreement to Establish Secretariat' (1965) 4 *International Legal Materials* 1108.

[53] Sir D Dawson and M Nicholls, 'Sir Owen Dixon and Judicial Method' (1986) 15 *Melbourne University Law Review* 543, 547; T Josev, '*Parker v The Queen* and Dixon's Diminishing Confidence

As modest as such departures might now seem, to Anglo-Australians of Menzies' and Dixon's generation, they represented a necessary recognition – if an unwelcome one – that the global and societal transformations of the middle decades of the century had bequeathed a world in which Australians could no longer look to the United Kingdom as the ultimate authority on wisdom and standards.

III. THE COMMONWEALTH AFTER BRITISH AUSTRALIA

The Commonwealth probably played a part in easing Australia's transition to a post-imperial order after Menzies' retirement in early 1966. Its capacity to play such a role was likely assisted by the long reign of Queen Elizabeth II, which included her role as Head of the Commonwealth, one she performed with high seriousness. Moreover, at least by the 1970s, the Commonwealth provided a relatively comfortable and, especially through the regular Commonwealth Heads of Government Meeting (CHOGM), a familiar forum in which Australian leaders could project a very different image of their country from that associated with Menzies, the British Empire and the White Australia Policy. This shift was also accompanied by a new approach to the question of Aboriginal rights at home; one of the key impulses behind a new liberalism in that field was a fear of international criticism, including in a multiracial Commonwealth.[54] Australian politicians could achieve a prominence within the Commonwealth that was almost impossible elsewhere, such as in the United Nations. They could rub shoulders with African and Asian leaders and express views on Rhodesia or South Africa and gain a hearing. They could seem progressive and internationalist in outlook – as they usually were after Menzies – mixing naturally with national leaders who, just a few years before, would have failed even to gain entry into Australia under the White Australia Policy if they had applied as migrants to do so. There is surely something in the historian DA Low's remark, in a 1984 lecture, that '[f]or all its shortcomings the Commonwealth … provides much the most convenient, ready made, connection that any country can possess, if it is to orient itself sensibly to very large parts of its common humanity'.[55] It could also shore up national pride. At the Commonwealth Games, such as those hosted by Brisbane in 1982, Australians could flatter themselves that they were giant-killers on the track and in the pool even when, in Olympic competition, they came home empty-handed. For a succession of prime ministers from Gough Whitlam (1972–75) through Malcolm Fraser (1975–83) – probably the most vigorous champion

in the Privy Council' in J Eldridge and T Pilkington (eds), *Sir Owen Dixon's Legacy* (Alexandria, Federation Press, 2019).

[54] J Clark, '"Something to Hide": Aborigines and the Department of External Affairs' (1997) 83 *Journal of the Royal Australian Historical Society* 71.

[55] DA Low, 'The Contraction of England: An Inaugural Lecture 1984' in DA Low, *Eclipse of Empire* (Cambridge, Cambridge University Press, 1991) 337.

of the Commonwealth in Australian politics during the modern era – to Bob Hawke from 1983 through to 1991, the Commonwealth still mattered. It was seen as a valuable if not essential part of Australia's engagement with the rest of the world, at a time when engagement with the claims of the 'Third World' to a New International Economic Order was increasingly demanded of developed nations. Fraser was even apparently in favour of an idea that had been kicked around for some years: the appointment of Prince Charles, who had spent a term studying at Geelong Grammar, as Governor-General of Australia in the wake of the damage done to the office by Sir John Kerr's dismissal of the Whitlam Labor Government in 1975.[56] But three factors in particular have combined to reduce the importance of the Commonwealth in Australian public life.

First, there has been the drastic decline of the Commonwealth as a factor in the defence of the region – East Asia – in which Australia has been most interested. Scholars of Australian defence policy have emphasised the continuing importance of the Commonwealth – the term 'Fourth British Empire' has been used – to Australia into the post-Second World War era.[57] Rocket and atomic bomb testing on Australian territory are the most vivid collective memory of this relationship, but these activities were part of a broader defence partnership that would see Australia send troops to Borneo in 1965 to defend Malaysia against Indonesia at about the same time as a battalion was being deployed to Vietnam alongside the United States. In early 1968, the Wilson Labour Government announced the withdrawal of all forces East of Suez by 1971. While Australia tried to persuade the British to extend the duration of their involvement in the region, by this time even the United States was moving away from direct military intervention in Asia. As Australia's traditional great and powerful friends retreated from the region in the late 1960s, it was becoming clear that Australia's foreign and defence policy would, in future, be necessarily more independent, and certainly less concerned with the British Empire.[58] The Five Power Defence Arrangement between Britain, Australia, New Zealand, Malaysia and Singapore continued, but Australia withdrew most of its presence from the Butterworth Air Force Base in Malaysia in the 1980s. The Five Eyes intelligence arrangements between the United Kingdom, United States, Canada, Australia and New Zealand continue to emphasise old associations, mutual understanding and trust, and notions of an Anglosphere gained a boost when Australia found itself alongside Britain and the United States in a 'coalition of the willing' in Iraq, as they would in 2021 with the signing of the AUKUS agreement. But this is all a far cry from the days in which Australia saw its security as being underwritten by its membership of the British Empire.

[56] Murphy, *Monarchy and the End of Empire*, above n 42, 150–51.

[57] W Reynolds, 'Loyal to the End: The Fourth British Empire, Australia and the Bomb, 1943–5' (2002) 33 *Australian Historical Studies* 38.

[58] A Benvenuti, *Anglo-Australian Relations and the 'Turn to Europe', 1961–1972* (Woodbridge, Royal Historical Society/Boydell Press, 2008); Goldsworthy, above n 13, ch 8.

A further reason for the decline of the Commonwealth in Australian consciousness and calculations was the transition to Black majority rule in Rhodesia, now Zimbabwe, and in South Africa, in 1980 and 1994 respectively. Australian governments of both stripes, Left and Right, had expressed forthright views through the Commonwealth on these issues, something that gave the organisation a sense of genuine moral purpose in the Australian context. Fraser played a prominent role in the Rhodesia–Zimbabwe negotiations of the late 1970s and, as a former prime minister, he was appointed by the Hawke Government as Australia's nominee to the Eminent Persons group formed in the mid-1980s to promote dialogue on the ending of apartheid in South Africa.[59] That issues such as South Africa placed daylight between Australian and British governments during the Thatcher era underlined the reality that Australia's Commonwealth connection was now very different from old imperial ties; it was certainly not about deference to Britain, or British policy, an approach consistent with that of the organisation's Secretary-General of this era, Sonny Ramphal (1975–90). Indeed, the Commonwealth was fundamentally no longer primarily about Australia's relationship with the United Kingdom at all. All the same, the Commonwealth, at least until the 1990s, seemed to emphasise those things that many Australians understood as aspects of the British tradition, such as a respect for individual rights, a belief in tolerance, the rule of law and political rights – while setting aside a legacy of racism and violence.[60] But the transition to Black majority rule in South Africa in the early 1990s, while a vindication of the Commonwealth's relevance in one sense, also removed an issue that had helped give it a continuing sense of purpose.[61]

A third reason why the Commonwealth possibly loomed rather smaller in Australian consciousness from the early 1990s was Australia's growing emphasis on regionalism, especially in economic matters. While Britain remains a major source of investment in Australia, trade declined dramatically in the 1950s and 1960s as Japan emerged as Australia's most important export market. Australia also consolidated its regional economic relationship with New Zealand via the Closer Economic Relations (CER) Agreement of 1983, a process that was independent of the Commonwealth relationship. The formation of APEC (Asia-Pacific Economic Cooperation) in 1989 created a multilateral forum whose significance, for various reasons, Australian governments have chosen to emphasise. In the circumstances, there was less space in Australian public culture for the Commonwealth. Australia's most natural regional and economic relationships are mainly with the nations of south-east and north-east Asia – but with South Asia rising in importance – and in the Pacific.

[59] P Ayres, *Malcolm Fraser: A Biography* (Richmond, William Heinemann Australia, 1987) 379–94, 447–71.

[60] The Commonwealth, 'Harare Declaration, 1991': thecommonwealth.org/harare-declaration-1991.

[61] Murphy, *Monarchy and the End of Empire*, above n 42, 188.

Australian republicanism has had little role to play as an ingredient in this mix, for republicans invariably favour remaining within the Commonwealth. While the relationship between de-dominionisation and republicanism defies easy analysis and has been different in each of Canada, Australia and New Zealand, the rise of republicanism in the early 1990s reflected the declining significance of Australia's relationship with Britain.[62] Yet there is also a sense in which republicanism, in its very preoccupations with completing the task of achieving full independence from Britain, is one of the ways that Australians are still reminded of their historic relationship to Empire and Commonwealth.[63]

IV. CONCLUSION

Empire and Commonwealth indeed provided an informal constitutional context for the development of Australia's relations with the rest of the world for much of the settler history of Australia up to the 1960s. To the researcher conscious of the reduced significance of the Commonwealth today, what is striking about the period between about 1918 and 1950 in particular, is the amount of intellectual, political and diplomatic effort that went into shaping formulas that both described and – as gently as possible – prescribed how self-governing countries who shared the monarchy and thought of themselves as part of a free association of 'British' countries could function internationally as self-governing states.

Leo Amery, the British Round Tabler and Conservative politician, was more inclined to such activity than most; in the 1920s, as Secretary of State for Dominion Affairs, he had described the developing tendency to think in terms of the Dominions as separate kingdoms, with the King as the head of state of each rather than of all, as a 'fatal heresy'.[64] Nevertheless, in the late 1940s his formula for keeping republics in the Commonwealth, set out in a letter to British Labour Prime Minister, Clement Attlee, in November 1948, underlines the intellectual gymnastics to which Commonwealthmen were prepared to resort in the era of decolonisation. The sheer intellectual effort is impressive, in the way that enthusiasts for slot-cars or trainspotting are capable of such exertions, but in this case it was a quest to shore up a faltering vision of Empire:

> I have been thinking a good deal of what it might be possible to get the Indians to include in their constitution in order to give some real and formal expression to their desire to remain in the Commonwealth, and at any rate in association with the Crown. I do not think it likely that one can get them to drop the word 'Republic' from the preamble to the draft constitution or any formula in relation to the Crown which would suggest that the Head of the Indian State owed a personal allegiance to the King. The best, I think, that could be secured would be a declaration of free

[62] ibid 8.
[63] J Hirst, *A Republican Manifesto* (Melbourne, Oxford University Press, 1994).
[64] Quoted in Murphy, *Monarchy and the End of Empire*, above n 42, 2.

> association with the Commonwealth and with the Crown as the historic symbol of that association and, if possible, a further declaration that that Crown is represented or personified by the Head of the Indian State … Up till 1837 the King here was also the wearer of the Hanover Crown and the two crowns only became separated by the Salic Law when Queen Victoria succeeded. Similarly, in the Austro-Hungarian Empire there was the separate Austrian Imperial Crown and the Hungarian Crown of St Stephen held by one person. So it is not altogether too fanciful to think in terms of a single crown of the Commonwealth even if its representative in one part were not the King himself.[65]

The ambitions that often attached to such efforts now seem quite as misdirected and far-fetched as the historical precedents being cited: that a newly independent and republican India would be prepared to limit its sovereignty by treating its president as representative of the British Crown; that a Commonwealth so preserved could underwrite a continuing world role for a United Kingdom overstretched by its global commitments and economically devastated by the war. Yet Australia, too, invested much in this fantasy of a Fourth British Empire which, after the accession of Queen Elizabeth II in 1952, translated into the conceit of a 'New Elizabethan Age'.

Now, we find the Commonwealth taking its place in a cynically fabricated industry in political nostalgia, one generated by fantasies about the rise of a new Anglosphere in the 1990s, and more recently by Brexit. Max Beloff remarked in the early 1970s: 'The Commonwealth – a good idea. A pity it failed'.[66] It is hard to disagree with the commentators who predict that it will no more be able to play its ordained role in a post-Brexit Britain than it was able to serve some of the more ambitious earlier purposes envisaged for it. The Commonwealth, with the monarchy at its head, has long ceased to be a kind of 'British Shintoism'.[67] Nevertheless, it did have a place on Australia's path to post-imperial independence in the twentieth century, and it was surprisingly resilient as a prism through which Australian elites understood the international community of states. Popular sentiment is harder to judge, but at least until the intensified globalisation and regionalisation of the later 1980s and 1990s, Australia's Commonwealth membership seems to have had some presence in political discourse and civic life – a matter worthy of further historical research. And the deeper legacies of these older connections and networks for identity, law, language and culture remain, even if often less tangible than for earlier generations. It is, after all, a condition of settler colonialism that origins remain embedded in the deepest structures of a society, even once that society has announced itself as post-imperial.

[65] Letter from LS Amery to C Attlee on 30 November 1948 (Bodleian Libraries, MS Attlee dep 76, fols 238–40): archives.bodleian.ox.ac.uk/repositories/2/resources/3194/index.
[66] Quoted in Low, *Eclipse of Empire*, above n 55, 332.
[67] Murphy, *Monarchy and the End of Empire*, above n 42, 3–4.

4

'Treat-Them-Gently-at-All-Costs-and-Please-the United Nations': The UN Trusteeship Council and Capital Punishment and Clemency in Papua and New Guinea, 1954–65

MURRY CHISHOLM

I. THE RELATIONSHIP BETWEEN AUSTRALIA, PAPUA AND NEW GUINEA AND THE UN TRUSTEESHIP COUNCIL

THIS CHAPTER EXAMINES Australia's relationship with the United Nations Trusteeship Council (UNTC) by analysing Papuan and New Guinean capital cases considered for clemency by the Commonwealth Executive Council and Governor-General between 1954 and 1965. In this period, the Australian Governor-General exercised the royal prerogative of mercy in the Australian territories of Papua and New Guinea under advice from the Commonwealth Executive Council. Capital case files were first assembled by the Papua New Guinea (PNG) law office for the Administrator of PNG. The Administrator provided an analysis in a cover letter with his recommendations and forwarded it to the Department of Territories. Territories' officials and the minister then adapted the file to present to the Commonwealth Executive Council with an analysis and recommendations from the minister. The minister's reformulation of the case file and recommendations were used to inform the Commonwealth's clemency decisions.[1]

[1] See, eg, 'Commutation of Sentences on Natives in Papua and New Guinea' (National Archives of Australia, NAA, Series A518, Control Symbol CQ840/1/3 Part 1, Item ID 3252669). Until 1954 Commonwealth oversight of the prerogative varied. The Lieutenant-Governors of Papua and New Guinea (until 1945), and then the administrator of the unified territories (until 1954), exercised it independently or with advice. After 1965, mandatory sentence of death ended and so there were no more death sentences.

This chapter will examine the capital case files relating to the Telefomin killings of 1953, the murderer Usamando in 1954, the murderers Gaumbu and Aro in 1957, and the Tariga killings of 1961. Capital punishment and clemency were high-profile acts of colonial governance and these files reveal that one reason why Australian authorities usually chose clemency and twice capital punishment for the murder of Papuan and New Guineans was to cultivate legitimacy for their control of PNG within the UNTC by making just and legal decisions.[2] Australia's policy decisions were designed to avoid the notice of the Trusteeship Council so that Australia could continue to pursue a colonial policy that they felt was appropriate to the needs of the people of Papua and New Guinea and was also in Australian interests. Clemency for Papuan and New Guinean offenders would not draw international attention to, and criticism of, Australia's ongoing colonial project, despite the international move to decolonisation. However, in two out of 822 cases it was decided that execution was more just than clemency. These decisions minimised attention and cultivated legitimacy.

The UNTC territories replaced the League of Nations Mandates after the Second World War. Founded on the agreement that trusteeship over a colonial territory was temporary, the Council held debates about how and when trusteeships would end.[3] After the war against fascist imperialism, as Martin J Weiner and Peter Gibbon argued, colonialists felt pressure to conform to the rhetoric of the UNTC goal of 'the political, economic, social, and educational advancement of the inhabitants of the trust territories'.[4]

Australia's intention to achieve the 'advancement of the inhabitants' arose out of self-interest in maintaining PNG as a capitalist, westernised bastion to the north, and out of moral duty to wartime allies.[5] Australia was granted

[2] For other reasons, see M Chisholm, *Capital Punishment, Clemency and Colonialism in Papua New Guinea 1954–1965* (Canberra, ANU Press, 2024).

[3] WJ Hudson, *Australia and the Colonial Question at the United Nations* (Honolulu, East-West Centre Press, 1970) 12–13; I Downs, *The Australian Trusteeship, Papua New Guinea 1945–75* (Canberra, Australian Government Publishing Service, 1980) 240; C Waters, '"Against the Tide": Australian Government Attitudes to Decolonisation in the South Pacific, 1962–1972' (2013) 48 *Journal of Pacific History* 194; C Waters, 'The Last of Australian Imperial Dreams for the Southwest Pacific: Paul Hasluck, 'The Department of Territories and a Greater Melanesia in 1960' (2016) 51 *Journal of Pacific History* 169.

[4] Charter of the United Nations, Art 76(b) (UN Charter); P Hasluck, *A Time for Building* (Melbourne, Melbourne University Press, 1976) 5, 45–47; MJ Wiener, *An Empire on Trial: Race, Murder, and Justice Under British Rule, 1870–1935* (Cambridge, Cambridge University Press, 2009) 233; P Gibbon, 'Lineages of Paternalism: An Introduction' (2014) 14 *Journal of Agrarian Change* 165; M Barnett, *Empire of Humanity: A History of Humanitarianism* (Ithaca, NY, Cornell University Press, 2011) table 1.

[5] On moral duty, see, eg, H Nelson, 'From Kanaka to Fuzzy Wuzzy Angel' (1978) 35 *Labour History* 172; N Brown, *Governing Prosperity: Social Change and Social Analysis in Australia in the 1950s* (Cambridge, Cambridge University Press, 2009) ch 2. On geostrategic interest, see, eg, T Moss, *Guarding the Periphery: The Australian Army in Papua New Guinea, 1951–75* (Cambridge, Cambridge University Press, 2017) 23; Downs, above n 3, xviii; B Essai, *Papua and New Guinea; A Contemporary Survey* (Oxford, Oxford University Press, 1961) 57; Waters, 'The Last of Australian Imperial Dreams for the Southwest Pacific', above n 3, 171; D Lowe, *Menzies and the 'Great World Struggle': Australia's Cold War 1948–1954* (Sydney, UNSW Press, 1999) 54.

Papua, the south-eastern quarter of the archipelago, as a Crown colony by the United Kingdom in 1902. However, New Guinea, the north-eastern quarter of the island chain, was controlled as a UN Trust Territory. Australia had seized German New Guinea at the beginning of the First World War and was granted the League of Nations Mandate at the Paris Peace Conference. The Second World War had taught Australia the importance of Papua and New Guinea and its people to its own defence. As a result, both major parties agreed to increase Australia's commitment in PNG. General Thomas Blamey, the former Australian Commander-in-Chief during the Second World War, wrote a 1946 report on PNG's future for the Labor Chifley Government and argued that Australia's colonialism was 'one of those rare moments in history when morality coincides with expediency'.[6] Australia's strategic interests were serviced by more actively colonising and funding the 'advancement' of Papuans and New Guineans.[7] Similarly, the Liberal Minister for Territories, Paul Hasluck, who was responsible for PNG from 1951 to 1963 spoke in 1951 of a new kind of relationship between PNG and Australia that was not colonial, but 'an attempt at cooperation and mutual service between two peoples of a type never seen before: governance that was a product of Australia's gratitude.[8] Yet, Peter Fitzpatrick questioned the rhetoric of Australian colonialism noting that '[i]ndeed, the exploitative relations of any colonialism was so manifestly at odds with the egalitarian nature of Australia's self-image, that they appear to have to deny that they were colonists at all'.[9] While Papua and New Guinea had been separately administered before the war, one result of the bipartisan agreement to develop and advance PNG was the joint administration of the territories from 1949, which was a change taken with the UNTC's permission. Australia tied the future of the two territories together in the perceived interests of the nation to be, and Australia.[10]

Yet, to meet the duty to 'advance' the people, Australians projected a long possession due to officials' views of Papuans and New Guineans as primitive and unready for modern nationhood. It was thought that advancement would take generations, rather than the 10 or 15 years argued for by many members of the UNTC.[11] One solution to that conflict of intention, as Ian Downs and WJ Hudson have noted, was to avoid the notice of the United Nations (UN) by making unremarkable policy when attention might otherwise have been drawn to

[6] Thomas Blamey, cited in S MacWilliam, 'Papua New Guinea in the 1940s: Empire and Legend' in D Lowe (ed), *Australia and the End of Empires: The Impact of Decolonisation in Australia's Near North, 1945–65* (Melbourne, Deakin University Press, 1996) 33.

[7] Downs, above n 3, 13–14.

[8] Brown, above n 5, 74.

[9] P Fitzpatrick, *Law and State in Papua New Guinea* (London, Academic Press, 1980) 68.

[10] Hasluck, *A Time for Building*, above n 4, 78; LP Mair, *Australia in New Guinea* (Melbourne, Melbourne University Press, 1970) 44.

[11] See RT Stella, *Imagining the Other: Representation of the Papua New Guinean Subject* (Honolulu, University of Hawaii Press, 2006); R Gore, *Justice Versus Sorcery* (St Lucia, Jaracranda Press, 1965) 218.

their colonial practices.[12] Accordingly, Australian colonial policy-makers made some efforts to appear just and fair and comply, and appear to comply, with UNTC obligations and international law. These obligations, including working for the advancement of the people towards independence, making annual reports to the Council, hosting triennial inspection tours by UNTC delegates, and implementing recommendations of the reports that the visiting delegations wrote (usually friendly reports largely drafted by Australian allies).

Yet, the Trusteeship Council was characterised both by Cold War tensions and the desire of newly independent states to extend liberation to peoples colonised by Western powers, such as the United Kingdom and Australia.[13] For example, India and the USSR raised their suspicions that Australia planned an annexation of New Guinea when Australia unified the administration of the territories. Further exposing Australia to UNTC critique, WJ Hudson noted that not all UNTC members accepted Australia's position that Papua was not subject to examination by the UNTC. Indeed, Hudson also showed that the UNTC gradually asserted a moral suasion over the administration of all colonies, as well as trust territories.[14] Consequently, the Commonwealth was subject to increasing scrutiny and commentary on Papua and New Guinea from unified administration in 1949 to the independence of PNG in 1975, particularly as the decolonisation movement strengthened. As such, Australian officials were also increasingly concerned to avoid adverse attention directed towards PNG in the UNTC.

Capital punishment and clemency as high-profile acts of colonial governance were carefully considered in Australia and PNG, as a matter of justice, as well as for possible reactions of the UNTC. As Stacey Hynd argued, 'the death penalty was a crucial element of a colonial state's coercive capabilities, but it was also a potential marker of its violence and inefficiency'.[15] As acts of benevolence or oppression, clemency or capital punishment could legitimise or delegitimise Australia's possession of New Guinea (NG) and PNG. Indeed, Australian officials in the 1950s and 1960s were well aware of that metric and considered it when making life and death decisions about PNG offenders.

Offenders found guilty of the capital crimes of wilful murder, and until 1959, the rape or attempted rape of a white female by a Papuan or New Guinean man, faced a mandatory sentence of death. Despite the mandatory sentence

[12] Hudson, above n 3, 37, 45–47; C Rowley, *The New Guinea Villager: A Retrospect from 1964* (Canberra, FW Cheshire, 1967) 1; Downs, above n 3, 240.

[13] GW Morrell, 'A Higher Stage of Imperialism? The Big Three, the UN Trusteeship Council, and the Early Cold War' in RM Douglas, MD Callahan and E Bishop (eds), *Imperialism on Trial: International Oversight of Colonial Rule in Historical Perspective* (Oxford, Lexington Books, 2006); Hudson, above n 3, ch 2; Rowley, above n 12, Introduction. On criticisms, see, eg, 'Member Refutes UN Statement' *South Pacific Post* (Port Moresby, 19 May 1954) 3; 'Minister Hits Back at Indian Critics' *South Pacific Post* (Port Moresby, 7 July 1954) 3.

[14] Hudson, above n 3, ch 2.

[15] S Hynd, 'Killing the Condemned: The Practice and Process of Capital Punishment in British Africa, 1900–1950s' (2008) 49 *Journal of African History* 403, 403.

of death on 822 people, only two men were hanged between 1954 and 1965. This was because in PNG, a judge could *record* a sentence of death and thus recommend clemency or *pronounce* a sentence of death and thus recommend the death penalty to the Governor-General. Between 1954 and 1965, Commonwealth law required that a pronounced sentence of death be passed to the Minister for Territories who took recommendations to the Cabinet sitting as Commonwealth Executive Council and the Governor-General who was empowered to exercise the royal prerogative of mercy in PNG and other Commonwealth Territories. They took into account the written recommendations of the judge and the Administrator of PNG, and any other information passed to them by the Department of Territories, such as political and administrative matters, in making the decision. In contrast, convention required that the Minister for Territories take recorded cases of death to the Governor-General for discussion and clemency. PNG diverged from other jurisdictions with the royal prerogative, such as Canadian provinces and the United Kingdom, by the strictly adhered to convention that recorded cases were always granted clemency by the Governor-General on the advice of the presiding judge and the Minister for Territories.[16] The discretion within this process in PNG was limited.[17] Largely with Commonwealth approval and confidence, judges almost always recorded death sentences in PNG in the average of 55 potentially capital cases a year between 1954 and 1965.

The royal prerogative of mercy, Douglas Hay argued, allowed the cultivation of political legitimacy among populations disadvantaged by existing power structures.[18] Tina Loo extended that argument to colonial Canada – that executive clemency for Aboriginal offenders legitimised colonisation to the metropole by representing it as gifting merciful justice to a savage land.[19] Hynd argued similarly that clemency in British African colonies could cultivate external perceptions of legitimacy.[20] That argument has explanatory power in understanding clemency and capital punishment in PNG, as one reason clemency was frequently enacted was to project the legitimacy of Australian colonial authority

[16] Attorney-General's Department Correspondence Files, 'Territory of Papua and New Guinea: General Question of Sentencing of Native Offenders Convicted of Willful Murder' (National Archives of Australia, NAA, Series A432, Control Symbol 1956/3371, Item ID 7801327).

[17] On discretionary justice, see, eg, C Strange, 'Discretionary Justice: Political Culture and Death Penalty in New South Wales and Ontario, 1890–1920' in C Strange (ed), *Qualities of Mercy; Justice, Punishment and Discretion* (Vancouver, University of British Columbia Press, 1996). For discretionary justice in colonies, see, eg, Wiener, above n 4, 158–59.

[18] D Hay, 'Property, Authority and the Criminal Law' in D Hay et al (eds), *Albion's Fatal Tree: Crime and Society in Eighteenth-Century England* (Harmondsworth, Penguin, 1977).

[19] T Loo, 'Savage Mercy: Native Culture and Modification of Capital Punishment in Nineteenth Century British Columbia' in C Strange (ed), *Qualities of Mercy: Justice Punishment and Discretion* (Vancouver, University of British Columbia Press, 1996).

[20] S Hynd, '"The Extreme Penalty of the Law": Mercy and the Death Penalty as Aspects of State Power in Colonial Nyasaland, c 1903–47' (2010) 4 *Journal of East African Studies* 542, 552; S Hynd, 'Murder and Mercy: Capital Punishment in Colonial Kenya, ca 1909–1956' (2012) 45 *International Journal of African Historical Studies* 81, 92.

to both Australian audiences and the UNTC.[21] Indeed, expatriates, the PNG administration, the Department of Territories, the Commonwealth executive, and the Australian public, discussed the actual and possible international reactions to execution and clemency in PNG, and Australia's obligations to advance the people under the UNTC.

II. CLEMENCY FOR THE TELEFOMIN KILLINGS

Demonstrating the use of clemency to legitimate Australian colonial practice and to minimise visibility to the UNTC was the executive's decision to grant clemency to 32 Telefomin men who killed four colonial officials in ambush attacks in November 1953.[22]

Some contemporary reportage developed a narrative of the savage violence committed by Telefomin men. Others emphasised cruel and unfair governance in the district and that the violence had justification.[23] Indeed, according to contemporary reports by the Telefomins' defence lawyer, William Lalor, and later research by anthropologist Barry Craig, some people in the district resented the colonial maladministration and Australian control in their area more broadly.[24] Officials realised there was the possibility that the events in Telefomin might be seen as a rebellion against injustices in Australian colonialism: a narrative that would endanger the legitimacy of Australian occupation of the territories. As such, they began to develop a policy response and counter-narrative.

The situation coincided with the 1954 meetings of the UNTC and UN General Assembly, during which the Visiting Mission's report into Australia's conduct as trustee in New Guinea for 1953 was scheduled. Consequently, Australian officials from the Department of External Affairs sought to amplify the justness of Australia's legal processes in PNG with information about the Telefomin situation. Officials were concerned that 'the Trusteeship Council's report [had]

[21] See, eg, Chisholm, above n 2.

[22] 'Fifth Menzies Ministry Second System Cabinet Submissions No 91-115' (National Archives of Australia, NAA, Series A4906, Control Symbol Volume 4, Item ID 209114).

[23] 'New Guinea Patrol Officer Killed by Natives' *Sun-Herald* (Sydney, 8 November 1953) 1; 'Geoffrey Harris' *Sun-Herald* (Sydney, 8 November 1953) 2; 'Lost on Patrol: Fears of 2nd NG Murder' *Courier-Mail* (Brisbane, 10 November 1953) 1; 'Second NG Patrol Officer Missing' *Advertiser* (Adelaide, 10 November 1953) 1; 'Danger Point in NG' *Courier-Mail* (Brisbane, 12 November 1953) 2; 'New Guinea Patrol Locates Bodies of Murdered Men' *Mercury* (Hobart, 16 November 1953) 8; 'Hunt Murderers in NG Jungles' *Courier-Mail* (Brisbane, 17 November 1953) 1; 'Report on NG Massacre' *Sydney Morning Herald* (2 December 1953) 5; 'White Prestige Must Be Restored' *Courier-Mail* (Brisbane, 18 January 1953) 2; Stella, above n 11, 139.

[24] B Craig, 'The Telefomin Murders: Whose Myth?' in B Craig and D Hyndman (eds), *Oceania Monograph: Children of Afek* (Sydney, Oceania Press-University of Sydney, 1990) 133–34; WA Lalor, 'Investigation Made by Myself for the Purpose of the Defence of the Accused Natives in the Telefomin Trials' (26 August 1954) in Annexure No 2, 'Fifth Menzies Ministry Second System Cabinet Submissions No 91-115' (National Archives of Australia, NAA, Series A4906, Control Symbol Volume 4, Item ID 209114).

yet to come before the 4th Committee of the Assembly and questions might be asked and possibly exaggerated criticisms made by Soviet representatives'.[25] Anticipating those critiques, Hasluck sought to represent Australia as fulfilling moral and UNTC obligations. Indeed, he requested frequent updates from colonial administration officials in Port Moresby to organise the representation of events, so 'he [Hasluck] will be in the best possible position to avoid pitfalls in shaping his replies'.[26] Hasluck was wary of decisions and reportage, the 'pitfalls' that might delegitimise Australian colonialism in PNG. In response to suggestions of rebellion against injustice, the PNG administration, Department of Territories and the Department of External Affairs cooperated on building a narrative on the Telefomin killings in which Australia was tolerant of savage irrationality and acted consistently with its project to advance the people, as was its obligation under the UNTC. Clemency corresponded with that narrative.

After the Telefomin killings, there was criticism of Australian colonialism by the families of the dead officers, by Australian papers, and by opposition Australian Labor Party politicians. While some criticised the responsible minister, Paul Hasluck, for not fulfilling Australia's obligation to support a path to independence, others complained of too much haste in meeting the directions of the UNTC and decolonisation. For example, the *Courier-Mail* criticised UN influence on Australian policy and Australian compliance as too rapid and not suitable for the 'primitive' and difficult nature of PNG and Papuans and New Guineans. While they lamented that fulfilment, they did not doubt Australia was attempting to comply with the UNTC requirement to advance PNG towards independence and meet human rights obligations:

> There is a connection between the murders which have taken place in the New Guinea Mountains and the talk which goes on in the conference chambers of the United Nations … they were the first to be murdered since the post war edict, 'treat-them-gently-at-all-costs-and-please-the United Nations' came into force.[27]

Critics such as the *Courier-Mail* concluded, erroneously, that hamstringing Patrol Officers with soft policies and frequent clemency had resulted in a rise in violence, particularly against Australians.[28] Advocates for continuing colonialism and perhaps future annexation saw connections between Australia's rapid expansion to control new areas and increased violence and instability.

Prior to the war, much of Australia's control of Papua and New Guinea was nominal only and substantial occupation limited to coastal areas. Australian officials had never visited or actually controlled large swathes of the interior and its population. To meet the obligations for advancement under the UN

[25] The report went before the Council during the trial the next year: Department of Territories (National Archives of Australia, NAA, 1956/1166, 11 November 1953) 24, cited in Craig, above n 24, 133–34.

[26] Cited in Craig, above n 24, 133–34.

[27] 'White Prestige Must Be Restored' *Courier-Mail* (Brisbane, 18 January 1954) 2.

[28] In fact, there was no rise in violence in the 1950s. See especially Chisholm, above n 2.

Charter, Australia invested in expanding its control to the interior much more quickly after the war. The first step was to establish patrols of new areas by officials called Patrol Officers and Assistant Patrol Officers. These armed officers were trained for a role in law, anthropology and colonial administration at the Australia School of Pacific Administration connected to the Australian National University (ANU). Supported by a few Papuan and New Guinean paramilitary constables, they conducted censuses, enforced Australian law and Native Regulations by being both the police force and magistrates.[29] They enforced health policy and the building and maintenance of airfields, tracks and roads by local people. They were required to build the confidence of the people in Australian administration and also be the spearhead for subsequent expansion of administrative control including, agricultural development, the expansion of health and education services, the promotion of some labour rights, and enmeshing Papuans and New Guineans in capitalism. Part of that confidence building and engagement was the use of clemency and imprisonment to punish offenders, rather than execution, which was too similar to the vendetta system common across much of PNG.[30] The negative influence of the UNTC on the rapid expansion of colonial reach, and in moderating the violent enforcement of law, was regarded as a common wisdom among the Australians who advocated for a continuation of the pre-war mode of colonialism and who were doubtful about international demands for decolonisation.[31]

Indeed, in this case the officials who advised Minister for Territories Paul Hasluck and his Cabinet colleagues accepted that maladministration of the Telefomin had occurred. They acknowledged the resentment of a previously independent people who chafed under colonial control.[32] The District Officer S Elliott-Smith and a Baptist missionary in the Telefomin area, Norm Draper, advised strongly that executions would not cultivate the cooperation of the people, nor enhance an understanding of the administration. To Cabinet, Hasluck emphasised their advice that to cultivate the legitimate occupation of the Telefomin land, the Commonwealth and the administration would need to send a conciliatory message through clemency.[33] They concluded the administration needed to pacify the people, rather than make abstract statements about

[29] AIL Kituai, *My Gun, My Brother: The World of the Papua New Guinea Colonial Police, 1920–1960* (Honolulu, University of Hawaii Press, 1998).

[30] Hasluck, *A Time for Building*, above n 4, 80–83.

[31] Downs, above n 3, ch 7.

[32] P Hasluck, 'Cabinet Submission Summary' in 'Fifth Menzies Ministry Cabinet Submissions No 91-115' (National Archives of Australia, NAA, Series A4906, Control Symbol Volume 4, Item ID 209114).

[33] S Elliott-Smith, as transmitted in DM Cleland to the Hon PMC Hasluck: 'The Telefomin Murders Recommendations as to Sentence, 30 Aug 1954' in 'Fifth Menzies Ministry Cabinet Submission No 91-115' (National Archives of Australia, NAA, Series A4906, Control Symbol Volume 4, Item ID 209114) 3–4; ibid 2–4.

Australian justice through the use of capital punishment. A district in rebellion would not be emblematic of legitimate colonialism that the UNTC would favour.

The decision to commute the sentences of the Telefomin killers was consciously taken by the Commonwealth Executive Council in the way that Loo, Hynde and Hay suggested. Clemency legitimised the authority of Australia in PNG by presenting to external audiences in Australia and the UNTC the need for benevolent and merciful colonialism for a violent and primitive people.[34] Clemency was also useful because it was a just outcome for local people and one that might cultivate acceptance of Australian authority and stabilise the region.

III. DECISIONS TO EXECUTE USAMANDO AND ARO

In addition to the grant of clemency in response to violence, the Commonwealth executive used capital punishment to maximise the perception that Australian colonialism was just and in conformity with its international moral and legal obligations.[35] In this way, the Commonwealth sought to anticipate and pre-empt international and UNTC criticisms of Australian control in PNG.

One example of this practice is the execution of the multiple murderer Usamando in Port Moresby in 1954. Usamando's sentence for four previous murders had been commuted, and clemency for his fifth murder was considered. Wally Watkins, head of the PNG Law Department, wrote a report for the capital case file handed to the Administrator of PNG, Donald Cleland, to inform his recommendations to the Minster for Territories, Paul Hasluck. Watkins argued for the Commonwealth executing a Papuan or New Guinean for a murder of a Papuan or New Guinean, so that a Papuan or New Guinean could be executed for the murder of a white person, without both injustice and concerns of unjust inconsistency being raised:[36]

> At any time a case may arise of a murder by a native of a European, or by a native of a European woman or girl, where the executive would feel strongly that the sentence of death should be carried out. A commutation in Usamando's case would be a powerful precedent to the contrary, and if in the later cases the sentence were executed, it would be very hard to rebut the criticism that there is one law for the protection of the European and another for the native.[37]

[34] See especially Stella, above n 11, 139.

[35] See generally Rowley, above n 12, 1; EP Wolfers, *Race Relations and Colonial Rule in Papua New Guinea* (Brookvale, Australian and New Zealand Book Company, 1975) 125–27; H Nelson, *Papua and New Guinea; Black Unity of Black Chaos* (Ringwood, Pelican-Penguin, 1972) 127.

[36] Walter Watkins to His Honour the administrator, regarding 'Prisoner Usamanda [sic], 13 November 1954': 'Territory of Papua New Guinea: Sentence of Death on the Native Usamando: Decision 207' (National Archives of Australia, NAA, Series A4906, Control Symbol 205, Item ID 4678943).

[37] ibid 4.

There was also concern that the regular use of clemency was undermining the precedent for execution to punish wilful murder. It was implicit to that reasoning that a Papuan or New Guinean should be executed for murdering an Australian as a matter of justice, indicating a dynamic of race and justice in the colonial practices of Australians that valued white lives more highly than Papuan and New Guinean lives. Yet, Watkins was aware UNTC members would disapprove of execution only being used in the cases of rapes or murders of whites and that a race-based approach to sentencing would characterise Australia as unjust and therefore illegitimately controlling PNG. Watkins' PNG Law Department was enmeshed in the process of using punishment to send messages about the legitimate nature of Australia's colonial administration in PNG.

Reporting on Usamando's execution indicated that government statements had focused on the legitimising force of clemency, as it was represented as a just outcome for an extreme criminal in a usually clement system. The Australian Associated Press's (AAP) report, picked up by many Australian papers as well as in the London *Times*, highlighted the media perception of the execution as just, and legitimate:

> Police officials at Lae this morning hanged a New Guinea native, Usamando, who was found guilty on August 30 of having willfully murdered a fellow prisoner, Kago, at Lae on June 22. Usamando had a record of four previous murders dating back to 1928. He was hanged for having killed Kago while he was a prisoner in the Lae Gaol. The last natives to be hanged in New Guinea were three on February 2, 1937, and a Papuan native hanged in 1938.[38]

The AAP report made it apparent that official statements had emphasised the rarity of execution to indicate that the Australian PNG administration was a just government able to differentiate between levels of criminality. Usamando as the killer of five people was a likely candidate for execution in any jurisdiction with capital punishment. The effect was to legitimise the administration.

Similarly, Australia cultivated legitimacy and pre-empted international reactions when Commonwealth and administration officials discussed the cases of *R v Gaumbu* (1957) and *R v Aro of Rupamanda* (1957). Aro had brutally killed his two wives with an axe while filled with jealous resentment. Gaumbu had viciously murdered a woman who resisted his attempts to rape her.[39] Officials

[38] The AAP report appeared in 'Native Hanged in New Guinea' *Canberra Times* (17 December 1954) 8; 'New Guinea Native Goes To Gallows' *West Australian* (Perth, 17 December 1954) 15; 'First NG Hanging for 16 Years' *Advertiser* (Adelaide, 17 December 1954) 28; 'Native Hanged for Murder' *Central Queensland Herald* (Rockhampton, 23 December 1954) 17; 'Native Hanged' *Townsville Daily Bulletin* (Townsville, 17 December 1954) 1. This reporting overlooks hangings conducted during the Second World War. See especially H Nelson, 'The Swinging Index: Capital Punishment and British and Australian Administration in Papua and New Guinea, 1888–1945' (1978) 13 *Journal of Pacific History* 130.

[39] 'Territory of Papua and New Guinea: Sentence of Death Recorded against the Native Gaumbu, Decision 889' (National Archives of Australia, NAA, Series A4926, Control Symbol 754, Item ID 4361140); Submission No 882 in 'Territory of Papua and New Guinea: Sentence of Death

again discussed the need to execute Papuans and New Guineans who killed Papuans and New Guineans to maintain the precedent for the execution of Papuans and New Guineans who killed whites. This was designed to show the world that Australia valued Papuan and New Guinean lives as well as white lives, and to deter crime for local security. They reversed the argument that clemency built legitimacy by arguing that a just execution could also legitimise Australia internationally. Indeed, the Australian Governor-General, former British colonial officer in India, and Second World War commander and war hero, Field Marshall Sir William Slim, argued to his advisers that they should hang men such as Gaumbu and Aro for reasons of simple justice as they killed so flagrantly.[40] In arguing for the execution of these men, Slim, like Watkins, also wanted to maintain the precedent of hanging for murder, so that they could execute a 'native murderer of a white woman' and so that PNG would not be, or appear to be, unjust by placing too little value on Papuan and New Guinean lives.[41] From 1954 to 1957, a fear of international criticism had been used to frame an argument for clemency. Slim turned that argument on its head when he argued for execution. He argued that a just, legitimate system used execution for wicked crimes, and that the precedent for execution must be maintained by executing Papuans and New Guineans for killing Papuans and New Guineans to allow for stern punishment for the murder of white women and men. Further, he argued that enforcing law and order would be productive of greater Australian power in the area.[42] Implicit in this argument was that order and compliance with Australian law would indicate to UNTC inspectors a successful project to 'advance' Papuans and New Guineans and thus further cultivate legitimacy. Aro of Rupamanda was hanged in 1957 using those arguments, although he was the last person hanged by Australians in PNG.[43] Slim did not succeed in hanging Gaumbu whose capital case review came in the context of the 1958 federal election. Apparently, executing a Papuan or New Guinean in the context of election would not cultivate a positive view of Australian colonialism to the domestic

on Native Aro: Decision 1035' (National Archives of Australia, NAA, Series A4926, Control Symbol 882, Item ID 4361268).

[40] W Slim, 'WJS to Minister for Territories, re: Rex v Gaumbu, 16/6/57' in 'Territory of Papua and New Guinea: Sentence of Death Recorded against the Native Gaumbu, Decision 889' (National Archives of Australia, NAA, Series A4926, Control Symbol 754, Item ID 4361140).

[41] ibid; P Hasluck, 'PH to the Secretary, re: The Queen v Gaumbu and the Queen v Korpil, 27/5/57' in 'Territory of Papua and New Guinea: Sentence of Death Recorded against the Native Gaumbu, Decision 889' (National Archives of Australia, NAA, Series A4926, Control Symbol 754, Item ID 4361140); DM Cleland, 'DM Cleland to The Secretary, Department of Territories, The Queen v Gaumbu, 11/7/57' in 'Territory of Papua and New Guinea, Sentence of Death Recorded against the Native Gaumbu, Decision 889' (National Archives of Australia, NAA, Series A4926, Control Symbol 754, Item ID 4361140).

[42] 'Sir William Slim to P Hasluck, 5/12/1957' in 'Capital Punishment [Territory of Papua and New Guinea]' (National Archives of Australia, NAA, Series M331, Control Symbol 8, Item ID 511120).

[43] 'Submission No 882' in 'Territory of Papua and New Guinea: Sentence of Death on Native Aro: Decision 1035' (National Archives of Australia, NAA, Series A4926, Control Symbol 882, Item ID 4361268).

electorate. Neither did the argument for using capital punishment to meet international obligations succeed in the future.

Similarly to Usamando's execution, the representations of the execution of Aro and the reporting of official statements on this execution indicated which reasons found their way into public discussions.[44] The *Canberra Times* and PNG's *South Pacific Post* reported on the execution. The differences in their representations of the execution indicate another attempt to project different, yet both just and legitimate, images for Australian colonialism to domestic and international audiences.

For the expatriate audience in Port Moresby and Rabaul, the *South Pacific Post* led with the fact that a group of *Luluais*, village leaders, from Aro's area came to witness Aro's execution. This local witnessing of the ritual of execution, Tim Castle, and others such as Daniel A Cohen and Karen Halttunen argued, signified approval of the ideas and processes of execution. They theorised that the cooperation with the execution confirmed to the broader audience the moral standards of the institutions of punishment.[45] Using that conceptualisation, the *South Pacific Post* report then confirmed to the predominantly expatriate readers the Papuan and New Guinean and expatriate acceptance of Australia's authority, rule of law and the moral correction through hanging. In addition, the newspaper reported the comments of the Administrator Donald Cleland who spoke to expatriate concerns expressed through the *South Pacific Post* after some well-publicised failures in policing and trial processes in 1957. Cleland emphasised the decisiveness and sternness of the administration: '[t]his is the second hanging in the territory in the last two years' Cleland said, Usamando having been hanged in 1955.[46] This stern tone addressed a community anxious about issues such as unsolved murders and the widespread yet erroneous perception of a growth in violence against women.[47] As the *South Pacific Post* did not circulate much beyond PNG, this was clearly directed at Australians in PNG.

There was a different representation of the execution to Canberra audiences, which featured the diplomatic community, via the *Canberra Times*. This representation focused on building legitimacy. The *Canberra Times* gave few details of the crime, context or region. It was content to cite Aro's crime of murdering his two wives. The problems of administrative control and law and order were not highlighted. For a Canberra audience, it would seem that a double

[44] The official statements were not preserved in the files.

[45] See, eg, T Castle, 'Constructing Death: Newspaper Reports of Executions in Colonial New South Wales, 1826–1837' (2007) 9 *Journal of Australian Colonial History* 51; K Halttunen, *Murder Most Foul: The Killer and the American Gothic Imagination* (Harvard, MA, Harvard University Press, 1998); DA Cohen, *Pillars of Salt and Monuments of Grace* (Amberst and Boston, University of Massachusetts Press, 2006).

[46] 'Native Murderer Hanged at Lae' *South Pacific Post* (Port Moresby, 20 November 1957) 1.

[47] See, eg, 'Smith Acquitted' *South Pacific Post* (Port Moresby, 23 January 1957) 1; 'Tolais Seek Murderer' *South Pacific Post* (Port Moresby, 13 February 1957) 1; 'Women Attacked in Port Moresby' *South Pacific Post* (Port Moresby, 24 April 1957) 12; 'Man Discharged: Interpreter Says He Would Falsify Evidence' *South Pacific Post* (Port Moresby, 6 January 1957) 9.

murder, implicitly, was justification enough for an execution. Certainly, in mainland Australia, sane, multiple murderers were usually hanged.[48] The *Canberra Times* article also noted that few executions had ever been carried out in PNG: '[a]lthough many sentences of death have been passed on natives during the post-war period this is only the second occasion the sentence has been carried out'.[49] Thus the *Canberra Times* article cited issues useful to the defence of the just and merciful character of Australian justice to the Australian and diplomatic audience of Canberra. The effect of citing the heinous crime and then citing the rarity of execution suggested to the domestic and international audiences that Australian justice was capable of reaching just verdicts appropriate to the situation; that it was working well.

Ultimately, the newspapers in their presentation of the executions found the execution acceptable, but for different reasons. This suggests either journalists selected material that seemed to them to be of most interest to their audiences, or that the Department of Territories in Port Moresby and Canberra produced differently worded public statements.[50] Either way, it clearly indicates the differing demands on making clemency decisions. Territories and the PNG administration were walking the narrow path between two different audiences and tailoring the representation of the same phenomena to be both tough on crime, while usually clement, and in both, legitimately just. The scrutiny of the international community and the need to justify the benevolence of Australia's role to the UNTC affected both execution and clemency decisions in these cases, and many more.

IV. PETITIONING THE UN TRUSTEESHIP COUNCIL

Another reason why Australia's international obligations affected its decisions on punishment in PNG was that Australia had had to answer criticisms about Australian colonial justice during UNTC meetings and it made them wary. In defending Australian justice to the UNTC, they argued that the system was clement and just and that imprisonment for offenders was used as a mechanism for 'advancing' Papuans and New Guineans by acculturating them to the West and educating offenders in language, capitalism and vocational skills. An example of this was when the Kilsyth, Victoria, branch of the Communist Party and the Victorian Trades Hall Council sent a petition to the Secretary-General of the UN and Minister Hasluck on 8 May 1961 protesting capital sentences for a group of Papuans from Tariga for wilful murder.[51] Members of the UNTC

[48] See, eg, *Sodeman v The King* (1936) 55 CLR 192; GM Irving, 'Sodeman, Arnold Karl (1899–1936)' *Australian Dictionary of Biography*: www.adb.anu.edu.au/biography/sodeman-arnold-karl-8574.

[49] 'Death Penalty Carried out on NG Native' *Canberra Times* (18 November 1957) 7.

[50] The official statements were not preserved in the files.

[51] Department of Territories, 'Petition to United Nations from Kilsyth Communist Party and Others, Re: Sentence of Death Passed on Papua and New Guinea Natives' (National Archives of Australia, NAA, Series A452, Control Symbol 1961/4256, Item ID 3500477).

received the petition on 8 June 1961 and so Australian officials coordinated a response among their own departments and Australia's allies on the UNTC.[52] This issue was significant enough that correspondence was exchanged at the ministerial level beyond the usual deliberations over clemency.

The Kilsyth and Victorian Trades Hall Council petition complained that the Tariga men had been condemned to death despite the fact that they were in a 'primitive' state, that is, they had had little contact with the colonial administration.[53] Petitioners called for differentiating punishment for 'primitive' people. Ironically, this differentiation was the long-term colonial practice that Minister Hasluck had been removing in response to the UNTC Visiting Missions' criticisms of racially based legal differentiations in PNG, and his belief in universal 'English law' principles.[54] Hasluck had wanted a more racially blind sentencing culture, insisted on sentencing oversight by Canberra, and had appointed a Chief Justice from Victoria in an attempt to change the culture.[55] Consequently, such a call to differentiate was galling. Nevertheless, the petition to the Council demonstrates the petitioners' perception of the impact of the UNTC on Australian colonialism, a perception that was borne out by the seriousness with which the minister and others reacted.

The Australian delegate at the UNTC accused the Soviet delegate, who used the petition as an opportunity to challenge Australia's continued administration of PNG, of ignoring the usually merciful Australian system, with which the UNTC was familiar:

> Mr Uberemko [the USSR representative] has also referred to reports of recent sentences in a certain area, which incidentally is a part of Papua. This reference is clearly tactical only, for he should know as well as I do myself – and I believe he does – that there is merely a legal form involved here; that in the whole post-war period in the territory, only two such sentences have been carried out. In this particular case, I am now able to report that in accordance with the standard procedure, the sentences have been reviewed and have now been commuted to terms of imprisonment of some three years in each case.[56]

The PNG Law Department report, written in response to the petition, argued Australian justice was clement and successfully rehabilitated killers. They argued that the prison system's success at westernising and educating people meant it was always going to be in Australia's interests to imprison rather than execute

[52] ibid.

[53] 'Trades Hall to Hasluck Letter with Clipping, 4 May 1961' in Department of Territories, 'Petition to United Nations from Kilsyth Communist Party and Others, Re: Sentence of Death Passed on Papua and New Guinea Natives' (National Archives of Australia, NAA, Series A452, Control Symbol 1961/4256, Item ID 3500477).

[54] Hasluck, *A Time For Building*, above n 4, 185–91.

[55] ibid 344–45.

[56] Extract from 'Concluding Statement by Special Representative Mr Dudley McCarthy at Twenty Seventh Session of Trusteeship Council (handwritten note) 15 June 1961' in Department of Territories, 'Petition to United Nations from Kilsyth Communist Party and Others', above n 53.

offenders.[57] Indeed, the head of the Law Department, Wally Watkins, argued that officials used law and punishment pedagogically in PNG, and prisons acculturated offenders to Australia.

Watkins argued that incarceration and successful rehabilitation were consistent with UNTC goals of advancement and this was exemplified by the Telefomin killers while they were held in the Boram Corrective Institution.[58] They had learned agricultural skills, pidgin and some had become qualified bricklayers while building their own prison. Indeed, three of the Telefomin killers wished to be employed as bricklayers by the Department of Public Works on their release and had been involved in training prisoners in other prisons in brickmaking and bricklaying.[59] Watkins argued this was the benefit of imprisoning Papuans and New Guineans: they came to understand Australian, capitalist ways, as well as gaining knowledge and skills. This policy was given as a reason why Australia hanged very few offenders. Clemency and incarceration were advancing Papuans and New Guineans, thus legitimising Australian colonialism.

V. CONCLUSION

When the Commonwealth executive made the political calculation to hang or to grant clemency to Papuan and New Guinean offenders they considered the impact such decisions would have upon the legitimacy of Australia's possession of PNG under the UNTC. They used the royal prerogative, both in the interests of justice and Australian strategic concerns. Australians, at many levels of government and society, were deeply interested in achieving positive reactions from UNTC members. While they were not necessarily interested in the UN's goals as a matter of principle, they were certainly interested in compliance with the UNTC as a matter of pragmatism. This had a real impact on the likelihood of Papuans and New Guineans experiencing carefully considered justice and clemency within the colonial justice system.

[57] 'From Crown law Officer W Watkins to the Secretary, Department of Territories, Reply to memorandum 28 February 1962' in Department of Territories, 'Petition to United Nations from Kilsyth Communist Party and Others', above n 53.

[58] ibid.

[59] ibid.

5

Australia, Timor-Leste and International Law

CLINTON FERNANDES

I. INTRODUCTION

How would Australian governments engage with the international community if they enjoyed an overwhelming advantage in power?[1] Would they uphold a 'rules-based international order', in the rhetoric of contemporary cultural management?[2] Would they be a 'good international citizen', to borrow from the rhetoric of an earlier period?[3] An enquiry into Australia's relations with Timor-Leste provides valuable answers to these questions. Eight decades of interaction with a neighbour over whom it enjoys a vast disparity of power constitutes a rich body of evidence. This chapter examines Australia's conduct towards Timor-Leste in an international law context. It is organised around a number of key episodes in the bilateral relationship, beginning during the Second World War and extending to 2021. It uses the terms 'Timor-Leste', 'East Timor' and 'Portuguese Timor' interchangeably, depending on context. They refer to the same geographical area.

II. THE AUSTRALIAN INVASION OF EAST TIMOR

East Timor lies approximately 240 nautical miles to the northwest of Australia. Portugal colonised it in the sixteenth century. For much of the twentieth century, Portugal's fascist *Estado Novo* (New State) was Western Europe's most enduring authoritarian system. The Portuguese regime banned strikes and permitted

[1] This chapter is dedicated to the late Dr Andrew McNaughtan.

[2] Australian Government, '2017 Foreign Policy White Paper' (White Paper, November 2016) www.fpwhitepaper.gov.au/.

[3] G Evans, 'Making Australian Foreign Policy' (Melbourne, Australian Fabian Society, Pamphlet No 50, 1989).

only one political party, União Nacional (National Union). It conferred special privileges on the Catholic Church in the areas of law and education. The same system prevailed in East Timor, then known as Portuguese Timor; the Church enjoyed special privileges and only one political party was permitted – the Ação Nacional Popular (People's National Action), which was the União Nacional under a different name.[4]

Australia had not shown much interest in Portuguese Timor before the Second World War. Portugal and Britain had one of the oldest continuing political and military alliances – the ancient Anglo-Portuguese Treaty of 1373, reaffirmed in 1386 as the Treaty of Windsor. The Australian colonies, shielded by British power and developed by British investments, were reflexively supportive of European rule over Asian colonies rather than of any campaign for freedom or national liberation in the Asian colonies. In 1915, Prime Minister Andrew Fisher suggested acquiring the territory from Portugal to develop it as a summer holiday location. Nothing came of this suggestion because northern Australians were 'far more likely' to come south to escape the summer and 'have the advantage of the society of their friends and relatives than go to such a place as Timor'.[5] Britain invoked the Treaty of Windsor during the Second World War to obtain the use of Portugal's bases in the Azores (an archipelago of nine widely separated islands in the mid-Atlantic). Portugal consented but remained neutral during the war.

After the Japanese attack on Pearl Harbor on 7 December 1941, Lord Cranbourne, Britain's Secretary of State for Dominion Affairs, instructed Prime Minister John Curtin to send Australian troops to Portuguese Timor, stating that Portugal had agreed to the plan. Australia had not yet adopted Britain's decade-old Statute of Westminster, preferring to remain a Dominion rather than become an independent state.[6] Having subordinated its defence policy to British imperial strategy, Australia complied with Britain's instructions and ordered its forces to land in East Timor. However, Portugal's Secretary-General Dr L Teixeira de Sampaio reacted in a 'violently unfavourable' manner to the operation.[7] He stated that Portugal's 'position with regard to the conflict is one of strict neutrality', and 'no aggression of any sort has taken place in our territory'.[8] The Governor of Portuguese Timor, Mr M de A Ferreira de Carvalho, cabled Curtin in strident terms, saying that he 'protests vigorously

[4] J Dunn, *Timor: A People Betrayed* (Milton, Jacaranda Press, 1983) 60.

[5] A Hunt, Memorandum to the Minister of External Affairs (25 May 1915) in 'Portuguese Timor Question of Disposal to Other Powers' (National Archives of Australia, NAA, Series A981, Control Symbol TIM P 15, Item ID 181035), cited in W Way (ed), *Australia and the Indonesian Incorporation of Portuguese Timor, 1974–1976* (Melbourne, Melbourne University Press, 2000) 17.

[6] W Hudson and M Sharp, *Australian Independence: Colony to Reluctant Kingdom* (Melbourne, Melbourne University Press, 1988); F Bongiorno, 'The Rise and Fall of "a Hyphenated Condition": Australia, the British Empire and the Commonwealth', ch 3 in this volume.

[7] WJ Hudson and HJW Stokes (eds), *Documents on Australian Foreign Policy 1937–4, Vol 5: July 1941–June 1942* (Canberra, Australian Government Publishing Service, 1982) document 202.

[8] Mr M de A Ferreira de Carvalho, 17 December 1941: ibid document 200.

against the aggression, absolutely contrary to the principles of law, being carried out against this part of Portuguese territory'.[9]

Lord Cranbourne requested Australia to not mention that Britain was in any way involved even though the plan was primarily a British one. Although annoyed at being placed in this difficult position, the Australians agreed. Cranbourne tried to minimise his own part in the affair by telling the Portuguese government that 'Japanese submarine activity off Portuguese Timor' had created 'an unavoidable necessity'.[10] He apologised to the Portuguese for the actions of 'Allied military authorities on the spot', implying that lower-level tactical commanders from Australia and the Netherlands had acted hastily.[11] But, Japan respected Portuguese neutrality. During its march through Asia, it never included Portuguese Timor or Portugal's other colony of Macau on its list of war objectives. Once Australian and other Allied troops had violated Portuguese neutrality in Timor, Japan, after an agonising debate between its navy and army, decided, reluctantly, to deploy troops there too.[12]

Australian commandos (known as Independent Companies) waged a guerrilla war against the Japanese in Portuguese Timor. The Royal Australian Air Force and its allies conducted aerial bombing operations against Japanese forces in Portuguese Timor. The costs of this conflict for the largely subsistence-farming peasant society were severe, with as many as 60,000 deaths.[13] No international investigation was ever conducted into war crimes committed by Australian or Japanese forces against the people of East Timor, who never received war reparations for their suffering in this conflict. In 2010, Australia's Foreign Minister dismissed questions about these events, saying he was 'not proposing to engage in a running commentary about Australia or East Timor or Indonesia's view of history'.[14] The phrase 'Australia invaded East Timor' is accurate but virtually inexpressible. Instead, most discussion of these events refers to the 'Japanese invasion'.[15]

III. DECOLONISATION AND PORTUGUESE TIMOR

Portugal under the fascist *Estado Novo* was a founding member of NATO. Its military bases in the Azores were a valuable air bridge between Europe and

[9] Ferreira de Carvalho to Curtin, 18 December 1941: ibid document 200.

[10] Lord Cranbourne, 17 December 1941: ibid document 202.

[11] Lord Cranbourne, 27 December 1941: ibid documents 202, 233.

[12] H Frei, 'Japan's Reluctant Decision to Occupy Portuguese Timor, 1 January 1942–20 February 1942' (1996) 27 *Australian Historical Studies* 281.

[13] The population of East Timor in 1930 was 472,221. Seventeen years later, the population had fallen by 38,809. James Dunn allows for a normal population growth to show that the loss of life was up to 60,000: see Dunn, above n 4.

[14] 'East Timor PM Says Foreign Aid "Squandered on Consultants"' (*Radio Australia*, 12 April 2010).

[15] C Fernandes, 'Two Tales of Timor' in C Stockings (ed), *Zombie Myths of Australian Military History* (Sydney, NewSouth Publishing, 2010).

North America. When Portugal joined the United Nations (UN) in 1955, it did not comply with UN policy on non-self-governing territories, wherein states responsible for territories whose people had not yet attained 'a full measure of self-government' must transmit to the Secretary-General 'statistical and other information of a technical nature relating to economic, social and educational conditions in the territories'.[16] Portugal argued that its colonies, including East Timor, were not colonies but 'overseas provinces', and thus beyond the authority of the United Nations.[17] This attitude resulted in considerable activity at the United Nations about decolonisation, with many newly independent states insisting that the age of European empires was over and that Portugal should not be an exception.

In light of the decolonisation debate, Australian defence planners re-evaluated Portuguese Timor's strategic importance. Their assessment was that 'whether controlled by Portugal or Indonesia, Portuguese Timor has no military importance to Australia'.[18] They felt that Portuguese rule was 'at serious variance with policies in non-self-governing Australian territories'. They were concerned that African and Asian countries might mistake Australia's recognition of Portuguese sovereignty in Timor for Australia's *approval* of Portuguese *policies* in Timor. If Indonesian control could be achieved 'by means short of war and with the support of the Timorese', then Australia's 'general interest in the stability of the region would be served by the removal of a potential trouble spot'.[19] Indonesia, however, showed little interest in acquiring the territory, having only recently recovered from US and Australian-sponsored separatist rebellions.[20]

In 1969, Australia granted five exploration permits for petroleum over parts of the seabed that lay closer to the coast of Portuguese Timor than to the coast of Australia. Each permit was granted for an initial six-year term, and all would be renewed for five years in 1975.[21] Portugal had also granted an oil exploration concession over these parts of the seabed, prompting Australian protests.[22] Australia and Indonesia negotiated the Seabed Treaty in 1972 based on a natural prolongation of the continental shelf, resulting in a boundary much closer to Indonesia than to Australia. Australia had thus gained the lion's share of any oil and gas resources that might be discovered in the seabed. And, two years

[16] Charter of the United Nations, Art 73(e) (UN Charter).

[17] RS Clark, 'The "Decolonisation" of East Timor and the United Nations Norms on Self-Determination and Aggression' (1980) 7 *Yale Journal of International Law* 2.

[18] Joint Intelligence Committee, 'Military Importance of Portuguese Timor to Australia' (National Archives Australia, NAA, Series A1838, Control Symbol TS666/61/75, Item ID 1732758).

[19] ibid.

[20] G Kahin and A Kahin, *Subversion as Foreign Policy: And Getting Better All the Time* (New York, New Press, 1995); B Toohey and W Pinwill, *Oyster: The Story of the Australian Secret Intelligence Service* (Port Melbourne, Heinemann, 1989); K Conboy and J Morrison, *Feet to the Fire* (Annapolis, Naval Institute Press, 1999).

[21] Commonwealth, *Parliamentary Debates*, House of Representatives, 1 December 1976 (response by Minister for Natural Resources (Mr Nixon) to Question on Notice from EG Whitlam).

[22] Portuguese Timor: Seabed Boundary (26 September 1974): Way, above n 5, document 38.

after the Seabed Treaty, the Greater Sunrise field was discovered just 0.7 nautical miles from the Seabed Treaty boundary at its closest point.[23] Perhaps alluding to Australia's considerably greater experience in geoscience, Indonesia's Minister for Foreign Affairs later told Australia's Ambassador to Jakarta that Australia had 'taken Indonesia to the cleaners'.[24] Australia had rebuffed Portugal's interest in these negotiations.[25] The maritime boundary with Portuguese Timor remained unresolved, resulting in what was known as the Timor Gap, the area between the eastern and western parts of the Australia–Indonesia seabed boundary to the south of Portuguese Timor.

On 25 April 1974, a group of Portuguese military officers known as the Armed Forces Movement overthrew the *Estado Novo* and committed Portugal to a decolonisation process. Portuguese Timor's independence was now on the agenda. In its assessment of these developments, Australia's Department of Foreign Affairs said that there were 'good possibilities' for the discovery of oil or natural gas deposits in Portuguese Timor, and 'the likelihood of increased revenues would increase the reluctance of Portugal to relinquish control over the territory'.[26] By contrast, it said, we should

> bear in mind that the Indonesians would probably be prepared to accept the same compromise as they did in the negotiations already completed on the seabed boundary between our two countries. Such a compromise would be more acceptable to us than the present Portuguese position.[27]

An Indonesian takeover of Portuguese Timor soon had its advocates in the Department. John McCredie in the Australian Embassy in Jakarta wrote that 'Indonesian absorption of Timor makes geopolitical sense' and would 'help confirm our seabed agreement with Indonesia'. The passage of time entailed risks: '[t]he problem with waiting and seeing is that time may turn against us'.[28] The Embassy moved quickly. Australia's Ambassador to Jakarta spoke to Harry Tjan, an Indonesian political operative who headed the Centre for Strategic and International Studies (CSIS). The CSIS was close to key Indonesian military and intelligence personnel – people who 'viewed massacres and psychological warfare operations and political intrigue as legitimate and normal modes of governance'.[29] Tjan submitted a report to Indonesian President Suharto

[23] J Sheehy, 'Law and Diplomacy, Sovereignty and Consent: A Reflection on the First-Ever Compulsory Conciliation under the Law of the Sea' (2021) 6 *Asia-Pacific Journal of Ocean Law and Policy* 5.

[24] Richard Woolcott, 'Fixed Relations' *The Australian* (New South Wales, 15 March 1997).

[25] K McGrath, *Crossing the Line: Australia's Secret History in the Timor Sea* (Carlton, Schwartz Publishing, 2017) 42.

[26] Policy Planning Paper, 3 May 1974: Way, above n 5, document 3.

[27] ibid.

[28] Letter from McCredie to Feakes, 29 May 1974: ibid document 9.

[29] J Roosa, *Pretext for Mass Murder* (Madison, WI, University of Wisconsin Press, 2006) 225.

'recommending that Indonesia mount a clandestine operation in Portuguese Timor to ensure that the territory would opt for incorporation into Indonesia'.[30]

Australia's position was influential. According to a subsequent memoir by a leading CSIS figure (and close friend of Tjan), 'this was all very low-key and certainly not something [President] Suharto himself was interested in'.[31] Things changed decisively after Prime Minister Whitlam met President Suharto on 6 September 1974. Whitlam advised Suharto that he was 'in favour of incorporation but obeisance has to be made to self-determination'.[32] Until Whitlam's visit to Jakarta, Indonesian officials 'had been undecided about Timor', said Major-General Ali Murtopo, a confidant of the President. 'However, the Prime Minister's support for the idea of incorporation into Indonesia had helped them to crystallise their own thinking and they were now firmly convinced of the wisdom of this course'.[33]

Before these developments, Indonesia had 'categorically abjured' any claim to Portuguese Timor.[34] When Indigenous political organisations emerged in the territory after the overthrow of the *Estado Novo*, the Indonesian establishment was not opposed to the prospect of independence. In June 1974, Indonesia's Foreign Minister provided written assurances in support of Portuguese Timor's right to self-determination, saying that 'independence' was 'the right of every nation with no exception for the people in Timor', and that 'whoever will govern in Timor in future after independence can be assured that the government of Indonesia will always strive to maintain good relations, friendship and cooperation for the benefit of both countries'.[35] However, Australian diplomacy and the popularity of an Indigenous organisation known as the Revolutionary Front for an Independent East Timor (Frente Revolucionária de Timor Leste Independente – FRETILIN) led to Indonesian hostility.

FRETILIN's calls for decolonisation, land reform, administrative reform and popular education ran counter to the Suharto regime's opposition to grassroots political mobilisation. The regime's view was that 'people in the villages' of Indonesia should not 'spend their valuable time and energy in the political struggles of parties and groups' but should 'be occupied wholly with development efforts'.[36] FRETILIN's energetic commitment to mobilising East Timorese villagers would have created a popular democratic alternative within the Indonesian archipelago. This was intolerable to the Indonesian regime, as regional policymakers acknowledged. Michael Curtin, the head of the Indonesia section at

[30] Letter from Furlonger to Feakes, 3 July 1974: Way, above n 5, document 12.

[31] J Wanandi, *Shades of Grey: A Political Memoir of Modern Indonesia, 1965–1998* (Jakarta, Equinox Publishers, 2012).

[32] Minute from Woolcott to Renouf, 24 September 1974: Way, above n 5, document 37.

[33] ibid document 45 (14 October 1974).

[34] D Weatherbee, 'Portuguese Timor: An Indonesian Dilemma' (1966) 6 *Asian Survey* 683.

[35] Clark, above n 17.

[36] A Murtopo, '25 Years of Accelerated Modernisation' in D Bourchier and V Hadiz, *Indonesian Politics and Society: A Reader* (London, Routledge, 2003) 45–46.

Australia's Department of Foreign Affairs, wrote that FRETILIN was 'the sort of party we would have welcomed, even encouraged, anywhere else than in Timor'.[37] But, 'an independent and politically radicalised East Timor ... would certainly become something for discontented Indonesians to look to'.[38]

Given the geopolitical context of the Cold War, Indonesia described FRETILIN as communists. The reality, as Australian intelligence observed, was that most of its leaders 'were practicing Catholics; of the ten main FRETILIN leaders, at least four attended mass daily ... few members of the Central Committee seemed familiar with Marxist philosophy'.[39] However, Indonesia's President Suharto had come to power by eliminating the Indonesian Communist Party. He created a more permissive environment for international financial institutions and business corporations. Suharto therefore earned the support of the United States (US) and Australia. The effect of this support was to suppress East Timor's right to self-determination. Indonesia mounted a campaign of covert destabilisation against East Timor. According to an adviser to President Suharto, the 'original idea was to train locals ... to subvert and then fight FRETILIN, and through that process to take over'. But, FRETILIN had too much support, he wrote, and 'our miscalculations, in hindsight, were obvious'.[40]

Australia supported Indonesia diplomatically at the United Nations even though the people of East Timor desired self-determination and were entitled to it under international law. East Timor was geographically separate and ethnically and culturally distinct from Portugal, the country responsible for its administration. Accordingly, it met the criteria set out in UN General Assembly Resolution 1541(XV) regarding the status of non-self-governing territories.[41] When the UN Decolonisation Committee circulated a draft resolution expressing the hope that the 'necessary steps will soon be taken' to help the people of Timor to 'exercise their right to self-determination and independence',[42] Australia's Mission to the United Nations worked with Indonesia to have the words 'soon' and 'independence' deleted from the draft.[43] The Decolonisation Committee Chair was advised that Australia supported a 'measured and deliberate' approach.[44] Furthermore, Australian diplomats were careful to avoid using the word 'independence' – they spoke of Timor's 'emergence into complete freedom', and suggested that this could mean that the Timorese 'will wish to associate themselves with Indonesia. If this was so, Australia would accept it provided that the decision was based on a well-prepared process of

[37] M Curtin, 15 October 1975: Way, above n 5, document 260.
[38] Curtin, ibid.
[39] Joint Intelligence Organisation, 'The Indonesian Integration of East Timor' (National Archives of Australia, NAA, Series A13685, Control Symbol 1/1978, Item ID 30485074).
[40] Wanandi, above n 31, 205.
[41] Clark, above n 17.
[42] Way, above n 5, document 139 (5 June 1975).
[43] ibid document 140 (6 June 1975).
[44] ibid.

self-determination'. Notable here are the deliberate choice of words: 'accept' rather than 'welcome', 'well-prepared' instead of 'internationally acceptable', and 'process of self-determination' instead of 'act of self-determination' – thus enabling a bogus, West Papuan-style 'consultation' rather than a plebiscite.[45]

The Department of Foreign Affairs' internal legal advice, as early as February 1975, was that an

> Indonesian invasion of Portuguese Timor would be contrary to art 2(3) and (4) of the [UN] *Charter* which provides that international disputes shall be settled by peaceful means and obliges members to refrain from the threat or use of force, against the territorial integrity or political independence of another State.[46]

However, although this advice stated that 'Indonesian action would fall into the category of outright aggression',[47] Australia's Ambassador to Indonesia argued that the aim of Australian foreign policy should be to 'do our best to contain the damage to the Australian/Indonesia relationship and act to limit a recrudescence of latent hostility to Indonesia in Australia'. Australian principles, according to this view, 'should be tempered by the proximity of Indonesia and its importance to us and by the relative unimportance of Portuguese Timor'.[48] Prime Minister Gough Whitlam noted in the margin of this cable, 'Woolcott is right'.[49] Subsequently, the Department of Foreign Affairs focused its energies inwards, on containing Australian domestic opinion rather than outwards, on Indonesian behaviour. The Australian government ordered the surveillance of activists who campaigned for East Timor and restricted the entry of East Timorese independence campaigners to Australia.[50]

There were policy alternatives available. Australia could have called for an internationally supervised referendum on independence at any time after the 1974 coup in Portugal. It could also have called for a decolonisation process under UN auspices, internationalising the issue and thwarting an Indonesian initiative. Australia could have recognised FRETILIN and other East Timorese political parties, and insisted on their inclusion in a decolonisation process.[51] Australia could also have informed its allies in the UN Security Council that it preferred an independent East Timor. All these options were compliant with international law. But, Australia's stance, expressed often in the internal documentary record, was that responsibility for East Timor 'rests primarily with

[45] ibid document 134 (26 May 1975). In 1969, Indonesia selected 1,022 West Papuans – approximately one-tenth of 1% of the West Papuan population – who voted unanimously to join Indonesia.

[46] ibid document 91 (21 February 1975).

[47] ibid.

[48] ibid document 166 (14 August 1975).

[49] ibid.

[50] P Job, *A Narrative of Denial: Australia and the Indonesian Violation of East Timor* (Melbourne, Melbourne University Publishing, 2021) 130.

[51] M Booth, 'Pritchett's Prediction: Australian Foreign Policy toward Indonesia's Incorporation of East Timor, 1974–1999' (MPhil Thesis, University of New South Wales, 2017).

Portugal and the Timorese, with Indonesia occupying the next place because of its predominant interest. Australia should not be a party principal'.[52]

In September 1975, Indonesia launched an armed, covert action involving as many as 3,800 soldiers. It briefed Australian embassy officials in advance, telling them that President Suharto 'had made it clear that "no Indonesian flag" could ever be used in the operation'.[53] It said the main thrust of the operation would be through the border towns of Balibo and Maliana. The next month, five Australian journalists entered the border region and attempted to report from Balibo. If successful, they would have exposed the Indonesian military's covert activities. Indonesian special forces captured them on 16 October 1975 and murdered them. In 2007, a coronial inquest into their deaths was held in Sydney. The governor of Jakarta, Lieutenant-General Sutiyoso, happened to be visiting Sydney at the time. He was a former soldier reported to have been present at Balibo when the journalists were killed. The coronial inquest requested his presence as a witness. Australia's Department of Foreign Affairs and Trade (DFAT) objected that Sutiyoso enjoyed state immunity, attempting to shield him from the inquest. As Ben Saul observed, 'one wonders whether interviewing a local mayor would really impair the conduct of international relations or interfere in the sovereign equality, dignity or independence of Indonesia'.[54] Sutiyoso did not appear at the inquest, and no prosecutions were ever launched even though the inquest identified two individuals as responsible for the murders.[55]

Indonesia launched a full-scale military invasion on 7 December 1975. Australian diplomats shielded Indonesia from criticism at the United Nations. They said their 'immediate diplomatic problem and task' was 'to do what we can to reduce the pressure on the Indonesians'.[56] Australia's Deputy Representative to the United Nations, Duncan Campbell, expressed 'understanding and sympathy for Indonesia's position', saying that Indonesia was 'inevitably touched and troubled by the tragedy in Timor'. Although Indonesia's use of force was 'a matter for deep regret and concern on the part of the Australian government', the fault, he said, was with Portugal, which 'remains responsible' for the 'anarchy across the border'. He said that Portugal's 'deficiencies in its role in the territory … have been the basic factor contributing to the present crisis'.[57] Australia's Mission to the United Nations reported that

> Campbell's skilled and pertinacious negotiation in the Fourth Committee has kept the 'ASEAN plus' group together and a relatively mild resolution seems to be

[52] Way, above n 5, document 118 (31 March 1975).
[53] ibid document 258 (13 October 1975).
[54] B Saul, 'Prosecuting War Crimes at Balibo under Australian Law: The Killing of Five Journalists in East Timor by Indonesia' (2009) 31 *Sydney Law Review* 83.
[55] D Pinch, 'Inquest into the Death of Brian Raymond Peters' (Report, Sydney, 2007).
[56] Way, above n 5, document 369 (9 December 1975).
[57] ibid document 373 (11 December 1975).

> emerging which will … avoid condemnation of Indonesia [and] avoid recognition of the so-called Democratic Republic [of East Timor.[58]

In this way, Indonesia was shielded from international criticism and its leaders assured of Australia's support. Indonesia's military operations caused food shortages and illnesses, forcing the East Timorese to come down from the mountains and surrender. The surrendering population was detained in camps that were ill-suited to their welfare. Often, there were no toilets and the only shelter was under trees. Indonesia prevented detainees from growing food. No medical care was available. Diseases such as cholera, diarrhoea and tuberculosis ensured that most people who were sick subsequently died.[59] A detailed demographic study later concluded that East Timor's death toll as a result of the occupation was approximately 204,000 or 31 per cent of the population.[60] This is the largest death toll relative to total population since the Holocaust. Most deaths occurred during a 19-month period in 1978 and 1979.

The Australian government 'denied the seriousness of the situation, distorted the historical narrative [and] deflected blame from Indonesia'.[61] It ordered the arrest of activists who tried to communicate by radio with East Timor, the interdiction of supply boats carrying humanitarian aid to Timor, and the denial of a visitor's visa to East Timorese independence campaigners.[62] Successive Australian governments continued in this vein. Australia did not support UN General Assembly resolutions in favour of East Timor's self-determination between 1976 and 1981. The Department of Foreign Affairs avoided obtaining formal legal advice regarding recognition of Indonesian sovereignty over Timor 'for fear of getting an embarrassing answer which would make it difficult to sustain the declared policy of the Australian government'.[63] In February 1979, Australia gave de jure recognition to Indonesian control over the territory and began negotiations with Indonesia over the seabed boundary with East Timor.

Indonesia refused to accept the same compromise over the Timor Gap as it had in the 1972 Seabed Treaty. A decade of negotiations ensued, resulting in the Timor Gap Treaty in 1989.[64] It divided the Timor Gap into three 'revenue

[58] ibid document 369 (9 December 1975).

[59] Commission for Reception, Truth and Reconciliation in East Timor, 'Chega! Final Report of the Commission for Reception, Truth and Reconciliation in East Timor (CAVR)' (Report, 7 February 2007) vol II, pt 7.3 See 'Forced Displacement and Famine' at 1253.

[60] S Staveteig, *How Many Persons in East Timor Went 'Missing' during the Indonesian Occupation? Results from Indirect Estimates* (Austria, International Institute for Applied Systems Analysis, 2007) 14.

[61] P Job, 'The Evolving Narrative of Denial' (2018) 50 *Critical Asian Studies* 442, 442.

[62] ibid 462–63.

[63] 'Political Relations between Australia and Indonesia' (British Archives, Reference No FCO 24/2208). Conversation with Alf Parsons, First Assistant Secretary in the Southeast Asia and Papua New Guinea division of the Department of Foreign Affairs.

[64] Treaty on the Zone of Cooperation in an Area between the Indonesian Province of East Timor and the Northern Territory, Timor-Leste-Northern Territory (adopted 11 December 1989, entered into force 9 February 1991) 1654 UNTS 105.

sharing' zones, in which Indonesia and Australia would jointly issue exploration and exploitation permits and share revenues.

IV. THE FIRST CASE BEFORE THE INTERNATIONAL COURT OF JUSTICE

Portugal had never abandoned its legal claim to East Timor. It remained committed to a decolonisation process that respected East Timor's right to self-determination. It contested the validity of the Timor Gap Treaty at the International Court of Justice (ICJ) in *East Timor (Portugal v Australia)*.[65] Portugal argued that there was a general obligation for states to not recognise East Timor's annexation and that Australia was therefore obliged not to deal with Indonesia in respect of the territory. It contended that Australia had 'failed to observe the obligation to respect the duties and powers of Portugal as the administering Power of East Timor and the right of the people of East Timor to self-determination and the related rights'.[66] It was unable to confront Indonesia directly because Indonesia had not accepted the Court's compulsory jurisdiction.

Foreign Minister Gareth Evans briefed the Australian Cabinet in confidence that the Solicitor-General, Gavan Griffiths, regarded the outcome as 'uncertain' and that ICJ judges could criticise Australia in a way that would 'have implications for our policy'. Australia would have to 'address aspects of the self-determination argument which the Government had so far avoided'.[67] Ever conscious that East Timor's right of self-determination was a major obstacle to its case, Australia forewarned the Indonesian government that it would be forced to acknowledge the continued existence of this right.[68] It demonstrated its ongoing support for the occupation of East Timor by making Indonesian Foreign Minister Ali Alatas an Honorary Officer of the Order of Australia on 30 March 1995.

Australia claimed that it was being sued in place of Indonesia – the real target of Portugal's claim. It argued that for the ICJ to rule on Australia's conduct, it would first have to rule on the lawfulness of Indonesia's invasion and occupation of East Timor. This would violate the principle articulated in the *Monetary Gold* case – that the Court cannot adjudicate on a dispute involving a third state where that state's legal interests 'would form the very subject-matter of the decision'.[69] Since Indonesia had not accepted the ICJ's jurisdiction, it submitted that the ICJ could not adjudicate on the matter. Australia's legal representatives

[65] *East Timor (Portugal v Australia)* (Judgment) [1995] ICJ Rep 90. For further discussion of this case, see M Young, 'Australia and the International Court of Justice', ch 8 in this volume.

[66] *East Timor*, above n 65, 92.

[67] 'Evans' views on East Timor ICJ case' *The Australian* (New South Wales, 7 February 1995).

[68] ABC Radio, 'Australia's Arguments in Court' (*Radio Australia*, 7 February 1995).

[69] *East Timor*, above n 65, 100–01.

stated that Australia still recognised that East Timor was a non-self-governing territory under Chapter XI of the UN Charter and that its people retained their right to self-determination.[70] They said that Australia recognised this right even before Portugal accepted it in 1974, and it dealt with Portugal as the colonial power because general international law imposed no obligations on itself not to deal with Portugal. Similarly, they argued, Australia was dealing with Indonesia because general international law imposed no obligations on itself not to deal with Indonesia.[71]

Portugal attempted to answer Australia's objection in two ways. First, it argued that since the right of self-determination was an obligation *erga omnes*, Australia was obliged to respect East Timor's right of self-determination irrespective of the obligations of Indonesia.[72] In a majority verdict, the ICJ accepted Portugal's argument but denied the implications that were said to flow from it, stating that 'the *erga omnes* character of a norm and the rule of consent to jurisdiction are two different things'.[73] It could not adjudicate upon Australia's conduct without first deciding on the lawfulness of Indonesia's conduct. Given the 'fundamental principle' in the ICJ's Statute that it could only exercise jurisdiction over a state with its consent, the Court concluded that it could not rule on Portugal's claims.[74] Portugal's second argument was that the United Nations had already decided that East Timor possessed the right to self-determination despite Indonesia's ongoing occupation. The ICJ's majority view of this argument was that General Assembly and Security Council resolutions nominating Portugal's role as the administering power of East Timor did not compel Australia to deal exclusively with it as regards the continental shelf of East Timor. It noted that 'several States have concluded with Indonesia treaties capable of application to East Timor but which do not include any reservation in regard to that Territory'.[75]

Two judges dissented from the majority position. Judge Weeramantry and Judge *ad hoc* Skubiszewski took the view that Australia had a duty not to recognise East Timor's annexation, and that such a verdict against Australia did not imply a finding against the rights of Indonesia.[76] The ICJ's majority verdict was clearly influenced by the fact that UN Member States were not overwhelmingly in favour of East Timorese independence. The verdict may well have been different had the situation been less ambivalent. It may also have been different had Portugal advanced a different legal argument: the obligation to not recognise

[70] ibid 96.

[71] Counter-Memorial of the Government of Australia, *East Timor (Portugal v Australia)* (1 June 1992) 165.

[72] *East Timor*, above n 65, 102.

[73] ibid.

[74] ibid 101, 105.

[75] ibid 104.

[76] ibid 220–23 (Dissenting Opinion of Judge Weeramantry) 273–77 (Dissenting Opinion of Judge Skubiszewski).

a change of territory acquired by force. All states are obliged not to recognise a change of territory acquired by force, regardless of the legality of the use of force.[77] The ICJ would only have needed to find that Indonesia's occupation resulted from the use of force, whether or not that force was unlawful. In James Crawford's analogy,

> it does not matter whether Israel was acting in self-defence in occupying the West Bank and the Gaza Strip during the Six Day War: whether or not it was then acting lawfully, third States are obliged not to recognise its sovereignty over those territories pending a final settlement.[78]

However, the ICJ made an important observation by declaring that 'Portugal's assertion that the right of peoples to self-determination … has an *erga omnes* character, is irreproachable' and that 'for the two Parties, the Territory of East Timor remains a non-self-governing territory and its people has the right to self-determination'.[79] It is worth noting that since the ICJ had decided that the case could not proceed to merits because of Indonesian interests, it need not have made any additional comments on self-determination. The fact that the ICJ made such comments showed that it wanted to place these points on the record as a judicial determination.

For two decades, Australian governments were protected by a bipartisan consensus: no parliamentary opposition would argue seriously for self-determination for the East Timorese. In 1997, the Australian Labor Party's spokesman on foreign affairs, Laurie Brereton, fractured the bipartisan consensus by arguing that 'a form of self-determination under the auspices of the UN' was 'the only real solution to the problem of East Timor'.[80] In January 1998, that view became official Labor Party policy.[81] The policy change opened up vital political space for East Timor campaigners and forced the government to defend its pro-occupation stance to an increasingly agitated public. The Asian Financial Crisis and the resignation of President Suharto four months later added to pressures for an act of self-determination. Suharto's successor, President Habibie, faced dire economic circumstances and needed to jettison the diplomatic burden of defending the occupation of East Timor. He agreed to grant the Timorese a referendum: they could choose special autonomy within

[77] Declaration on Principles of International Law Concerning Friendly Relations and Co-operation among States in Accordance with the Charter of the United Nations, UNGA Res 2625 (XXV) (24 October 1970); Declaration on the Strengthening of International Security, UNGA Res 2734 (CCV) (16 December 1970); Declaration on the Enhancement of the Effectiveness of the Principle of Refraining from the Threat or Use of Force in International Relations, UNGA Res 42/22 (18 November 1987).

[78] J Crawford, *The Creation of States in International Law* (Cambridge, Cambridge University Press, 2006) 168–72.

[79] *East Timor*, above n 65, 102, 105–06.

[80] C Fernandes, *The Independence of East Timor* (Brighton, Sussex Academic Press, 2011) 169.

[81] Australian Labor Party, *Platform, Resolutions and Rules as Approved by the National Conference* (Barton, ALP Secretariat, 1998).

Indonesia or independence. The referendum, called a 'popular consultation', was held on 30 August 1999 under the auspices of the United Nations: 78.5 per cent of registered voters opted for independence from Indonesia. Under mounting international pressure, Indonesia withdrew from the territory after destroying much of its infrastructure and deporting 250,000 East Timorese across the border to West Timor. On 15 September 1999 the UN Security Council passed Resolution 1264, authorising a multinational force with full Chapter VII powers to restore peace and security in East Timor. Led by an Australian Major-General, INTERFET (International Force – East Timor) entered the territory on 20 September and secured it quickly. Neither the United Nations nor most states contributing troops to INTERFET recognised Indonesian sovereignty over East Timor. Their view was that East Timor remained a UN-designated non-self-governing territory. The notable exception was Australia, which had given de jure recognition to Indonesian rule over East Timor in 1979. Australia entered into a Status of Forces Agreement with Indonesia. Other contributing states adopted a different approach. New Zealand, for example, argued that the Status of Forces Agreement was a bilateral issue between Australia and Indonesia and did not bind New Zealand. Its view was that UNSC Resolution 1264 provided the legal authority for the deployment and that New Zealand forces were immune from the local jurisdiction and the enforcement of local laws on the basis of customary international law. The United Nations followed an approach of constructive engagement with Indonesia by acknowledging its de facto control of East Timor without prejudice to the sovereignty question.[82] The Security Council passed Resolution 1272 (1999) establishing the UN Transitional Administration of East Timor (UNTAET) on 25 October 1999.

The Democratic Republic of Timor-Leste became an independent state on 20 May 2002. The Timor Gap Treaty between Australia and Indonesia had to be renegotiated because East Timor's leaders made it clear they were 'not going to be a successor to an illegal treaty'.[83] Andrew McNaughtan, an Australian medical doctor and supporter of East Timor, arranged for a legal opinion of Timor-Leste's potential maritime entitlements by three experts in international maritime law: Professor Vaughan Lowe of the University of Oxford, Commander Chris Carleton of the UK Hydrographic Office and Australian barrister Chris Ward. Their opinion showed that Timor-Leste's potential maritime boundaries – and therefore its oil and gas resources – were significantly larger than Australia alleged.[84] It referred, inter alia, to the ICJ's ruling in the *Libya–Malta* case of 1985, which held that both countries had rights based on

[82] MJ Kelly et al, 'Legal Aspects of Australia's Involvement in the International Force for East Timor' (2001) 83 *International Review of the Red Cross* 101, 118.

[83] Karen Polglaze, 'Future of Timor Gap Treaty Thrown into Doubt' *Sydney Morning Herald* (30 November 1999).

[84] C Ward, C Carleton and V Lowe, *In the Matter of East Timor's Maritime Boundaries* (11 April 2002): www.laohamutuk.org/OilWeb/Company/PetroTim/LegalOp.htm.

equidistance regardless of the undersea geology.[85] The ICJ dismissed Libya's reliance on the principle of natural prolongation of its continental shelf.[86] This meant that Australia's reliance on the same principle would have to give way to Timor-Leste's reliance on rights based on equidistance.

Drafts of the Ward, Carleton and Lowe opinion were in circulation in March 2002, three months before Timor-Leste was to gain formal independent statehood.[87] The Australian government withdrew immediately – and without notifying Parliament – from the maritime boundary jurisdiction of the ICJ and the International Tribunal on the Law of the Sea.[88] DFAT's internal analysis stated that there had been 'no consultation outside Federal Government' about the decision to withdraw because '[p]ublic knowledge of the proposed action could have led other countries to pre-empt the declaration by commencing an action against Australia in relation to sea boundary delimitation'.[89] That is, the Australian government did not wish to risk a legal challenge.

DFAT later stated that it was 'common practice for States to make a declaration', that 'many other countries have made similar declaration' to the Law of the Sea Convention (UNCLOS) and that 'eight countries have made a reservation to the International Court of Justice statute specifically regarding maritime boundaries'.[90] In fact, of the 21 states that made declarations under Article 298(1)(a) of UNCLOS, only nine also made declarations under Article 36(2) of the ICJ Statute. And out of these nine, only Australia explicitly excluded sea boundary delimitation disputes from the jurisdiction of the ICJ. A declaration made only under Article 298(1)(a) of UNCLOS does not exempt a state from the ICJ's jurisdiction because Article 282 of UNCLOS provides that an agreement to submit a dispute to a specified procedure may be reached 'otherwise'. A state must specifically make another declaration under Article 36(2) of the ICJ Statute because 'otherwise' includes a standing offer to settle disputes in the ICJ.[91] And, only Australia made both declarations and furthermore explicitly excluded sea boundary delimitation disputes from ICJ jurisdiction in

[85] *Case Concerning the Continental Shelf (Libyan Arab Jamahiriya/Malta)* (Judgment of 3 June 1985) [1985] ICJ Rep 13.

[86] ibid.

[87] A McNaughtan, Submission to the Joint Standing Committee on Treaties Concerning the Agreement Relating to the Unitisation of the Sunrise and Troubador Fields (16 June 2003); Joint Standing Committee On Treaties, 'Report 53: Treaties Tabled in May and June 2003' (Report, August 2003). The date of their final version is April 11, 2002.

[88] International Court of Justice, 'Declarations Recognising the Jurisdiction of the Court as Compulsory: Australia' (22 March 2002): www.icj-cij.org/en/declarations.

[89] DFAT, 'Australian Declarations under Articles 287(1) and 298(1)(a) of the United Nations Convention on the Law of the Sea 1982, Lodged at New York on 22 March 2002' (18 June 2022): www.laohamutuk.org/Oil/Boundary/2002/unclonia.pdf.

[90] DFAT, Submission to the Senate Foreign Affairs, Defence and Trade References Committee's Inquiry into Australia's Declarations Made under Certain International Laws (February 2020) (Submission to Inquiry into Australia's Declarations Made under Certain International Laws).

[91] A Sheehan, 'Dispute Settlement under UNCLOS: The Exclusion of Maritime Delimitation Disputes' (2005) 24 *University of Queensland Law Journal* 165.

its Article 36(2) declaration.[92] DFAT also stated it 'considers negotiation of maritime delimitation disputes to be the best approach'.[93] This is technically true; negotiations are typically the preferred method of solving disputes; litigation is typically the last resort. It failed to explain what, if anything, was so unique about maritime boundary disputes that litigation had to be ruled out entirely. Fear that Timor-Leste might have a strong legal case is a more plausible explanation.

Australia informed the government of the newly independent Timor-Leste that the oil and gas project in the Bayu-Undan field 135 nautical miles south of Timor-Leste would not go ahead unless it signed the Timor Sea Treaty on 20 May 2002. Timor-Leste's government needed the funds from the Bayu-Undan project because it had no source of revenues other than foreign aid. But Australia refused to ratify the Timor Sea Treaty unless the Timor-Leste government signed an International Unitization Agreement (IUA) that gave Australia the lion's share of the much more valuable Sunrise and Troubadour gas fields (together called Greater Sunrise). Needing the revenues from Bayu-Undan, the Timor-Leste government signed the IUA but did not submit it for parliamentary ratification for several years.

Well aware of Timor-Leste's financial predicament, Australia's Foreign Minister Alexander Downer told Timor-Leste's Prime Minister in November 2002 that he was willing to hold up the flow of gas from the Timor Sea for decades. 'We don't have to exploit the resources', he said. 'They can stay there for 20, 40, 50 years. We are very tough. We will not care if you give information to the media. Let me give you a tutorial in politics – not a chance'.[94] The transcript of these talks was later leaked to the media.[95] One year later, the first round of talks was held in Darwin in November 2003. Timor-Leste sent a full team of negotiators with a mandate to engage in substantive negotiations about a permanent maritime boundary. By contrast, Australia sent a team of three. Timor-Leste requested discussions on a monthly basis, but – straining credulity – Australia claimed it had only enough resources for two rounds of discussions per year. Timor-Leste offered to fund Australia's expenses, but the offer was not taken up.[96]

[92] C Fernandes, Supplementary Submission: Senate FADT Inquiry into Australia's Declarations Made under Certain International Laws (2 December 2019).

[93] DFAT, Submission to Inquiry into Australia's Declarations Made under Certain International Laws, above n 90.

[94] James Irwin, 'Asia: Australia Accused' (*Energy Compass*, 5 December 2003).

[95] See La'o Hamutuk, 'Meeting between East Timorese Prime Minister Mari Alkatiri and Australian Foreign Minister Alexander Downer' (2002): www.laohamutuk.org/OilWeb/TSTreaty/Downer.htm, for the record of the meeting on 27 November 2002. See also Jonathan Steele, 'Anger in Timor-Leste as Australia Plays Tough over Gas Reserves' *Guardian* (14 October 2003).

[96] Shawn Donnan, 'Australia Accused of Stalling Boundary Talk' *Financial Times* (27 November 2003); James Ensor, 'Coalition Credibility with Australia's Elastic Borders' *Sydney Morning Herald* (27 November 2003).

The government turned to the Australian Secret Intelligence Service (ASIS), its intelligence espionage agency that collects intelligence outside Australia. According to information that became public some years later, ASIS allegedly used the cover of an aid project to install listening devices in Timor-Leste's ministerial offices.[97] The espionage operation is said to have provided Australia with secret access to Timor-Leste's internal deliberations and negotiating positions. The combined weight of overt and covert pressure forced Timor-Leste to sign a Treaty on Certain Maritime Arrangements in the Timor Sea (CMATS) in 2006 and ratify it in 2007. Known as CMATS, it imposed a 50-year moratorium on maritime boundary claims in the Timor Sea.

Professor Andrew Serdy, a Law of the Sea expert and former officer in the Sea Law, Environmental Law and Antarctic Policy Section of DFAT, described the process leading to CMATS as 'suggestive of a persistent policy failure'. He stated that Australia had 'departed from its usual and hitherto fruitful policy of settling its maritime boundaries on a permanent basis'. It 'would have made more sense, and led to far less rancor in the interim' had Australia acted differently.[98] He later observed that 'senior officials at all times simply assumed – whether because of direction to that effect by Ministers or their offices I do not know – that the national interest was identical to Woodside's (the operator of the Greater Sunrise joint venture)'.[99] As Australia's Foreign Minister during the espionage operation against Timor-Leste said, '[t]he Australian government unashamedly should be trying to advance the interests of Australian companies'.[100] The head of technical operations for ASIS complained to the Inspector-General of Intelligence and Security about a changed culture within ASIS. One example of the change was 'an operation he had been ordered to execute in Dili, Timor-Leste'.[101] The full ramifications of the changed culture in ASIS, of which the Dili operation was only one illustration, remains a closely guarded secret. The ASIS officer was referred to an ASIS-approved lawyer named Bernard Collaery, a former Attorney-General of the Australian Capital Territory. Collaery had, coincidentally, been a long-time supporter of East Timor's right to self-determination and his law practice had among its clients the government of Timor-Leste.

[97] Marian Wilkinson and Peter Cronau, 'Drawing the Line' (*ABC, Four Corners*, 2014): www.abc.net.au/4corners/drawing-the-line/5328634. The name of the hotel does not appear in the transcript of the program, but the film footage showed its name on-screen. The photo of the hotel comes from La'o Hamutuk: 'The La'o Hamutuk Bulletin Vol 6, No 1–2: April 2005': www.laohamutuk.org/Bulletin/2005/Apr/bulletinv6n1.html#Solidarity_Central.

[98] A Serdy, Submission to the Joint Standing Committee on Treaties Inquiry into Certain Maritime Arrangements: Timor-Leste (13 March 2007).

[99] A Serdy, Supplementary Submission to the Senate Foreign Affairs, Defence and Trade References Committee's Inquiry into Australia's Declarations Made under Certain International Laws (2019).

[100] Wilkinson and Cronau, above n 97.

[101] Response by Mr Bernard Collaery to a speech made by Senator Brandis in the Senate on 4 December 2013: Senate Committee of Privileges, '156th Report: Person Referred to in the Senate' (Report, 15 May 2014).

V. THE SECOND CASE BEFORE THE INTERNATIONAL COURT OF JUSTICE

In 2013, Timor-Leste launched proceedings against Australia at the Arbitral Tribunal constituted by the 2002 Timor Sea Treaty.[102] It sought a declaration that the 2006 CMATS Treaty was induced by fraud, due to the espionage operation in 2004.[103] The ASIS officer, now retired, would be a witness. It brought a separate arbitration under the Timor Sea Treaty regarding whether the jurisdiction awarded to Australia over the pipeline connecting the Bayu-Undan field to Darwin was exclusive or must be shared with Timor-Leste.[104] On 3 December 2013, the day before the ex-ASIS officer was to give evidence in The Hague via video link in the Timor Sea Treaty Arbitration, the Australian Security Intelligence Organisation raided his home and the home and office of his lawyer, Bernard Collaery. They seized a number of documents relating to the case. On 17 December 2013, Timor-Leste brought a case before the ICJ seeking an order for provisional measures that (1) Australia shall not use the seized material; (2) the documents shall be kept under seal; and further that (3) Australia shall not interfere in any way in communications between Timor-Leste and its legal advisers in connection with the Timor Sea Treaty Arbitration.[105]

Australia opposed the application for provisional measures on grounds of sovereignty and national security.[106] It stated, inter alia, that the ICJ 'cannot, or in any event should not, take on the responsibility of ordering provisional measures in circumstances where another forum – the Arbitral Tribunal constituted under the Timor Sea Treaty – has already convened'. It argued that the ICJ had 'no inherent priority' over the Arbitral Tribunal. It had to admit that 'Australia contests the jurisdiction of the Tribunal' as well, but 'that question is evidently a matter for the Tribunal'.[107] In March 2014, the ICJ decided 12:4, 12:4, 15:1 respectively, in Timor-Leste's favour. In an unconvincing attempt to save face, Australia's Attorney-General said he was 'pleased with the decision' and called it a 'good outcome'.[108] Lawyers for both sides were set to argue their cases before the ICJ in September 2014. Less than two weeks before the case began, the two

[102] *Arbitration under the Timor Sea Treaty (Timor-Leste v Australia)* (Permanent Court of Arbitration, Case No 2013-16, 23 April 2016).

[103] DK Anton, 'The Timor Sea Treaty Arbitration: Timor-Leste Challenges Australian Espionage and Seizure of Documents' (2014) 18 *American Society of International Law* (online): www.asil.org/insights/volume/18/issue/6/timor-sea-treaty-arbitration-timor-leste-challenges-australian-espionage.

[104] *Arbitration under the Timor Sea Treaty (Timor-Leste v Australia)* (Permanent Court of Arbitration, Case No 2015-42, 15 September 2015).

[105] *Questions Relating to the Seizure and Detention of Certain Documents and Data (Timor-Leste v Australia)* (Provisional Measures, Order of 3 March 2014) [2014] ICJ Rep 147 (*Documents Seizure Case*). For further discussion of this case see, Young, ch 8 in this volume.

[106] Counter Memorial of Australia, *Questions Relating to the Seizure and Detention of Certain Documents and Data (Timor-Leste v Australia)* (28 July 2014).

[107] Verbatim Record, *Questions Relating to the Seizure and Detention of Certain Documents and Data (Timor-Leste v Australia)* (International Court of Justice, CR 2014/2, 21 January 2014) 40 (J Crawford).

[108] Attorney-General, 'ICJ Decision: Timor-Leste v Australia' (Press Release, 4 March 2014).

countries agreed to a six-month postponement in order to try to resolve their differences amicably.

In 2015, Timor-Leste and Australia engaged in 'structured engagement' – a phrase designed to avoid the CMATS moratorium on maritime boundary negotiations. Little came out of this process. Australia continued to resist negotiations on boundaries, preferring to keep discussing provisional resource sharing treaties.

VI. COMPULSORY CONCILIATION

In April 2016, Timor-Leste launched the first known compulsory conciliation under Article 298 of UNCLOS. This previously little-known procedure is enlivened when a state does not accept the procedures provided for in section 2 of Part XV of UNCLOS with respect to maritime boundary delimitation. Timor-Leste argued that Australia's jurisdictional reservation over maritime boundaries and its refusal to negotiate these boundaries bilaterally met the test. It nominated two Commissioners. Australia accepted the notice commencing compulsory conciliation, and also nominated two Commissioners, but stated that it would be disputing the competence (or jurisdiction) of the Conciliation Commission. The four Commissioners settled on a fifth Commissioner in order to constitute the five-member Conciliation Commission.

Australia made six objections to the compulsory conciliation.[109] The Commission dismissed them all. It relied on the dispute settlement provisions within UNCLOS, grouped in Part XV (Articles 279–99). It rejected Australia's arguments that CMATS precluded compulsory conciliation. Since it owed its own existence to UNCLOS, not CMATS or the Timor Sea Treaty, the Commission held that it had no authority to give effect to a treaty other than UNCLOS except where UNCLOS itself provided for this situation. A press release from Australia's Foreign Minister noted that 'Australia accepts the Commission's decision and will continue to engage in good faith' saying, as foreign ministers frequently do, that this was 'consistent with our support for the rules-based international order'. But it added that any report the Commission would produce 'is not legally binding'.[110]

However, the Australian government was now under pressure as a result of three factors. The first was a new policy in 2015 from the opposition Labor Party, committing a future Labor government to renewed boundary negotiations with Timor-Leste, including binding third-party dispute resolution if necessary. This

[109] T Koh, 'The Conciliation Commission's Decision on Competence' in HD Phan, T Davenport and R Beckman (eds), *The Timor-Leste/Australia Conciliation* (Singapore, World Scientific Publishing, 2019).

[110] J Bishop, 'Timor Sea Conciliation' (Media Release, 26 September 2016): www.foreignminister.gov.au/minister/julie-bishop/media-release/timor-sea-conciliation.

policy change was reminiscent of Labor's fracturing of the bipartisan consensus in 1998. It reduced the government's margin of political comfort. The second was the government's frequent proclamations of the importance of a rules-based international order, notably in the context of China's non-participation in arbitral proceedings with the Philippines regarding the South China Sea.[111] Some commentators equated China's rejection of these proceedings with Australia's own conduct towards Timor-Leste.[112] This had become a diplomatic liability, resulting in the third factor: the US House Armed Services Committee's National Defense Authorization Act pointed to 'the strategic importance of the Indo-Asia-Pacific region' and stated that 'negotiations between Australia and Timor-Leste to establish permanent maritime boundaries sends a positive signal to other states in the region regarding adherence to a rules-based international order'.[113]

Australia could no longer maintain its rejection of compulsory conciliation.[114] In September 2017, the Conciliation Commission announced that the two countries had reached an agreement. It stated that the comprehensive agreement included maritime boundaries and addressed the legal status of the Greater Sunrise gas field.[115] The result of the agreement was a Maritime Boundary Treaty that established the border largely along a median line between the two countries without affecting any rights possessed by Indonesia.[116] The Treaty Between Australia and the Democratic Republic of Timor-Leste Establishing their Maritime Boundaries in the Timor Sea entered into force on 30 August 2019. There would be no compensation for Australia's past exploitation of the oil and gas fields in the Timor Sea – including those that would have rightfully gone to Timor-Leste, had a median line been drawn in 2002. Timor-Leste vacated its case at the ICJ during the Conciliation Commission-sponsored negotiations; the Australian government was now at liberty to authorise prosecutions against the ASIS officer and his lawyer, Bernard Collaery, without whose disclosures Timor's legal strategy would not have been possible.

[111] *The South China Sea Arbitration (The Republic of Philippines v The People's Republic of China)* (Award) (Permanent Court of Arbitration, Case No 2013-19, 12 July 2016).

[112] Tom Clarke, 'Australia Is Guilty of Same Misconduct as China over Our Treatment of East Timor' *Sydney Morning Herald* (14 July 2016).

[113] MZ Bordallo (Guam), *Amendment to HR 2810 National Defense Authorization Act for Fiscal Year 2018*, 115th Congress, 1st Session, Report 115-200: www.govinfo.gov/content/pkg/CRPT-115hrpt200/pdf/CRPT-115hrpt200.pdf.

[114] Michael Leach, 'Timor-Leste: Architect of its Own Sunrise' (*Inside Story*, 8 March 2018): insidestory.org.au/timor-leste-architect-of-its-own-sunrise/.

[115] Permanent Court of Arbitration, 'Timor-Leste and Australia Achieve Breakthrough in Maritime Boundary Conciliation Proceedings' (Media Release, 1 September 2017): pcacases.com/web/sendAttach/2230.

[116] Treaty between Australia and the Democratic Republic of Timor-Leste Establishing their Maritime Boundaries in the Timor Sea (adopted 6 March 2018, entered into force 30 August 2019) ATS 2019 16.

The Australian government has not confirmed or denied allegations of its espionage operation against Timor-Leste in 2004 but Australia has acted in a manner consistent with the allegations being true, including its appearance in proceedings in the Permanent Court of Arbitration in the Hague; its appearance in proceedings at the ICJ; and its bringing of prosecutions against the two men in proceedings held largely in secret due to national security claims. In July 2022, a new Attorney-General of Australia, Mark Dreyfus QC, discontinued the prosecution of Bernard Collaery under section 71 of the Judiciary Act 1903 (Cth). The former ASIS officer had received a three-month suspended sentence in 2021.

VII. CONCLUSION

This chapter began by asking how Australian governments would engage with the international community if they enjoyed an overwhelming advantage in power. It subsequently reviewed eight decades of interactions with Timor-Leste – a rich body of relevant evidentiary material. It showed that Australia cooperated with Indonesia to block Timor-Leste's claim to self-determination. Australia rejected adjudication at the ICJ when Portugal commenced an action against it in the Court. It withdrew from the relevant jurisdiction of the ICJ to prevent an independent Timor-Leste commencing an action in relation to sea boundary delimitation. It eventually entered into compulsory conciliation after the failure of its jurisdictional objections.

As the preceding paragraphs have shown, being a 'good international citizen' and upholding a 'rules-based international order' is not the best way to describe the nature and practice of Australia's foreign relations. It is perhaps more accurate to describe Australian foreign policy as sub-imperial: fitting into the geostrategy of an imperial power while exerting considerable influence among smaller states in its own region. The Australian invasion of East Timor during the Second World War is a good illustration of the first aspect; the power exerted over Timor-Leste exemplifies the second. The chapter illustrates how a smaller state can sometimes reduce the disparity in power if it receives assistance and solidarity from citizens in a more powerful one.

Part II

Australia and Institutions

6

Australia and the United Nations

ALISON PERT

I. INTRODUCTION

THIS CHAPTER PRESENTS an overview of Australia's relationship with the United Nations (UN), from the drafting of the Charter of the United Nations to the present day. It takes a chronological approach, providing a snapshot of the depth of engagement by Australia from time to time, and how it has changed – or not – under different governments.[1] It will be seen that the level of engagement has tended to vary according to the government of the day's attitude to multilateralism more broadly. As Labor governments have generally been more multilateralist in outlook, so they have placed a higher priority on the United Nations than have conservative governments. But it will also be seen how particular individuals within government have greatly influenced the relationship.

II. AUSTRALIA'S EARLY PARTICIPATION IN THE UNITED NATIONS

Australia's attitude to the creation of the United Nations in 1945 was inevitably framed by its position in the world at the time. In 1939, Australia was still a Dominion of the United Kingdom. Over the previous 20 years there had been great changes in the status of the Dominions within the British Empire: they had been permitted to join the League of Nations, and had gradually acquired more treaty-making powers.[2] The Irish Free State and South Africa declared themselves independent in the 1930s, but Australia was much slower to embrace these developments, declining even to pass the Statute of Westminster[3] which, when

[1] For a more detailed, thematic approach, see, eg, J Cotton and D Lee, *Australia and the United Nations* (Barton, Longueville Books, 2012).

[2] See, eg, AB Keith, *The Dominions as Sovereign States: Their Constitutions and Governments* (London, MacMillan and Co, 1938).

[3] Statute of Westminster 1931 (22 & 23 Geo 5 c 4). The Statute required adoption by enactment of the parliaments of Australia and New Zealand before having any effect there – it was finally passed by Australia in 1942: Statute of Westminster Adoption Act 1942 (Cth).

enacted, would severely constrain Imperial control over dominion legislative powers. Thus on the eve of the Second World War, Australia had a large degree of practical and legal autonomy, but was still nestled firmly in the bosom of the 'mother country'.[4] While it had shaken off many aspects of its erstwhile parent–child colonial status, it might be viewed at that time as a teenager still living at home, albeit in a granny flat out the back. It looked to Britain for security, and to a large degree for foreign policy direction, conscious of the need for Imperial unity. But the Second World War had a profound effect on Australia's relationship with the United Kingdom. In the space of just three or four years, Australia grew up, to continue the metaphor. The fall of the supposedly impregnable fortress of Singapore in 1942, and the British preparedness to sacrifice Australia to the Japanese in order to 'beat Hitler first',[5] made it painfully obvious that Britain could not be relied on to guarantee Australia's security.

The Prime Minister, John Curtin, complained frequently of the lack of consultation by the United Kingdom over the conduct of the war and related matters. A particularly egregious example occurred in 1943 when, without reference to either of the two Pacific Dominions (Australia and New Zealand), Britain, the United States (US) and China issued the Cairo Declaration determining the future of Japan's Pacific possessions after the war.[6] Dr HV Evatt, who was the Australian Attorney-General and Minister for External Affairs from 1941 to 1949, was especially outraged at this decision.[7] One consequence was the conclusion of the ANZAC Agreement[8] with New Zealand in 1944, in which Australia and New Zealand not only asserted their interest in the South West and South Pacific, but also declared that it was

> a matter of cardinal importance that they should both be associated, not only in the membership, but also in the planning and establishment, of the general international organisation referred to in the Moscow Declaration of October 1943 [the United Nations], which organisation is based on the principle of the sovereign equality of all peace-loving States and open to membership by all such States, large or small, for the maintenance of international peace and security.[9]

[4] For a detailed account, see A Pert, 'The Development of Australia's International Legal Personality' (2016) 34 *Australian Year Book of International Law* 149.

[5] A Watt, *The Evolution of Australian Foreign Policy 1938–1965* (London, Cambridge University Press, 1967) 34, 43, 51.

[6] ibid 73; P Hasluck, *The Government and the People, 1942–1945* (Canberra, Australian War Memorial, 1970) 487.

[7] Evatt was 'greatly agitated' by the Declaration: P Hasluck, 'Australia and the Formation of the United Nations' (1954) XL(III) *Royal Australian Historical Society Journal and Proceedings* 135, 149.

[8] Australian–New Zealand Agreement 1944 (adopted 21 January 1944, entered into force 21 June 1944) 18 UNTS 357; N Mansergh, *Survey of British Commonwealth Affairs: Problems of Wartime Co-operation and Post-War Change 1939–1952* (Oxford, Oxford University Press, 1958) 181. It seems to have been the first non-trade treaty made by Australia: Hasluck, 'Australia and the Formation of the United Nations', above n 7, 151.

[9] Australian–New Zealand Agreement 1944, above n 8, Art 14.

Pursuant to this Agreement,[10] in late 1944 Australia and New Zealand conferred on the draft charter for a new general international organisation, to be known as the United Nations Organisation,[11] which had been produced by the United States, the United Kingdom, the Union of Soviet Socialist Republics (USSR) and China at Dumbarton Oaks a few weeks earlier.[12] The Dumbarton Oaks draft formed the basis of negotiations at San Francisco where the UN Charter was agreed in June 1945. It seems that Evatt personally did not turn his mind to the detail of the Dumbarton Oaks draft until arriving in London for a Commonwealth conference in advance of the San Francisco meeting, but he quickly mastered the papers and the issues.[13]

III. EVATT AT SAN FRANCISCO

This mastery of detail came to the fore at San Francisco.[14] The Prime Minister, John Curtin, had not made it clear whether Evatt or Frank Forde, Deputy Prime Minister, was to lead the Australian delegation.[15] Evatt nevertheless behaved as the formal leader, and certainly came to be regarded as such by the other delegations. A brilliant lawyer,[16] Evatt ensured that Australia was represented on as many committees and sub-committees as possible,[17] and the combination of his

[10] Hasluck, 'Australia and the Formation of the United Nations', above n 7, 149, 157.

[11] The term 'United Nations' had been coined in 1941 by President Roosevelt to describe the US, Great Britain and their allies; it was used formally in the 'Declaration by United Nations' of 1 January 1942: 'Declaration by United Nations' (1942) 36 (S3) *American Journal of International Law* 191, 191–92.

[12] 'Proposals for the Establishment of a General International Organization': WJ Hudson, *Australia and the New World Order: Evatt at San Francisco, 1945* (Canberra, Australian Foreign Policy Publications Program, 1993) 26. The Proposals are set out in a Department of External Affairs document of 25 October 1944: Department of Foreign Affairs and Trade (DFAT), *Documents on Australian Foreign Policy 1937–1949* (Department of Foreign Affairs and Trade, 1975–2001) vol 7, doc 311.

[13] Hudson, *Australia and the New World Order*, above n 12, 44. The conference took place from 4 to 13 April 1945.

[14] The United Nations Conference on International Organization, met at San Francisco from 25 April to 26 June 1945 to settle, using the Dumbarton Oaks draft as a basis, the constitution of 'a general international organization for the maintenance of international peace and security': see, eg, Hasluck, 'Australia and the Formation of the United Nations', above n 7, 169.

[15] The Australian delegation was unique in not admitting to having a chairman, instead listing both ministers for the purposes of membership of the Steering Committee which provided overall direction of the conference and comprised the chairmen of all delegations: see, eg, ibid 160; Hudson, *Australia and the New World Order*, above n 12, 43–44, 60–61; DFAT, *Documents on Australian Foreign Policy 1937–1949*, above n 12, vol 8, doc 64 (diary note of Bruce, 2 April 1945) vol 8, doc 74 (letter from Bruce to McDougall, 20 April 1945).

[16] Evatt graduated BA (in mathematics, English and philosophy), MA and LLB, each with first-class honours, LLD, and numerous prizes including two University Medals; at the age of 36 he became the youngest High Court Judge in the history of the British Empire: A Dalziel, *Evatt the Enigma* (Melbourne, Lansdowne Press, 1967) 5–6.

[17] Membership of the conference commissions and committees was open to all delegations, but Australia was appointed to many sub-committees 'because of the energetic way in which the

intellect, training (in constitutional law), zeal and inexhaustible energy meant that:

> If any really big issue arose on a committee, a message would be sent to Dr Evatt, and he would arrive in a hurry to handle it ... he was so wrapped up in the Charter that he could move from point to point, and at a few minutes notice enter into a new fight on any article in the draft. It was an amazing display of physical energy and sustained combativeness on a dozen different fronts.[18]

Evatt applied this furious energy to pursuing the goals he had outlined in late 1944,[19] many concerning the roles of, and balance of power between, the proposed Security Council and General Assembly. He rejected the idea that 'the settlement of international disputes should be left entirely to the arbitrary decision of the suggested Security Council',[20] and believed that the General Assembly should have more powers to function as the organisation's central body, that far more attention should be given to the 'welfare side' of the organisation dealing with social, economic and humanitarian problems, that the Security Council should include as members at least eight powers other than the 'Big Four',[21] and that Member States should 'declare the principles they were prepared to uphold and to enter into specific undertakings regarding their duties as members'.[22] These were the policies he pursued at San Francisco, and as Hudson summarised, 'Evatt expended every ounce of his considerable intellectual muscle at San Francisco to give the world a political structure which would preserve the peace and improve the lives of its people'.[23]

A. The Veto Power

Limiting the veto power – the ability of a permanent member of the Security Council to block a resolution – became one of Evatt's causes célèbres during the conference. He fought desperately to confine the use of the veto to decisions

Australian delegation performed and the diversity of its interests ... and thus the Ministers and officials were committed to constant meetings, morning, afternoon and night, and to constant labour in preparing material and drafting resolutions in readiness for them': Hasluck, 'Australia and the Formation of the United Nations', above n 7, 171.

[18] ibid 170.

[19] Parliament of the Commonwealth of Australia, *United Nations Conference on International Organization, Report by the Australian Delegates* (1945) 7–8, paras 4–10; DFAT, 'Cablegram Australian Delegation to Commonwealth Government 29 April 1945': dfat.gov.au/about-us/publications/historical-documents/Pages/volume-08/80-australian-delegation-san-francisco-conference-to-commonwealth-government.aspx. See, eg, Evatt's Ministerial Statement in the House of Representatives on 8 September 1944: HV Evatt, *Foreign Policy of Australia* (Sydney, Angus & Robertson, 1945) 209.

[20] *Report by the Australian Delegates*, above n 19, 8 para 8.

[21] The US, UK, USSR and China.

[22] *Report by the Australian Delegates*, above n 19, 8 para 8; Evatt, *Foreign Policy*, above n 19, 209.

[23] Hudson, *Australia and the New World Order*, above n 12, 152.

under what is now Chapter VII of the Charter, that is, to matters concerning international peace and security.[24] As is well known, he was unsuccessful. He and others submitted a long questionnaire to the P5-elect[25] asking whether the veto could or would be used in a number of given situations. This was not answered; the P5 did issue a statement on how they envisaged the voting procedure would work in practice – the so-called 'San Francisco Declaration'[26] – but it changed nothing of substance. There was merely an implied assurance that the veto power would only be used properly: 'It is not to be assumed … that the permanent members, any more than the non-permanent members, would use their "veto" power wilfully to obstruct the operation of the Council'.[27]

This was ignored almost immediately after the creation of the organisation, and continues to be.[28]

B. Greater Powers for the General Assembly

Evatt did succeed in gaining greater power for the General Assembly, and therefore for the smaller states.[29] Essentially the P5 wanted the Assembly to have as little power as possible, and Evatt, and the smaller nations behind him, wanted the exact opposite. Negotiations on the issue lasted over a month, in the latter stages pitting Andrei Gromyko of the Soviet delegation directly against Evatt.[30] Evatt won in almost every respect:

> The most vital amendment [was] to extend the assembly's right of discussion and recommendation to all matters and questions within the scope of the charter (which necessarily includes preamble, purposes, principles, and all the activities of the organs).[31]

[24] *Report by the Australian Delegates*, above n 19, 16–18, paras 55–72; G Sawer, 'The United Nations' in G Greenwood and N Harper (eds), *Australia in World Affairs 1950–1955* (Melbourne, FW Cheshire, 1957) 95 (The United Nations 1950–1955).

[25] The proposed permanent members of the Security Council: the US, UK, USSR, China and France.

[26] Statement at San Francisco by the delegations of the four Sponsoring Governments (China, the UK, the US and the USSR) on 'The Yalta Formula' on Voting in the Security Council 8 June 1945, *Documents of the United Nations Conference on International Organization, San Francisco, 1945* (New York, United Nations, 1945) vol XI, 710–14.

[27] ibid para 8.

[28] In 1946 alone, the USSR exercised the veto five times over the admission of new members of the UN: see also Sawer, 'The United Nations 1950–1955', above n 24, 106. More recent illustrations are the US serial use of the veto to block resolutions condemning Israel, and by Russia to block condemnation of the Syrian government in relation to the Syrian civil war: see United Nations, 'Security Council: Veto List': research.un.org/en/docs/sc/quick.

[29] At the final meeting of the conference Steering Committee, for example, the Peruvian delegate moved a special vote of thanks, carried 'amid cheering', to Evatt as 'the greatest champion of the small powers': Hasluck, 'Australia and the Formation of the United Nations', above n 7, 174.

[30] See, eg, Hudson, *Australia and the New World Order*, above n 12, 92–110.

[31] Commonwealth, *Parliamentary Debates*, House of Representatives, 30 August 1945, 5031.

The Assembly was not, however, to have power over any matter being dealt with by the Security Council, as now provided for in Article 12 of the Charter.

This episode more than any other crowned Evatt as the champion of the smaller nations at San Francisco, and elevated his status such that he was negotiating directly with not only Gromyko but also Edward Stettinius of the US delegation.[32] '[T]he great powers came to see Evatt as the delegate who must be satisfied if the conference as a whole would be satisfied'.[33]

C. Other Significant Drafting Achievements

Evatt's goal '[t]o declare that justice and the rule of law shall be the principles guiding the action of the security council and for this purpose to require the maximum employment of the permanent court in determining the legal aspects of international disputes'[34] was reflected in additions to Article 1 (Purposes) of the Charter, such as the provision 'that peaceful settlement shall proceed not arbitrarily but in conformity with the principles of justice and international law'.[35]

His demand for more emphasis on social and economic welfare as a major aim of the organisation found expression in the 'Australian Pledge', by which Member States committed to working towards full employment, in Articles 55 and 56 of the Charter, along with commitments to other economic and social development and the protection of human rights.[36]

Evatt was largely responsible for what is now Article 2(7) of the Charter, the 'domestic jurisdiction' provision – mainly, it must be said, to protect the White Australia policy.[37] The Dumbarton Oaks draft[38] and early proposed amendments[39] would have had the effect of permitting Security Council intervention in domestic affairs (such as migration) as soon as a threat to the peace arose. Evatt succeeded in confining this power to enforcement measures under what is now Chapter VII: 'the clause as adopted is a recognition, among other things, that the decision of any nation as to such internal matters as migration cannot become the subject of any action by the United Nations'.[40] 'In particular', Evatt wrote, 'it assures the retention of the general principle that it is for

[32] Hudson, *Australia and the New World Order*, above n 12, 108.

[33] ibid.

[34] Commonwealth, *Parliamentary Debates*, above n 31, 5023.

[35] ibid 5031.

[36] See generally, Hudson, *Australia and the New World Order*, above n 12, 123–36.

[37] Sawer, 'The United Nations 1950–1955', above n 24, 96.

[38] 'The provisions of paragraph 1 to 6 of Section A should not apply to situations or disputes arising out of matters which by international law are solely within the domestic jurisdiction of the state concerned.'

[39] *Report by the Australian Delegates*, above n 19, para 148.

[40] ibid para 153.

each nation to determine for itself – without outside intervention – the composition of its own population'.[41]

D. Evatt's Contribution to the United Nations

Evatt's personal role in shaping the UN Charter, and therefore the United Nations itself, is undeniable. While impossible to measure exactly, it is clear that through Evatt's frenetic activity at the San Francisco conference in 1945, Australia was 'one of the two or three most effective nations in the writing of the version of the Charter finally accepted'.[42] At the time, the *New York Times* described him as 'the most brilliant and effective voice of the small powers, a leading spokesman for the world's conscience'.[43] The international stature he had gained was recognised in several appointments in the new organisation, including Australia's election to the first Security Council (1946–47)[44] and, most significantly, Evatt's election as President of the UN General Assembly for its third session (1948–49).[45] Other appointments included Evatt's chairing of the Atomic Energy Commission established by the very first resolution passed by the General Assembly,[46] and Australia's election to the governing body of the International Labour Organization (ILO) in 1945,[47] the Central Committee of the Council of UNRRA (the UN Relief and Rehabilitation Administration) in 1946,[48] and the Economic and Social Council (ECOSOC) in 1948.[49]

IV. THE CONSERVATIVE GOVERNMENTS 1949–72

Evatt's idealism was not shared by many of his Labor colleagues, nor by the conservative government which took office under Robert Menzies in 1949.[50] The

[41] HV Evatt, *Australia in World Affairs* (Sydney, Angus & Robertson, 1946) 51–52.

[42] C Hartley Grattan, *The United States and the Southwest Pacific* (Cambridge, MA, Harvard University Press, 1961) 199.

[43] 'Evatt Acclaimed for Parley Work: Australian's Fight for Rights of Small Powers Gives Him a World Role' *New York Times* (27 June 1945) 11.

[44] Evatt, *Australia in World Affairs*, above n 41, 192.

[45] Hudson, *Australia and the New World Order*, above n 12, 5.

[46] Establishment of a Commission to Deal with the Problems Raised by the Discovery of Atomic Energy, UNGA Res 1(I) (24 January 1946) UN Doc A/RES/1(I); HV Evatt, *The United Nations* (London, Geoffrey Cumberlage, 1948) 84. The Commission was superseded by the Disarmament Commission three years later: United Nations, *Repertory of Practice of United Nations Organs 1945–1954* (United Nations) vol 2, 55–56.

[47] Evatt, *Australia in World Affairs*, above n 41, 170.

[48] DFAT, *Documents on Australian Foreign Policy 1937–1949*, above n 12, vol 9, doc 141 note 1 (Cable Brigden to DEA, 24 March 1946).

[49] United Nations, *Repertory*, above n 46, vol 3, 193.

[50] N Harper and D Sissons, *Australia and the United Nations* (New York, Manhattan Publishing Co, 1959) 289–90.

attitude to the United Nations of Evatt's successors as Minister for External Affairs, Percy Spender[51] and Richard Casey,[52] was less than enthusiastic; the 'Spender–Casey'[53] view was that 'the scope of the United Nations activities should be restricted, its jurisdiction more carefully defined',[54] and Australian participation in those activities should be more selective, although Spender did serve as Vice-President of the General Assembly in 1955 and Australia was elected to ECOSOC from 1953 to 1955 and to the Security Council again in 1955.[55] In 1957, Spender was elected to the International Court of Justice for a nine-year term from 1958; for the last three years he was President, and until 2015 was the only Australian to have been elected to the Court.[56] Australia's reputation at the United Nations was damaged when Spender used his casting vote as President to deny the claims of Ethiopia and Liberia against South Africa in the *South West Africa* cases[57] on the basis of lack of standing;[58] the resultant dismay of Afro-Asian nations ensured the rejection of Australia's next candidate for election, Sir Kenneth Bailey.[59]

[51] Sir Percy Claude Spender was Minister for External Affairs 1949–51, Ambassador to the United States 1951–58, where he represented Australia at the United Nations, and judge of the International Court of Justice 1958–67, including three years as its president 1964–67: P Spender, *Politics and a Man* (Sydney, Collins, 1972) 261, 271, 304.

[52] Richard Gavin Gardiner (later Lord) Casey entered Parliament in 1931 and resigned in 1940 on his appointment by Menzies as Australia's first Minister to Washington; in 1942, Churchill appointed him British minister of state in the Middle East and, in 1944, Governor of Bengal; he re-entered Parliament in 1949 and was Liberal Minister for External Affairs from 1951 until his resignation in 1960 and was made a British life peer the same year; in 1965, Menzies appointed him Governor-General, the first appointment of an Australian to the position by a non-Labor government: WJ Hudson, 'Casey, Richard Gavin Gardiner [Baron Casey] (1890–1976)' in J Ritchie (ed), *Australian Dictionary of Biography: Volume 13 1940–1980* (Carlton, Melbourne University Press, 1993) 381–85.

[53] This shorthand term was often used since both men were Ministers for External Affairs and when Casey was Minister, Spender was the Australian representative at the United Nations and exerted a powerful influence on UN affairs: see, eg, Watt, above n 5, 113; G Sawer, 'The United Nations' in G Greenwood and N Harper (eds), *Australia in World Affairs 1956–1960* (Melbourne, FW Cheshire, 1963) 145 (The United Nations 1956–1960).

[54] Sawer, 'The United Nations 1950–1955', above n 24, 115. Australia supported 'a more frequent and rigid insistence on the application of Article 2(7)': at 116; and it was 'the general view of the political Right that many United Nations activities were a waste of time and money': Sawer, 'The United Nations 1956–1960', ibid 165.

[55] Sawer, 'The United Nations 1950–1955', above n 24, 115–16.

[56] International Court of Justice, 'All Members': www.icj-cij.org/en/all-members.

[57] *South West Africa (Ethiopia v South Africa; Liberia v South Africa), Second Phase* (Judgment) [1966] ICJ Rep 6. See discussion in M Young, 'Australian and the International Court of Justice', ch 8 in this volume.

[58] *South West Africa*, above n 57; WJ Hudson, 'The United Nations' in G Greenwood and N Harper (eds), *Australia in World Affairs 1966–1970* (Vancouver, UBC Press, 1974) 220 (The United Nations 1966–1970).

[59] ibid 225; H Burmester, 'Australia and the International Court of Justice' (1996) 17 *Australian Year Book of International Law* 19, 28–29; E McWhinney, 'The Role and Mission of the International Court in an Era of Historical Transition' in N Jasentuliyana (ed), *Perspectives on International Law* (London, Kluwer, 1995) 221. Bailey had also missed election to the Court in 1946: DFAT, *Documents on Australian Foreign Policy 1937–1949*, above n 12, vol 9, doc 79 (cable Australian delegation at the UN to DEA, 7 February 1946).

Australia took less interest in the United Nations in the 1960s: the UN's composition had changed dramatically with an exponential increase in membership (doubling 1945–60) due mainly to decolonisation, the organisation failed to deal with significant conflicts in Australia's region such as the Indonesia–Malaya confrontation and the Vietnam war, and it struggled financially.[60] The Australian UN mission in the years from 1961 to 1966 was substantial in size, ranking eighteenth out of 100 analysed, but from having held five General Assembly offices (President, committee chairmen, vice-chairman and rapporteurs) from 1946 to 1959 (only 18 states held more), Australian participation dropped to only one from 1960 to 1966 and none from 1966 to 1970.[61] Having had a seat on the Security Council from 1946 to 1947 and 1956 to 1957, Australia chose not to seek election in the 1960s, but in 1972 the Coalition Government decided Australia should take its forthcoming 'turn'[62] – '[t]he Security Council, for all its indifferent record of achievement, is still the prestigious forum. In 1972, it will be Australia's turn to stand for election to a seat on it; there is likely to be some pressure on us to do so and some incomprehension if we decline'[63] – and Australia was duly elected for 1973 to 1974.

The differing priority accorded to the United Nations is reflected in Australian foreign policy statements from this time.[64] While Evatt placed the United Nations first on his list of priorities, Spender in 1950 placed it fourth, and McMahon in 1970 omitted the United Nations altogether.[65]

V. THE WHITLAM LABOR GOVERNMENT 1972–75

Federal government attitudes changed radically on the election of the Whitlam Labor Government in late 1972. E Gough Whitlam was a liberal internationalist, a strong believer in multilateralism[66] who 'brought new vigour and new intentions' to matters of foreign policy.[67] He was also Foreign Minister for the

[60] G Sawer and WJ Hudson, 'The United Nations' in G Greenwood and N Harper (eds), *Australia in World Affairs 1961–1965* (Vancouver, UBC Press, 1968) 235.

[61] Hudson, 'The United Nations 1966–1970', above n 58, 227.

[62] C Clark, 'The United Nations' in WJ Hudson (ed), *Australia in World Affairs 1971–1975* (Sydney, George Allen & Unwin, 1980) 126. The 'Coalition' Government refers to the coalition between the Liberal and Country/National parties.

[63] 'Notes for Introduction of the Agenda Item 'Australia and the United Nations'', attached to a letter dated 5 October 1971 from McIntyre in New York to Secretary, DFAT (National Archives of Australia, NAA, Series A1838, Control Symbol (CS) 907/5 Part 1, Item ID 1608942).

[64] Hudson, 'The United Nations 1966–1970', above n 58, 206.

[65] ibid; D Lee, 'The Curtin and Chifley Governments: Liberal Internationalism and World Organisation' in D Lee and C Waters (eds), *Evatt to Evans: The Labor Tradition in Australian Foreign Policy* (Sydney, Allen & Unwin, 1997) 55.

[66] J Curran, *The Power of Speech: Australian Prime Ministers Defining the National Image* (Melbourne, Melbourne University Press, 2004) 2–3.

[67] JDB Miller, 'Problems in Australian Foreign Policy, July to December, 1972' (1973) 19 *Australian Journal of Politics & History* 1.

first year of his government, and maintained a strong influence over foreign policy throughout his term.[68] His revival of Australian interest in the United Nations was enhanced by Australia's election to the Security Council, 1973–74, the first since 1956–57.[69] This had been initiated by the outgoing Coalition Government, but in addition there was an immediate increase in not only political but also financial support for the United Nations, with Australia's voluntary contributions to 'the UN Family' rising from $4 million in 1971 to 1972 to over $18 million in 1974 to 1975.[70]

Most notable was an immediate change in voting policy at the United Nations. Whitlam was elected on 2 December 1972, towards the end of the twenty-seventh annual session of the UN General Assembly, but just in time to vote on a flurry of UN resolutions being dealt with before Christmas. Under the previous, Conservative, governments Australia had drawn criticism from developing states, particularly the Afro-Asian group in the General Assembly, by voting against or abstaining on many issues such as the regular condemnation of apartheid by the General Assembly, insisting they were matters of domestic concern.[71] Within days of Whitlam's election, Australia voted to condemn South Africa's role in Namibia, and announced a string of new measures including banning visits by racially segregated sporting teams from South Africa, closing the Rhodesian Information Centre in Australia, and becoming party to numerous treaties on nuclear disarmament and human rights.[72] This was part of a wider policy 'to reflect the new Australian Government's … determination to condemn colonialism and racial discrimination',[73] and the expression of more support for developing countries rather than its previous habit of voting with the United States and United Kingdom.[74] As Whitlam declared in 1973, '[n]ever again are we going to be put in the position of finding ourselves siding with Britain, France, Portugal, South Africa and the US, while all our neighbours are on the other side'.[75]

Whitlam's term of office was short, but it abruptly brought Australia out of the torpor of two decades of conservative rule:

[68] TB Millar, 'From Whitlam to Fraser' (1977) 55 *Foreign Affairs* 854, 856, 857.

[69] Australia has been a member of the Security Council for the two-year periods 1946–47, 1956–57, 1973–74, 1985–86 and 2013–14: see, eg, United Nations Security Council, 'Countries Elected Members: List of All Countries Which Have Been Elected As Members of the Security Council at Least Once since 1946': www.un.org/securitycouncil/content/countries-elected-members.

[70] Commonwealth of Australia, *Official Year Book of Australia: No 61, 1975 and 1976* (Australian Bureau of Statistics, 1976) 127. Contributions to all UN bodies rose from under $8 million in 1971–72 to over $26 million in 1974–75: Clark, above n 62, 159.

[71] G Greenwood, 'Australian Foreign Policy in Action' in G Greenwood and N Harper (eds), *Australia in World Affairs 1956–1960* (Melbourne, FW Cheshire, 1963) 50–51.

[72] JDB Miller, above n 67, 8–9.

[73] Commonwealth of Australia, *Official Year Book of Australia: No 59, 1973* (Australian Bureau of Statistics, 1974) 117.

[74] Clark, above n 62, 129.

[75] DJ Murphy, 'Problems in Australian Foreign Policy, January to June, 1973' (1973) 19 *Australian Journal of Politics and History* 331, 340–41, citing *The Age* (Melbourne, 7 June 1973).

> Labor restored some dignity to the conduct of our national affairs at a time when we had all come more or less to expect nothing but ill from political action. Without precedent in the history of British-style governments, it set out to make up for lost time by immediately implementing its campaign promises. Australians blinked as within weeks we recognised China, ended conscription, abolished race as a criterion of our immigration policy, began reform of the health system, supported equal pay for women, banned racially selected sporting teams, abolished federal British honours, increased arts subsidies, put contraceptives on the medical benefits list, took the tax off Australian wine, moved to stop the slaughter of kangaroos and crocodiles, and searched for a new national anthem.[76]

The reinvigoration of Australia's engagement with the United Nations epitomised this new direction.

VI. THE FRASER COALITION GOVERNMENT 1975–83

The foreign policy of the new Coalition Government was dominated by Fraser himself, and while the fairly active level of Australian participation in the United Nations did not change significantly,[77] there was an immediate downgrading of the United Nations in foreign policy priorities. In a major foreign policy statement in 1977, the Minister for Foreign Affairs mentioned the United Nations only briefly towards the end of his speech, after discussing the trade and security importance of Japan, the United States and Europe.[78] Its importance to Australia was described in utilitarian terms:

> [T]he United Nations provides our only means of constant and ready contact with close on half the countries of the world. In terms of the need for access, therefore, the United Nations is of great benefit to us.[79]

The government's voting policies did not revert to pre-Whitlam days, but Australia did abstain on significant issues such as calling on the Security Council to impose sanctions on South Africa because of its continuing apartheid policies.[80] Australia was at pains to express its condemnation of apartheid, but objected to the 'extreme language' of many of these resolutions, and the naming of individual states.[81] The Fraser Government took a much more active role against

[76] R Drewe, 'The New Nationalism' *The Australian 40 Years* (New South Wales, 2004) 10 (edited version of an article originally published in *The Australian* on 9 April 1973).

[77] R Harry, 'Australian Multilateral Diplomacy' in PJ Boyce and JR Angel (eds), *Independence and Alliance: Australia in World Affairs 1976–1980* (Sydney, George Allen & Unwin, 1983) 87.

[78] Commonwealth, *Parliamentary Debates*, House of Representatives, 15 March 1977, 209 (A Peacock).

[79] ibid.

[80] See, eg, UNGA Res 36/172 (17 December 1981) UN Doc A/RES/36/172.

[81] See, eg, the Australian representative's explanation of its vote in UNGA, 'Report of the Special Political Committee' UN GAOR 36th Session 102nd Plenary Meeting UN Doc A/RES/36/172 (17 December 1981) 1857.

the white minority regime in Southern Rhodesia, but using the Commonwealth, rather than the United Nations, as the vehicle. Fraser personally played a key role in negotiating a peaceful transition of power to Zimbabwean independence in 1979.[82]

One small but telling indicator of the prominence given to the United Nations by successive governments is the length of the 'United Nations' entry in the Commonwealth Year Book of Australia. In 1972, for example, towards the end of the 23-year Coalition reign, the UN entry rated barely 70 words.[83] Two years later, under Whitlam, it was greatly expanded, to over 900 words.[84] Under the Fraser Government, it shrank to a third of that.[85]

VII. THE HAWKE (1983–91) AND KEATING (1991–96) LABOR GOVERNMENTS

Under Bob Hawke, the Labor Party won the 1983 federal election with a landslide. The Labor election platform gave prominence to support for the United Nations, in contrast to the Liberal Party which scarcely mentioned it.[86] In addition to the traditional multilateralist leanings of all Labor governments, a number of other factors contributed to particularly active involvement with the United Nations of the governments of Hawke and his successor, Paul Keating.

One of the Hawke Government's early steps was to appoint an Ambassador for Disarmament, because of its concern at the prospect of nuclear proliferation and the continuing nuclear tests being conducted, notably by France in the Pacific.[87] Australia was one of only 40 UN members (then totalling 159) holding a seat at the annual UN Conference on Disarmament, where it earned respect for its vigorous attempts to achieve consensus on a treaty prohibiting nuclear tests.[88] These were ultimately successful, with Australia a lead sponsor of the 1996

[82] R Higgott, 'Australia and Africa' in PJ Boyce and JR Angel (eds), *Independence and Alliance: Australia in World Affairs 1976–1980* (Sydney, George Allen & Unwin, 1983) 247–51; D Schreuder, 'The Commonwealth Connection: A Contemporary History and Prospect' in PJ Boyce and JR Angel (eds), *Diplomacy in the Marketplace: Australia in World Affairs 1981–90* (Melbourne, Longman Cheshire, 1992) 303.

[83] Commonwealth of Australia, *Official Year Book of Australia: No 58, 1972* (Australian Bureau of Statistics, 1972) 114.

[84] Commonwealth of Australia, *Official Year Book of Australia: No 60, 1974* (Australian Bureau of Statistics, 1975) 124–25.

[85] Commonwealth of Australia, *Official Year Book of Australia: No 62, 1977–78* (Australian Bureau of Statistics, 1978) 90; Commonwealth of Australia, *Official Year Book of Australia: No 66, 1982* (Australian Bureau of Statistics, 1982) 73–74.

[86] D Combe, G Hartung and G Hawker (eds), *Platforms for Government* (Canberra, Yarralumla Soft, 1982) 133 (Labor), 38 (Liberal).

[87] The first appointee was Richard Butler: see, eg, R Butler, 'Nuclear Disarmament: Does Australia Have a Role?' (1987) 59 *Australian Quarterly* 91.

[88] The Conference was created in 1978 as 'the single multilateral disarmament negotiating forum of the international community' and has met annually since then: United Nations Office for Disarmament Affairs, 'Conference on Disarmament': www.un.org/disarmament/conference-on-disarmament/. Australia maintains an ambassador and a disarmament delegation in Geneva:

General Assembly resolution adopting the Comprehensive Nuclear-Test-Ban Treaty.[89]

In 1984 Australia was elected to the Security Council for 1985 to 1986 (with the highest number of votes of any candidate), and in 1988 Gareth Evans became Minister for Foreign Affairs and he held that position until 1996.[90] Evans' tenure coincided with the end of the Cold War, with renewed interest in – and hope for – the United Nations and the role it could play in maintaining international peace and security. Evans himself was a former academic of Evatt-like energy and intelligence;[91] he wrote prolifically on foreign policy matters, and developed ideas to improve the UN's work on collective security.[92] Much like Evatt and Whitlam before him, Evans personally had an enormous influence on Australian foreign policy. Both the Hawke and Keating governments maintained the usual Labor support for multilateralism, but Evans took this further with his promotion of the concept of good international citizenship. This concept had been in existence for a few decades, but Evans brought it into common parlance, and made it a stated goal of Australia's foreign policy.[93] For Australia, this meant setting an example in areas such as compliance with international law, having generous international aid programmes, being a 'world leader' in the fight to ban chemical weapons, and its strong commitment to multilateral solutions to international problems generally and the United Nations in particular.[94] Australia's work in promoting universal human rights was of especial importance,[95] and included encouraging other states to ratify the fundamental human rights treaties, reporting on Australia's own implementation of those agreements, and striving to consolidate and expand existing standards and institutions.[96]

Australia in Switzerland: Bern and Geneva, 'Australian Permanent Mission to the Office of the United Nations in Geneva': geneva.mission.gov.au/gene/un.html.

[89] Comprehensive Nuclear-Test-Ban Treaty, UNGA Res 50/245 (17 September 1996) UN Doc A/RES/50/245.

[90] Commonwealth of Australia, *Parliamentary Handbook of the Commonwealth of Australia 2020*, 35th edn (Canberra, Department of Parliamentary Services, 2020) 642–49.

[91] Richard Woolcott, Secretary of DFAT under Evans, considered Evans to be 'our most active Foreign Minister' to 2008: T Wilson and G Cooke (eds), *Steady Hands Needed: Reflections on the Role of the Secretary of Foreign Affairs and Trade in Australia 1979–1999* (Acton, ANU E Press, 2008) 42.

[92] The books were *Australia's Foreign Relations in the World of the 1990s*, with Bruce Grant, first published in 1991 with a second edition in 1995, and *Cooperating for Peace: The Global Agenda for the 1990s and Beyond*, published in 1993 and drawing heavily on papers prepared mainly within his Department which were subsequently published as K Clements and R Ward (eds), *Building International Community: Cooperating for Peace: Case Studies* (Canberra, Allen and Unwin, 1994). The prizewinning paper was G Evans, 'Cooperative Security and Intrastate Conflict' (1994) 96 *Foreign Policy* 1.

[93] A Pert, *Australia as a Good International Citizen* (Sydney, Federation Press, 2014) 5.

[94] See, eg, G Evans, 'Australia and the United States in the New World Order' (1991) 3 *Sydney Papers Conference 1991* 95, 99.

[95] G Evans, 'Australia in Asia: Looking Back and Looking Forward' in *Ideas for the Future of a Civil Society* (Sydney, ABC Books, 2001).

[96] ibid.

Evans argued that this was not mere idealism, but in the national interest: 'being, and being seen to be, a good international citizen'[97] furthered Australia's national interests in at least two ways: 'the promotion of an international legal order and of an effective multilateral system is essential for [Australia's] strategic, trade and humanitarian concerns and interests';[98] and being recognised as a good international citizen increases Australia's international standing and ability to influence other members of the international community.[99]

One of Evans' greatest achievements was the peace plan for Cambodia that was finally agreed in 1992. The genocidal Pol Pot regime had been removed by a Vietnamese invasion in late 1978 and Cambodia had descended into civil war, with different parties supported by China, the USSR and the United States, among others. Early Australian suggestions for a negotiated peace were not widely supported, but negotiations resumed in 1987 and a peace conference was held in 1989. Some issues proved intractable, particularly whether the proposed transitional administration would include members of the Khmer Rouge.[100] To overcome this, Evans proposed that the United Nations itself should be the administering authority – the first time it had undertaken this kind of role – and he and his department launched an intensive diplomatic campaign to sell the plan to the parties, interested states, the General Assembly and the Security Council. They produced a series of options papers (the 'Red Book') which formed the basis of continuing discussions, and in 1992 the UN Transitional Authority in Cambodia (UNTAC) was established to administer Cambodia until elections were held in late 1993. Evans described Australia's role as 'crucial … in particular through producing and selling diplomatically the so-called "Red Book" in January 1990 which broke the deadlock, shaped the final settlement, and created conditions for peace'.[101] This was elsewhere noted as 'one of Australia's most important diplomatic achievements';[102] in recognition of his contribution, Evans was nominated for a Nobel Peace Prize in 1991, and an Australian was appointed as UNTAC's military force commander.[103]

In this period Australia also engaged more closely with the United Nations on human rights matters. It acceded to both optional protocols of the International

[97] See, eg, G Evans, 'Making Australian Foreign Policy' (Melbourne, Australian Fabian Society, Pamphlet No 50, 1989) 9.

[98] G Evans, 'International Law and Australia's Interests' [1989] *Monthly Record* 91, 92.

[99] Evans, 'Making Australian Foreign Policy', above n 97, 12, 31; Evans, 'International Law', above n 98, 92; Commonwealth, *Parliamentary Debates*, House of Representatives, 28 September 1999 10763 (G Evans).

[100] D Lee, 'Australia and the Security Council' in J Cotton and D Lee (eds), *Australia and the United Nations* (Barton, Department of Foreign Affairs and Trade, 2012) 87.

[101] G Evans, 'Labor's Foreign Policy' (Speech to the Rotary International World Understanding Month Dinner, 15 February 1996): www.gevans.org/speeches/old/1996/150296_labour_foreign_policy.pdf.

[102] Lee, 'Australia and the Security Council', above n 100, 86.

[103] Commonwealth, *Parliamentary Debates*, House of Representatives, 7 November 1991, 2605 (RJL Hawke); UNTAC, 'Cambodia: Background': peacekeeping.un.org/sites/default/files/past/untacbackgr2.html.

Covenant on Civil and Political Rights (ICCPR) in 1990; in 1993, it accepted the individual complaints mechanisms under the ICCPR, the Racial Discrimination Convention, and the Convention Against Torture, and overall adopted seven human rights instruments.[104] This increased treaty participation also extended to conventions on drugs and other penal matters, the 1986 Vienna Convention on the Law of Treaties between States and International Organizations or between International Organizations, three disarmament treaties, nearly all the major environmental instruments, and 14 ILO conventions.

Evans argued strongly for increased funding of the United Nations and for reform of the organisation, particularly of the composition and operation of the Security Council, and for more attention to be given to conflict prevention.[105] His ideas were elaborated in his book *Cooperating for Peace*, copies of which he distributed to all delegations attending the UN General Assembly session in 1993.[106] What is also noteworthy about this era is that Evans made multilateralism, good international citizenship and support for the United Nations a prominent part of his, and his government's, speeches and policies. Together with his indefatigable activism, this gave Evans a very high international profile, recognised in many subsequent appointments such as to the UN Secretary General's High Level Panel on Threats, Challenges and Change in 2004.[107] This made the contrast with the succeeding government of John Howard all the more stark.

VIII. THE HOWARD GOVERNMENT 1996–2007

The Howard Government's relationship with the United Nations started badly and only deteriorated thereafter. Elected in March 1996, it inherited the Keating Government's bid for election to the Security Council for the 1997 to 1998

[104] A declaration under Art 41 recognises the competence of the Human Rights Committee to hear complaints of non-compliance from other States Parties: International Convention on the Elimination of All Forms of Racial Discrimination (adopted 7 March 1966, entered into force 4 January 1969) 660 UNTS 195. A declaration under Art 14 enables individuals to bring complaints directly to the Committee on the Elimination of Racial Discrimination (CERD). Article 21 recognises the competence of the Committee Against Torture to hear complaints of non-compliance from other states parties; Art 22 enables individuals to bring complaints directly to the Committee. Each declaration was made on 28 January 1993: United Nations, 'Multilateral Treaties Deposited with the Secretary-General: Chapter IV': treaties.un.org/Pages/ParticipationStatus.aspx.

[105] See, eg, Evans's Statements to the 47th and 48th sessions of the UN General Assembly, 28 September 1992 and 27 September 1993: G Evans, 'The United Nations: New Opportunities, New Challenges' (Address to the Forty Seventh Session of the General Assembly of the United Nations, 28 September 1992): www.gevans.org/speeches/old/1992/280992_fm_unnewopportunities.pdf; G Evans, 'The United Nations: Cooperating for Peace' (Address to the Forty Eighth General Assembly of the United Nations, 27 September 1993): www.gevans.org/speeches/old/1993/270993_fm_uncooperatingforpeaces.pdf.

[106] G Evans, 'The United Nations: Cooperating for Peace', above n 105.

[107] UNGA, 'Note by the Secretary-General: Follow-Up to the Outcome of the Millennium Summit' UN GAOR 59th Session Agenda Item 55 UN Doc A/59/565 (2 December 2004).

term. But shortly before the UN vote, in September 1996, Pauline Hanson, the leader of the One Nation Party, gave her maiden speech in Parliament in which she complained about the 'privileges' accorded to Indigenous Australians, the United Nations, immigration and multiculturalism, declaring that 'we are in danger of being swamped by Asians'.[108] The negative image of Australia that this projected was exacerbated by the government's refusal to condemn these sentiments. Indeed, Howard poured fuel on the fire by praising his government's restoration of free speech instead of 'political correctness': 'people do feel free to speak a little more freely and a little more openly about what they feel'.[109] Within Australia a xenophobic debate about race and immigration ensued, with extreme anti-immigration views given free rein in the media. At the same time, Howard was refusing to apologise formally to the 'stolen generations' of Indigenous Australian children who had been taken from their families by successive governments in the twentieth century.[110] Internationally Howard's inaction and the apparent electoral support for Hanson's racism were interpreted as Australia reverting to the White Australia policy,[111] and were undoubtedly a factor in Australia's humiliating defeat in the Security Council election.[112]

In its foreign policy, the Coalition Government gave primacy to its idea of the national interest, with 'a more selective approach to ... multilateral issues, concentrating on areas where Australia's national interests are closely engaged'.[113] Its regard for the United Nations bordered on hostility, especially towards human rights treaty bodies. During the Coalition's term of office, Australia was found in violation of its human rights treaty obligations in 18 cases,[114] and in September 1998 Australia became the first Western state

[108] Commonwealth, *Parliamentary Debates*, House of Representatives, 10 September 1996, 3862–63 (P Hanson).

[109] J Howard (Speech to Queensland Liberal Party, 22 September 1996), quoted in I Ward, 'Commonwealth Political Chronicle: July–December 1996' (1997) 43 *Australian Journal of Politics and History* 216.

[110] An inquiry was established by Labor in 1995 and reported in 1997: Human Rights and Equal Opportunity Commission, *Bringing them Home: Report of the National Inquiry into the Separation of Aboriginal and Torres Strait Islander Children from Their Families* (Report, 1997).

[111] P Kelly, *The March of Patriots: The Struggle for Modern Australia* (Melbourne, Melbourne University Press, 2009) 370–71.

[112] Jose Ramos-Horta, quoted in T Hyland, 'Timor Not Decisive in Australia's UN Debacle' *AAP* (Melbourne, 22 October 1996). Other possible factors were Australia's perceived pro-American stance and the personal standing of the Australian ambassador to the UN at the time: ibid; Cynthia Banham, 'UN Mission is an Uphill Battle' *Sydney Morning Herald* (6 September 2008) 31; DM Malone, 'Eyes on the Prize: The Quest for Nonpermanent Seats on the UN Security Council' (2000) 6 *Global Governance: A Review of Multilateralism and International Organizations* 3, 15.

[113] Minister for Foreign Affairs and Minister for Trade, 'Joint Statement on Foreign and Trade Policy White Paper' (Media Release, 28 August 1997); Commonwealth of Australia, 'In the National Interest: Australia's Foreign and Trade Policy' (White Paper, 1997) iii, 49; D Goldsworthy, 'An Overview' in J Cotton and J Ravenhill (eds), *The National Interest in a Global Era: Australia in World Affairs, 1996–2000* (South Melbourne, Oxford University Press, 2001) 12.

[114] For a comprehensive list of all cases, their outcomes and government responses, see Bayefsky, 'The United Nations Human Rights Treaties': www.bayefsky.com.

called to explain its race policies to the Committee on the Elimination of Racial Discrimination (CERD), arising out of amendments to the Native Title Act 1993 (Cth).[115] In 2000 the Minister for Immigration and Multicultural Affairs was outraged at his treatment by CERD when he appeared personally before it, decrying its 'blatantly political and partisan approach'.[116] The government immediately reviewed its participation with the treaty bodies and announced that until they were reformed, Australia would not allow committee visits except for compelling reasons; its reporting to and representation at treaty committees would be 'more economical and selective'; and (among other measures) it would not sign the Optional Protocol to the Convention on the Elimination of All Forms of Discrimination against Women (CEDAW), which created an individual complaints mechanism.[117]

Towards the end of its term, the Howard Government was one of only four states (with Canada, New Zealand and the United States) to vote against the UN Declaration on the Rights of Indigenous Peoples,[118] arguing that its references to Indigenous customary law and self-determination would lead to the development of separate Indigenous and non-Indigenous nations.[119]

A more positive engagement with the United Nations arose out of the conflict in East Timor.[120] After nearly 25 years of Indonesian rule, a referendum was held in 1999 in which the people of East Timor voted overwhelmingly for independence. Before and after the referendum, pro-Indonesian militia reacted violently. Australia was asked to lead a multinational force to halt the violence, providing the force commander and almost half the personnel.[121] Australia also contributed a major component of the subsequent peacekeeping force, part of the multifunctional UN Transitional Authority in East Timor.[122] When violence flared again in 2006 and East Timor requested assistance, Australia and New Zealand formed an International Stabilisation Force, working

[115] Goldsworthy, above n 113, 29; CERD, 'Report of the Committee on the Elimination of Racial Discrimination' UN GAOR 53rd Session Supp No 18 UN Doc A/53/18 (11 August 1998) 18 (Decision 1(53) on Australia).

[116] A Downer, 'Government to Review UN Treaty Committees' (Media Release, 30 March 2000).

[117] A Downer, D Williams and P Ruddock, Improving the Effectiveness of United Nations Committees' (Joint Media Release, 29 August 2000).

[118] UNGA, 'Resolution Adopted by the General Assembly on 13 September 2007' 61st Session Agenda Item 68 UN Doc A/RES/61/295 (13 September 2007). For a discussion of Australia's relationship with UNDRIP, see L Malezer, 'The Increasing Results of Indigenous Peoples' Engagement in International Law and Geopolitics, ch 7 in this volume.

[119] The Declaration was signed by the Labor government on 3 April 2009: R McClelland, Attorney-General, 'Remarks in Support of the United Nations Declaration on the Rights of Indigenous Peoples' (3 April 2009).

[120] For a discussion of Australia's troubled relationship with East Timor/Timor-Leste, see C Fernandes, 'Australia, Timor-Leste and International Law', ch 5 in this volume.

[121] INTERFET (International Force for East Timor), established under UN Charter ch VII: UNSC Res 1264 (15 September 1999) UN Doc S/RES/1264; Kelly, above n 111, 510.

[122] J Cotton and J Ravenhill, 'Australia in World Affairs 1996–2000' in Cotton and Ravenhill (eds), above n 113, 225; Senate Standing Committee on Foreign Affairs, Defence and Trade, *Australia's Involvement in Peacekeeping Operations* (2008) 8. UNTAET was established by UNSC Res 1272 (25 October 1999) UN Doc S/RES/1272.

(not always smoothly)[123] in conjunction with the UN Integrated Mission in Timor-Leste.[124]

A low point in terms of Australia's regard for the United Nations came with the invasion of Iraq in 2003. The invasion by the United States, United Kingdom, Australia and others occurred in March 2003, without the authorisation of the Security Council. Australia was an enthusiastic contributor, arguing (unpersuasively) that legal authority to use force could be derived from the Security Council's resolutions over a decade earlier, when responding to Iraq's 1990 invasion of Kuwait.[125] The refusal of the Security Council to pass the necessary resolution in 2003 only reinforced Australia's dim view of that body, with the Foreign Minister commenting:

> Multilateral institutions need to become more results oriented if they are to serve the interests of the international community, including Australia. We are prepared to join coalitions of the willing that can bring focus and purpose to addressing the urgent security and other challenges we face. Sovereignty in our view is not absolute.[126]

The Howard Government's lack of respect – at times, contempt – for the United Nations and the multilateral system[127] was clear in its 2004 decision not to seek election to the Security Council for 2008 to 2009.[128] The effect of over nine years of 'conspicuous anti-multilateralism'[129] was that by 2005 Australia was considered 'virtually unelectable' to the Security Council anyway.[130]

[123] See, eg, Nautilus Institute for Security and Sustainability, 'United Nations Integrated Mission in Timor-Leste (UNMIT)': nautilus.org/publications/books/australian-forces-abroad/east-timor/united-nations-integrated-mission-in-timor-leste-unmit/.

[124] United Nations Peacekeeping, 'UNMIT: United Nations Integrated Mission in Timor-Leste': peacekeeping.un.org/mission/past/unmit/.

[125] UNSC, 'Letter Dated 20 March 2003 from the Permanent Representative of Australia to the United Nations addressed to the President of the Security Council' (20 March 2003) UN Doc S/2003/352; B Campbell and C Moraitis, 'Memorandum of Advice to the Commonwealth Government on the Use of Force' (2003) 4 *Melbourne Journal of International Law* 178.

[126] A Downer, 'Security in an Unstable World' (Speech at the National Press Club, 26 June 2003).

[127] See, eg, M Hanson, 'Issues in Australian Foreign Policy, January to June 2005' (2005) 51 *Australian Journal of Politics & History* 564, 574–77. In a 2003 speech, Downer, 'Security in an Unstable World', above n 126, made this clear: 'What underpins our approach to foreign and trade policy is a determination to advance the national interest in a pragmatic and hard headed way. We look for outcomes not just empty form and posturing … We can not afford to spend time and effort on processes and institutions that are marginal to our interests … Some multilateral institutions will remain important to our interests. But increasingly multilateralism is a synonym for an ineffective and unfocused policy involving internationalism of the lowest common denominator'.

[128] Downer was in favour, but Howard decided that the cost ($35 million) was too high: Phillip Coorey, 'No Chance of UN Seat until 2018' *Sydney Morning Herald* (3 March 2008) 5.

[129] A Kent, 'Australia and International Human Rights' in J Cotton and J Ravenhill (eds), *Trading on Alliance Security: Australia in World Affairs 2001–2005* (Melbourne, Oxford University Press, 2007) 249.

[130] R Woolcott, *Lecturing More and Listening Less: Recent Australian Attitudes Towards Multilateralism* (Centre for Policy Development, 5 Septemer 2005): cpd.org.au/2005/09/lecturing-more-and-listening-less-recent-australian-attitudes-towards-multilateralism/.

IX. THE RUDD/GILLARD/RUDD GOVERNMENTS 2007–13

In November 2007, the Labor Party won the federal election and Kevin Rudd, Labor leader for less than a year, became Prime Minister. The strong popular support he enjoyed in his first two years plummeted in 2010, leading the Party to replace him as Prime Minister with Julia Gillard. The Party struggled to regain popularity and shortly before the 2013 election, Rudd was again installed as Prime Minister, but was unable to save the Party from defeat: Labor obtained the lowest primary vote since 1903 in the 2013 election.[131]

Rudd had a special interest in international relations, having been a diplomat and then Shadow Minister for Foreign Affairs for several years during the Howard era. He condemned Howard's spurning of multilateralism and, in keeping with long-standing Labor policy, vowed to re-engage with the world once in government, and to restore Australia's reputation as a good international citizen.[132] The first and most obvious sign of Australia's recommitment to multilateralism was Rudd's very public ratification of the Kyoto Protocol[133] on his first day in office.[134] John Howard had steadfastly refused to ratify the Protocol, arguing that the economic cost was too high and that the Protocol would only be effective if developing countries were also required to reduce their greenhouse gas emissions.[135]

Membership of the United Nations was described in the Party platform as one of the three pillars of Labor foreign policy,[136] and this took tangible form almost immediately. Within weeks of becoming Prime Minister, both Rudd and his Minister for Foreign Affairs visited the United Nations in New York, and Rudd announced that Australia would bid for a seat on the Security Council for 2013 to 2014 – Australia had not held such a seat since 1986.[137] Australia's

[131] J Wanna, 'Political Chronicles July to December 2013' (2007) 60 *Australian Journal of Politics & History* 279, 280–83.

[132] See, eg, Commonwealth, *Parliamentary Debates*, House of Representatives, 11 November 1992, 162 (K Rudd); Commonwealth, *Parliamentary Debates*, House of Representatives, 2 October 1997, 9059 (L Brereton, Shadow Minister for Foreign Affairs); Commonwealth, *Parliamentary Debates*, House of Representatives, 26 August 1999, 9281 (S Smith, Shadow Minister for Communications); S Crean, 'Australia and Asia: New Partnerships, New Directions' (Speech to the Asia-Australia Institute, 22 April 2002); R McClelland, 'Time to Repair Our Reputation: The Rise and Fall of Australia as a Good International Citizen' (Media Release, 14 March 2007).

[133] Kyoto Protocol to the United Nations Framework Convention on Climate Change (adopted 11 December 1997, entered into force 16 February 2005) 2303 UNTS 162.

[134] K Rudd (Address to the UN Bali Conference on Climate Change, 12 December 2007): australianpolitics.com/2007/12/12/rudd-address-to-bali-climate-change-conference.html.

[135] L Elliott, 'Pragmatism, Prosperity, and Environmental Challenges in Australia's Foreign Policy' in Cotton and Ravenhill (eds), above n 129, 222–23.

[136] Membership of the United Nations was the first of the three 'fundamental pillars' of Labor's national security policy in the 2004, 2007 and 2009 party platforms: Australian Labor Party, *National Platform and Constitution* (2004) 232, para 4 (ALP Platform, 2004); Australian Labor Party, *National Platform and Constitution* (2007) 227, para 1 (ALP Platform, 2007); Australian Labor Party, *National Platform and Constitution* (2009) ch 10, para 14.

[137] DFAT, *Annual Report 2007–2008* (Report, 2008) 115–16. Both Smith and Rudd also attended the opening of the 63rd session of the General Assembly in September that year: DFAT, 'Annual Report 2008–2009' (Report, 2009) 116. In New York, … the return of multilateralism to the

financial contribution to the United Nations doubled between 2007 and 2010, and doubled again by 2012.[138]

In further contrast to the previous Howard Government, Rudd moved quickly to ratify the 2006 Convention on the Rights of Persons with Disabilities, and its Optional Protocol, to accede to the 1999 Optional Protocol to CEDAW, to sign the 2002 Optional Protocol to the Convention against Torture (OPCAT), and to give formal support to the UN Declaration on the Rights of Indigenous Peoples.[139] The Rudd Government also issued a standing invitation to UN human rights Special Rapporteurs and other experts to visit Australia.[140] Coming after Rudd's widely praised apology to the Stolen Generations, these actions further evidenced Australia's retreat from the Howard Government's exceptionalism and its re-engagement with the international community.

Rudd personally expended great energy in trying to achieve international consensus on action to combat climate change, which he described as 'one of the greatest moral, economic and environmental challenges of our age'.[141] He led a large delegation to the UN Conference of Parties on Climate Change in Bali in December 2007, and to the unsuccessful Copenhagen summit in December 2009.[142] For this he won international acclaim,[143] but lost domestic support when he first proposed, and then abandoned, plans for an emissions trading scheme (ETS) which would have given effect to the reduction targets.[144] Legislation setting a fixed price on emissions with a view to a cap-and-trade ETS in the longer term was eventually passed by the Gillard Government

vocabulary of Australian diplomacy drew warm applause': R Leaver, 'Issues in Australian Foreign Policy January to June 2008' (2008) 54 *Australian Journal of Politics & History* 597, 605.

[138] OECD: Australia, Multilateral Contributions to UN Agencies, Total Flows by Donor: stats.oecd.org/Index.aspx#. In current prices, the contributions were US$79 million in 2007, US$163m in 2010 and US$299m in 2012.

[139] UNGA Res 61/295 (13 September 2007) UN Doc A/RES/61/295; J Macklin, 'Statement on the United Nations Declaration on the Rights of Indigenous Peoples' (Canberra, 3 April 2009): www.un.org/esa/socdev/unpfii/documents/Australia_official_statement_endorsement_UNDRIP.pdf. The other states that initially voted against the Declaration were the United States, Canada and New Zealand, but they all subsequently endorsed it: United Nations, 'United Nations Declaration On The Rights Of Indigenous Peoples': social.desa.un.org/issues/indigenous-peoples/united-nations-declaration-on-the-rights-of-indigenous-peoples. The Howard Government had opposed the Declaration, above n 119 and accompanying text.

[140] See, eg, R McClelland, 'Strengthening Human Rights and the Rule of Law' (Speech to the Human Rights Law Resource Centre, Melbourne, 7 August 2008) 11: parlinfo.aph.gov.au/.

[141] eg, in Rudd, above n 134; and a speech to US Brookings Institution: AAP, 'Rudd Calls on US to Ratify Kyoto Protocol' *Sydney Morning Herald* (21 April 2007).

[142] Andrew Charlton, 'What We Learned in Copenhagen' *The Monthly* (28 November 2011). The purpose of the Copenhagen summit was to agree on a framework for action once the Kyoto Protocol expired in December 2012, but states could not agree on any binding commitments: R Leaver and M Kelton, 'Issues in Australian Foreign Policy January to December 2009' (2010) 56 *Australian Journal of Politics & History* 259, 272–73.

[143] A O'Neil, 'Regional, Alliance and Global Priorities of the Rudd–Gillard Governments' in J Cotton and J Ravenhill (eds), *Middle Power Dreaming: Australia in World Affairs 2006–2010* (Melbourne, Oxford University Press, 2011) 286.

[144] See, eg, Lenore Taylor, 'Rudd's ETS Flip-Flop Sparks Climate Chaos' *Sydney Morning Herald* (29 April 2010).

in 2011,[145] but it was repealed by the incoming Coalition Government in 2014.[146]

Julia Gillard did not take the same interest in foreign affairs, but Rudd was Foreign Minister for much of her term, and continued to exert considerable influence over foreign policy. The rehabilitation of Australia's international reputation was confirmed when in late 2012 it won a Security Council seat for 2013 to 2014 with 'a big, juicy, decisive win' of 140 votes.[147] A more prosaic explanation was that the actor Hugh Jackman was responsible, after the Australian mission in New York organised a pre-election trip for two dozen senior female diplomats to see his Broadway show and meet him afterwards.[148]

In September 2013, the Liberal–National Coalition came to power in Australia under Tony Abbott, but as the change of government had no palpable effect on its approach to and in the Security Council, the Security Council term is dealt with in a single section here.

In a nod to Evatt, Australia's campaign slogan was 'Making a Difference for the Small and Medium Countries of the World' – to be achieved through reform of the Council and greater transparency in its working methods.[149] One step in this direction was a programme of events organised by the Australian mission, to engage all UN Member States and civil society in the work of the Council; another was its chairing of the Al-Qaeda, Iran and Taliban sanctions committees, where it encouraged greater transparency and co-sponsored a review of the effectiveness of sanctions.[150]

During Australia's term the Council was busier than ever, with a record number of meetings.[151] Australia played a significant role in relation to many of the crises coming before the Council, such as that in Syria, and the downing of Malaysian Airlines flight MH17 over Ukraine.

As the civil war in Syria worsened, Russia and China had consistently blocked the Security Council from taking any action, even to alleviate the dire humanitarian situation. In August 2013, it was alleged that the Syrian government had used chemical weapons, and the United States was considering military action in response.[152] Gary Quinlan, Australia's highly skilled ambassador to the United Nations, used his position as President of the Council to encourage private

[145] Clean Energy Act 2011 (Cth).

[146] Clean Energy Legislation (Carbon Tax Repeal) Act 2014 (Cth).

[147] B Carr, Minister for Foreign Affairs, quoted in Tony Eastley and Lisa Millar, 'Australia Wins Seat on UN Security Council' (*ABC News*, 19 Oct 2012).

[148] Nick Bryant, 'Australia at the UN Security Council' (*The Monthly*, November 2013).

[149] Commonwealth of Australia, 'Australia: Candidate for the United Nations Security Council 2013–14' (Commonwealth of Australia, 2011) 1.

[150] DFAT, 'Australia's Term on the United Nations Security Council 2013–14: Achievements' (February 2015) 5: www.dfat.gov.au/about-us/publications/international-relations/Pages/australias-term-on-the-united-nations-security-council-2013-14-achievements.

[151] ibid.

[152] See, eg, Arms Control Association, 'Timeline of Syrian Chemical Weapons Activity, 2012–2020' (May 2021): www.armscontrol.org/factsheets/Timeline-of-Syrian-Chemical-Weapons-Activity.

negotiations between the United States and Russia, leading to an agreement for Syria to destroy its chemical weapons under UN supervision.[153] He also persuaded the Council to authorise the delivery of humanitarian aid into Syria, without the consent of the Syrian government.[154]

In July 2014, Malaysian Airlines flight MH17 was shot down over Ukraine, killing all on board including 38 Australians. Australia took the lead in drafting a Security Council resolution that condemned the incident, and demanded a full investigation and unrestricted access to the crash site.[155] Australia was able to negotiate wording acceptable to all members of the Council and the resolution was passed unanimously, described as a 'diplomatic triumph' for Australia.[156]

The UN Association of Australia (UNAA) published a 'report card' assessing Australia's performance in 2013 and awarded it an 'A' for its work on the Security Council and in the General Assembly, where it played a leading role in the negotiations for the Arms Trade Treaty.[157] In the Security Council, Australia gained respect for its constructive approach and strong advocacy: '[a]fter a decade during which Australia's support for multilateralism and its standing in the UN had declined, the situation has improved markedly and Australia is now an active, productive and positive contributor to the political work of the UN'.[158] The UNAA, not often a fan of Australia's performance at the United Nations, concluded in 2015 that Australia had 'developed a reputation as an active, pragmatic UNSC member by pursuing solutions to difficult and sensitive international issues involving peace and security'.[159]

X. THE ABBOTT/TURNBULL/MORRISON COALITION GOVERNMENTS 2013–22

The Coalition Government under Tony Abbott had opposed Labor's bid for a seat on the Security Council, and in its first foreign policy statement made a point of emphasising the primary importance of the national interest: '[w]e will ensure that for the remainder of its term on the United Nations Security Council

[153] Nick Bryant, 'Heavy Lifting' *The Monthly* (November 2014). The agreement is made mandatory by UNSC Res 2118 (27 September 2013) UN Doc S/RES/2118.

[154] DFAT, Australia's Term on the United Nations Security Council 2013–14: Achievements', above n 150; UNSC Res 2165 (14 July 2014) UN Doc S/RES/2165.

[155] UNSC Res 2166 (21 July 2014) UN Doc S/RES/2166.

[156] M Conley-Tyler, S Scott and D Dao, 'Australia's Engagement with the UN, G20 and International Law' in M Beeson and S Hameiri (eds), *Navigating the New International Disorder: Australia in World Affairs, 2011–2015* (South Melbourne, Oxford University Press, 2017) 88.

[157] United Nations Association of Australia, *Australia and the United Nations: Report Card 2013* (Report, October 2013) 7: www.unaa.org.au/wp-content/uploads/2015/07/Australia-and-the-UN-Report-Card-2013.pdf.

[158] ibid 7.

[159] United Nations Association of Australia, 'Australia's 2013–2015 Seat on the UN Security Council': www.unaa.org.au/wp-content/uploads/2015/07/UNAA_Aus_security_council.pdf.

Australia serves with distinction and advances genuine national interests'.[160] As noted, however, there was no obvious change in New York. The incoming Minister for Foreign Affairs, Julie Bishop, was an active participant in UN affairs, addressing the General Assembly barely a week after becoming minister, and playing a particularly prominent role in relation to the MH17 incident.[161]

Bishop retained the Foreign Affairs portfolio until 2018, providing a much-needed element of continuity when Tony Abbott was replaced as Prime Minister by Malcolm Turnbull in September 2015. The perceived value of the United Nations to Australia was confirmed by the announcement that month that Australia would again stand for election to the Security Council for 2029 to 2030.[162] The minister also affirmed the previous Labor government's decision to stand for election to the Human Rights Council for 2018 to 2020,[163] then regarded as somewhat ambitious given Australia's poor international reputation on human rights, especially its treatment of asylum seekers and Indigenous Australians:[164] Australia had been found in violation of its human rights treaty obligations 43 times.[165] But the bid was successful, and while Australian policies on detention of asylum seekers did not change, there was a conscious move towards greater transparency, with an open invitation to visits from human rights Special Rapporteurs, and a long-delayed ratification of the OPCAT, permitting inspection of detention facilities.[166]

In 2016, Australia had the opportunity to gain, indirectly, more international recognition when former Prime Minister Kevin Rudd sought nomination as a candidate for UN Secretary-General. Julie Bishop supported this, but Turnbull refused, citing (without detail) Rudd's unsuitability for the role.[167]

[160] Liberal Party of Australia and National Party of Australia, *The Coalition's Policy for Foreign Affairs* (Policy, September 2013): lpaweb-static.s3.amazonaws.com/Coalition%202013%20Election%20Policy%20–%20Foreign%20Affairs%20-%20final.pdf.

[161] J Bishop, 'United Nations General Assembly High Level Debate: Building Global Security and Prosperity' (Speech, 27 September 2013): www.foreignminister.gov.au/minister/julie-bishop/speech/united-nations-general-assembly-high-level-debate-building-global-security-and-prosperity. See, eg, Nick O'Malley, 'MH17: UN Votes Unanimously to Support Australia's Resolution for Access to Crash Site' *Sydney Morning Herald* (22 July 2014).

[162] J Bishop, 'National Statement: United Nations General Assembly 70th Session' (Speech, 29 September 2015): www.foreignminister.gov.au/minister/julie-bishop/speech/national-statement-united-nations-general-assembly-70th-session.

[163] ibid.

[164] See, eg, Sarah Joseph, 'Australia's Bid for the UN Human Rights Council' *The Conversation* (30 September 2015). For a discussion of Australia's policies towards asylum-seeker children, see J Silverstein, 'Child Refugees, Child Rights: Sidestepping International Law in Australian Policy-Making', ch 12 in this volume.

[165] See Bayefsky, 'The United Nations Human Rights Treaties': www.bayefsky.com/bycategory.php/state/9; United Nations Human Rights Treaty Bodies, 'The UN Treaty Body Database': tbinternet.ohchr.org/_layouts/15/TreatyBodyExternal/TBSearch.aspx?Lang=en&DocTypeID=17&DocTypeCategoryID=6.

[166] DFAT, 'Pillars and Priorities': www.dfat.gov.au/international-relations/international-organisations/un/unhrc-2018-2020/pillars-and-priorities/Pages/pillars-and-priorities.

[167] Stephanie Anderson, 'Kevin Rudd: Malcolm Turnbull Rules Out Nominating Former PM for UN Secretary-General Job' (*ABC News*, 29 July 2016); 'Should Australia Have

The prime ministership changed yet again in 2018, and with it the rhetoric on multilateralism: the new Prime Minister, Scott Morrison, decried the 'new variant of globalism that seeks to elevate global institutions above the authority of nation states to direct national policies', asserting that '[w]e can never answer to a higher authority than the people of Australia', let alone 'an unaccountable internationalist bureaucracy'.[168] Morrison maintained his predecessors' lack of enthusiasm for UN efforts to combat climate change, becoming more intransigent with time and refusing to commit to long-term targets on emissions reductions.[169] In 2021, Australia was ranked last of all 193 UN Member States for action taken to reduce emissions.[170] In similar vein, and contrary to Bishop's general support of multilateral fora, the Coalition governments declined even to attend the UN negotiations towards a treaty banning nuclear weapons, and did not sign the resultant Treaty on the Prohibition of Nuclear Weapons.[171]

XI. THE ALBANESE GOVERNMENT 2022–2025

The Morrison Government's internationally isolated stance on climate change was increasingly at odds with domestic public opinion, and was a major factor in its May 2022 electoral loss to Labor, led by Anthony Albanese.[172] At the time of writing, the Albanese Government has been in office for barely a year and, facing issues such as a deteriorating economy, the lingering effects of the COVID-19 pandemic, the Russian invasion of Ukraine, and rising aggression from China, there has been little overt attention paid to the United Nations itself. However, in her address to the General Assembly in September 2022, the Foreign Minister, Penny Wong, emphasised the Labor government's new direction on climate change and recommitted Australia to multilateralism and to the

Nominated Kevin Rudd for UN Secretary-General?', Analysis (Australian Institute of International Affairs, 4 August 2016): www.internationalaffairs.org.au/australianoutlook/should-australia-have-nominated-kevin-rudd-for-un-secretary-general/.

[168] S Morrison, 'The 2019 Lowy Lecture' (Speech, 3 October 2019): www.lowyinstitute.org/publications/2019-lowy-lecture-prime-minister-scott-morrison.

[169] See, eg, Greg Brown, 'Politics of Carbon Has Ended, Scott Morrison Declares' *The Weekend Australian* (22 January 2021).

[170] Michael Mazengarb, 'Australia Ranked Dead Last in World for Climate Action in Latest UN Report' (*Renew Economy*, 1 July 2021): reneweconomy.com.au/australia-ranked-dead-last-in-world-for-climate-action-in-latest-un-report.

[171] Treaty on the Prohibition of Nuclear Weapons (adopted 7 July 2017, entered into force 22 January 2021) 3380 UNTS; Tim Wright, 'Australia's Opposition to a Nuclear Weapon Ban' (*International Campaign to Abolish Nuclear Weapons*, 16 October 2016): www.icanw.org/australia_s_opposition_to_a_nuclear_weapon_ban. The Austalian government regarded the treaty as incompatible with reliance on the US nuclear umbrella, which was considered essential for Australia's protection: Stephen Dziedzic, 'Australia's Stance on the Nuclear Weapons Ban Treaty and Why Our Diplomats Were Labelled "Weasels"' (*ABC News*, 3 June 2017).

[172] Patricia Karvelas, 'How Scott Morrison Lost the Election as Anthony Albanese Triumphs in a Sea of Teal' (*ABC News*, 21 May 2022): www.abc.net.au/news/2022-05-21/election-2022-scott-morrison-loses-albanese/101087832.

United Nations and its reform.[173] The minister confirmed that Australia would be standing for election to the Security Council for the 2029 to 2030 term, and that it would be seeking reform of the Council to include more permanent members from Africa, Latin America and Asia.[174]

Among the more subtle changes in Australian policy at the United Nations has been the attitude to the Treaty on the Prohibition of Nuclear Weapons. Since the Treaty's conclusion in 2017, the UN General Assembly has passed an annual resolution urging members to become parties. Australia is still not a party (despite it being Labor policy),[175] but in late 2022 it changed its vote from regularly opposing the resolution to abstaining – widely regarded as a positive move.[176] To date the government appears to be acting consistently with its electoral platform statement: '[w]e believe strongly in the rule of international law and remain strong supporters of the United Nations'.[177]

XII. CONCLUSIONS

It can be seen from the above chronology that the level of Australia's engagement with the United Nations has, in general, varied according to the government in power. Labor has invariably embraced multilateralism, and the United Nations as the paradigm multilateral institution, while conservative governments have tended to distrust the United Nations and to relegate multilateralism by varying orders of magnitude behind the national interest. This oscillation has often had less of a tangible effect than might be expected from the attendant rhetoric,[178] but several exceptions stand out. Whitlam in 1972 immediately changed Australia's voting policy at the United Nations, increased its financial contributions, and became party to a number of treaties on human rights and disarmament. Hawke, to some extent, but Gareth Evans to a much greater

[173] P Wong, 'National Statement to the UN General Assembly, New York' (Speech, 23 September 2022): www.foreignminister.gov.au/minister/penny-wong/speech/national-statement-un-general-assembly-new-york.

[174] ibid.

[175] The ALP National Platform contains a somewhat qualified commitment to becoming a party to the Treaty: Australian Labor Party, 'ALP National Platform: As Adopted at the 2021 Special Platform Conference' (Report, March 2021) 117: alp.org.au/media/2594/2021-alp-national-platform-final-endorsed-platform.pdf.

[176] 'Australia's Reassessment of the Treaty on the Prohibition of Nuclear Weapons' (*International Campaign to Abolish Nuclear Weapons*, 10 November 2022): icanw.org.au/australias-reassessment-tpnw.

[177] 'ALP National Platform', above n 175, 3.

[178] A fairly consistent theme in the periodic reviews of Australian participation at the UN is that variations in government attitudes to the UN do not always translate into a radical change in Australian conduct in New York, such as voting policies: see, eg, A Pert and H Nasu, 'Australia and International Organisations' in DR Rothwell and E Crawford (eds), *International Law in Australia*, 3rd edn (Pyrmont, Lawbook Co, 2017). See also the chapters on the UN in the 'Australia in World Affairs' series cited in this chapter.

degree, made Australia a significant player in resolving international crises such as Cambodia, and worked hard, and constructively, to reform the United Nations. The Hawke and Keating Labor governments, like Whitlam, stepped up the treaty participation rate, and Evans personally worked tirelessly to promote the virtues of good international citizenship.

With John Howard, the pendulum swung violently in the opposite direction: his government explicitly rejected cooperation with the United Nations in areas such as human rights, and ignored the Security Council in the 2003 invasion of Iraq. An equally sharp swing back to multilateralism occurred under Kevin Rudd in 2007: he signalled Australia's return to the UN fold by initiating the bid for election to the Security Council, catching up on treaty participation in human rights and environment matters, and reopening the door to human rights inspections.

The changes wrought since 2013 have not been quite as obvious. Tony Abbott, Prime Minister from 2013 to 2015, was openly disdainful of the United Nations but inherited a seat on the Security Council where Australia acquitted itself well, due largely to the skills and efforts of Julie Bishop and Gary Quinlan, Australia's Ambassador to the United Nations. Malcolm Turnbull (2015–18) was, like Bishop, a liberal internationalist, and maintained a generally positive relationship with the United Nations. His successor, Scott Morrison, was more in the Howard/Abbott mould; he also inherited an existing UN seat, this time on the Human Rights Council, but more vigorously pursued an 'Australia first' agenda on multilateral issues, particularly action on climate change. This has been reversed by the Albanese Government which, in Labor tradition, is following a more multilateralist approach.

One final observation that flows from the chronology is while these changes are due to the political colour of the government of the day, the intensity of those changes is due to particular individuals. Governments, of course, comprise individuals, but some have put their personal stamp on Australia's engagement with the United Nations to a remarkable degree. The obvious candidates here are Evatt, Whitlam, Evans and Rudd – all Labor politicians, and, curiously, all men of great self-belief, driven and (with the possible exception of Whitlam) irascible. Australia seems to have a history of producing such men – at the Versailles Peace Conference Billy Hughes was described by US President Wilson as a 'pestiferous varmint'.[179] Fortunately, such characteristics are not a prerequisite for Australia to play an active and constructive role in the United Nations. Since 2013, all Australian foreign ministers have been women (Julie Bishop (2013–18), Marise Payne (2018–22) and Penny Wong (since 2022)), and Bishop and Wong in particular have ensured that Australia remains an engaged and supportive member of the United Nations.

[179] S Bonsal, *Suitors and Suppliants: The Little Nations at Versailles* (New York, Prentice-Hall, 1946) 229. Not that Hughes was a multilateralist – quite the opposite: Pert, *Australia as a Good International Citizen*, above n 93, 40. For Hughes' views on President Wilson's proposals for the League of Nations, see A Duxbury, 'Participation in the "Gilded Ball": Australia and the Council of the League of Nations', ch 2 in this volume.

7

The Increasing Results of Indigenous Peoples' Engagement in International Law and Geopolitics

LES MALEZER

PREFACE

I HAVE PREPARED this chapter to reveal the international framework that has developed to promote and protect the rights of Indigenous Peoples. I am privileged to have participated in the development of this framework during the last 50 years and believe that the rights of Indigenous Peoples worldwide are now able to be exercised and protected as a result of the developments that have taken place. Much still remains to be addressed but the machinery for change is in place.

My involvement as a human rights defender for Indigenous Peoples began with the early years of my life. Racial discrimination, both overt and covert, impacted upon my development. I was a high achiever during my teen years, succeeding at schooling to be a high achiever as a sportsman, an academic and a leader, only to experience shock in trying to get employment, service and accommodation in the 'outside world'.

I am an Aboriginal person, proud of myself, but needing in my formative years identity, self esteem and goals. I was very fortunate as fate placed me in the Australian Public Service as one of very few Aboriginal people at a time that the Australian government decided to modernise policies to accept the international human rights standards into domestic laws, programmes and administration.

I was to the forefront of the 'winds of change' in the 1980s, able to function as an influential person at the national level. My skills as a bureaucrat were interlinked with my work as an advocate for our people. I travelled far and wide in Australia, making connections with Aboriginal communities and Torres Strait Islander communities in even the remotest of regions. Outside my professional work I became a community activist to defeat governments and laws that embedded racism in the lives of our people.

At 20 years of age, I helped to establish the Foundation for Aboriginal and Islander Research Action (FAIRA). This organisation was formed at the request of the Aboriginal and Torres Strait Islander Peoples in the State of Queensland who continued to live under the 'Black Acts' which had been in place since 1897. When enacted these laws led to the round-up of the entire population to live on more than 30 reserves around the State.

I was elected as Chairperson of FAIRA and continued to be elected to that position whenever my employment did not cause a conflict of interest. FAIRA is formally accredited to the United Nations (UN) as a Non-Government Organisation with Special Consultation status.

I fight for 'Land Rights', an ideology entailing the two key components for our wellbeing: connection to country, and self-determination. When Australia rejected the promise of national Land Rights laws in 1985, and then later legislated to defeat the High Court's ruling to recognise 'Native Title' in 1998, I turned to the United Nations for legal support, becoming acquainted with the scope of international law and universal human rights.

From the 1980s onwards I chose to work in community-controlled organisations, including in national representative bodies like the National Aboriginal Conference, as Secretary-General; the Aboriginal and Torres Strait Islander Commission, as Assistant to the Chairperson; and the National Congress of Australia's First Peoples, as Co-Chairperson.

In 1998 I decided to concentrate my time and energy at the United Nations, as well as other intergovernmental organisations such as the Commonwealth of Nations and International Labour Organization.

* * *

On late morning, 13 September 2007, the composed atmosphere in the Assembly Hall of the United Nations General Assembly suddenly erupted with loud cheering and hand clapping. The disruption came from diverse crowds of Indigenous Peoples who had filled the gallery to witness the vote for the Declaration on the Rights of Indigenous Peoples.

When order was restored, I was invited by the President of the General Assembly to come to the podium to speak on behalf of the Indigenous Peoples of the world. I was the coordinator for the delegations of the Indigenous Peoples from all regions of the world. My words for the 10-minute speech were carefully chosen:

> Today's adoption of the Declaration occurs because the United Nations and the Indigenous Peoples have found the common will to achieve this outcome. The Declaration does not represent solely the viewpoint of the United Nations, nor does it represent solely the viewpoint of the Indigenous Peoples. It is a Declaration which combines our views and interests and which sets the framework for the future. It is a tool for peace and justice, based upon mutual recognition and mutual respect.

It was important to emphasise the status of Indigenous Peoples in international law, as a 'peoples' with the right to self-determination:

> As Indigenous Peoples we now see a guarantee that our rights to self determination, to our lands and territories, to our cultural identities, to our own representation and to our values and beliefs will be respected at the international level. The Declaration is a framework for States to link and integrate with the Indigenous Peoples, to initiate new and positive relations but this time without exclusion, without discrimination and without exploitation.

It was also important to reject and denounce the accusations that self-determination is a right to secede from the state:

> Territorial Integrity of States, wrongly bandied about by opponents to the Declaration as a restraint on the exercise of self-determination, does not pose a limitation for Indigenous Peoples to achieve the ends of the Declaration. We realise that a number of States have insisted that the Declaration affirm 'territorial integrity' (which by the way is not a human right) as defined in the Declaration on Principles of International Law concerning Friendly Relations and Co-operation among States and in the Vienna Declaration.
>
> We confirm that 'territorial integrity' in fact obligates every State to promote realisation of the principle of equal rights and self-determination of peoples, and to bring a speedy end to colonialism, with due regard to the freely expressed will of the peoples concerned. 'Territorial integrity' also requires that a State represent the whole people without distinction, and reaffirms that subjection of peoples to alien subjugation, domination and exploitation constitutes a violation of the principle, as well as a denial of fundamental human rights, and is contrary to the Charter.

To conclude my speech I called upon the Member States of the United Nations to form collaborative and cooperative relationships with the representatives of the Indigenous Peoples to ensure that the rights contained in the Declaration are protected and promoted.

While the event at the General Assembly is a significant high point in my work to have the human rights of Indigenous Peoples respected, it is only a small marker of my international work to end injustices and racism against Indigenous Peoples.

It was more than 50 years ago that I set out to fight for justice in Australia, beginning with campaigns against the racist laws of Queensland, known as 'the Black Acts'. Around that time my organisation filed an international complaint of racism in Australia to the Committee on the Elimination of Racial Discrimination (CERD).

In 1981 I attended my first international gathering organised by Indigenous Peoples from around the world. It was the Third Assembly of the World Council of Indigenous Peoples and I was the editor of a national Aboriginal and Torres Strait Islander magazine, *Identity*. I attended again in 1984 at the Fourth Assembly, this time as the Secretary-General of the National Aboriginal Conference. These were heady times, to realise that from around the world Indigenous Peoples were organising and planning to get international attention for human rights abuses against their population.

My involvement with the National Aboriginal Conference in the 1980s, the Aboriginal and Torres Strait Islander Commission from the 1990s, and the

National Congress of Australia's First Peoples (2010–16) kept me at the forefront of the Indigenous movement worldwide. Clearly, there was a lot to learn at the international level, where the movement for rights of Indigenous Peoples had broken away from domestic appeals to national governments.

In 1995 I decided to scale up my advocacy at the United Nations, participating in UN meetings of Indigenous Peoples. I built my knowledge as an advocate for human rights and learnt much more about human rights in international law and the UN system.

I was at all possible times a participant in the meetings of the Global Indigenous Caucus. These fora of Indigenous Peoples played an important part in the preparation and organisation of Indigenous Peoples from around the world. The Indigenous Caucus became, and continues to be, an effective structure for Indigenous Peoples to share information and unify efforts for change.

The Indigenous Caucus also grew to become a conduit for resolution of conflicts or dissent among delegations. Problems were often handled through regional meetings of Indigenous Peoples' delegations where problem-solving was easier to put into practice.

My efforts at Caucus level were to share high-level information, often obtained through the UN system, state ambassadors and regional caucus contacts. As the drafting of the Declaration on the Rights of Indigenous Peoples progressed towards completion, I became a spokesperson for our Indigenous Caucus from the Pacific Region. As the Draft Declaration went to the General Assembly for final resolution, I was accepted to become the Coordinator of the representative delegations from each of the seven regions of the world. It was in this capacity that I found myself at the podium before the UN General Assembly.

In preparing this chapter on Indigenous Peoples in international law I chose to provide a timeline of developments which demonstrated the change in the status of Indigenous Peoples at the international level, along with corresponding developments in international human rights law. The major goal sought by Indigenous Peoples at the international level has been achieved, I believe, but states are yet to show they have adjusted in accordance with international law and their obligations under the Charter of the United Nations, to see equality and justice for the exploitation and colonisation, where it occurred and still exists, of Indigenous Peoples.

I have chosen to present the information from the viewpoint of an observer rather than based on my personal experiences, views and activism. I believe that the information presented in this chapter can speak for itself and not be weighted by my enthusiasm or disappointments. However, I take the liberty to predict a better future.

While it is frustrating that states have not made enough progress – in quick time and with remorsefulness – in acknowledging and recognising the status of Indigenous Peoples, I take solace that the international structures created to support the rights of Indigenous persons will bring about change. The loud calls for actions coming from the UN system are a request for states to now *work in cooperation with* Indigenous Peoples.

'Consultation' has become the excuse of the coloniser, and a mask to hide the intention to maintain power over the Indigenous Peoples, because consultation is the tool of the holder of power and control. The character of consultation raises the challenge of 'how long is a piece of string?'

I believe in international human rights law, and the principles of the UN Charter. The world has made a commitment under that treaty to promote and protect the human rights of all Peoples. In addition, the Charter recognises, without distinction, the rights of 'All' (sic) Peoples to self-determination and peaceful resolution of disputes.

The UN Charter vests the responsibility of both promoting and protecting human rights in Member States. The states are well and truly vested with that responsibility and therefore they need to be held to account by peoples and civil society in all its formations and appearances.

Indigenous Peoples have reported and continue to report that states are not promoting and protecting their human rights. The UN system now recognises the truth and severity of that situation. The Member States of the UN do not represent the Indigenous Peoples of the world, but those Member States control their lands, territories and resources in the most destructive and unaccountable ways.

This what I have learned from the wise and forward-looking Charter of the United Nations.

I. INTRODUCTION

'You have a home at the United Nations'.

These were the words of UN Secretary-General, Kofi Annan, on 24 May 2002, as he welcomed representatives of Indigenous Peoples to the new body created within the United Nations, the Permanent Forum on Indigenous Issues. This new entity represented an important achievement, signalling an end to colonisation around the world, and bringing change that, in international law, is of no lesser importance than the defeat of slavery:

> With the inauguration of this Forum, indigenous issues assume their rightful place – higher on the international agenda than ever before. We begin a new chapter in the history of indigenous peoples at the United Nations. It is entirely appropriate that as victims of discrimination, and as some of the world's poorest of the poor, indigenous peoples have a platform where they can raise their concerns.[1]

[1] United Nations, 'You Have a Home at the United Nations' says Secretary-General, as Indigenous Forum Concludes First Session' (24 May 2002), available at: press.un.org/en/2002/sgsm8249.doc.htm.

The journey for equality and self-determination of Indigenous Peoples began in 1945 when the 'treaty of nations', the Charter of the United Nations, affirmed the universality of human rights and included obligations requiring Member States to promote and respect those rights.[2] The additional structures and procedures were necessary given these purposes, and the creation of the Permanent Forum on Indigenous Issues opened the doors to the UN for Indigenous Peoples. Nevertheless, for Indigenous Peoples, the journey took over 50 years to arrive at the first session of the UN Permanent Forum on Indigenous Issues.

In 2002, the Secretary-General recognised that:

> Indeed, you have rights, needs and aspirations that can and must be addressed by the world Organization. And you have knowledge, vision, values, skills and many other attributes that can and must help us at the United Nations, and indeed all of humankind, to achieve our long-sought goals of development and peace.[3]

A number of significant changes have been made since 2002 to ensure Indigenous Peoples hold a pronounced place on the world stage. Before these changes are examined, it is important to look back to the earliest encounters between Western states and Indigenous populations around the world, and the more recent efforts by Indigenous Peoples to engage with the international community to seek status and justice under international law.

II. HISTORICAL CONTEXT

The era of colonisation extended from the 1500s to 1900. During this period Western European countries competed for the riches and resources, newly discovered in Africa, Asia and the Americas, as they seized the lands, territories and resources of Indigenous populations. International law of the time was generated by the aggressors using religious and moral justifications to subjugate 'inferior' populations, expand their territories and take the natural resources. Indigenous populations, unprepared and vulnerable to this exploitation, were devastated by colonisation. These colonisers generated great economic power and military strength as nation states.

A. A Treaty for Peaceful Settlement of International Disputes

The competition between the European powers culminated in the early twentieth century when tensions and disputes over territories erupted into 'the Great War' of 1914–1918. The human and economic costs of the First World War were unprecedented, demanding a new world order for regulating the excesses of

[2] Charter of the United Nations, Arts 1 and 55 (UN Charter).
[3] United Nations Human Rights Office of the High Commissioner, above n 1.

colonial powers and an international court to resolve disputes in international law. The Treaty of Versailles, signed in 1919, set out the conditions for peace between Germany and the Allies, led by the United States, France and the United Kingdom. The League of Nations was formed under terms in the treaty. This League was the first worldwide intergovernmental organisation whose principal mission was to maintain world peace by preventing wars through negotiations and arbitration.

Through the League, some Indigenous Peoples from the British settler-colonies attempted to have their claims heard. From Australia, for example, Pearl Gibbs, then Secretary of the Aboriginal Progressives Association, wrote to the League to protest about the treatment of Aboriginal People. The League took no action in response.[4] First Nations Americans saw an opportunity to discuss the treaties that they had made with Western nations. The Iroquois believed their rights of sovereignty were recognised in treaties and should be protected in international law, viz the 1794 Jay Treaty and the 1814 Treaty of Ghent, signed by Great Britain and the United States of America. But the Canadian government proposed in the 1900s to bypass treaty arrangements, and to use the Indian Act to alter the legal foundation and status of governance for the Iroquois.

Levi General, chief of the Younger Bear clan of the Cayuga Nation, was an eloquent speaker, fluent in all six languages of the Iroquois. His title was Deskaheh, and he arrived in Geneva in late 1923 to prepare petitions and hold meetings with officials and representatives. Great Britain, representing Canada at the League of Nations, had the Iroquois request taken off the agenda of the League of Nations. The delegation from the Iroquois Peoples failed to have their rights weighed and protected under international law:

> [W]e went to the League of Nations at Geneva, with its covenant to protect little peoples, and to enforce respect for treaties by its members and we spent a whole year patiently waiting but got no hearing.[5]

Indigenous Peoples' efforts to engage at the international level did not arise again until 60 years later, many years after the conclusion of the Second World War. The UN Charter, signed in June 1945 by 50 states, remains in place today with 193 Member States. According to the Charter, UN Member States must accept the obligation to respect the sovereign equality, territorial integrity and political independence of all Members:

> All Members, in order to ensure to all of them the rights and benefits resulting from membership, shall fulfill in good faith the obligations assumed by them in accordance with the present Charter.[6]

[4] S Rigney, 'On Hearing Well and Being Heard Well: Indigenous International Law at the United Nations' (2021) 2 *TWAIL Review* 122, 134–35.

[5] Deskaheh (10 March 1925). *Rochester Radio*, available at: rochester.indymedia.org/node/878.

[6] Charter of the United Nations, above n 2, Art 2(2).

The UN Charter sets the UN's purposes as, inter alia, to maintain international peace and security, to develop friendly relations among nations based on principles of equal rights and self-determination of peoples, and to encourage respect for human rights and fundamental freedoms among the peoples of Member States and their territories.[7] These purposes have major importance for Indigenous Peoples, as they look for the highest levels of support to take on the discriminatory policies, laws and actions that are embedded in the constitutions and laws of states.

B. Indigenous Peoples of the World

In the 1970s Indigenous Peoples again undertook international action to challenge systemic injustices that continue to impact upon their lives and livelihoods. The initial stages saw Indigenous leaders making contact with Indigenous Peoples in other regions to build alliances and unify actions. The most important contact began with the National Indian Brotherhood (NIB) in Canada under the leadership of George Manuel. The NIB was the first Indigenous Non-Government Organisation (NGO) to be accredited to the United Nations, in anticipation of alliances with other Indigenous Peoples.

George Manuel had gained experience through establishing the NIB as a pan-aboriginal organisation across Canada and attending international meetings and events with delegations of the Canadian government. He also had earlier experiences in gaining access to the United Nations in the 1960s. After establishing the national profile for the Indigenous rights movement, Manuel set his focus on organising an international forum of Indigenous Peoples from around the world. In 1975 the National Indian Brotherhood hosted a General Assembly of the World Council of Indigenous Peoples (WCIP) in Port Alberni, Canada. Indigenous Peoples attended from 24 different countries around the world:

> Now, we come from the four corners of the earth,
> we protest before the concert of nations
> that, We are the Indigenous Peoples, we who have
> a consciousness of culture and peoplehood …
> We vow to control again our own destiny and
> recover our complete humanity and
> pride in being Indigenous people.[8]

[7] ibid Art 1(1)–(3).

[8] World Council of Indigenous People, First International Conference on Indigenous Peoples, 'Solemn Declaration' (Port Alberni, October 1975), available at: digital.library.manoa.hawaii.edu/items/show/31240.

Two key items discussed at this first General Assembly were a charter for the World Council of Indigenous Peoples and accreditation for Indigenous Peoples to send representatives to the United Nations. The workshops and plenary sessions at the WCIP discussed many important topics for Indigenous Peoples, including social, economic and political justice, cultural identity, and land and natural resources. A second meeting of the WCIP was held two years later.

This time the General Assembly was hosted by the Saami Peoples in Kiruna, Samiland, Sweden, in September 1977. At this second General Assembly there was increased participation from the Indigenous Peoples of Latin America. These participants were not keen to engage with states at the international level, having experienced direct threats and hostilities for participating in international dialogues with other Indigenous Peoples. For example, Professor of Law, Douglas Sanders, reported that delegates from Latin America faced imprisonment and torture upon their return from the WCIP General Assembly and were not confident that the World Council would be able to achieve results at the international level through engagements at the United Nations.

The Sami, the North American Indians, the Maoris and the Australian Aborigines could understand each others' situations quite easily. But the relationships between those groups and their national governments were paradoxical, perhaps incomprehensible to the delegates from most of Latin America:

> Correspondingly, the political tension within which Indian organizations functioned in Latin America was difficult for the other delegates to appreciate ... The basic elements of indigenous culture were mutually understood – but the political differences between governments in Latin America and the industrialized west had given the two groups of delegates radically different experiences with national governments.[9]

This second General Assembly of the World Council did not secure a consensus on strategies for engagement with states at the United Nations. The WCIP third General Assembly was hosted in Canberra, Australia, by Aboriginal and Torres Strait Islander Peoples, in April 1981. For this third gathering, a draft document for a convention on Indigenous Peoples had been prepared, but did not get called upon in the agenda for consideration or for further action. This draft document made reference to the right to self-determination and other principles elaborated in the international human rights treaties adopted in the 1960s, namely the International Covenant on Civil and Political Rights (ICCPR) and the International Covenant on Economic, Social and Cultural Rights (ICESCR).[10]

A fourth General Assembly of the WCIP was held in Panama in 1984, where the *Panama Declaration of Principles* was adopted. It contained 17 principles

[9] D Sanders, 'Background Information on the World Council of Indigenous Peoples: The Formation of the World Council of Indigenous Peoples' (WCIP-Secretariat Document, April 1980), available at: www.cwis.org/wp-content/uploads/documents/wcipinfo.txt.

[10] 'The Need for International Conventions' (A World Council of Indigenous Peoples Concept Paper, April 1981), available at: cwis.org/wp-content/uploads/documents/intconv.txt.

consistent with existing international human rights law and reiterated basic rights that were taken for granted in democratic states but routinely denied to Indigenous populations:

> Principle 1: All indigenous peoples have the right of self-determination. By virtue of this right they may freely determine their political status and freely pursue their economic, social, religious and cultural development …
>
> Principle 5: All indigenous people have the right to determine the person or group of persons who are included within its population …
>
> Principle 7: The institutions of indigenous peoples and their decisions, like those of states, must be in conformity with internationally accepted human rights both collective and individual …
>
> Principle 9: Indigenous people shall have exclusive rights to their traditional lands and resources, where the lands and resources of the indigenous people have been taken away without their free and informed consent such lands and resources shall be returned.[11]

While Indigenous Peoples were holding international meetings to discuss their organisation and development, the United Nations was strongly pursuing its agenda to promote universal human rights and the right to self-determination for all peoples.

III. WHO ARE INDIGENOUS PEOPLES?

UN interest in the situation of Indigenous Peoples began with the study of discrimination against Indigenous populations authorised by the Economic and Social Council (ECOSOC) in 1971. The purpose of the study was to examine:

> [T]he problem of discrimination against indigenous populations and to suggest the necessary national and international measures for eliminating such discrimination, in cooperation with the other organs and bodies of the United Nations and with the competent international organizations.[12]

In 1946 ECOSOC created the Commission on Human Rights as the UN's central policy organ in the human rights field. The Commission had a subsidiary body, the Sub-Commission on the Prevention of Discrimination and Protection of Minorities (the Sub-Commission), which was made up of individual human rights experts. Jose R Martinez Cobo, an expert member of the Sub-Commission, was appointed as Special Rapporteur to undertake a study

[11] General Assembly of the World Council of Indigenous Peoples, 'Declaration of Principles' (1984) *WCIP Fourth General Assembly*.

[12] UN ECOSOC, 'The problem of indigenous populations' 50th Session 1771st Plenary Meeting, UN Doc E/RES/1589(L) (2 May 1971).

on the problem of discrimination against Indigenous populations. The study was a long and difficult task, taking a decade to complete due to remoteness and geographical diversity, diversity in cultures and societies, and the historical and political experiences of the Indigenous populations. The Sub-Commission received annual progress reports from the Special Rapporteur between 1973 and 1980 and examined chapters for his final report during 1981 and 1983. The full report by the Special Rapporteur consisted of 21 chapters and was completed in 1984.[13] Upon receiving and considering the report ECOSOC requested the UN Secretary-General to widely distribute the full report to governments, specialised agencies and academic and research institutions.[14]

One of the first questions to be asked was: who are Indigenous Peoples? Cobo's Study on the Problem of Discrimination against Indigenous Populations recommended that there be no definition of 'Indigenous Peoples', concluding that Indigenous Peoples are, and should continue to be, self-identifying as Indigenous Peoples.[15] His report does however include text describing common characteristics of Indigenous populations:

> Indigenous communities, peoples and nations are those which, having a historical continuity with pre-invasion and pre-colonial societies that developed on their territories, consider themselves distinct from other sectors of the societies now prevailing in those territories, or parts of them. They form at present non-dominant sectors of society and are determined to preserve, develop and transmit to future generations their ancestral territories, and their ethnic identity, as the basis of their continued existence as peoples, in accordance with their own cultural patterns, social institutions and legal systems.[16]

It is now estimated that there are between 500 million and 800 million Indigenous People living in every geographical and climatic region of the world. There are the Inuit Peoples and the Saami Peoples in the Arctic region. In Africa Indigenous Peoples include the San, the Maasai, the Samburu and the Imazighen. Many tribal peoples such as the Jummas, the Jarawa and forest dwellers and island peoples live in the Asia region. The Pacific region includes Melanesian, Micronesian and Polynesian nations and peoples, as well as the Aboriginal peoples of Australia. Native American peoples exist across the entire North American region. In Central and South America there are the Awa, Enxet, Guarani, Yanomami and Wichi peoples. This is but a quick and brief account of the Indigenous Peoples of the world.

[13] J Martínez Cobo, 'Study of the Problem of Discrimination Against Indigenous Populations: Final report submitted by the Special Rapporteur, Mr José Martínez Cobo', UN Doc E/CN.4 Sub.2 /1983/21/Add.8 (30 September 1983); the other chapters of the Cobo Report are available at: www.un.org/development/desa/indigenouspeoples/publications/2014/09/martinez-cobo-study/.

[14] UN ECOSOC, 'Study of the problem of discrimination against indigenous populations' 1st Regular Session 25th Plenary Meeting, UN Doc E/1985/85 (30 May 1985).

[15] Cobo, above n 13, 5, para 21.

[16] ibid 50, para 379.

Indigenous Peoples have identifying characteristics that clearly distinguish them from other populations and nation states. These distinguishing features are racial, linguistic, social, ideological, political, economic and religious. Indigenous Peoples also have a global identity based upon their shared experience involving ancient cultures and viable relationships with their territories and environment, in contrast to modern political entities of nation states and consumer cultures. As the Cobo study reached its final stages, three initiatives combined to bring the delegations of Indigenous Peoples to the United Nations in Geneva.

The first of these was the establishment in 1982 of the Working Group on Indigenous Populations (WGIP; the Working Group), the first body within the United Nations to respond to the situation of Indigenous Peoples around the world.[17] The Working Group adopted a procedure allowing any person to speak at its sessions, to gain information and achieve common understanding.

The second development was the access provided for Indigenous Peoples' delegations to attend the sessions of the Working Group. ECOSOC had already adopted a resolution to allow formal arrangements to accredit civil society representatives to participate in its meetings and the meetings of its subsidiary organisations.[18] The resolution provided that:

> Consultative arrangements are to be made, on the one hand, for the purpose of enabling the Council or one of its bodies to secure expert information or advice from organizations having special competence in the subjects for which consultative arrangements are made, and, on the other hand, to enable international, regional, sub-regional and national organizations that represent important elements of public opinion to express their views.[19]

However, most Indigenous Peoples' representatives, keen to participate in sessions of the Working Group, were neither resourced nor structured to seek formal consultative status with ECOSOC.

The third development was the creation of a voluntary trust fund to assist Indigenous delegates to travel to the United Nations. The UN Voluntary Fund for Indigenous Peoples was authorised by the General Assembly in 1985.[20] The General Assembly accepted that many Indigenous Peoples would need financial assistance if they were to attend the sessions of the Working Group. The Voluntary Fund receives donations from states and various institutions, to enable travel and accommodation costs to be paid for approved persons to attend Working Group sessions. The General Assembly provided that:

[17] UN ECOSOC, 'Study of the problem of discrimination against indigenous populations' 1st Session 28th Plenary Meeting, UN Doc E/RES/1982/34 (7 May 1982) 26–27, para 1.

[18] UN ECOSOC, 'Consultative relationship between the United Nations and non-governmental organizations' Substantive Session 49th Plenary Meeting, UN Doc E/RES/1996/31 (25 July 1996).

[19] ibid para 20.

[20] UNGA, 'United Nations Voluntary Fund for Indigenous Populations' 116th Plenary Meeting, UN Doc A/RES/40/130 (13 December 1985).

> The purpose of the Fund shall be to assist representatives of indigenous communities and organizations to participate in the deliberations of the Working Group on Indigenous Populations by providing them with financial assistance, funded by means of voluntary contributions from Governments, non-governmental organizations and other private or public entities.[21]

The Fund continues to exist and has been expanded over time by various resolutions, to widen support for participation in those UN mechanisms, sessions and processes relevant to Indigenous Peoples. With these three developments, Indigenous Peoples have been able to successfully engage with the United Nations.

IV. WORKING GROUP ON INDIGENOUS POPULATIONS

The proposal for a working group was motivated by the reports of Jose R Martinez Cobo, Special Rapporteur for the study into the Problem of Discrimination against Indigenous Populations. As the Cobo study was coming to conclusion, the Sub-Commission successfully recommended that five of its members form a 'Working Group on Indigenous Populations'.[22] The Working Group on Indigenous Populations was authorised by ECOSOC in 1982 to:

a. [R]eview developments pertaining to the promotion and protection of human rights and fundamental freedoms of indigenous populations, including … non-governmental organisations in consultative status, particularly those of indigenous peoples … and to
b. give special attention to the evolution of standards concerning the rights of indigenous populations, taking account of both the similarities and the differences in the situations and aspirations of indigenous populations throughout the world.[23]

The Working Group sessions were held over five working days in July of each year with over 600 delegates arriving from almost every region on earth. The Working Group was designed to be 'open and accessible' and to 'encourage a dialogue … in order to advance, as a collective enterprise, the evolution of and respect for standards safeguarding the reasonable concerns of indigenous populations'.[24] The primary concern of the Working Group was, from the outset, to 'give special attention to the evolution of standards concerning the rights of indigenous

[21] ibid para (b).

[22] UN ECOSOC, above n 17; J Martínez Cobo, 'Study of the Problem of Discrimination Against Indigenous Populations: Volume V Conclusions, Proposals and Recommendations', UN Doc E/CN.4/Sub.2 /1986/7/Add.4 (1987) 4, para 8.

[23] UN ECOSOC, above n 17, paras 1 and 2.

[24] UN ECOSOC, 'Study of the problem of discrimination against indigenous populations: Report of the Working Group on Indigenous Populations on its first session' 35th Session, Agenda item 12, UN Doc E/CN.4/Sub.2/1982/33 (25 August 1982) 22, para 111.

populations'.[25] The Working Group took note of the discriminatory divide between the lives of the Indigenous Peoples and the societies that dominated Indigenous Peoples' territories, and stated that there should be firm protection of the land rights of Indigenous populations, and these populations should play a central role in the planning and execution of development projects affecting the territories in which they live. Standards to be developed could concern:

- The right to maintain own culture, language, and way of life.
- Land and mineral rights.
- Self-management, consultation, participation, self-government or self-determination.
- Freedom of religion and traditional religious practices.[26]

The Working Group agreed not to be diverted by dealing with the complaints of Indigenous Peoples as that would detract from standard-setting discussions and could lead to quasi-judicial functions that would be unhelpful in building UN support for the needs of Indigenous Peoples.[27] The UN system had already established structures and procedures to handle complaints of abuse of human rights. Indigenous Peoples' complaints are mostly accounts of historical and contemporary discrimination by states which failed to respect the fundamental human rights of Indigenous populations.

The UN Charter supports the principle of 'territorial integrity' of states, but individual UN Member States were not supportive of complaints to the UN system where Indigenous Peoples claim rights over lands, territories and resources within state boundaries. Under the UN Charter, Member States hold prime responsibility and a duty to promote and protect the human rights of populations within their respective territories,[28] and this also extends to the protection of Indigenous Peoples' human rights.

The Working Group on Indigenous Populations was well aware that its role required an appreciation of the relations between Indigenous Peoples and states and responded to that challenge by concentrating on the identification of a new human rights standard, to reinforce the principles of equality and non-discrimination, in relation to protecting the human rights of Indigenous Peoples. With that aim in mind, by 1994 the Working Group on Indigenous Populations completed the text for a Draft Declaration on the Rights of Indigenous Peoples.[29]

[25] UN ECOSOC, above n 17, para 2.

[26] Working Group on Indigenous Populations on its first session, n 24, 23, paras 123 and 124.

[27] ibid 22, para 114.

[28] See eg, UNGA, 'Resolution Adopted by the General Assembly on the report of the Third Committee (A/53/625/Add.2): Declaration on the Right and Responsibility of Individuals, Groups and Organs of Society to Promote and Protect Universally-Recognized Human Rights and Fundamental Freedoms' 53rd Session 85th Plenary meeting, Agenda item 110(b), UN Doc A/RES/53/144 (9 December 1998) Art 2(1).

[29] See Commission on Human Rights, Sub-Commission on Prevention of Discrimination and Protection of Minorities, 'Discrimination against indigenous peoples: Report of the Working Group

The Draft Declaration was accepted and endorsed by the Sub-Commission and submitted to the Commission on Human Rights for consideration, thus completing a key task assigned to the Working Group in 1982. After the Draft Declaration was submitted to the Commission, the continued sessions of the Working Group on Indigenous Populations generated reports and recommendations for actions within the United Nations. The members of the Working Group completed expert studies on the relationship between Indigenous Peoples and Lands, Treaties, Heritage and Natural Resources.[30] The expert papers generated from the Working Group built awareness and a knowledge base within the UN system and created wider interest in the situation of Indigenous Peoples. In addition to the expert papers, the Working Group conducted discussions at its sessions and themes under consideration within ECOSOC, the General Assembly and relevant international organisations.

Also associated with the sessions of the WGIP was the formation of the 'Caucus' of Indigenous Peoples. The Indigenous Caucus was a gathering of Indigenous Peoples' representatives convened prior to each session of the WGIP. It has continued to operate whenever Indigenous Peoples meet at the United Nations, or even at international organisations within the UN system.

A preliminary 'caucus' gathering is usually convened to coordinate by sharing information and expectations. It is the Indigenous Caucus that helps to clarify the goals and strategies for Indigenous Peoples' relations with the UN system. However, the Caucus does not try to control or limit inputs from Indigenous Peoples' delegations; rather it promotes cooperative, cohesive relationships which strengthens engagement with the United Nations. Each Caucus gathering is also a ceremonial occasion, a gathering of Indigenous Peoples from all regions recalling traditional and spiritual connections with 'mother earth' and the commitments to past and future generations. The Indigenous Peoples Caucus had been influential in winning support from Member States and encouraging change within the UN system.

By the time of its Tentieth session in 2002, the Working Group on Indigenous Populations had overseen a number of structural developments, studies and landmark reports:

1985 Voluntary Trust Fund for Indigenous Peoples.

1993 International Year for the World's Indigenous Peoples.

1995 International Decade for World's Indigenous Peoples (1995–2004).

on Indigenous Populations on its eleventh session' 45th Session, Agenda item 14, UN Doc E/CN.4/SUB.2/1993/29 (23 August 1993) Annex I.

[30] See, eg, M Martínez, 'Study on treaties, agreements and other constructive arrangements between States and indigenous populations' 47th Session, Agenda Item 14, UN Doc E/CN.4/Sub.2/1995/27 (31 July 1995); E Daes, 'Protection of the heritage of indigenous people' 47th Session, Provision Agenda Item 15, UN Doc E/CN.4/Sub.2/1995/26 (21 June 1995).

1996 Open Ended Inter Sessional Working Group on the Draft Declaration on the Rights of Indigenous Peoples.

1996 Report of the Special Rapporteur on the Protection of the heritage of indigenous people.[31]

1999 Study on treaties, agreements and other constructive arrangements between States and indigenous populations.[32]

2001 Final working paper – Indigenous peoples and their relationship to land.[33]

2002 Appointment of Special Rapporteur on the situation of the human rights and fundamental freedoms of indigenous people.

2002 Establishment of the Permanent Forum on Indigenous Issues.

V. DECLARATION ON THE RIGHTS OF INDIGENOUS PEOPLES

Although a draft of the Declaration had been completed in 1994 by the Working Group on Indigenous Populations little progress was being made in the second phase of drafting, requested by the Commission on Human Rights. The draft Declaration had been forwarded by the Working Group on Indigenous Populations and endorsed by the Sub-Commission on Prevention of Discrimination and Protection of Minorities.[34] However, the Commission on Human Rights did not adopt the draft Declaration as received, but established a new, second working group in 1995 to revise the text before final consideration by the Commission. This new process enabled states to further scrutinise the text before endorsing a final version. Indigenous Peoples were not happy with this review, claiming that states were able to participate in the preparation of the draft declaration, and that the final version as submitted to the Commission represented the consensus reached between states and Indigenous Peoples, as drafted by the qualified human rights experts of the Working Group on Indigenous Populations.

The Commission's new Working Group was formally called the Working Group of the Commission on the Draft Declaration on the Rights of Indigenous

[31] E Daes, 'Protection of the heritage of indigenous people: Supplementary report of the Special Rapporteur, Mrs Erica-Irene Daes, submitted pursuant to Sub-Commission resolution 1995/40 and Commission on Human Rights resolution 1996/63' 48th Session, Provisional Agenda Item 14, UN Doc E/CN.4/Sub.2/1996/22 (24 June 1996).

[32] M Martínez, 'Study on treaties, agreements and other constructive arrangements between States and indigenous populations: Final report by Miguel Alfonso Martínez, Special Rapporteur' 51st Session, Provisional Agenda Item 7, UN Doc E/CN.4/Sub.2/1999/20 (22 June 1999).

[33] E Daes, 'Indigenous peoples and their relationship to land: Final working paper prepared by the Special Rapporteur, Mrs Erica-Irene A Daes' 53rd Session, Provisional Agenda Item 5, UN Doc E/CN.4/Sub.2/2001/21 (11 June 2001).

[34] Working Group on Indigenous Populations on its eleventh session, above n 29.

Peoples.[35] It was an 'open-ended' 'inter-sessional' body and its existence signalled that closer scrutiny would come from Member States. The procedure under this second Working Group did not curtail engagement from representatives of Indigenous Peoples, who were widely represented and participated in large numbers. A chairperson was appointed, having full authority over the process and being responsible for reporting back to the Commission.

It was a unique experience within the United Nations as Indigenous Peoples participated on an equal level with Member States; the only population group to directly participate with UN members to define their human rights. The procedure to further work on the text of the draft Declaration would take a decade to conclude, and even then controversy continued as political actions stalled final adoption of the Declaration. Indigenous Peoples concertedly supported the draft Declaration and refused to accept proposals put forward by states to change the provisions.

The draft Declaration had been assembled in nine parts, including those on life, integrity and security; culture; religious and linguistic identity; economic and social rights; and land resources.[36] The Chairperson of the Working Group called for agreement by consensus on each of the articles by all participants to ensure a successful adoption by the General Assembly at the end of the process.

There was resistance from certain states which were strongly opposed to the right of Indigenous Peoples to self-determination, and to the right of ownership over lands, territories and resources.[37] Some states were convinced that the right to self-determination provided Indigenous Peoples with a right to secession.[38] Other states had firm opposition to the principle that Indigenous Peoples retained the right to own lands, and to exercise control over developments on their lands and territories. Discussions on these particular rights occurred over a number of sessions. During the process, states became more aware of the importance of these rights to Indigenous Peoples and gained information regarding the history of Indigenous Peoples and the relevance of particular articles in the draft Declaration. A majority of states supported the available text

[35] Commission on Human Rights, 'Establishment of a Working Group of the Commission on Human Rights to Elaborate a Draft Declaration in Accordance with Paragraph 5 of General Assembly Resolution 49/214 of 23 December 1994', UN Doc E/CN.4/1995/32 (1995).

[36] Working Group on Indigenous Populations on its eleventh session, above n 29.

[37] See, eg, the comments of Australia, Canada and Czechoslovakia, in Sub-Commission on Prevention of Discrimination and Protection of Minorities, 'Analytical compilation of observations and comments received pursuant to Sub-Commission resolution 1988/18' 41st Session, Provisional Agenda Item 13, UN Doc E/CN.4/Sub.2/1989/33/Add.1 (20 June 1989).

[38] M Davis, 'To Bind or Not to Bind: The United Nations *Declaration on the Rights of Indigenous Peoples* Five Years On' (2012) 19 *Australian International Law Journal* 17, 22–23, citing S Pritchard, 'Working Group on Indigenous Populations: Mandate, Standard-Setting Activities and Future Perspectives' in S Pritchard (ed), *Indigenous Peoples, United Nations and Human Rights* (Sydney, Federation Press, 1998) 46; R Falk, 'Groups Claims within the United Nations System: The Rights of Indigenous Peoples' in R Falk, *Human Rights Horizons* (Oxford, Routledge, 2000) 128; A Xanthaki, *Indigenous Rights and the United Nations Standards: Self-Determination, Culture and Land* (Cambridge, Cambridge University Press, 2007) 110.

and expressed their support for the text as drafted. Despite engaging with early drafts that referred to the right to self-determination, ultimately Australia did not support the draft text.[39]

After a number of sessions, patience was wearing thin over the lack of progress within the Working Group as the target date for adoption, towards the end of the International Decade of the World's Indigenous Peoples (1995–2004), had passed. These concerns were shared by the High Commissioner for Human Rights, Louise Arbour, who in 2004 noted that she had been informed that 'to date the working group set up by the Commission has been able to adopt only 2 of the 45 articles at first reading'.[40] The adoption of the draft Declaration was in jeopardy as actions were taken by a minority of UN members to bring the Declaration into disrepute.

By 2006, completion of the draft Declaration by the Working Group was imminent, as the Chairperson introduced a version cited as the 'Chairman's Text', which he believed represented a fair balance of the supported text, taking account of all proposals from participants. He called upon the participants to accept this version of the draft Declaration as the consensus from the sessions.[41] Consensus was achieved at the last session of the Working Group, held in early 2006. The Working Group was able to submit a recommendation to the Commission on Human Rights that the draft Declaration be forwarded for adoption by the General Assembly.

However, the Canadian government undertook to discredit the draft Declaration by contacting the capitals of many UN members to express their strong opposition to the final draft of the Declaration. The New Zealand government also raised their objections to Indigenous Peoples' right to self-determination. These objections were political actions to deny human rights. Both governments had previously expressed support for the right to self-determination and Canada, in particular, had led the majority bloc of Member States who were in support of the draft Declaration. The politically motivated message from these Member States was that the right of self-determination would lead to secession by Indigenous Peoples from the state. Australia shared similar concerns about the possible scope and consequences of the draft Declaration's wording on self-determination.[42]

[39] See the discussion in Catherine J Iorns, 'The Draft Declaration of the Rights of Indigenous Peoples' (1993) 1 *Murdoch University Electronic Journal of Law*, available at: www5.austlii.edu.au/au/journals/MurUEJL/1993/2.html.

[40] L Arbour, 'Working Group on Indigenous Populations Twenty Second Session' (Opening Statement to the Working Group on Indigenous Populations' Twenty Second Session, 19 July 2004), available at: www.ohchr.org/en/statements/2009/10/working-group-indigenous-populations-twenty-second-session.

[41] See the Chairman's proposals in L Chávez, 'Human rights and indigenous issues: Report of the working group established in accordance with Commission on Human Rights resolution 1995/32 of 3 March 1995 on its eleventh session' 62nd Session, Provision Agenda Item 15, UN Doc E/CN.4/2006/79 (22 March 2006).

[42] UN Human Rights Council, Joint Statement by Australia, New Zealand and the United States of America, 'On the Chair's Text on the Declaration on the Rights of Indigenous Peoples' (June 2006).

Fortunately, and in a timely manner, major reform within the United Nations to achieve a more robust human rights framework occurred during the early years of the new millennium. The UN General Assembly decided to strengthen the framework for promotion and protection of human rights worldwide.[43] The Commission on Human Rights, positioned under ECOSOC, was replaced by a new, more powerful body, the Human Rights Council, as a subsidiary body of the General Assembly. The First Session of the Human Rights Council considered the draft Declaration on the Rights of Indigenous Peoples as the second item on its agenda.[44] When the Declaration was put for adoption by consensus, Canada rose from the floor to call for a vote by the members of the Human Rights Council. A vote was called, and the Declaration was adopted on 29 June 2006 by a majority vote of Council members.[45]

The Declaration on the Rights of Indigenous Peoples was forwarded to the General Assembly for endorsement. The General Assembly decided to delay a vote on the Declaration until certain Member States, including the Africa Group, had time to further review the draft Declaration. The Africa Group in particular were concerned by claims that the Declaration supported secession and felt that political implications arising from the draft document needed to be further examined.[46] The President of the Human Rights Council argued that the General Assembly should not take a vote on the Declaration because the new role and authority of the Human Rights Council, setting and promoting universal standards on human rights, should not be subject to the political machinations of the General Assembly. The General Assembly did not agree and insisted that the Declaration be further examined by the General Assembly. Other members continued to agitate for defeat of the Declaration out of concern regarding articles addressing the right to self-determination and rights to land, territories and resources. At this time the prime ministers of Canada and Australia were known to be campaigning internationally for the Declaration to be defeated.[47]

[43] UNGA, 'Resolution adopted by the General Assembly on 15 March 2006: 60/251. Human Rights Council' 60th Session 72nd Plenary Meeting, Agenda Items 46 and 120, UN DOC A/RES/60/251 (15 March 2006).

[44] Human Rights Council, 'Resolution 1/2. Working group of the Commission on Human Rights to elaborate a draft declaration in accordance with paragraph 5 of the General Assembly resolution 49/214 of 23 December 1994', UN Doc A/HRC/RES/1/2 (29 June 2006).

[45] ibid.

[46] UNGA, 'Resolution adopted by the General Assembly on 20 December 2006: 61/178. Working group of the Commission on Human Rights to elaborate a draft declaration in accordance with paragraph 5 of General Assembly resolution 49/214 of 23 December 1994' 61st Session 82nd Plenary Meeting, Agenda Item 68, UN DOC A/RES/61/178 (20 Dec 2006); African Union African Commission on Human & Peoples' Rights, 'Advisory Opinion of the African Commission on Human and Peoples' Rights on the United Nations Declaration on the Rights of Indigenous Peoples' 41st Ordinary Session (16–30 May 2007).

[47] Australian Cabinet, 'Cabinet Submission JH03/0212 – Draft Declaration on the Rights of Indigenous Peoples – Decision JH03/0212/CAB' Series Number A14370, Document Item ID 32711252 (30 May 2003–10 June 2003); Australian Cabinet, 'Cabinet Memorandum JH02/0267 – Draft Declaration on the Rights of Indigenous Peoples – Decision JH02/0267/CAB' Series Number A14370, Document Item ID 203019479 (1 August 2002–26 August 2002).

One year after the Human Rights Council had adopted the Declaration there was still no response from the General Assembly. However, the Africa group eventually became comfortable with the Declaration's text once they were aware that Article 46 in the General Provisions of the Declaration would be amended to include text on 'territorial integrity':

> Nothing in this Declaration may be interpreted as implying for any State, people, group or person any right to engage in any activity or to perform any act contrary to the Charter of the United Nations or construed as authorizing or encouraging any action which would dismember or impair, totally or in part, the territorial integrity or political unity of sovereign and independent States.[48]

This inclusion was agreed upon by Indigenous Peoples' delegations at the General Assembly session because the new text contributed nothing new in international law and, again, because a right to secession does not exist. In any event, the added text repeated the principle included in the UN Charter.[49] The concerns of African states had arisen because contemporary boundaries (or territories) of states in Africa continue to be based upon colonial boundaries created by the European nations, and these boundaries divide peoples and tribal communities.

However, states' concerns were for the most part resolved. The Declaration on the Rights of Indigenous Peoples was finally adopted on 13 September 2007 with 143 Member States voting in favour and four members – Australia, Canada, New Zealand and the United States – voting against because of fundamental disagreements with the Declaration's framing of a number of issues, including self-determination, rights to land and other resources, and the need for free, prior and informed consent of Indigenous Peoples on measures relevant to them.[50] The four states which cast negative votes have since pledged support for the Declaration.[51]

The draft Declaration prepared by the Working Group on Indigenous Peoples in 1994 included an important principle: the definition of Indigenous Peoples as 'peoples' equal to all other peoples of the world. This invokes Article 1(2) of the UN Charter which establishes that the purpose of the United Nations is 'to develop friendly relations among nations based on respect for the principle of equal rights and self-determination of peoples'. Some states remain reticent about Article 3 of the Declaration, which affirms 'Indigenous Peoples have the right to self-determination'. However, the Declaration on the Rights of Indigenous

[48] UNGA, 'Resolution adopted by the General Assembly on 13 September 2007: 61/295. United Nations Declaration on the Rights of Indigenous Peoples' 107th Plenary Meeting 61st Session, Agenda Item 68, UN Doc A/RES/61/295 (13 September 2007) Annex, Art 46(1).

[49] Charter of the United Nations, above n 2, Art 2(4).

[50] UNGA (2007) GAOR 61st Session, UN Doc A/61/PV.107 11–12.

[51] United Nations Department of Economic and Social Affairs, 'United Nations Declaration on The Rights of Indigenous Peoples' (website): social.desa.un.org/issues/indigenous-peoples/united-nations-declaration-on-the-rights-of-indigenous-peoples.

Peoples is a compilation of the human rights that have been historically denied to Indigenous Peoples. These are rights that most peoples enjoy and take for granted. For Indigenous Peoples, they are rights that uphold the legitimacy of their systems of governance and juridical institutions, their autonomy and sustainability, and their survival and wellbeing. The right to self-determination is particularly vital to Indigenous Peoples, who insist upon the ability to exercise their rights to autonomy, sustainable livelihood and future development.

VI. HUMAN RIGHTS TREATIES AND INDIGENOUS PEOPLES

Since the adoption of the Declaration almost two decades ago, the rights of Indigenous Peoples, including the right to self-determination, have become evident in customary international human rights law. The rights of Indigenous Peoples have been promoted through consideration and elaboration by international human rights treaty bodies, UN special mechanisms on human rights, individual human rights experts and juridical bodies.

The International Labour Organization (ILO) created and ratified an international treaty on the human rights of Indigenous Peoples in 1989. The ILO is a uniquely a tripartite organisation, as an international organisation comprised of representatives from governments, businesses and workers. As early as 1957, the ILO adopted the Indigenous and Tribal Populations Convention.[52] Indigenous Peoples' delegations attending the UN in the 1980s examined this Convention (C107) for its suitability as a standard for human rights and decided that it 'had an inherent assimilationist orientation'.[53] The ILO formed a Committee of Experts to update the C107, and the new Indigenous and Tribal Peoples Convention (C169) was adopted in 1989.[54]

C169 addressed a number of issues that were important to Indigenous Peoples, including consultation and participation; rights to land; employment and vocational training; education; health and social security; customary law; traditional institutions; and cross-border cooperation. For example, Article 15 provided that:

1. The rights of the peoples concerned to the natural resources pertaining to their lands shall be specially safeguarded. These rights include the right of

[52] Convention concerning the Protection and Integration of Indigenous and Other Tribal and Semi-Tribal Populations in Independent Countries (adopted 26 June 1957, entered into force 2 June 1959) International Labour Organization Convention No 107.

[53] International Labour Organization, 'International labour standards regarding indigenous and tribal peoples' (website): www.ilo.org/resource/international-labour-standards-regarding-indigenous-and-tribal-peoples.

[54] Convention concerning Indigenous and Tribal Peoples in Independent Countries (adopted 27 June 1989, entered into force 5 September 1991) International Labour Organization Convention No 169.

these peoples to participate in the use, management and conservation of these resources.

2. In cases in which the State retains the ownership of mineral or sub-surface resources or rights to other resources pertaining to lands, governments shall establish or maintain procedures through which they shall consult these peoples … The peoples concerned shall wherever possible participate in the benefits of such activities.[55]

Indigenous Peoples' right to self-determination was not affirmed in ILO Convention No 169, so despite the vast improvements in the updated Convention, Indigenous Peoples are still hesitant to support the treaty. C169 has been ratified by 24 states, between 1990 (Norway) and 2021 (Germany), but many states remain reluctant to consider the treaty and the contemporary human rights standards therein. Australia, for example, has not ratified the Convention.

The Economic and Social Council's Permanent Forum on Indigenous Issues calls upon Member States annually, in the resolutions on Indigenous Peoples, to ratify ILO Convention No 169.[56] The right of Indigenous Peoples to exercise self-determination continues to be disputed and redefined by some states and scholars, usually as an attempt to retain state authority and to imply limitations and control over Indigenous Peoples' actions and freedoms.

However Indigenous Peoples are 'peoples' by definition and have the same right to self-determination as all peoples as contained in Article 1 of ICESCR and the ICCPR.[57] This right must be consistently interpreted through the provisions in the UN Charter, international treaties, the International Court of Justice and a number of UN Declarations and Resolutions, including Article 2 of the UN Declaration on the Rights of Indigenous Peoples.

The Human Rights Committee, as the body of experts which monitors the ICCPR, has stated that Article 1 of the Covenant 'imposes specific obligations on States parties, not only in relation to its own peoples but vis-a-vis all peoples which have not been able to exercise or have been deprived of the possibility of exercising their right to self-determination'.[58]

The Committee on the Elimination of Racial Discrimination (CERD), the treaty body for the International Convention on the Elimination of All Forms of Racial Discrimination, plays a significant role in monitoring the implementation of the rights of Indigenous Peoples. Although the Convention does not include

[55] ibid, Art 15.

[56] See, eg, Economic and Social Council, 'Permanent Forum on Indigenous Issues: Report on the sixteenth session' 16th Session Official Records 2017 Supplement No 23, UN Doc E/2017/43 (24 April – 5 May 2017) 7, para 19.

[57] International Covenant on Economic, Social and Cultural Rights (adopted 16 December 1966, entered into force 3 January 1976) 993 UNTS 3, Art 1; International Covenant on Civil and Political Rights (adopted 16 December 1966, entered into force 23 March 1976) 999 UNTS 171, Art 1.

[58] UN Human Rights Committee, 'CCPR General Comment No 12: Article 1 (Right to Self-determination) The Right to Self-determination of Peoples' 21st Session (13 March 1984) para 6.

the right to self-determination, CERD has adopted General Recommendation No 23 (1996) on the Rights of Indigenous Peoples, General Recommendation No 21 (1996) on Self-Determination and General Recommendation No 32 (2009) on Special Measures.[59] Thus, the human rights treaty bodies are giving close attention to the rights of Indigenous Peoples, and may even require State parties to report on Indigenous Peoples' right to self-determination.

VII. OTHER INTERNATIONAL MECHANISMS ON HUMAN RIGHTS OF INDIGENOUS PEOPLES

A. Special Rapporteur on the Rights of Indigenous Peoples

The human rights of Indigenous Peoples are also monitored under the special mechanisms and special procedures of the UN Human Rights Council. Special Procedures can have a thematic scope or focus on a single country; and such procedures provide a report and recommendations to the Council every year.

In 2001, the Commission on Human Rights responded to the increased complaints of human rights abuses from Indigenous Peoples by adopting a resolution to establish a Special Rapporteur on the rights of Indigenous Peoples.[60] Rodolfo Stavenhagan, a renowned sociologist, professor/researcher in Mexico, and former Deputy Director General of UNESCO, was the first appointee, in 2002. Since his appointment there have been three further appointments, with each expert being an Indigenous person: James Anaya (2008–14), Vicky Tauli-Corpuz (2014–20) and Jose Francisco Cali Tzay (appointed in 2020).

The role of the Special Rapporteur has become an important component in the field of human rights of Indigenous Peoples. The Special Rapporteur is called upon to not only provide an annual report to the Human Rights Council, but also give a presentation on an annual basis to the General Assembly. The Special Rapporteur's expertise and balanced perspective on the situation of human rights of Indigenous Peoples has had wide influence within the UN system.

The mandate of the Special Rapporteur includes to:

- Promote good practices, including new laws, government programmes, and constructive agreements between Indigenous Peoples and states, to implement international standards concerning the rights of indigenous peoples.

[59] CERD, 'General Recommendation XXI on the right to self-determination' CERD General Recommendation No 21 48th Session (1996); CERD, 'General recommendation XXIII on the rights of indigenous peoples' CERD General Recommendation No 23 51st Session (1997); CERD, 'General recommendation No 32: The meaning and scope of special measures in the International Convention on the Elimination of All Forms Racial Discrimination' 75th Session, UN Doc CERD/C/GC/32 (24 September 2009).

[60] UNCHR Res 2001/57 (2001) UN doc E/CN.4/2001/57.

- Report on the overall human rights situations of Indigenous Peoples in selected countries.
- Address specific cases of alleged violations of the rights of Indigenous Peoples through communications with governments and others.
- Conduct or contribute to thematic studies on topics of special importance regarding the promotion and protection of the rights of Indigenous Peoples.
- Engage with the Permanent Forum on Indigenous Issues and the Expert Mechanism on the Rights of Indigenous Peoples, to develop a regular cooperative dialogue with all relevant actors.[61]

As an individual expert, and with the capacity to investigate and report on any human rights issue, the Special Rapporteur complements the human rights agenda at the national, regional and global levels, and can interact with any of the international organisations and bodies of the United Nations. The Special Rapporteur has issued one report on Australia. This report was critical of Australia's policies and practices on Indigenous Peoples, observing a failure to respect the right to self-determination, and failing to meet targets on Indigenous health, education and employment.[62]

B. Permanent Forum on Indigenous Issues

The creation of the Special Rapporteur position by the Commission on Human Rights coincided with the decision by ECOSOC to establish a 'permanent forum' to give voice to Indigenous Peoples at the UN Headquarters in New York.

In July 2000, ECOSOC received a recommendation from the Commission on Human Rights to establish a more permanent and improved structure, following the successful Working Group on Indigenous Populations. The Permanent Forum on Indigenous Issues was established by ECOSOC Resolution 2000/22[63] and represented another step forward for Indigenous Peoples' status in international affairs. The Permanent Forum operates at a much higher level in the United Nations than did the Working Group on Indigenous Populations, by reporting directly to ECOSOC. States and Indigenous Peoples are able to jointly determine the members of the Permanent Forum. Of the 16 members, half are elected by ECOSOC from nominations received from Member States. The other eight members are appointed, by the President of ECOSOC, from nominations

[61] UN Human Rights Council, 'Resolution adopted by the Human Rights Council on 6 October 2022: 51/16. Human rights and Indigenous Peoples: mandate of Special Rapporteur on the rights of Indigenous Peoples' 51st Session 41st Meeting Agenda Item 3, UN Doc A/HRC/RES/51/16 (12 October 2022).

[62] See UNHRC, 'Report of the Special Rapporteur on the Rights of Indigenous Peoples on her Visit to Australia' (11–29 September 2017), UN Doc A/HRC/36/46/Add.2.

[63] UN ECOSOC, 'Establishment of a Permanent Forum on Indigenous Issues: Economic and Social Council Resolution 2000/22' 45th Plenary Meeting, UN Doc E/2000/22 (28 July 2000).

received from Indigenous Peoples. Appointment of Indigenous Peoples' nominees is made on the basis of broad consultations with Indigenous organisations and taking into account the diversity and geographical distribution of Indigenous populations.[64] Indigenous individuals make up the majority of the 16 members of the Permanent Forum, because ECOSOC prefers to elect Indigenous persons if possible. In 2002, the President of ECOSOC, Ivan Simonovic, claimed the establishment of the Permanent Forum as 'a great victory and a cause for celebration'.

Simonovic recalled giving his personal support during the 1993 World Conference on Human Rights in Vienna, when the Permanent Forum was first recommended, and expressed his satisfaction that the work of the Permanent Forum was about to commence:

> The Permanent Forum is an innovative organ. It is characterised by its unique membership, composed of indigenous and non-indigenous experts, and by the principle of inclusion of all concerned in its work. Since the work of the Permanent Forum is open to all indigenous representatives, whether or not they belong to organizations accredited with ECOSOC, we can conclude that we have created a very open, transparent and participatory body.[65]

Mary Robinson, the UN High Commissioner for Human Rights, had two years earlier provided her ideas for the role and modus operandi of the Permanent Forum. She referred to the growing agenda in the United Nations relating to Indigenous Peoples, but at that stage there was no formal mechanism for sharing information and experiences, or for coordinating and strengthening activities of interest to Indigenous Peoples. Her view was that

> a formal UN body in which all interested parties, including governments, indigenous peoples, UN specialised agencies, NGOs experts and others, able to discuss all relevant matters such as health, education, development, environment and human rights will contribute to a more transparent and coordinated institutional approach by the international community.[66]

Kenneth Deer, Chairman of the Indigenous Caucus, expected positive outcomes for the Permanent Forum:

> There is no other body quite like [the Permanent Forum] in the entire UN at such a high level. It is the only one where Indigenous persons have equal status to other international experts. It is not a seat in the UN General Assembly but it's a notch closer. To

[64] ibid para 1.

[65] I Simonovic, 'Address to the first session of the Permanent Forum on Indigenous Issues, 13 May 2002', available at: www.un.org/en/ecosoc/president/statement_2002/simonovic_13may_02.pdf.

[66] M Robinson, 'Opening statement by Mary Robinson, United Nations High Commissioner for Human Rights to the Open-ended working group on the permanent forum for indigenous people' (Address to the High 2nd meeting of Working Group on the Permanent Forum on Indigenous Issues, 14 February 2000), available at: cendoc.docip.org/collect/cendocdo/index/assoc/HASH014a.dir/001_as.pdf.

> get a seat in the UN is a totally political process which would require the acceptance as a member from all the member states of the UN; not likely at this time. But the Permanent Forum is useful in bringing our concerns to the highest levels of the UN.[67]

Erica-Irene Daes, former Chairperson of the Working Group on Indigenous Populations, identified key tasks based on her experiences and her lobbying for the successful establishment of the Permanent Forum. Madam Daes considered that land and resource issues were of great importance and that specified actions should be taken to support the needs of Indigenous Peoples, including the creation of a number of bodies, including (1) a 'fact-finding body, with a mandate to make site visits and to prepare reports concerning particular indigenous land and resource issues'; (2) 'an indigenous land and resource ombudsman or office which could provide response, mediation and reconciliation services'; and (3) 'a complaint mechanism or procedure for human rights violations that pertain to indigenous land and resource situations'.[68]

An interesting step was taken by the Permanent Forum in 2009 when, two years after the General Assembly had adopted the Declaration on the Rights of Indigenous Peoples, the Permanent Forum issued a General Comment on the effect of Article 42 of the Declaration on the Rights of Indigenous Peoples.[69] The Permanent Forum contended that the Declaration is 'an international law instrument of a human rights character', and the Declaration becomes part of the legal framework of the Permanent Forum along with ECOSOC resolution 2000/22.[70] In the Forum's view:

> The Declaration is a human rights standard elaborated upon the fundamental rights of universal application and set in the cultural, economic, political and social context of indigenous peoples.[71]

The General Comment concludes with the assertion that the Permanent Forum has a duty to see the Declaration as a set of norms that ought to be applied in national jurisdictions.[72] No further comments have been issued by the Permanent Forum since the General Comment of 2009. This may be because the Human Rights Council created a new human rights mechanism to monitor and report on the rights of Indigenous Peoples.

[67] K Deer, 'Not a seat in the UN, but …' (*The Eastern Door*, Kahnawake, 31 May 2002) vol 11, no 19, available at: www.tomifobia.com/mohawk_kendeer2.html.

[68] E Daes, 'Human Rights of Indigenous Peoples: Indigenous peoples and their relationship to land Final working paper prepared by the Special Rapporteur, Mrs Erica-Irene A Daes' 52nd Session Provisional Agenda Item 7(a), UN Doc E/CN.4/Sub.2/2000/25 (30 June 2000).

[69] Permanent Forum on Indigenous Issues, 'Follow-up to the recommendations of the Permanent Forum on Indigenous Issues on implementation of the United Nations Declaration on the Rights of Indigenous Peoples and on dialogue with the Special Rapporteur on the situation of human rights and fundamental freedoms of indigenous peoples and other special rapporteurs' 8th Session Agenda Items 4(a) and (b), UN Doc E/C.19/2009/L.3 (22 May 2009) Annex.

[70] ibid para 3.

[71] ibid para 8.

[72] ibid para 25.

C. Expert Mechanism on the Rights of Indigenous Peoples

When the Commission on Human Rights was replaced by the Human Rights Council, the Working Group on Indigenous Populations, as a subsidiary of the Commission, ceased to exist. The Permanent Forum, as a subsidiary of ECOSOC, did not have connection to the Human Rights Council. Indigenous Peoples had consequently submitted to the Human Rights Council that a subsidiary mechanism composed of experts from Indigenous Peoples was a necessary part of the Human Rights Council network. Thus, in December 2007 the Human Rights Council created the Expert Mechanism on the Rights of Indigenous Peoples (EMRIP),[73] two months after the General Assembly had adopted the Declaration on the Rights of Indigenous Peoples.

EMRIP was structured to provide thematic advice to the Council based on research and studies. The body would consist of five independent experts, giving due regard to experts of 'Indigenous origin'.[74] EMRIP would meet once a year and, to avoid duplication with other procedures and mechanisms, was to invite the Special Rapporteur on the rights of Indigenous Peoples and a member of the Permanent Forum on Indigenous Issues to attend and contribute to its annual meetings. The work of EMRIP was further enhanced in September 2016 when the Human Rights Council adopted a resolution to widen and strengthen the role of EMRIP.[75] The strengthened role of EMRIP followed on from the UN World Conference on Indigenous Peoples. The Australian government has expressed support for EMRIP and the mechanism's potential to create 'better outcomes for Indigenous Peoples'.[76]

D. World Conference on Indigenous Peoples

The United Nations hosts world conferences to bring focus to a particular theme, such as Indigenous Peoples, and to bring attention to and build momentum for the theme by inviting 'high-level' attendance from governments. The UN World Conference on Indigenous Peoples (WCIP) was convened in 2014, seven years after the Declaration on the Rights of Indigenous Peoples was adopted. It was seen as an opportunity to encourage UN members to increase efforts to achieve the ends of the Declaration on the Rights of Indigenous Peoples. On this

[73] Human Rights Council, 'Resolution 6/36. Expert mechanism on the rights of indigenous peoples' 34th Meeting (14 December 2007), available at: ap.ohchr.org/documents/E/HRC/resolutions/A_HRC_RES_6_36.pdf.

[74] ibid para 3.

[75] Human Rights Council, 'Resolution adopted by the Human Rights Council on 30 September 2016: 33/25. Expert Mechanism on the Rights of Indigenous Peoples' 33rd Session 41st Meeting, UN Doc A/HRC/RES/33/25 (30 September 2016).

[76] Australian Government, Department of Foreign Affairs and Trade, 'Statement on the Expert Mechanism on the Rights of Indigenous Peoples (CANZ)', United Nations Human Rights Council (28 September 2022).

occasion, the World Conference was arranged as a high-level plenary meeting of the UN General Assembly.

The goal of the World Conference was to adopt an 'Outcome Document', as a plan of action for Member States to assist Indigenous Peoples to achieve the ends of the Declaration. However, when Indigenous Peoples became aware of this world conference there was some concern that, as a meeting of states' representatives, it would work against Indigenous Peoples' interests and have a negative result on efforts to achieve self-determination. As a result, Indigenous Peoples decided to hold an Indigenous preparatory conference to prepare a report for presentation at the UN World Conference.

The 'Global Indigenous Preparatory Conference' was held in Alta, Norway, from 10 to 12 June 2013. The Outcome Document prepared from the Alta conference presented recommendations from which Indigenous Peoples would accept results from the UN World Conference:

> We reaffirm the peremptory norms of international law, including on equality and non-discrimination, and assert that the realization of the rights of Indigenous Peoples, including those affirmed in the Declaration, must be upheld by States, individually and collectively, free from all forms of discrimination including discrimination based on race, ethnicity, religion, gender, sexual orientation, age and disability. We also reaffirm that the Declaration must be regarded as the normative framework and basis for the Outcome Document and its full realization.
>
> We affirm that the inherent and inalienable right of self determination is pre-eminent and is a prerequisite for the realization of all rights. We Indigenous Peoples, have the right of self determination and permanent sovereignty over our lands, territories, resources, air, ice, oceans and waters, mountains and forests.[77]

At the World Conference, states cooperated with Indigenous Peoples during the drafting stages of the Outcome Document, but were not happy to be excluded from the last round of drafting. The Outcome Document was adopted by consensus of states in the General Assembly on 22 September 2014.[78] The resolution adopted by the General Assembly readily affirmed a commitment by Member States to work in a spirit of cooperation with Indigenous Peoples of the world:

> We, the Heads of State and Government, ministers and representatives of Member States, reaffirming our solemn commitment to the purposes and principles of the Charter of the United Nations, in a spirit of cooperation with the indigenous peoples of the world, are assembled at United Nations Headquarters in New York on

[77] S Solíz et al, 'Letter dated 10 September 2013 from the Permanent Representatives of the Plurinational State of Bolivia, Denmark, Finland, Guatemala, Mexico, New Zealand, Nicaragua, Norway and Peru to the United Nations addressed to the Secretary-General' 67th Session, Agenda Item 66, UN Doc A/67/994 (13 September 2013) 4.

[78] UNGA, 'Resolution adopted by the General Assembly on 22 September 2014 [without reference to a Main Committee (A/69/L.1)] 69/2. Outcome document of the high-level plenary meeting of the General Assembly known as the World Conference on Indigenous Peoples' 69th Session 4th Plenary Meeting, Agenda Item 65, UN Doc A/RES/69/2 (22 September 2014).

> 22 and 23 September 2014, on the occasion of the high-level plenary meeting of the General Assembly known as the World Conference on Indigenous Peoples, to reiterate the important and continuing role of the United Nations in promoting and protecting the rights of indigenous peoples.[79]

The resolution was clear in expressing commitments by states to achieve the ends of the Declaration on the Rights of Indigenous Peoples:

> We commit ourselves to taking, in consultation and cooperation with indigenous peoples, appropriate measures at the national level, including legislative, policy and administrative measures, to achieve the ends of the Declaration and to promote awareness of it among all sectors of society, including members of legislatures, the judiciary and the civil service.[80]

Following the outcomes from the UN World Conference on Indigenous Peoples the Human Rights Council accepted recommendations from EMRIP and Indigenous Peoples to strengthen the mandate of the Expert Mechanism to improve the efforts to achieve the ends of the Declaration on the Rights of Indigenous Peoples.[81] The number of experts on EMRIP increased to seven members, and the mandate was upgraded so EMRIP could engage more directly with members to achieve the ends of the Declaration, and to implement recommendations to Member States arising from the Human Rights Council's Universal Periodic Review process.

VIII. CONCLUSION

Indigenous Peoples have affirmed their rightful identity and equal status as peoples and, in the process, gained full and authoritative acknowledgement and appreciation of their human rights. However, UN Member States, including Australia, continue to show reluctance to incorporate the rights of Indigenous Peoples in their constitutions and legal systems. States have not implemented the Declaration, because the peoples represented by the states are the dominant society that displaces the Indigenous Peoples. It is the dominant people who feel threatened by the rights of Indigenous Peoples, and who are concerned that their wellbeing and livelihoods will be adversely affected if the Indigenous Peoples are empowered and are able to reclaim any of their lands, territories and resources.

The Declaration is not legally binding upon states, but it does carry the weight of a universal human rights standard and is backed by the moral support of the international community. Instruments such as ILO Convention 169 are there to assist states to achieve the ends of the Declaration on the Rights of Indigenous

[79] ibid para 1.
[80] ibid para 7.
[81] Human Rights Council, Expert Mechanism on the Rights of Indigenous Peoples, above n 75.

Peoples and to fulfil their obligations under the UN Charter to promote and protect the human rights of all peoples, including Indigenous Peoples. As well, new challenges exist for states and Indigenous Peoples at all levels of governance – local, national, regional and international. As Madam Daes pointed out two decades ago, work must continue to end discrimination against Indigenous Peoples. That discrimination is not just racial discrimination, it is an economic discrimination depriving them of lands, territories and resources.

The leadership of Indigenous Peoples still feels the weight of discrimination from UN Member States. Despite the international recognition of their right to self-determination and the obligations of members under the UN Charter, Indigenous Peoples are still classified as 'non-government organisations' and are demoted in the UN system to participate as if they are 'civil society', and not self-governing peoples.

Indigenous Peoples have sought higher accreditation to participate in the work of the United Nations when representing their peoples' right to self-determination. For example, they have requested 'observer status' at the General Assembly and at the Human Rights Council. In 2017 the General Assembly considered a request from Indigenous Peoples for enhanced participation and asked the President of the General Assembly to consult with Member States, Indigenous Peoples and mechanisms of the United Nations on necessary measures to enable Indigenous Peoples to participate in UN meetings.[82] Some UN members have challenged the idea of higher participation by Indigenous Peoples, believing that states alone should be represented in Assembly sessions, while a number of other members, including Australia, are supportive of the idea.[83]

The Human Rights Council is also considering this request for higher participation in Council sessions and has taken steps to consider enhanced participation. It has decided to organise 'a dialogue on concrete ways to enhance the participation of Indigenous Peoples in the work of the Human Rights Council'.[84] The results of this challenge for increased status for Indigenous Peoples in the United Nations remain to be seen. International law continues to evolve as jurisprudence on Indigenous Peoples and human rights develops. Indigenous Peoples continue to edge closer towards full self-determination through stronger structures and improved partnerships with states. Thus, the idea that Indigenous Peoples may hold seats at the United Nations could be closer than anyone realises.

[82] UNGA, 'Resolution adopted by the General Assembly on 8 September 2017 [without reference to a Main Committee (A/71/L.82)] 71/321. Enhancing the participation of indigenous peoples' representatives and institutions in meetings of relevant United Nations bodies on issues affecting them' 71st Session 96th Plenary Meeting, Agenda Item 65 (8 September 2017).

[83] Australian Government, Department of Foreign Affairs and Trade, James Larsen, 'Statement at the General Discussion on Indigenous Peoples' UNGA 3rd Committee (9 October 2023).

[84] Human Rights Council, 'Resolution adopted by the Human Rights Council on 11 October 2023 54/12. Human rights and Indigenous Peoples' 54th Session 46th Meeting, Agenda Item 3, UN Doc A/HRC/RES/54/12 (11 October 2023) 5–6, para 16.

8

Australia and the International Court of Justice

MARGARET A. YOUNG*

I. INTRODUCTION

WHAT IS AUSTRALIA'S role in, and attitude towards, the International Court of Justice (ICJ; the Court)? The principal judicial organ of the United Nations (UN), established by the Charter of the United Nations (UN Charter) in 1945[1] and imbued with hopes for peace, stability and legal certainty after the Second World War, has heard almost 150 contentious cases. In two of these cases, Australia has pursued litigation against other states.[2] In three of these cases, other states have pursued litigation against Australia.[3] In about a quarter of the Court's almost 30 advisory opinions, Australia has submitted written or oral statements.[4] The relevant international disputes have involved matters that can be variously described as regional discord over natural resource exploitation, environmental stewardship, or misaligned security ambitions. Indeed, how to classify the underlying disputes is one of the questions animating this chapter, especially as the answer reveals as much about the stated interests of Australia as it does about the role and function of the ICJ.

* This research was supported by the Australian Research Council's Discovery Projects funding scheme. The author gratefully acknowledges the intellectual leadership and comments of Hilary Charlesworth, who was the principal investigator of their jointly held project DP180101318 until her election to the International Court of Justice. The usual disclaimer applies.

[1] Charter of the United Nations, Art 92.

[2] *Nuclear Tests (Australia v France)* (Judgment) [1974] ICJ Rep 253; *Whaling in the Antarctic (Australia v Japan: New Zealand intervening)* (Judgment) [2014] ICJ Rep 226.

[3] *Certain Phosphate Lands in Nauru (Nauru v Australia)* (Preliminary Objections) [1992] ICJ Rep 240; *East Timor (Portugal v Australia)* (Judgment) [1995] ICJ Rep 90; *Questions relating to the Seizure and Detention of Certain Documents and Data (Timor-Leste v Australia)* (Request for the Modification of the Order Indicating Provisional Measures of 3 March 2014: Order) [2015] ICJ Rep 556.

[4] See also H Charlesworth and MA Young, 'Australian Encounters with the Advisory Jurisdiction of the International Court of Justice' (2021) 21 *Melbourne Journal of International Law* 698.

This chapter seeks to understand the course of Australia's relationship with the ICJ, from what is shown to be an early enthusiasm to a more cautious – even reticent – approach. Confidence and trust in an independent judicial body is essential for any functioning legal system. Setting the rules and procedures for this arrangement at the international level is crucial and difficult, especially given the disparities of power and wealth among states, and this chapter seeks to understand Australia's considerable leadership at the time of the Court's establishment. It explores the link to Australia's new-found independence and the idealism of individuals who have been portrayed by the late Australian Judge Crawford as 'dreamers of the day'.[5] It investigates whether this position has continued over the Court's 80-year history, during Australia's own milestones such as the abolition of appeals from domestic litigation to the Privy Council, and the dismantling of colonial arrangements in its region.

The chapter draws on cases, memorials and other documents publicly available from the Court's website, as well as secondary literature and archival research.[6] Perspectives of legal advisers, eminent counsel and the Court itself are canvassed. This method comes from an awareness (described elsewhere)[7] that the study of national encounters with the Court contributes to an understanding of the potential and limits of the ICJ in resolving disputes and contributing to the evolution of international law.

The chapter is structured in five parts. After this introduction, I examine Australia's role in constituting the Court. Section II considers the Court's jurisdiction, constrained as it is by the so-called 'optional' clause, by which States parties to the Statute of the International Court of Justice (Statute) choose to declare that they agree to the jurisdiction of the Court.[8] The appointment of judges is also essential in the constitution of the Court, and the three Australian individuals elected as judges by the General Assembly and the Security Council (Judge Percy Spender, Judge James Crawford and Judge Hilary Charlesworth) merit special attention. In section III, I turn to Australia's role as a litigant before the Court, giving context to the cases in which Australia has appeared as an applicant and a respondent. In section IV, I contrast Australia's readiness to participate in the Court's contentious jurisdiction with its reticence towards the Court's advisory jurisdiction, in which

[5] J Crawford, '"Dreamers of the Day": Australia and the International Court of Justice' (2013) 14 *Melbourne Journal of International Law* 520.

[6] This chapter is part of a broader project on 'The Potential and Limits of International Adjudication' funded by the Australian Research Council (DP180101318) and the author acknowledges the intellectual contribution of her co-investigator Professor (now Judge) Hilary Charlesworth and the project's Research Fellow, Dr Emma Nyhan.

[7] H Charlesworth and MA Young, 'National Encounters with the International Court of Justice: Introduction to the Special Issue' (2021) 21 *Melbourne Journal of International Law* 502.

[8] Statute of the International Court of Justice, Art 36(2).

the Court answers legal questions posed by the General Assembly or other duly authorised UN bodies. Section V concludes.

II. CONSTITUTING THE COURT

This section investigates Australia's contribution to the building of the ICJ. I juxtapose Australia's leadership at the UN Conference on International Organization in San Francisco in 1945 (San Francisco Conference) with the later changes in Australia's approach to the 'optional clause'. This section also points to the unmistakeable (and highly divergent) global influence of the Australian nationals who have sat as ICJ judges.

A. Constructing a System for Peaceful Dispute Settlement

Australia played a significant role in the transition to the ICJ from the League of Nation's Permanent Court of International Justice (PCIJ), which also sat at the Peace Palace in The Hague. In contrast to its lack of involvement in the PCIJ (having never appeared before that Court),[9] Australia demonstrated leadership at the San Francisco Conference. The influence of the personalities of Dr Herbert Vere Evatt, Sir Kenneth Bailey and Sir Paul Hasluck have been well documented, including by James Crawford in the Melbourne Law School annual lecture which bears Sir Kenneth's name.[10] Writing before his own election to the bench (more on that below), Crawford gave credit to remarkable individuals in Australia's history who 'comprehended the value of the Court and – perhaps more importantly – its potential, such that the dream of a functioning system of international justice might be enacted with open eyes'.[11]

As Crawford noted, Australia's position at the San Francisco Conference extended to advocating that an obligation be inserted into the Charter which would require states to carry out decisions of the Court in cases in which they were parties.[12] Crawford sees the eventual Charter provision requiring compliance by disputing parties with ICJ decisions[13] as 'probably Australia's main contribution to the system of international justice as it currently stands'.[14] Australia had emerged from the Second World War with a foreign

[9] WJ Hudson, *Australia and the League of Nations* (Sydney, Sydney University Press, 1980) 129.
[10] Crawford, 'Dreamers of the Day', above n 5.
[11] ibid 549.
[12] ibid 525.
[13] Charter of the United Nations, Art 94.
[14] Crawford, 'Dreamers of the Day', above n 5, 525.

policy position distinct from the United Kingdom (UK) and with a broad support for international organisations.[15]

B. Jurisdiction and the Optional Clause

As part of its robust advocacy during the San Francisco Conference, Australia – through Sir Kenneth Bailey – gave initial broad support for a court with compulsory jurisdiction with respect to all justiciable disputes. A number of states indicated support for compulsory jurisdiction, but others, including the major powers France, the Union of Soviet Socialist Republics, the United Kingdom, the United States and China, supported an 'opt-in' system instead. Ultimately, the Statute provides for an optional clause procedure,[16] for which Australia ultimately voted in order to avoid a stalemate.[17]

It is useful to take a backward step to contextualise these institutional developments in terms of Australia's position as an independent state and its attitude towards the judicial function. The role of adjudication preoccupied the former colonies as they transitioned to the Australian federation, as evidenced by the parliamentary debates on the Commonwealth of Australia Constitution Bill in 1900. In his speech introducing the Bill to the House of Commons, Joseph Chamberlain, Secretary of State for the Colonies, referred to the proposed external affairs power of the new federation in section 51(xxix) of the Constitution and stressed that 'measures of this kind, which may involve the Imperial Government in the most serious responsibility, should be interpreted by a tribunal in which all parties have confidence'.[18]

This need for the confidence of *all* parties – imperial and Dominion – led the Secretary of State to call for the preservation of appeals from Australian courts to the Privy Council,[19] an arrangement that lasted well after the formal independence of Australia and even after Australia's first complaint against another state to the ICJ, in the *Nuclear Tests* case assessed below. The Secretary of State's views on adjudication demonstrates the link between a burgeoning independence of an Australian federation (as developed through the foreign affairs

[15] ibid 522.

[16] Statute of the International Court of Justice, Art 36(2).

[17] Summary Report of Seventeenth Meeting of Committee IV/1, Doc 759 IV/1/59 (2 June 1945) in *Documents of the United Nations Conference on International Organization* (London, United Nations Information Organizations, 1945) vol 13, 251, cited in Crawford, 'Dreamers of the Day', above n 5, 525.

[18] HC Deb 14 May 1900, vol 83, cols 54–55.

[19] ibid. This was supported by Attorney General Sir Robert Finlay: HC Deb 21 June 1900, vol 84, cols 647–58). Viscount Finlay was later to be nominated by Britain for election to the PCIJ, which Australia followed: Hudson, above n 9, 129. Australia's nomination of a British national led to questions in the Commonwealth Parliament: Commonwealth, *Parliamentary Debates*, House of Representatives, 29 September 1921, 11583.

powers) and the need to maintain confidence and control in the tribunal which would interpret those powers.

Australia's optional clause declaration was initially carried over from its PCIJ declaration,[20] according to the terms of the ICJ Statute.[21] This was terminated in 1954,[22] and a new declaration contained several substantive reservations, including the exclusion of disputes concerning the continental shelf. The declaration maintained Australia's PCIJ-era declaration's exclusion from compulsory jurisdiction disputes with any governments that were members of the British Commonwealth of Nations.[23] This so-called 'Commonwealth reservation' is attributable to the *inter se* doctrine, which holds that relations between Commonwealth members were less than fully international in character due to the indivisible Crown to which their common allegiance was owed.[24]

These reservations were removed in 1975 by Prime Minister Gough Whitlam, who provided a new declaration containing a general submission to jurisdiction with no substantive reservations.[25] This removal of the Commonwealth reservation was followed by New Zealand in 1977. (As will be discussed below, the suit against Australia in 1991 by Nauru, then an 'associate member' of the Commonwealth', was thus unhampered by a Commonwealth reservation.)

Australia's openness towards the jurisdiction of the Court was narrowed by Alexander Downer, minister in the Coalition Government led by John Howard, in 2002, the form of which remains to this day.[26] The 2002 declaration contains a reservation relating to disputes 'concerning or relating to the delimitation of maritime zones, including the territorial sea, the exclusive economic zone and the continental shelf', reflecting the preference to negotiate rather than

[20] For the 1929 declaration regarding the Commonwealth of Australia, see declaration signed by Granville Ryrie on 20 September 1929: Parliament of the Commonwealth of Australia, *League of Nations: Tenth Assembly (2nd September to 26th September, 1929)* (Canberra, HJ Green, 1930) 633. See 'Australia' signed by SM Bruce, London, 21 August 1940: law.unimelb.edu.au/__data/assets/pdf_file/0019/3043513/2.-Australias-Declaration-Recognising-Compulsory-Jurisdiction-1940.pdf. See also H Burmester, 'Australia and the International Court of Justice' (1996) 17 *Australian Year Book of International Law* 19, 20.

[21] Statute of the International Court of Justice, Art 36(5).

[22] Declaration Recognizing as Compulsory the Jurisdiction of the International Court of Justice, in Conformity with Article 36, Paragraph 2, of the Statute of the International Court of Justice (adopted 6 February 1954, entered into force 6 February 1954) 186 UNTS 77.

[23] ibid 80.

[24] NA Sims, 'The Commonwealth and the International Court of Justice' (2002) 89 *The Round Table* 205. See also JDB Miller, 'The Decline of *Inter Se*' (1969) 24 *International Journal* 765.

[25] The only exception related to 'any dispute in regard to which the parties thereto have agreed or shall agree to have recourse to some other method of peaceful settlement': Declaration Recognizing as Compulsory the Jurisdiction of the International Court of Justice, in Conformity with Article 36, Paragraph 2, of the Statute of the International Court of Justice (signed 13 March 1975) 961 UNTS 183. See also Crawford, 'Dreamers of the Day', above n 5, 539.

[26] Declaration Recognizing as Compulsory the Jurisdiction of the International Court of Justice, under Article 36, Paragraph 2, of the Statute of the International Court of Justice (signed 21 March 2002) 2175 UNTS 493.

adjudicate upon maritime boundaries.[27] An accompanying press release noted the contemporary unresolved maritime boundaries,[28] many of which reflected the imperial origins of Australia and surrounding countries. The 2002 declaration also constrained the conditions of reciprocity required to invoke Australia's declaration.

Australia's reservation continues to prompt reflection on Australia's motivations and self-interest within the region. Just as Japan modified its optional declaration after losing the *Whaling* case to exclude disputes relating to living marine resources from the Court's jurisdiction,[29] Australia's reservation has been linked to contemporaneous maritime boundary negotiations and general relations with Timor-Leste. In 2020, a Senate committee was established to inquire into, among other things, reports from non-government committee members of the Joint Standing Committee on Treaties (JSCOT) that 'the ICJ declaration … damages Australia's international reputation and may not be in Australia's long-term national interests' as it 'may be interpreted as an effort to intimidate and limit the options of neighbouring countries in relation to any future maritime border disputes'.[30] The Senate committee recommended against revoking Australia's 2002 declaration under the optional clause.[31] In dissent, one Senate committee member claimed:

> The 2002 declaration was made to allow Australia to steal oil and gas from the newest and one of the most impoverished countries in the world. The Committee politely alludes to this in circumstances where brutal frankness should prevail.[32]

In the course of the inquiry, the Chief Legal Officer of the Department of Foreign Affairs and Trade (DFAT) pointed out that only 74 of a total of 193 states have accepted the compulsory jurisdiction of the ICJ, and 50 of those 74 states have made declarations limiting that jurisdiction.[33] DFAT submitted that:

> Like most countries accepting the compulsory jurisdiction to the ICJ – including the United Kingdom, Canada and New Zealand – Australia does so with limitations. Eight countries have made a reservation to the ICJ statute specifically regarding maritime boundaries including Germany, India and Malta.[34]

[27] See also B Campbell, 'Australia's Engagement with the International Court of Justice: Practical and Political Factors' (2021) 21 *Melbourne Journal of International Law* 596, 603.

[28] D Williams and A Downer, 'Changes to International Dispute Resolution' (News Release, 25 March 2002).

[29] Japan, 'Declaration Recognizing the Jurisdiction of the Court as Compulsory' (International Court of Justice, 6 October 2015): www.icj-cij.org/en/declarations/jp.

[30] Foreign Affairs, *Defence and Trade References Committee, Australia's Declarations Made under Certain International Laws* (Report, February 2020) 1 [1.1(1)(f)].

[31] ibid 22 [2.41]. See also Campbell, 'Australia's Engagement', above n 27, 603.

[32] Foreign Affairs, Defence and Trade References Committee, above n 30, 25 [1.14] (dissenting comments by Senator Rex Patrick: Pushing the Boundaries Too Far).

[33] ibid 14 [2.5].

[34] ibid 14 [2.5].

Of the countries noted in this quote, it is perhaps salient to observe that the United Kingdom expanded its reservation in 2017,[35] after the Marshall Islands nuclear weapons case, ensuring among other things that any dispute related to nuclear disarmament or nuclear weapons could only be brought if all other nuclear weapon owning states participated. The United Kingdom had also expanded its Commonwealth reservation in 2004, ensuring that it would not recognise the jurisdiction of the ICJ as compulsory for 'any dispute with the government of any other country which is *or has been* a Member of the Commonwealth'.[36] The declaration was also amended to restrict the timeline of applicable disputes, which formerly covered disputes arising after 24 October 1945, but which was restricted to disputes arising after 1 January 1974. These changes were a response to Mauritius's aspirations to challenge the UK's sovereignty over the British Indian Ocean Territory,[37] which culminated in the advisory opinion proceedings detailed below.

While the optional clause is not the only way to enliven the Court's jurisdiction – and the compromissory clause of a treaty, or a special agreement between the parties, are increasingly used by countries – the declarations of states remain important signals of their tolerance for adjudication in particular areas. Indeed, it is common for states to make no declaration at all: of the five Security Council permanent members, Russia has never submitted a declaration while China, France and the United States have withdrawn theirs.[38] Larger states have proved unwilling to relinquish their power to such a tribunal. Even where declarations are made, reservations attenuate the jurisdiction of the Court in sensitive issues that are not far from imperial legacies, as the experience of Australia and other countries demonstrates.

C. Australian Judges on the Court

This review of Australia's role in constituting the ICJ is incomplete without regard to the appointment of judges. The bench is made up of 15 judges, who are each elected for a nine-year term by the General Assembly and the Security

[35] United Kingdom of Great Britain and Northern Ireland, 'Declarations Recognizing the Jurisdiction of the Court as Compulsory' (International Court of Justice, 22 February 2017): www.icj-cij.org/en/declarations/gb.

[36] See the UK's declaration registered on 5 July 2004: '4. Declarations Recognizing as Compulsory the Jurisdiction of the International Court of Justice under Article 36, Paragraph 2, of the Statute of the Court' (United Nations Treaty Collection): treaties.un.org/. Note that a revision was also made to the UK's declaration on 31 December 2014.

[37] M Wood, 'The United Kingdom's Acceptance of the Compulsory Jurisdiction of the International Court of Justice, 2006' in JM Barrett and JP Gauci (eds), *British Contributions to International Law, 1915–2015: An Anthology Set* (Leiden, Brill Nijhoff, 2021) 3279–80.

[38] MA Young, E Nyhan and H Charlesworth, 'Studying Country-Specific Engagements with the International Court of Justice' (2019) *Journal of International Dispute Settlement* 582, 583.

Council.[39] Moreover, countries are entitled to appoint a judge *ad hoc* in cases where they appear as a party, if there is no sitting judge of their nationality.[40] In all cases, judges exercise their powers impartially,[41] independently of their country of nationality.[42] While *ad hoc* judges have been influential in disputes involving Australia (with Australian *ad hoc* judges twice joining the majority and twice issuing dissents),[43] the remainder of this section concentrates on the impact of three Australians in their capacity as elected judges:[44] Sir Percy Spender, James Crawford and Hilary Charlesworth.[45]

The seismic impact on the Court of Sir Percy Spender, a former Australian politician, has been carefully documented, especially as archives have opened in recent times.[46] Scholars have delved into his nomination by the Australian government in which he served[47] – when he was selected over Sir Kenneth Bailey – and his subsequent elevation to the presidency of the Court. It was Sir Percy's influence in the *South-West Africa* cases,[48] brought by Ethiopia and Liberia, that caused that greatest setback to the prestige of the Court in its history. The case related to South Africa's implementation of apartheid policy and was heralded as an opportunity for the World Court to deliver international justice. Sir Percy, together with Sir Gerald Fitzmaurice, pressured Pakistan's judge Sir Muhammad Zafrulla Khan to recuse himself.[49] Even more significantly (and

[39] Statute of the International Court of Justice, Art 4.

[40] ibid Art 31(2)–(3). Australia has appointed as *ad hoc* judges Sir Garfield Barwick (*Nuclear Tests*), Sir Ninian Stephen (*East Timor*), Hilary Charlesworth (*Whaling in the Antarctic*) and Ian Callinan (*Seizure and Detention*). In *Certain Phosphate Lands*, no *ad hoc* judge was nominated by agreement of both parties.

[41] Statute of the International Court of Justice, Art 20.

[42] ibid Art 2.

[43] For a broader discussion of the role of dissent in international adjudication, see JL Dunoff and MA Pollack, 'The Road Not Taken: Comparative International Judicial Dissent' (2022) 116 *American Journal of International Law* 340.

[44] On Australia's process of nominating individuals for election and the role of national groups, see Burmester, 'Australia and the International Court of Justice', above n 20, 26–28.

[45] Outside the scope of analysis is the important contribution of Sri Lankan jurist and former Vice President of the ICJ, His Excellency Judge CG Weeramantry, who was a Professor of Law at Monash University, Australia, before his election to the Bench. See generally, A Anghie and G Sturgess (eds), *Legal Visions of the 21st Century: Essays in Honour of Judge Christopher Weeramantry* (The Hague, Kluwer Law International, 1998); A Anghie, 'CG Weeramantry at the International Court of Justice' (2001) 14 *Leiden Journal of International Law* 829, 848.

[46] See V Kattan, 'Decolonizing the International Court of Justice: The Experience of Judge Sir Muhammad Zafrulla Khan in the *South West Africa* Cases' (2015) 5 *Asian Journal of International Law* 310; V Kattan, '"There Was an Elephant in the Court Room": Reflections on the Role of Judge Sir Percy Spender (1897–1985) in the *South West Africa Cases* (1960–1966) after Half a Century' (2018) 31 *Leiden Journal of International Law* 147.

[47] In Australia, Sir Percy had played a role in developing the security alliance with New Zealand and the United States, and in the Colombo Plan for Asia-Pacific co-operation: Crawford, 'Dreamers of the Day', above n 5, 530.

[48] *South West Africa Cases (Ethiopia v South Africa; Liberia v South Africa) (Second Phase)* (Judgment) [1966] ICJ Rep 6, 28–29. Note also the request for Khan to recuse himself: Crawford, 'Dreamers of the Day', above n 5, 535–36; Kattan, 'Decolonizing the International Court of Justice', above n 46, 318.

[49] Kattan, 'Decolonizing the International Court of Justice', above n 46, 318.

more transparently at the time), Sir Percy used his casting vote as President to reject the claim on the basis that Ethiopia and Liberia had not established any legal rights opposable against South Africa in the context of the League system. The decision has been seen by the highest of authorities as 'an aberration',[50] and caused a lasting loss of confidence in the Court, particularly from the developing world.

The election of James Crawford to the bench in November 2014 almost 50 years later was as consequential for the Court and international law, but in a very different way. Crawford, noted for his rigorous and encyclopaedic understanding of the law, displayed sensitivity to matters of colonisation and international law throughout his career.[51] He was the intellectual and practical leader guiding the International Law Commission (ILC) to recognise in 2001 that 'any state other than an injured state is entitled to invoke the responsibility of another state for breaches of obligations owed *erga omnes*'.[52] Walking past the bust of Sir Percy when at the Court, Crawford would reflect on the need to rehabilitate Australia's reputation.[53] And indeed, in his decision in dissent in the preliminary objections phase of the Marshall Islands claim against nuclear weapon-owning states in 2016, he expressly sought to correct the inferences commonly drawn from the *South West Africa* cases. Crawford, in contrast with the majority, would have allowed the claim to proceed to the merits and emphasised that 'States can be parties to disputes about obligations in the performance of which they have no specific material interests'.[54] In his judgments and his service to the administration at the Court, Judge Crawford demonstrated unrelenting commitment to practical, rigorous and well-reasoned justice.[55]

[50] R Higgins, 'The International Court of Justice and Africa' in R Higgins, *Themes and Theories: Selected Essays, Speeches, and Writings in International Law* (Oxford, Oxford University Press, 2009) 1071.

[51] MA Young, 'Judge James Crawford AC SC FBA (1948–2021)' (2021) 22 *Melbourne Journal of International Law* i. See generally, D Guilfoyle, DR Rothwell and MA Young, 'James Crawford: His Legacy and Impact on International Law in Australia and Globally' (2023) 40 *Australian Year Book of International Law* 25, and the other contributions to the special issue.

[52] See Article 48 of the ILC's Articles on State Responsibility: International Law Commission, Report of the International Law Commission: Fifty-Third Session (23 April–1 June and 2 July–10 August 2001) UN GAOR, 56th Session Supp No 10 UN Doc A/56/10, 318–19. See also JR Crawford, 'Responsibility to the International Community as a Whole' (2001) 8 *Indiana Journal of Global Legal Studies* 303. On Crawford's 'extraordinary stewardship and delivery' of the ILC Articles, see MEK Neuhaus and JM Jolly, 'A Race and Rage for Order: Judge James Crawford's Legacy at the International Court of Justice' (2023) 40 *Australian Year Book of International Law* 245, 247.

[53] Guilfoyle, Rothwell and Young, above n 51, 30.

[54] *Obligations concerning Negotiations Relating to Cessation of the Nuclear Arms Race and to Nuclear Disarmament (Marshall Islands v United Kingdom)* (Preliminary Objections) [2016] ICJ Rep 833, 1102 (Judge Crawford). See also *Obligations concerning Negotiations Relating to Cessation of the Nuclear Arms Race and to Nuclear Disarmament (Marshall Islands v India)* (Jurisdiction and Admissibility) [2016] ICJ Rep 255, 521 (Judge Crawford); *Obligations concerning Negotiations Relating to Cessation of the Nuclear Arms Race and to Nuclear Disarmament (Marshall Islands v Pakistan)* (Jurisdiction and Admissibility) [2016] ICJ Rep 552, 803 (Judge Crawford).

[55] See Neuhaus and Jolly, above n 52; R Cameron and J Sherman, 'Reflections on Judge Crawford's Contributions to the International Court of Justice' (2023) 40 *Australian Year Book of International*

Crawford's untimely death in 2021 cut short his term on the bench, and eminent Australian jurist Professor Hilary Charlesworth was nominated to fill his place, securing it through election by the General Assembly and Security Council and commencing on 5 November 2021. Their intellectual traditions and reputations as iconic Australians/cosmopolitans seemed aligned, and indeed one of the first cases for Judge Charlesworth was the preliminary objections in *The Gambia v Myanmar*.[56] The oral hearings had been held in 2019 when, among other things, counsel for The Gambia, Philippe Sands QC, replied to the submissions of counsel for Myanmar, Australian-born barrister Christopher Staker QC, by evoking the legacy of Sir Percy on the Court.[57] The decision of the Court on jurisdiction and admissibility, which Judge Charlesworth joined, upheld the legal interest and standing of The Gambia to bring Myanmar's alleged acts of genocide before the Court, as Judge Crawford no doubt would have done. The merits phase of the case is pending.

Judge Charlesworth brings to the Court the keen legal and critical analysis of a scholar renowned for feminist legal thought, human rights and public international law, as well as experience as an *ad hoc* judge.[58] Judge Charlesworth has been fearless in establishing matters of interpretation and justice, even if this requires her to issue a separate declaration or dissenting opinion. The dispute between Chile and Bolivia over a shared watercourse,[59] for example, saw Judge Charlesworth vote against the majority decision, which had been informed by a rather constrained view of the role of adjudication. The majority considered that the claim no longer had an object and that the Court was not called upon to give a decision. Judge Charlesworth disagreed

Law 218; J McIntyre, 'Crawford's Multilateralism and the International Court of Justice' (2023) 40 *Australian Year Book of International Law* 271.

[56] *Application of the Convention on the Prevention and Punishment of the Crime of Genocide (The Gambia v Myanmar)* (Preliminary Objections) General List No 178 [2022] ICJ 1.

[57] Verbatim Record, *Application of the Convention on the Prevention and Punishment of the Crime of Genocide (The Gambia v Myanmar)* (International Court of Justice, CR 2019/20, 12 December 2019) 29–30 [3] (Mr Sands): '[Mr Staker] cited numerous cases in support of that contention, but there was one that he did not mention. As he addressed the Court, in dulcet Australian tones, I shut my eyes and suddenly wondered if I was not hearing the voice of Sir Percy Spender, back in 1966, as he explained why he cast the decisive President's vote in favour of the Court's conclusion … That Judgment caused a scandal, it cast the Court into a wilderness for nearly two decades. This Court could, I suppose, if it wishes, rule that The Gambia has no legal interest in the case, but you will surely be aware that to take that approach will cast the Court into an incomparably more bleak wilderness, given that the overwhelming majority of the Members of the United Nations, having endorsed the reports of the UN Fact-Finding Mission, and other UN supported activities, will be truly shocked if this Court, 53 years after South West Africa, declines to indicate provisional measures in this case'.

[58] Judge *ad hoc* of the International Court of Justice in the *Arbitral Award of 3 October 1899 (Guyana v Venezuela)* case (2019–21); Judge *ad hoc* of the International Court of Justice in the *Whaling in the Antarctic (Australia v Japan: New Zealand intervening)* case (2011–14).

[59] *Dispute over the Status and Use of the Waters of the Silala (Chile v Bolivia)* (Judgment) [2022] ICJ Rep 61.

with this view, though she was in full agreement with the Court's reasoning on the rights and obligations of states sharing an international watercourse. She noted the utility for the parties of a declaratory judgment, especially in removing uncertainty from their legal relations.[60] Judge Charlesworth's decision is at once deeply practical and conceptually enlightened. The expressive function of international adjudication (and law more generally) is increasingly embraced in the literature,[61] and the Court's clear guidance is envisaged for contentious disputes and for the Court's advisory jurisdiction alike, as is further discussed in the next section.

III. AUSTRALIA AS LITIGANT

This section describes Australia's role as a litigant before the ICJ.[62] As an applicant in the 1970s, Australia requested a declaration on the unlawfulness of atmospheric testing of nuclear weapons by the respondent (France).[63] Forty years later, Australia instituted proceedings against Japan for breach of obligations under the International Convention for the Regulation of Whaling.[64] Regional activities involving grave environmental impacts were also a feature of the three disputes in which Australia has been a respondent. These are: (1) Nauru's claims regarding ruinous phosphate mining during Australian administration before Nauruan independence;[65] (2) Portugal's claims after Australia's 1989 treaty with Indonesia to cooperate in a shared maritime zone between East Timor and Australia, when East Timor was still regarded by Portugal and others as subject to illegal annexation by Indonesia;[66] and (3) after Timor-Leste's 2002 independence and its new 2002 treaty with Australia, its proceedings against Australia with regard to the seizure and subsequent detention 'by Agents of Australia of documents, data and other property' relating to a pending arbitration under that 2002 Treaty.[67] The subject matter of these cases hints at a lingering link with Empire. It is also important (but more difficult, methodologically), to point to disputes which never made it to the Court, and the section seeks to trace the cases not taken, or taken elsewhere.

[60] Declaration of Judge Charlesworth, ibid 667, 674 [19].

[61] See, eg, T Ginsburg and RH McAdams, 'Adjudicating in Anarchy: An Expressive Theory of International Dispute Resolution' (2004) 45 *William & Mary Law Review* 1229.

[62] For a separate and highly informative discussion of the practicalities in running Australia's cases, see Campbell, 'Australia's Engagement', above n 27.

[63] *Nuclear Tests (Australia v France)*, above n 2; *Nuclear Tests (New Zealand v France)* (Judgment) [1974] ICJ Rep 457.

[64] *Whaling in the Antarctic*, above n 2.

[65] *Certain Phosphate Lands in Nauru*, above n 3.

[66] *East Timor*, above n 3.

[67] *Seizure and Detention*, above n 3.

A. Two Times an Applicant: Nuclear Tests and Whaling

In both cases in which Australia has complained to the ICJ of breaches of international law, the proceedings were preceded by an election commitment on the part of an incoming prime minister.[68] Moreover, as with other international disputes, New Zealand was an applicant or an intervenor in support of Australia's claims, although that country's path to litigation before the world court has been distinct.[69]

The first case related to the French atmospheric nuclear testing in the Pacific, which threatened both national and regional impacts.[70] Australia had lodged diplomatic protests with France concerning its proposed nuclear tests in the 1960s,[71] along with other nations including New Zealand, Chile and Peru.[72] Within the Australian federation, the State Labor governments of Tasmania, South Australia and Western Australia commissioned legal opinions about the legality of France's actions from Professor DP O'Connell, which were obtained in 1972.[73] The federal opposition Labor Party committed to take the question of French atmospheric nuclear testing to the ICJ in a policy statement in November 1972,[74] and instituted proceedings after it won office.[75]

The case helped achieve the aims of Australia and New Zealand.[76] On 22 June 1973, each state was awarded provisional measures, inter alia, that 'the French Government should avoid nuclear tests causing the deposit of radioactive fall-out on Australian territory' and 'on the territory of New Zealand, the

[68] H Burmester, 'Civil Society and the Instigation of International Court Litigation: The Australian Experience' (2021) 21 *Melbourne Journal of international Law* 772, 775.

[69] K Keith, 'New Zealand and the International Court of Justice' (2021) 21 *Melbourne Journal of International Law* 516.

[70] *Nuclear Tests (Australia v France)*, above n 2; *Nuclear Tests (New Zealand v France)*, above n 63. Fiji also sought to participate: see *Nuclear Tests Case (New Zealand v France)* (Application by Fiji for Permission to Intervene: Order) [1973] ICJ Rep 324. On the collective nature of the claims, see M Fitzmaurice, 'The International Court of Justice and International Environmental Law' in CJ Tams and J Sloan, *The Development of International Law by the International Court of Justice* (Oxford, Oxford University Press, 2013) 358–59. On the Australian involvement, see generally H Burmester, 'Sir Elihu Lauterpacht QC and the *Nuclear Tests* Case' (2017) 35 *Australian Year Book of International Law* 41.

[71] R Rowe, 'The Diplomatic Dimension: Australia and the *Nuclear Tests* Case' (2021) 21 *Melbourne Journal of International Law* 536.

[72] AA D'Amato, 'Legal Aspects of the French Nuclear Tests' (1967) 61 *Australian Journal International Law* 66, 66.

[73] Burmester, 'Civil Society', above n 68, 777. Professor O'Connell, by then Chichele Professor of Public International Law at the University of Oxford, went on to assist as counsel in the proceedings before the Court, together with Lionel Murphy QC (Attorney-General of Australia), MH Byers QC (Solicitor-General of Australia) and Elihu Lauterpacht.

[74] Gough Whitlam (Speech, Blacktown, New South Wales, 13 November 1972): electionspeeches.moadoph.gov.au/speeches/1972-gough-whitlam, archived at www.perma.cc/7GUZ-KEED, cited in Burmester, 'Civil Society', above n 68, 777.

[75] Australia and New Zealand each instituted proceedings against France on 9 May 1973.

[76] *cf* France denied that the case played any part in its decision to cease nuclear testing in the atmosphere: see Burmester, 'Civil Society', above n 68, 786.

Cook Islands, Niue or the Tokelau Islands'.[77] These orders ceased at the merits stage, when, on 20 December 1974, the Court accepted that France had made unilateral declarations not to carry out further atmospheric nuclear tests in the South Pacific Ocean, and that these constituted an obligation as to conduct concerning the cessation of nuclear tests. The Court found, by nine votes to six, that 'the claim of Australia no longer has any object and that the Court is therefore not called upon to give a decision therein'.[78]

This finding was made despite a lack of submission to the Court by France, which did not accept the jurisdiction of the Court, and did not appoint an agent. In dissent, Australia's *ad hoc* judge Sir Garfield Barwick found the Court's decision not to proceed, and thus avoid deciding the matters before it, to be 'an unjustifiable course, uncharacteristic of a court of justice'; he could have no part in it and considered it 'failing to fulfil an essential obligation of the Court's judicial process'.[79] There are echoes of Judge Barwick's 'loyalty to the law and its administration',[80] albeit in different form, in the declaration of Judge Charlesworth in 2022, described above,[81] although she did not refer to Judge Barwick's dissenting opinion and instead demonstrated the important differences between the ultimate lack of legal object in *Nuclear Tests* and the claim in *Chile v Bolivia*.[82]

The *Nuclear Tests* cases support the oft-cited notion of a middle power depending on the Court much more than the major powers who can rely simply on their might.[83] The cases also hint at the aspirations of those major powers: France was deeply unhappy with Australia's decision to take the case, given that it considered its nuclear testing was part of a security initiative that directly benefited Australia, rather than an environmental or health problem.[84] When New Zealand sought to press its claim against France in 1995, after a purported decision by France to conduct a final series of nuclear weapons tests in the South Pacific, Australia intervened in support along with small island developing

[77] *Nuclear Tests (Australia v France)* (Request for the Indication of Interim Measures of Protection: Order) [1973] ICJ Rep 99, 106; *Nuclear Tests (New Zealand v France)* (Request for the Indication of Interim Measures of Protection: Order) [1973] ICJ Rep 135, 142.

[78] *Nuclear Tests (Australia v France)*, above n 2, 272. See also *Nuclear Tests (New Zealand v France)*, above n 63, 478.

[79] *Nuclear Tests (Australia v France)*, above n 2, 392. See also *Nuclear Tests (New Zealand v France)*, above n 63, 525–28.

[80] *Nuclear Tests (Australia v France)*, above n 2, 392.

[81] *Dispute over the Status and Use of the Waters of the Silala (Chile v Bolivia)*, above n 59.

[82] Declaration of Judge Charlesworth, above n 60, 671–74 [13]–[19].

[83] G Palmer, 'The ICJ in the Asia Pacific Region' in M Brewster and I Shearer (eds), *Colloquium to Celebrate the 50th Anniversary of the International Court of Justice* (Sydney, International Law Association, 1996) 55.

[84] See Burmester, 'Civil Society', above n 68, 545. Burmester has also reflected on which legal arguments never made it to the Court record. For example, Australia did not seek to challenge the French colonial arrangements over French Polynesia that formed the basis for its testing.

countries.[85] The case was dismissed, because the Court found that France's aims related to a series of underground tests, whereas the 1974 judgment was based on France's undertaking not to conduct any further atmospheric nuclear tests. The dissenting judges lamented the 1974 judgment and its missed opportunity to develop international environmental law, which New Zealand's Judge *ad hoc* Sir Geoffrey Palmer decried as a 'landmark of political caution, weak in law and logic'.[86]

Australia's second case as applicant was *Whaling in the Antarctic*, brought after diplomatic efforts failed to alter Japan's lethal whaling practices.[87] The case was based on the interest of every party to the International Convention on the Regulation of Whaling[88] to ensure compliance by every other party; New Zealand joined as an intervenor.[89] This emphasis on collective interest was not addressed by the Court; it was satisfied as to its jurisdiction based on the acceptance by both Australia and Japan of the optional clause.[90] (As noted above the Court has latterly addressed matters of standing and legal interest in The Gambia's claim against Myanmar,[91] and will do so again in Ukraine's current case against Russia, in which Australia has intervened.)[92]

By emphasising Australia's collective interest in Japan's treaty compliance, rather than any specific injury,[93] Australia avoided some of the diplomatic sensitivities that had accompanied domestic litigation on whaling, which had been based on violation of Australian federal environmental law in the Australian

[85] *Request for an Examination of the Situation in Accordance with Paragraph 63 of the Court's Judgment of 20 December 1974 in the Nuclear Tests (New Zealand v France) Case* [1995] ICJ Rep 288.

[86] ibid 419 [113]. See also the dissenting opinion of Judge Weeramantry, '[t]he Court has too long been silent on these issues and, in the words of ancient wisdom, one may well ask "If not now, when?"': ibid 362. See generally, T Stephens, 'Environmental Litigation by Asia Pacific States at the International Court of Justice' (2021) 21 *Melbourne Journal of International Law* 653, 660–61.

[87] *Whaling in the Antarctic*, above n 2.

[88] International Convention for the Regulation of Whaling (adopted 2 December 1946, entered into force 10 November 1948) 161 UNTS 72.

[89] As stated in Australia's oral submissions to the Court, delivered on 9 July 2013, '[e]very party has the same interest in ensuring compliance by every other party … Australia is seeking to uphold its collective interest, an interest it shares with all other parties': Verbatim Record, *Whaling in the Antarctic (Australia v Japan: New Zealand Intervening)* (International Court of Justice, CR 2013/18, 9 July 2013) 28 [19] (Mr Burmester).

[90] See generally CJ Tams, 'Roads Not Taken, Opportunities Missed: Procedural and Jurisdictional Questions Sidestepped in the *Whaling* Judgment' in M Fitzmaurice and D Tamada (eds), *Whaling in the Antarctic: Significance and the Implications of the ICJ Judgment* (Leiden, Brill Nijhoff, 2016); MA Young and SR Sullivan, 'Evolution through the Duty to Cooperate: Implications of the *Whaling* Case at the International Court of Justice' (2015) 16 *Melbourne Journal of International Law* 311.

[91] *The Gambia v Myanmar*, above n 56.

[92] Declaration of Intervention of the Government of Australia, *Allegations of Genocide under the Convention on the Prevention and Punishment of the Crime of Genocide (Ukraine v Russian Federation)* (International Court of Justice, 30 September 2022).

[93] See generally SV Scott, 'National Encounters with the International Court of Justice: Avoiding Litigating Antarctic Sovereignty' (2021) 21 *Melbourne Journal of International Law* 578, 585–87.

Whale Sanctuary of the Australian Antarctic Territory.[94] It might also be said that Australia was implicitly invoking the legal interests of the whales themselves, although of course international courts do not currently accord standing to animals.[95]

On 31 March 2014, the ICJ was unanimous in finding it had jurisdiction, and by a large majority it upheld Australia's claims on the merits.[96] Japan was found to have violated its treaty obligations, and the Court allowed for the evolution of international law – the case was heard almost 70 years after the 1946 whaling treaty's original objective of the 'orderly development of the whaling industry' – through the standard of conduct expected of states parties.[97] Voting with the majority, Judge *ad hoc* Charlesworth delivered a separate opinion that extended the Court's analysis of legal sources and principles. Australia's legal team attributed their success to the contribution of Professor Crawford, as he then was, as legal counsel.[98] Australia did not have this representation in the first case in which it appeared as a respondent, when Professor Crawford was counsel for Nauru, which I now discuss.

B. Three Times a Respondent: Certain Phosphate Lands, East Timor and Seizure and Detention

As respondent, Australia has faced legal challenge three times at the ICJ. Each time Australia has appeared at the Court. This contrasts with other states who have faced legal action, including major powers France and the United States, who refused to appear in the respective cases *Nuclear Tests* and *Nicaragua*, and who withdrew their acceptance of the optional clause immediately after those cases. Australia's acceptance of the Court's jurisdiction (via its optional clause declaration mentioned above) was the basis of jurisdiction for each of the three cases. For the reasons set out below, none of the cases led to judgment against Australia, though this is not to suggest the cases did not lead to change.

The first case was Nauru's claim relating to responsibility for phosphate mining. The *Certain Phosphate Lands in Nauru* case stemmed from the joint

[94] *Humane Society International Inc v Kyodo Senpaku Kaisha Ltd* [2004] FCA 1510 (Allsop J); *Humane Society International Inc v Kyodo Senpaku Kaisha Ltd* [2005] FCA 664 (Allsop J), revd (2006) 154 FCR 425 (Black CJ, Moore and Finkelstein JJ); *Humane Society International Inc v Kyodo Senpaku Kaisha Ltd* [2007] FCA 124 (Allsop J); *Humane Society International Inc v Kyodo Senpaku Kaisha Ltd* (2008) 165 FCR 510 (Allsop J).

[95] MA Young, 'International Adjudication and the Commons' (2019) 41 *University of Hawai'i Law Review* 353, 369–70.

[96] *Whaling in the Antarctic*, above n 2.

[97] See generally, Young and Sullivan, above n 90.

[98] B Campbell and S Ierino, 'James Crawford and the Australian Government' (2023) 40 *Australian Year Book of International Law* 195, 206. The other counsel were Philippe Sands QC, Laurence Boisson de Chazournes, then Solicitor-General, Stephen Gageler SC (now Justice Gageler of the High Court of Australia), Henry Burmester QC and Bill Campbell QC.

trustee mandate over the former German colonial territory of Nauru from 1923, which Australia shared with New Zealand and the United Kingdom[99] until Nauru's independence in 1966. The lucrative British Phosphate Commission administered by the three partner countries wrought catastrophic environmental damage, which was canvassed by a Commission of Inquiry into the Rehabilitation of Phosphate Lands.[100] The evidence of destruction amassed in this Inquiry formed the basis for Nauru's claim to the ICJ, filed in 1989, which sought reparations for the loss caused to Nauru as a result of the breaches of Australia's legal obligations.[101]

Australia challenged the Court's jurisdiction. Although Australia's 1975 amendment to the optional clause declaration, described above, served to remove Australia's reservation concerning disputes between members of the Commonwealth, Australia submitted that the Court had no jurisdiction, inter alia, because New Zealand and the United Kingdom were not parties to the proceedings. This relied on the fundamental principle that the ICJ cannot decide a dispute between states without the consent of those states to its jurisdiction.[102] The Court disagreed that the lack of participation by New Zealand and the United Kingdom served as a bar, holding that a finding on the responsibility attributed to Australia could be made without adjudicating on their interests.[103]

The ICJ's adverse decision against Australia at the Preliminary Objections stage on 26 June 1992 led Australia to reassess its approach. Cabinet was briefed that '[t]he prospect of an adverse finding of a breach of trusteeship obligations and exposure to substantial financial damages could attract considerable interest and criticism'.[104] The Australian government, led by Paul Keating, decided to

[99] See generally C Storr, '"*Imperium in Imperio*": Sub-Imperialism and the Formation of Australia as a Subject of International Law' (2018) 19 *Melbourne Journal of International Law* 335. The League of Nations mandate was updated on 1 November 1947, when Nauru was placed under the Trusteeship System provided for in ch XII of the Charter of the United Nations by a Trusteeship Agreement approved by the General Assembly.

[100] The Commission was chaired by CG Weeramantry before his election to the International Court of Justice: see generally, C Weeramantry, *Nauru: Environmental Damage under International Trusteeship* (Oxford, Oxford University Press, 1992). See also A Anghie, '"The Heart of My Home": Colonialism, Environmental Damage, and the Nauru Case' (1993) 34 *Harvard International Law Journal* 445; A Anghie, *Imperialism, Sovereignty and the Making of International Law* (Cambridge, Cambridge University Press, 2005). Much of the archival research for the Commission was completed by Deborah Cass in Melbourne, as detailed in A Anghie, 'Self-Determination and Beyond: Reflections on the Aftermath of the Nauru Case' in K Rubenstein (ed), *Traversing the Divide: Honouring Deborah Cass's Contributions to Public and International Law* (Canberra, ANU Press, 2021). On Judge Weeramantry's connection to Australia, see above n 45.

[101] *Certain Phosphate Lands in Nauru*, above n 3, 243–44.

[102] As confirmed in *Monetary Gold Removed from Rome in 1943 (Italy v France, United Kingdom of Great Britain and Northern Ireland and United States of America)* (Preliminary Objections) [1954] ICJ Rep 19, 32.

[103] *Certain Phosphate Lands in Nauru*, above n 3, 261.

[104] 'Cabinet Minute, 2 February 1992' in 'Cabinet Submission 914: Nauru: International Court of Justice (ICJ) Case: Decision 1565' (National Archives of Australia, NAA, Series A14217, Control Symbol 914, Item ID 32177313) 3.

settle the matter before it reached the merits stage.[105] It paid a cash settlement of A$107 million to Nauru,[106] to which New Zealand contributed A$12 million.[107] Australia and Nauru recorded their wish to 'respect and seek to build on existing bilateral, regional and other mutually beneficial arrangements in accordance with their shared commitment to constructive co-operation'.[108] Despite these sentiments, environmental rehabilitation has not ensued.[109] Instead, Nauru's economic activities have extended to revenue raising through detention facilities (where it has operated as a 'legal black hole' for asylum seekers to Australia)[110] and deep seabed mining.[111]

A second case against Australia involving trusteeship rights was working its way through the Court at this time. Indeed, some of the Australian arguments in *Certain Phosphate Lands* were adopted in its defence against Portugal's claim that it had illegally recognised Indonesian sovereignty over East Timor.[112] This challenge, filed by Portugal in 1991 (though without seeking the consent of the people of East Timor),[113] followed the 1989 Treaty between Australia and Indonesia to cooperate to exploit the resources of the Timor Gap (also concluded without the consent of the East Timorese).[114] The case was pursued alongside domestic legal challenges to Australia's recognition of Indonesian sovereignty in the High Court, which were refused on grounds of justiciability.[115]

The Court delivered its decision on 30 June 1995. It found it had no jurisdiction to grant Portugal the sought declaration as to 'the rights of the people of East Timor to self-determination, to territorial integrity and unity and to

[105] PJ Keating, 'Australia-Nauru Relations: Settlement of the ICJ Case' (Statement by the Prime Minister, 9 August 1993) in 'Nauru: Relations with Australia: International Court of Justice (ICJ) Case' (National Archives of Australia, NAA, Series A9737, Control Symbol 1990/3276 PART 3, Item ID, 8260122) 70.

[106] Agreement for the Settlement of the Case in the International Court of Justice concerning Certain Phosphate Lands in Nauru (signed 10 August 1993, entered into force 20 August 1993) 1770 UNTS 379. Australia had lodged its Counter-Memorial dealing with the merits of the case on 29 March 1993.

[107] Exchange of Letters constituting an Agreement between the Government of Australia and the Government of New Zealand relating to Nauru (entered into force 23 May 1994) ATS 1994 17.

[108] Joint Declaration of Principles Guiding Relations between Australia and the Republic of Nauru, [1993] ILM 1476.

[109] C Storr, *International Status in the Shadow of Empire: Nauru and the Histories of International Law* (Cambridge, Cambridge University Press, 2020) 248–52.

[110] Anghie, 'Self-Determination and Beyond', above n 100, 47.

[111] Storr, *International Status*, above n 109, 257–59.

[112] GJ Simpson, 'Judging the East Timor Dispute: Self-Determination at the International Court of Justice' (1994) 17 *Hastings International and Comparative Law Review* 323; CM Chinkin, 'East Timor Moves into the World Court' (1993) 4 *European Journal of International Law* 206.

[113] *East Timor*, above n 3, 135 (Judge Vereshchetin).

[114] Treaty between Australia and the Republic of Indonesia on the Zone of Cooperation in an Area between the Indonesian Province of East Timor and Northern Australia, executed on behalf of Australia and Indonesia in 1989 (adopted 11 December 1989, entered into force 9 February 1991) ATS 1991 9. For a broader history, see C Fernandes, 'Australia, Timor Leste and International Law', ch 5 in this volume.

[115] *Horta v Commonwealth* (1994) 181 CLR 183.

permanent sovereignty over its wealth and natural resources'.[116] Although the Court was careful to uphold its previous interpretation of self-determination and to recognise the right of self-determination as *erga omnes*,[117] it found it lacked jurisdiction to rule on Portugal's claim.[118] In contrast to *Certain Phosphate Lands*, the rights and obligations of a non-consenting third state – in this case, Indonesia – would constitute the very subject matter of the judgment.[119] Australia's *ad hoc* judge, Sir Ninian Stephen, voted with the majority and issued no separate declaration.

In an oral report to Cabinet on the ICJ's decision on 5 July 1995, the Minister for Foreign Affairs, Gareth Evans, noted the response of the Indonesian government and the Australian petroleum industry (although further details of this response are not recorded), and foreshadowed a submission about Australia's acceptance of the jurisdiction of the ICJ to be brought to Cabinet in due course.[120] (As it turned out, it was the John Howard-led Coalition Liberal Government, who defeated Prime Minister Paul Keating to come into power in 1996, that ultimately amended Australia's optional clause in 2002, as set out above.)

The 1995 decision of the Court was not without impact on the principle of self-determination, especially when considering the separate and dissenting opinions.[121] Interpretation of the UN Charter's concept of 'sacred trust'[122] led to an emphasis on consultation with the East Timorese people, and 'a concern to equalize cultures through participation'.[123] These jurisprudential developments had perhaps some relationship to the political changes in the region less than five years later. After a change of government in Indonesia, a referendum was held on independence for the East Timorese in 1999, and the Democratic Republic of Timor-Leste became a UN Member State in 2002.

The third case against Australia was Timor-Leste's claim that Australia had illegally seized and detained documents from Timor-Leste's legal advisers in Canberra. The claim stemmed from a raid by Australian agents on the law firm's office on 3 December 2013, which seized material relating to a pending arbitration between the two countries. That arbitration, administered by the Permanent Court of Arbitration, was being conducted under a 2002 treaty between Timor-Leste and Australia, and concerned a 2006 treaty relating to

[116] *East Timor*, above n 3, 94.
[117] ibid 102 [29].
[118] ibid 105 [35].
[119] ibid 104–05 [34].
[120] 'Cabinet Minute, 5 July 1995' in 'Cabinet Decision 4315: International Court of Justice (ICJ): Timor Gap Case: Without Submission' (National Archives of Australia, NAA, Series A14218, Control Symbol 4315, Item ID 32701599).
[121] See especially the separate opinion of Judge Vereschchetin and the dissenting opinions of Judge Weeramantry and Judge *ad hoc* Skubiszewski, which are discussed in K Knop, *Diversity and Self-Determination in International Law* (Cambridge, Cambridge University Press, 2002) 190–211.
[122] Charter of the United Nations, Art 73.
[123] Knop, above n 121, 210.

resources of the Timor Sea, the negotiations for which Timor-Leste believed had been tainted by clandestine bugging operations on the part of Australia.[124]

The case, which was launched on 17 December 2013, was a considerable embarrassment for Australia. It showcased the 'deep offence and shock' to Timor-Leste caused by the raid.[125] It also seemed to bemuse the Court, with one judge noting it as an example 'that the factual context of disputes lodged with an international tribunal like the International Court of Justice may well cross the threshold of human imagination'.[126] Timor-Leste's lawyers included British-born Sir Elihu Lauterpacht QC, who had served as the principal legal adviser to the Australian Department of Foreign Affairs from 1975 to 1977, and who had been highly influential in many matters of international law on behalf of Australia, including the *Nuclear Tests* case.[127] In oral submissions, noting his 'deep affection and high regard' for Australia, he described his sadness at being 'obliged to confront Australia in respect of conduct which inexplicably falls so far short of the high standards that prevailed in my time'.[128]

The Court indicated provisional measures on 3 March 2014, accepting in part the requests of Timor-Leste.[129] Contrary to the positive public statement made by the Abbott-led Coalition government, the ICJ decision was adverse to Australia.[130] The Court included orders that Australia 'shall ensure that the content of the seized material is not in any way or at any time used ... until the present case has been concluded'.[131] The dissenting opinions, by Judge Keith, Judge Greenwood and Australia's Judge *ad hoc* Callinan,[132] differed from the majority in their interpretation of the undertaking offered by Australia's Attorney-General, George Brandis, about safeguarding the seized documents and data,[133] which they considered to be sufficient. The provisional measures

[124] For background, see Sir Elihu Lauterpacht's opening remarks at the hearing in Verbatim Record, *Questions Relating to the Seizure and Detention of Certain Documents and Data (Timor-Leste v Australia)* (International Court of Justice, CR 2014/1, 20 January 2014) 15–25 [1]–[18]. See especially, 17–18 [5]–[7].

[125] ibid 14 [5] (Mr da Fonseca, Ambassador of the Democratic Republic of Timor-Leste to the United Kingdom). Timor-Leste's feelings of deep shock and regret were restated by Judge Keith in his dissenting opinion: *Questions Relating to the Seizure and Detention of Certain Documents and Data (Timor-Leste v Australia)* (Provisional Measures) [2014] ICJ Rep 147, 163.

[126] *Questions Relating to the Seizure and Detention of Certain Documents and Data (Timor-Leste v Australia)*, above n 125, 168 [1] (Judge Cançado Trindade).

[127] Burmester, 'Sir Elihu Lauterpacht QC', above n 70. See also J Crawford, 'International Law and the Public Service' (2017) 35 *Australian Year Book of International Law* 17.

[128] Verbatim Record, *Questions Relating to the Seizure and Detention of Certain Documents and Data (Timor-Leste v Australia)* (International Court of Justice, CR 2014/1, 20 January 2014) p 16 [2] (Sir Elihu Lauterpacht).

[129] *Questions Relating to the Seizure and Detention of Certain Documents and Data (Timor-Leste v Australia)* (Provisional Measures) [2014] ICJ Rep 147.

[130] Campbell, 'Australia's Engagement', above n 27, 617–18.

[131] *Seizure and Detention* (Provisional Measures), above n 129, 161.

[132] Dissenting opinions: ibid 163 (Judge Keith), 194 (Judge Greenwood), 214 (Judge *ad hoc* Callinan).

[133] The undertakings were described at ibid 155–57 [35]–[39].

set the scene for later political developments between the two countries. Some months later, Australia requested a modification of the Court's order so as to authorise the return of the documents and copies to Timor-Leste, and on 2 June 2015, Timor-Leste informed the Court that it wished to discontinue the proceedings.[134]

C. Cases Not Taken: Or Taken Elsewhere

The cases in which Australia has appeared before the ICJ do not demonstrate the full extent to which the ICJ has been influential in resolving Australia's international disputes. Australia was a potential respondent or applicant in a variety of scenarios, although evidence is difficult to locate. For example, Japan was poised to challenge Australia at the ICJ over pearl fishing in the 1950s, a position that was ultimately resolved by the collapse of the pearl shell industry amidst technological developments in plastic production.[135] Australia also contemplated instituting proceedings in the ICJ against Singapore and Indonesia, respectively, concerning the imposition of the death penalty on Australian citizens for drug trafficking.[136]

Some of the disputes leading to litigation at the ICJ have featured domestic legal issues, which have been pursued in Australian courts. Indeed, 'national encounters with the ICJ have often preceded, coincided with or developed subsequently to domestic litigation',[137] as was the case with *East Timor*[138] and *Whaling*.[139] These and other ICJ disputes have a continuing influence on domestic courts.[140]

Australia's international disputes have also been pursued by the parties in other international courts and tribunals.[141] These forums have sometimes been far more active than the ICJ, and the major powers that do not consent to the

[134] *Questions Relating to the Seizure and Detention of Certain Documents and Data (Timor-Leste v Australia)* (Order of 11 June 2015) [2015] ICJ Rep 572.

[135] E Nyhan, 'A Latent Encounter with the Court: How Australia and Japan Settled a Pearl Fisheries Dispute' (2021) 21 *Melbourne Journal of International Law* 553. See especially, 564, 576.

[136] Campbell, 'Australia's Engagement', above n 27, 600–01.

[137] Charlesworth and Young, 'National Encounters', above n 7, 506–07. See also C Ward, 'National and International Litigation: Partners or Competitors?' in N Klein (ed), *Litigating International Law Disputes: Weighing the Options* (Cambridge, Cambridge University Press, 2014).

[138] *Horta*, above n 115.

[139] See above n 94. Humane Society waited until the conclusion of the ICJ proceedings before relaunching its enforcement action; in late 2015, its application was heard at the Federal Court and the Japanese whaling firm was found to be in contempt and fined: *Humane Society International Inc v Kyodo Senpaku Kaisha Ltd* (2015) 238 FCR 209. Jagot J ordered the respondent to pay fines together totalling $1,000,000.

[140] See also N Klein and N Hughes, 'National Litigation and International Law: Repercussions for Australia's Protection of Marine Resources' (2009) 33 *Melbourne University Law Review* 163.

[141] See Charter of the United Nations, Art 95.

ICJ's jurisdiction might be more likely to appear.[142] Just as the Privy Council's role in Australia diminished *not* just because of the fall of the British Empire but because of the rise of the Australian High Court, Australia's attitude to the ICJ can be assessed against its attitude towards other tribunals – both international and domestic – during the relevant period. For example, Australia has been a complainant and respondent in multiple disputes arising from the law of the sea, including before ad hoc tribunals and the International Tribunal for the Law of the Sea. It has been a complainant and respondent in multiple disputes at the World Trade Organization (WTO). In accordance with investor–state dispute settlement provisions in investment agreements, it welcomes compulsory dispute settlement by ad hoc investment tribunals over matters of certain investor rights. This proliferation of adjudicative forums contributes to conflicts between rules and tribunals' overlapping jurisdiction.[143] For example, litigation over Australia's plain packaging tobacco legislation, which was challenged at the High Court, the WTO and at an investment arbitration, gave rise to legal uncertainty.[144] One solution calls for an enhanced role for the ICJ in delivering advisory opinions to support judicial reflexivity.[145] This recommendation makes Australia's early support for the greater use of the Court by the United Nations and its organs particularly prescient, as the next section discusses.

IV. REQUESTING ADVICE ON LEGAL QUESTIONS

Australia was an early supporter of the ICJ's advisory jurisdiction, recognising its utility in supporting the UN system. In 1947, Australia led a General Assembly resolution recommending that 'each UN organ and specialised agency regularly review challenging questions of international law generally within their competence and refer them to the ICJ seeking an advisory opinion'.[146] The

[142] For one example, see China discussed by N Klein, 'Stakeholders in Dispute Settlement under the UN Convention on the Law of the Sea' in MC Ribeiro, FL Bastos and T Henriksen (eds), *Global Challenges and the Law of the Sea* (Cham, Springer, 2020).

[143] J Crawford and P Nevill, 'Relations between International Courts and Tribunals: The "Regime Problem"' in MA Young (ed), *Regime Interaction in International Law: Facing Fragmentation* (Cambridge, Cambridge University Press, 2012).

[144] The potential for such arbitrations to interfere with decisions of Australian domestic courts has been noted by former Chief Justice of the High Court, Robert French, in an address to Australian judges: RS French, 'Investor–State Dispute Settlement: A Cut Above the Courts?' (Speech at the Supreme and Federal Courts Judges' Conference, 9 July 2014): www.hcourt.gov.au/assets/publications/speeches/current-justices/frenchcj/frenchcj09jul14.pdf.

[145] A Lang, 'The Role of the International Court of Justice in a Context of Fragmentation' (2013) 62 *International & Comparative Law Quarterly* 777.

[146] Need for Greater Use by the United Nations and its Organs of the International Court of Justice, UNGA Res 171(II) (14 November 1947) UN Doc A/RES/171(II). See also Crawford, 'Dreamers of the Day', above n 5, 527–28. The resolution was adopted 44 votes in favour, six votes against and two abstentions: UN GAOR 2nd Session 113th Plenary Meeting UN Doc A/PV.113 (14 November 1947).

Court's advisory jurisdiction is established by the UN Charter.[147] Unlike the Court's contentious jurisdiction, the advisory jurisdiction does not lead to decisions that are binding on states, but instead is intended to guide UN organs such as the General Assembly with answers to legal questions.[148] Almost 30 advisory opinions have been delivered by the Court in its seven decades.[149] In a quarter of these opinions, Australia has had some involvement, either through oral or written submissions or both.

Australia's practice on advisory opinion requests has moved through eras of caution, ambivalence and reticence.[150] In the first two decades of the ICJ, Australia showed cautious support for the advisory jurisdiction and its ability to shape the functions of UN organs. An example is Sir Kenneth Bailey's oral advocacy in proceedings relating to the funding of UN operations, which was notable in its vision for the international legal order.[151] Despite the distance, time and expense involved, Australia participated in the proceedings because it felt 'itself to have a great, indeed a vital, investment in the maintenance of an effective international organization'.[152]

In contrast, during the period of decolonisation, Australia retreated to a more ambivalent stance. It did not appear, for example, in the UN Security Council requested advisory opinion on the legal consequences of South Africa's continued presence in Namibia in 1970,[153] or the 1975 advisory opinion on the legal status of Western Sahara.[154] A memorandum of advice by Elihu Lauterpacht, then Legal Adviser to the Department of Foreign Affairs (as noted above), considered the latter case relevant only for Australia's territorial claims in the Antarctic, or for the move by Papua New Guinea towards independence.[155] By contrast, the Acting Deputy Secretary of the Attorney-General's Department noted that the issues of whether Western Sahara was a 'territory belonging to no one (*terra nullius*)', in general terms, 'could have a certain bearing on the legal aspects of the mode in which the Australian continent was acquired from the aboriginal inhabitants'.[156] This prediction proved correct 20 years later when

[147] Charter of the United Nations, Art 96. See further Charlesworth and Young, 'Australian Encounters', above n 4, 701–03.

[148] Statute of the International Court of Justice, Art 65.

[149] 'Advisory Proceedings' (International Court of Justice): www.icj-cij.org/en/advisory-proceedings.

[150] This argument is made in Charlesworth and Young, 'Australian Encounters', above n 4.

[151] *Certain Expenses of the United Nations (Article 17, Paragraph 2, of the Charter)* (Advisory Opinion) [1962] ICJ Rep 151. See also Charlesworth and Young, 'Australian Encounters', above n 4, 707–10.

[152] 'Oral Statement of Sir Kenneth Bailey', *Certain Expenses of the United Nations (Article 17, Paragraph 2, of the Charter)* (Advisory Opinion) [1962] II ICJ Pleadings 372, 372–73.

[153] *Legal Consequences for States of the Continued Presence of South Africa in Namibia (South West Africa) notwithstanding Security Council Resolution 276 (1970)* (Advisory Opinion) [1971] ICJ Rep 16.

[154] *Western Sahara* (Advisory Opinion) [1975] ICJ Rep 12.

[155] The relevant archival materials are canvassed in Charlesworth and Young, 'Australian Encounters', above n 4, 711–14.

[156] P Brazil, 'International Court of Justice: Status of the Western Sahara' (16 January 1975) in 'International Court of Justice' (National Archives of Australia, NAA, Series M132, Control

the High Court ruled on the legal fiction of *terra nullius* in Australia.[157] Around this time, Australia resumed its participation in advisory opinions, with written and oral submissions in the request for an advisory opinion on nuclear weapons, launched first by the World Health Organization[158] and then by the General Assembly.[159] Australia urged the Court to exercise its jurisdiction *not* to provide an opinion on procedural grounds, but, in the alternative, to hold substantively on the illegality of nuclear weapons.[160]

Australia's attitude to advisory opinions since the turn of the century has been one of reticence. It voted against a General Assembly resolution in 2003 requesting an advisory opinion on the legal consequences of Israel's construction of a barrier wall in the Occupied Palestinian Territory,[161] and against a General Assembly resolution requesting an advisory opinion on Israeli practices affecting the human rights of the Palestinian people in the Occupied Palestinian Territory, including East Jerusalem, in 2022.[162] Australia voted against a General Assembly resolution requesting an opinion on the *Legal Consequences of the Separation of the Chagos Archipelago from Mauritius in 1965* (*Chagos*) in 2017.[163] Australia participated in two of the three advisory proceedings resulting from these resolutions,[164] pressing the ICJ to exercise discretion not to give an opinion in the cases. Australia's position contrasts with the position of other states including small countries.[165]

The *Chagos* case related to the decolonisation of Mauritius in 1965 and the separation of the Chagos Archipelago by the British to create a 'British

Symbol 162, Item ID 5437557) [6]–[7], cited in Charlesworth and Young, 'Australian Encounters', above n 4, 714.

157 *Mabo v Queensland (No 2)* (1992) 175 CLR 1. See also Charlesworth and Young, 'Australian Encounters', above n 4, 711–14.

158 *Legality of the Use by a State of Nuclear Weapons in Armed Conflict* (Advisory Opinion) [1996] ICJ Rep 66.

159 *Legality of the Threat or Use of Nuclear Weapons* (Advisory Opinion) [1996] ICJ Rep 226.

160 Charlesworth and Young, 'Australian Encounters', above n 4, 715–19.

161 Illegal Israeli Actions in Occupied East Jerusalem and the Rest of the Occupied Palestinian Territory, UNGA Res ES-10/14 (12 December 2003, adopted 8 December 2003) UN Doc A/RES/ES-10/14. The recorded vote in the Assembly, which consists of all 191 UN Member States, was 90 in favour, eight against, with 74 abstentions: UN GAOR 10th Emergency Special Session 23rd Plenary Meeting Agenda Item 5 (8 December 2003) UN Doc A/ES-10/PV.23. Nineteen Member States did not vote.

162 Israeli Practices and Settlement Affecting the Rights of the Palestinian People and Other Arabs of the Occupied Palestinian Territory, UNGA Res 77/247 (9 January 2023, adopted 30 December 2022) UN Doc A/RES/77/247.

163 Request for an Advisory Opinion of the International Court of Justice on the Legal Consequences of the Separation of the Chagos Archipelago from Mauritius in 1965, UNGA Res 71/292 (22 June 2017) UN Doc A/RES/71/292; UN GAOR 71st Session 88th Plenary Meeting Agenda Item 87 (22 June 2017) (adopted by 94 votes to 15; 65 abstentions) UN Doc A/71/PV.88.

164 Australia did not file a written statement in *Legal Consequences arising from the Policies and Practices of Israel in the Occupied Palestinian Territory, including East Jerusalem* (Advisory Opinion of 19 July 2024): icj-cij.org/case/186.

165 See, eg, the vote of El Salvador ('as a small country, we are protected by international law. We do not have nuclear weapons; we do not have big armies to defend our sovereignty. It is international law that defends us, and as a result we have the obligation to support everything that is being done to enhance international law'): UN GAOR (A/71/PV.88), above n 163, 20.

Indian Ocean Territory'. Australia submitted that an advisory opinion 'would be inconsistent with the fundamental principle which requires the consent of both the United Kingdom and Mauritius'.[166] Counsel for Mauritius referred to Australia's position, 'given its own historical experience as a former colony', as 'resembl[ing] a form of abused child syndrome, in which the victim becomes the oppressor'.[167] The ICJ did not accept Australia's position, and delivered an advisory opinion which has become authoritative for the General Assembly and for other tribunals.[168] Its ruling that the Chagos Archipelago was not lawfully separated from Mauritius was ultimately influential for the UK's decision in late 2022 to open negotiations with Mauritius about the territory.

The reticence of Australia towards the Court's advisory jurisdiction may give way to a position resembling its original stance. In 2022, Australia indicated that it would support Vanuatu's campaign at the General Assembly for a vote to request from the ICJ an advisory opinion relating to obligations of states in respect of climate change.[169] The resolution was adopted in March 2023.[170] Australia filed a written statement, a written comment on other participants' statements, and made oral submissions.[171] Australia's submissions deviated in substance from many others including Vanuatu and the Melanesian Spearhead Group, and unlike many participants Australia did not file a written reply to the questions put by Judges Cleveland, Tladi, Aurescu and Charlesworth at the end of the hearing. Regardless of whether Australia's legal arguments are persuasive for the Court, its engagement with the climate proceedings has brought it closer to its attitude towards the Court's contentious jurisdiction, in which, as described above, it has been fully prepared to act as both applicant and respondent.[172]

[166] 'Written Statement of the Government of Australia', *Legal Consequences of the Separation of the Chagos Archipelago from Mauritius in 1965* (International Court of Justice, 27 February 2018) 1 [5].

[167] Verbatim Record. *Legal Consequences of the Separation of the Chagos Archipelago from Mauritius in 1965* (International Court of Justice, CR 2018/20, 3 September 2018) 78 [12] (Mr Sands).

[168] D Guilfoyle, 'The Chagos Archipelago before International Tribunals: Strategic Litigation and the Production of Historical Knowledge' (2021) 21 *Melbourne Journal of International Law* 749, 768.

[169] Ben McKay, 'Australia, NZ Sign up for ICJ Climate Case' *Canberra Times* (12 July 2022).

[170] Request for an Advisory Opinion of the International Court of Justice on the Obligations of States in Respect of Climate Change, UNGA Res 77/276 (4 April 2023, adopted 29 March 2023) UN Doc A/RES/77/276.

[171] Written Statement of Australia (22 March 2024): www.icj-cij.org/sites/default/files/case-related/187/187-20240326-wri-02-00-en.pdf; Written comments of Australia (15 August 2024): www.icj-cij.org/sites/default/files/case-related/187/187-20240815-wri-14-00-en.pdf; Oral Statements in: Verbatim Record, *Obligations of States in respect of Climate Change* (Request for advisory opinion submitted by the General Assembly of the United Nations) International Court of Justice, CR 2024/35, 2 December 2024, 35–52 (Mr Clarke, Mr Donaghue, Ms Partlett): www.icj-cij.org/sites/default/files/case-related/187/187-20241202-ora-02-00-bi_0.pdf.

[172] See Charlesworth and Young, 'Australian Encounters', above n 4, 724–25.

V. CONCLUSION

This chapter has demonstrated that Australia takes the position of the ICJ seriously. Since its establishment, Australia has recognised the merits of an international system of peaceful dispute settlement. Australia was active in debates that led to the ICJ's Statute, committing with ideas and resources to what was to become the primary judicial organ of the United Nations. Moreover, the Australian judges who have been elected to the bench have contributed in varied ways to the Court, with an important legacy of the terms of Judge Crawford and Judge Charlesworth currently taking shape.

The chapter has described how Australia utilised the Court as an applicant twice and participated as a respondent three times. Unlike more powerful nations, it has always 'turned up' when challenged at the Court, when its activities in the region have led to disputes with neighbours over sovereignty, natural resource exploitation and mining rehabilitation. While it has been prepared to rethink the terms of its consent to the Court's contentious jurisdiction when it has been on the losing side, also unlike more powerful nations it has never fully withdrawn its consent.

The current version of Australia's declaration accepting the jurisdiction of the Court – which has been in place since the distinctive sovereign developments in the region in 2002 (when East Timor voted on its independence) – maintains a preference for negotiation or mediation, rather than adjudication, for any dispute concerning or relating to the delimitation of its maritime zones. These other avenues of dispute settlement, endorsed by the UN Charter,[173] rely on relationships of trust and informality but are also subject to relative power imbalances wrought by a history of empire. Australia has more strength, through its size, economy and alliances, than many of its regional neighbours in the Asia-Pacific. Thus, while often considered as a middle-power that values independent international adjudication, Australia might also be described as a major-power in its region that eschews Court processes when it suits. Moreover, the context of the cases that have involved Australia, many of which have concerned disputes over the extraction of natural resources (mineral or living), indicate the ongoing relevance of imperial history.

The Court's advisory jurisdiction, which allows it to provide advisory opinions on legal questions referred to it by duly authorised UN organs and agencies, has provoked different reactions from Australia. This chapter has pointed to Australia's enthusiastic participation in early advisory proceedings, and a changing attitude that has been summarised as moving through caution, ambivalence and reticence.[174] Australia's practice of encouraging the Court to exercise its discretion to reject requests for advisory opinions has differed

[173] Charter of the United Nations, Art 33.
[174] Charlesworth and Young, 'Australian Encounters', above n 4.

from other countries and from the Court, which instead operates with a strong presumption of jurisdiction over advisory requests, as occurred with its highly consequential opinion in *Chagos*. The support by the newly elected Australian government for a long-awaited request for an advisory opinion on the obligations of states with respect to climate change shows that Australia's attitude to advisory opinions is not fixed.

The status of the ICJ is tested when a commitment to multilateralism and the United Nations gives way to power and force. In contrast, Australia's trust and confidence in the Court has been preserved by a respect for state consent and existing sovereign arrangements. At times, this respect has cleaved too closely to colonial-era affiliations. Ultimately, however, Australia recognises the importance of having an independent third-party dispute settlement system to hear legal claims and pronounce upon their validity, and the ICJ has benefited from the work of Australian individuals and successive governments who hold this view.

9

International Law in the Attorney-General's Department: 1901–2000

HENRY BURMESTER

I. INTRODUCTION

A STUDY OF any institution inevitably reflects its existence in the wider world, as well as the contribution of particular individuals who played a key role in it. The work of a government department is predictably affected by the politics of the day and, in particular, the ministers who were at relevant times responsible for the department. This chapter examines the work of the Australian Attorney-General's Department (the Department) in relation to international law, from its establishment in 1901, as one of the first departments of the new Commonwealth, until 2000. These decades saw the emergence of Australia into a fully developed international legal person and an active player in the international legal order, particularly as that order developed after the Second World War. It is inevitably a selective account of some of the main issues. Events after 2000 are dealt with elsewhere in this collection.[1]

In the period from Australia's establishment in 1901 until 2000, the world underwent enormous change in terms of the international legal framework in which nations operate. As Australia became an active participant in world affairs, departmental officers made a contribution to the development of international law in many new areas. The work and advice of such officers is often hidden behind the more public actions of the governments they serve. This makes an account of the Department's contribution in relation to international law more difficult. However, such an account can provide an insight into the changing priorities of various Australian governments in relation to the international legal order. A timeline accompanies this study which highlights key developments in this regard.[2]

[1] See B Campbell, 'Australian Government Practice of International Law in the Twenty-First Century', ch 10 in this volume.

[2] See Appendix to this chapter.

Prior to the Second World War, Australia's engagement with the rest of the world was rather limited and opportunistic. In most areas, it took its lead from the United Kingdom. The difficulty of overseas travel meant direct contributions by departmental officers at international conferences were somewhat restricted. However, officers of the Department played a key role in Australia's distinct contribution at the Versailles Conference. The Department was also very involved in the domestic implications of international law as Australia's status evolved to independent nation. In the post-Second World War era, the Department became actively engaged in promoting Australian international law positions, including at negotiations for the establishment of the United Nations (UN), at the First Law of the Sea Conference and during the development of human rights treaties in the 1950s and 1960s.

By the 1970s, departmental involvement in international law grew significantly as international law itself expanded into new areas, such as environmental law. Older areas, such as law of the sea, international criminal law and trade law, grew in their scope. This participation in the 1970s onwards also in part reflected the politics of the time, with the election of the Whitlam Government in 1972 creating exponential growth in Australia's international law engagement. Later, governments such as those led by Malcolm Fraser or John Howard may have been less inclined than Gough Whitlam to engage with international law, but world events have meant that every government since the 1970s has needed to be heavily involved with international law. By 1989, the growing demands for departmental input into international legal issues was reflected in the establishment within the Department of a separate Office of International Law (OIL; the Office).

Three main themes help to focus this study. The first is the important role of departmental officers in finding creative and constructive legal solutions to protect Australia's national interests, both on the international stage but also domestically. This leads to the two main departmental roles that will be explored. The first is the externally focused role of the Department, where officers were directly involved in international conferences and engaging with the outside world. In doing this, they worked closely with other departments and delegations from many other countries. The second is the way in which the Department was constantly involved in the translation of Australia's international obligations and international legal interests into domestic law – the internally focused role. This often required delicate negotiations with the States and Territories, and litigation in Australian courts. These concurrent roles by the Department have, in my view, been one of the reasons the Department's international law contributions have been so important and central to the Australian government's effective participation in the international legal order.

The study is dependent in part on personal recollections and does not pretend to be comprehensive. From 1972 onwards, I was involved in the Department's provision of international law advice and services. My personal recollections inform the account of this period. For the earlier period, the study is principally reliant on secondary materials. A detailed archival research project would be necessary to fully understand the contribution of the Department and its officers to Australia's international law efforts in this earlier period. For the most part this has not yet occurred.[3]

II. INSTITUTIONAL ARRANGEMENTS

Bureaucratic arrangements made by different countries for the provision of international law services within their governments vary widely around the world. Some countries, like the United States (US) and the United Kingdom tend to give a central place to separate offices of Legal Adviser in the State Department or Foreign Office. In Australia, the Attorney-General's Department has always had a central role. Two key factors gave the Attorney-General and the Department this central role in relation to international law from Federation. First, many of the issues in the early years after Federation were more intra-Empire issues as the constitutional relationships between the United Kingdom and its former colonies evolved. Secondly, Australia's federal system meant that many international law questions also raised significant domestic and constitutional law issues, for which the Attorney- General's Department had clear responsibility as the lead department on legal affairs. Also relevant is the fact that a well-resourced Department of External Affairs was not in existence until after the Second World War. For much of the period until 1935, that Department had not been a fully autonomous department with its own Secretary.[4] This reflected the general absence of Australian diplomatic missions and a willingness to follow Britain's lead on most international law issues. By contrast, the Attorney-General's Department was among the first departments established in 1901 and has always existed since that date.

However, the involvement of the Attorney-General's Department's in international legal issues has never been exclusive. The Department of External Affairs after the Second World War had officers responsible for treaties and diplomatic and consular relations and worked alongside the Attorney-General's Department on many of the emerging international law issues, including space law and the Antarctic. From the 1970s, the Department of Foreign Affairs (as it became in 1971; Foreign Affairs) devoted greater resources to the international legal area as did the Attorney-General's Department. In more recent times, with Australia's involvement in armed conflict, the Department of Defence has become closely involved in international law issues affecting Australia's military, such as the use of force and rules of engagement. Additionally, international

[3] An exception is A Devereux, *Australia and the Birth of the International Bill of Rights: 1946–1966* (Annandale, Federation Press, 2005).

[4] I Castles, *Year Book Australia: 1988* (Canberra, Australian Bureau of Statistics, 1988).

terrorism and the movement of people, has drawn other departments into the area of international law.

The precise demarcation of responsibilities for international law between departments has never been rigidly defined, although an attempt to allocate broad responsibilities between the Attorney-General's Department and Foreign Affairs was attempted in 1975. This occurred at the time of the appointment of Elihu Lauterpacht QC as Legal Adviser in Foreign Affairs. Professor James Crawford has analysed the arrangements made at that time.[5] These arrangements followed a period of tension between the two departments in the early 1970s, as Foreign Affairs sought to assert greater responsibility in relation to international legal affairs. The tension between the two departments was resolved pragmatically and in a way that recognised the respective policy strengths and expertise of the two departments. This approach and use of the best and most appropriate available expertise in the two departments for particular issues was, from my observation, the most consistent theme in departmental relations in this area from the mid-1970s to the end of the 1990s, when this chapter ends. The lack of any detailed delineation of responsibilities between the two departments has, at times, frustrated outside observers. However, this has meant responsibilities were able to evolve as resources, personnel and government priorities changed. In practice, the two departments worked very closely together in most areas. At relevant points in this study, further reference will be made to the way in which the division of responsibilities operated.

Within the Department, arrangements for the provision of international law services varied as the Department grew in size and the issues of concern expanded. At first, it was only the Secretary and one or two other officers who were involved. After the Second World War, a number of officers, mainly in the Advisings area, were included. In the 1970s, while the Advisings area, later called General Counsel Division, remained the core area, officers in specialised areas like trade law or criminal law became involved.

In 1989, a separate small OIL was created in the Department in recognition of the increasing importance of this area of law in the delivery of a full range of legal services to government. It increased in size as demands for its services grew. The focus of the Office was on legal advice on questions of international law having domestic relevance, such as treaty implementation, or the interpretation of legislation with international law aspects. The Office was also heavily involved in litigation in the International Court of Justice (ICJ; the Court), coordinating the work of the various legal teams led by the Solicitor-General. The Office was also involved in increasing numbers of cases in domestic courts raising international law issues. This is discussed further below.[6]

[5] J Crawford, 'International Law and the Public Service' (2017) 35 *Australian Year Book of International Law* 17.

[6] See section VI.C below.

The future of OIL was put under a cloud in 1991, when its abolition was proposed by the opposition Liberal Party prior to the 1993 election. The assumption behind the proposal appears to have been that the Office was duplicating work that was also being done in Foreign Affairs. Abolition never happened as the Opposition did not win the 1993 election. The policy seemed short-sighted and failed to appreciate the important and distinct role of OIL.

One other change that confronted the international law responsibilities of the Department in the early 1990s was the introduction of user pays for certain legal services provided by the Department. When this began in 1991, public international law and treaties services were not subject to the user pays system under which departments paid for certain legal services, even when provided by the Attorney-General's Department. This changed to some extent over time. For instance, when National Interest Analyses were required to accompany referral of proposed treaty actions to the parliamentary Joint Standing Committee on Treaties, the Office was entitled to charge for their preparation. When the Australian Government Solicitor (AGS) was formally separated from the Department in 1999, international law responsibilities remained with the Department, although some advice on treaty interpretation was given by AGS as was the negotiation of certain types of bilateral agreements such as those dealing with reciprocal social security.

III. THE CREATIVE INDIVIDUALS

The history of the Department's involvement in various issues dealt with below identifies a number of key individual officers who worked on particular matters. Most of the relevant officers were not international law specialists. Rather, they were able public law experts as much at ease with providing advice on constitutional or governmental law as on international law. What distinguished them was their ability to get on top of an issue and provide pertinent advice or help to craft an appropriate legal regime consistent with the policy positions of the relevant Australian government. While most had traditional legal training and no doubt reflected the innate conservatism of most lawyers of their time, my impression is that a commitment to finding creative and constructive solutions to often difficult issues was a defining characteristic of their work. This will be seen more readily in the discussion below.

Prior to the Second World War, international law was primarily handled by Sir Robert Garran, Secretary from 1901 to 1932,[7] or Sir George Knowles,

[7] RS Parker, 'Garran, Sir Robert Randolph' in B Nairn and G Serle (eds), *Australian Dictionary of Biography: Volume 8 1891–1939* (Melbourne, Melbourne University Press, 1976) 622. For a summary of his career, and further references, see S Gageler, 'Sir Robert Garran: Medeo Tuttissimus Ibis' (2018) 46 *Federal Law Review* 1, 1–4, 10–12.

Secretary from 1932 to 1946.[8] Their contributions are considered in section IV below. The appointment of Sir Kenneth Bailey as Secretary in 1946, a position he held until 1964, ensured the Department continued to play a central role in many of the international law issues affecting Australia. Bailey had been a key adviser to Attorney-General Evatt during the negotiations of the Charter of the United Nations. On his retirement as Secretary, Bailey was appointed as High Commissioner to Canada. He again missed out on election to the ICJ in the 1966 elections, despite his high repute.[9] In 1969, on his return to Canberra, Bailey was appointed as Special Adviser to both the Attorney-General's Department and the Department of External Affairs. He held that position until his death in 1972.

After Bailey's retirement, there were a number of key personnel changes in relation to international law in the Department. The new Secretary, Edwin Hook, was not an international lawyer. Sir Clarrie Harders became the main international lawyer, appointed as Deputy Secretary in 1965. He later was Secretary from 1970 to 1979. Patrick (Pat) Brazil was outposted to the Department of External Affairs from 1965 to 1969 as Legal Adviser. At the same time, Alfred Body, who had been Legal Adviser in that department, joined the Attorney-General's Department. Brazil as Legal Adviser participated in the Vienna Conference on Treaties in 1969 and then led the Australian delegation to the Second Session of that Conference in 1970.[10] His exposure to the debates at that Conference on treaty interpretation influenced his later enthusiasm for changes that supported use of extrinsic materials in the interpretation of statutes. This culminated in the 1984 amendments to the Acts Interpretation Act 1901 (Cth) that made clear that extrinsic materials, including treaties, could be taken into account in construing Commonwealth statutes.[11] Brazil also pushed for Australian ratification of the Vienna Convention on Treaties, achieved in 1974. The rules in that Treaty are used by Australian courts when seeking to ascertain the meaning of treaty provisions.

Another change with the retirement of Bailey was the appointment of a separate Solicitor-General. In 1964, Anthony Mason was appointed, a position he held until the end of 1969, when Robert Ellicott was appointed to take his place. As Solicitors-General, they were involved in international law issues, such as maritime delimitation with Indonesia. Ellicott, and his successors, Maurice Byers and Gavan Griffith, also were the day-to-day leaders of Australia's legal teams in various international cases, as well as major domestic cases involving

[8] EG Whitlam, 'Knowles, Sir George Shaw' in B Nairn and G Serle (eds), *Australian Dictionary of Biography: Volume 9 1891–1939* (Melbourne, Melbourne University Press 1978) 623.

[9] Bailey had been nominated previously in 1946. In 1956, Sir Percy Spender was nominated by Australia and was elected to take office in 1957. In 1966, on the expiry of Spender's term, Bailey was again nominated but he missed out on election, in part due to the way in which Spender had exercised his casting vote in the *South West Africa* case, which led to the case being dismissed. Crawford, 'International Law and the Public Service', above n 5, 537.

[10] See P Brazil, 'Some Reflections on the Vienna Convention on the Law of Treaties' (1975) 6 *Federal Law Review* 223.

[11] Acts Interpretation Act 1901 (Cth) s 15AB.

international law issues. They also represented Australia in international organisations like the UN Commission on International Trade Law (UNCITRAL) and the Hague Conference, with departmental lawyers assisting.

The election of the Whitlam Government in December 1972 saw a significant increase in international law work for the Department. The Department grew in size and international law work involved far more officers across different areas of the Department. For instance, Frank Mahony, Deputy Secretary, led Australia's delegation to the conferences that negotiated the 1977 Protocols to the Geneva Conventions on the laws of war. Brazil, as head of the Advisings Division, then Deputy Secretary and later Secretary became the central international law figure in the Department from 1972 until his retirement in 1989. Harders remained as Secretary until 1979 but could not devote much time to international law issues. However, on his retirement in 1979 he was appointed as Legal Adviser in Foreign Affairs, but left that position in 1980.

The Department recruited Gerard Brennan from the University of Melbourne in 1973. He worked largely on the law of the sea issues and was a member of the Australian Delegation to the many Third Law of the Sea Conference sessions from 1974 to 1982. In 1981, he was seconded to the Department of Foreign Affairs as Legal Adviser, a position he held until 1987. In this role, he worked mostly on nuclear safeguards issues.

Within the Department, a wide range of international law work up until 1989 was handled in the Constitutional and International Branch of the Advisings Division (renamed the Counsel 2 branch in the General Counsel Division in 1984). This branch was led by Alfred Body until 1980, then Geoffrey Dabb from 1981 to 1985 (he had previously been a senior legal adviser to Papua New Guinea and lead negotiator for them on the Torres Strait Treaty and the UN Convention on the Law of the Sea). In 1985, I was appointed to the position. I had left the Department in 1981 to take up an appointment at the Australian National University Law School and now returned. In 1989, when the separate OIL was created, I was appointed the initial head, and on my appointment as Chief General Counsel in 1995, I was succeeded by William (Bill) Campbell.

IV. PRE-SECOND WORLD WAR

The establishment of the Commonwealth of Australia in 1901 gave rise to many novel international legal issues. The first Secretary of the Department, Sir Robert Garran, was closely involved in advising successive Attorneys-General on these until his retirement in 1932. In the early days, the Attorney-General himself gave many of the significant opinions. This was certainly the case with Alfred Deakin, who was Attorney-General from 1901 to 1903. When Billy Hughes became Prime Minister as well as Attorney-General in 1915, he was too busy to give detailed attention to legal issues. In 1916, he appointed Garran as Solicitor-General in addition to his position as Secretary.

From the earliest days, the challenge of translating international law into the new Australian constitutional framework received attention. This included issues associated with whether treaties acceded to by individual Australian States, when colonies, continued to apply (they could but without prejudice to the rights of the Commonwealth). Other questions concerned whether Australia could accede for only some or all of the States in relation to treaties that had allowed parts of the British Empire to accede separately (it was not ruled out but as a matter of policy the Commonwealth may not wish to do this).[12]

Another early issue was the proper channel for communications from the British government concerning issues raised with it by foreign governments about the actions of State governments. The *Vondel* case in 1902 involved a complaint by Dutch authorities to the British government about the actions of South Australian officials in relation to Dutch seamen. South Australia argued the British should have approached it directly for a report rather than the Commonwealth.[13] This led to a firm assertion by the Commonwealth that such issues should be raised with it and not directly with the States. Attorney-General Deakin provided an opinion, and the Commonwealth position was supported by Joseph Chamberlain, the Colonial Secretary. It confirmed the responsibility of the new Commonwealth for external affairs. Garran worked closely with Deakin on the opinion by providing a draft that Deakin amended.[14] The position taken in the *Vondel* case was used as a precedent in relation to later incidents.[15] The early years saw the Department involved closely with Deakin in setting the legal foundation for the approach that would be followed subsequently as to the central responsibility of the Commonwealth and not the States for matters of foreign relations.

Early consideration was given to the scope of the external affairs power in the Constitution. Opinions by Attorney-General Deakin in 1901 and Attorney-General Isaacs in 1906 took a broad view in relation to the ability to implement treaties under the power.[16] This view was reaffirmed in later opinions, including by Garran in 1921.[17] Territorial issues also received early attention. In 1902, Deakin considered the extent of the territorial waters of Queensland. He confirmed that the lines defining the islands that formed

[12] *Selected Opinions of Attorneys-General of the Commonwealth of Australia with Opinions of Solicitors-General and the Attorney-General's Department 1901–1950* (Australian Government, 1981) nos 2, 25, 276, 312: www.legalopinions.ags.gov.au (Selected Opinions).

[13] L Zines, 'The Growth of Australian Nationhood and its Effect on the Powers of the Commonwealth' in L Zines (ed), *Commentaries on the Australian Constitution: A Tribute to Geoffrey Sawer* (Sydney, Butterworths, 1977) 16–19; *Selected Opinions*, ibid no 107.

[14] *Selected Opinions*, above n 12, no 107; J La Nauze, *Alfred Deakin* (Melbourne, Melbourne University Press, 1965) 269. See also Zines, above n 13, 16–20.

[15] *Selected Opinions*, above n 12, nos 224, 234, 267, 312.

[16] ibid nos 2 (Deakin), 244 (Isaacs).

[17] ibid nos 312 (Attorney-General Groom), 1041 (Garran).

Queensland did not define the territorial limits of Queensland.[18] He also suggested that in addition to waters within three nautical miles there was a strong case for regarding as within territorial limits, waters between and among closely connected islands or between the mainland and any group of islands forming a natural appendage. This obviously had implications for the waters of the Great Barrier Reef. Territorial issues would arise in other contexts, such as the status of the Coral Sea islands[19] and the acquisition of the Australian Antarctic Territory in 1933.

New legal issues arose from Australia's involvement in the First World War. As Garran relates, he resorted to some extent to the textbook by Pitt Cobbett, the first professor of law in the University of Sydney, which 'was the most practical and useful of all the textbooks'.[20] Interaction with the outside world on international law issues became a central focus as the war ended and the Versailles Peace Conference took place. Garran accompanied Prime Minister and Attorney-General Billy Hughes to meetings of the Imperial War Conference in April 1918 and went on in January 1919 to attend the Versailles Conference as a member of the Australian Division of the British Empire delegation. He served throughout as adviser and general assistant to the Prime Minister. They were well acquainted from Hughes' earlier tenure as Attorney-General starting in 1908. As one writer puts it, Garran 'worked on various drafting committees and provided Hughes with ingenious arguments, especially on reparations, and helped to formulate the mandate provisions of the League of Nations Covenant, including the proposal for the "C" Class mandate'.[21] The creative side of departmental officers was on display.

Among the issues that arose in the years after the First World War were the various Imperial conferences that considered the evolution of the separate components of the British Empire into fully fledged international legal persons. Of note in this regard was the Balfour Statement of 1926 and the Statute of Westminster 1932.[22] Garran attended the 1923 Conference and also the 1930 Conference with the then Attorney-General Frank Brennan. Their attendance at the latter Conference gave them a convenient opportunity to also attend the 1930 Assembly of the League of Nations in Geneva.

Garran's contribution can probably never be fully appreciated, but it was clearly substantial. In the advice and counsel he provided to successive

[18] ibid no 66.

[19] ibid nos 1337, 1640. This issue was not resolved until the Coral Sea Islands Act 1969 (Cth). See H Burmester, 'Outposts of Australia in the Pacific Ocean' (1983) 29 *Australian Journal of Politics & History* 14.

[20] R Garran, *Prosper the Commonwealth* (Sydney, Angus & Robertson, 1958) 220–21.

[21] Parker, above n 7, 623. See Garran's own account in Garran, above n 20, ch XIX. As to Australia's approach at Versailles and in the League see TB Millar, *Australia in Peace and War: External Relations, 1788–1977* (Canberra, Australian National University Press, 1978) 119–32.

[22] See generally A Pert, 'The Development of Australia's International Legal Personality' (2016) 34 *Australian Year Book of International Law* 149; Zines, above n 13, 25–35.

governments, he no doubt reflected the British view of the world shared by Australian governments of the time. However, as Milner has said, he 'had an instinctive sense of Australia's separate national interests, especially in the Pacific region' and he 'acted according to that instinct, with a keen sense of the practical reality of Australian autonomy, but he did so within the imperial framework'.[23] Sir George Knowles, who had acted as Secretary during Garran's lengthy absence overseas with Hughes from 1918 until 1919, was Garran's successor as Secretary and Solicitor-General from 1932 until 1946. He was, prior to that, involved in international law issues as adviser to the Australian delegation to the League of Nations Conference in 1920 and 1924, and Secretary for Australia in the British Empire delegation to the Washington Conference on the Limitation of Armaments from 1921 to 1922.[24]

In the period prior to the Second World War, governments took advantage of the presence in Europe of leading Australian academic lawyers to represent Australia at conferences where direct representation from Canberra was too difficult because of the slow pace of travel across the globe. Thus, in 1927, Professor Harrison Moore from Melbourne, an adviser particularly to federal conservative governments, attended the Rome Conference revising the Bonn Convention on artistic and literary copyright. He also was an Australian delegate to the League of Nations in 1928 and 1929 and played a significant role in the League Commission responsible for revising the rules of the Permanent Court of International Justice.[25]

Professor Kenneth Bailey, also from Melbourne, was another academic whose presence in England enabled Australian legal representation at conferences in Europe. He attended the 1937 International Law Congress in Paris as Australia's representative. In that same year, he was an adviser at the Imperial Conference and a member of Australia's delegation to the League of Nations Assembly. He later became an adviser at the San Francisco Conference in 1945 that drew up the Charter of the United Nations. Evatt, Foreign Minister and Attorney-General from 1941 to 1949, played an important role at the Conference in seeking to protect the interests of smaller states. Bailey was Australia's day-to-day representative in Commission IV, responsible in particular for the Statute of the International Court of Justice.[26] In May 1946, he was appointed Secretary of the Department and Solicitor-General on the retirement of Sir George Knowles.

[23] C Milner, 'Robert Randolph Garran and the Creation of the Australian Commonwealth' in J Beaumont and M Jordan (eds), *Australia and the World: A Festschrift for Neville Meaney* (Sydney, Sydney University Press, 2013) 138.

[24] Whitlam, above n 8.

[25] B Nairn and G Serle (eds), *Australian Dictionary of Biography: Volume 10 1891–1939* (Melbourne, Melbourne University Press, 1971) 573–75.

[26] J Crawford, '"Dreamers of the Day": Australia and the International Court of Justice' (2013) 14 *Melbourne Journal of International Law* 520, 542–43.

V. DEPARTMENTAL ENGAGEMENT WITH THE OUTSIDE WORLD POST-SECOND WORLD WAR

A. The Bailey Era: 1946–72

The appointment of Sir Kenneth Bailey as Secretary in 1946, a position he held until 1964, ensured the Department continued to play a central role in many of the international law issues affecting Australia. His influence remained significant up until his death in 1972. It, therefore, seems appropriate to still call the period up until 1972 the Bailey era. Among the areas where Bailey was particularly active was the newly developing law of the sea. Departmental officers were also heavily involved in the development of new human rights instruments. Other issues that engaged the Department in this period included the negotiation of the Antarctic Treaty, and the status of Nauru and New Guinea. A closer look at the Department's contribution to law of the sea and human rights during the Bailey era follows.

i. Law of the Sea

An area of international law that took major new shape after the Second World War was the law of the sea. Bailey was a central player in shaping Australia's approach to the new issues challenging the traditional freedom of the seas.

Bailey as early as September 1950 wrote to the Departments of External Affairs and Commerce and Agriculture suggesting an interdepartmental committee to consider the ramifications of the US declaration in 1945 of rights over the resources of the continental shelf.[27] This led to Australia claiming a continental shelf in 1953. Australia at this time was in dispute with Japan over pearl fishing and enacted legislation controlling this activity.[28] In 1954, Australia entered into a provisional regime with Japan to regulate pearl fishing while a contemplated case could be brought before the ICJ.[29] Australia made a new declaration under the optional clause to the Statute of the International Court of Justice ensuring that Japan could not unilaterally bring proceedings against Australia before the Court in relation to continental shelf resources including

[27] *Selected Opinions*, above n 12, nos 1906–07.

[28] See DP O'Connell, 'Australian Coastal Jurisdiction' in DP O'Connell (ed), *International Law in Australia* (Sydney, Law Book Co, 1966) 281–83.

[29] Agreement between Australia and Japan on a Provisional Regime to Regulate Pearling by Japanese Nationals pending the Final Decision of the International Court of Justice in the Dispute concerning the Application to Japanese Nationals of the Australian Pearl Fisheries Act 1952–1953 (adopted 24 May 1954, entered into force 24 May 1954) 191 UNTS 125. See E Nyhan, 'A Latent Encounter with the Court: How Australia and Japan Settled a Pearl Fisheries Dispute' (2021) 21 *Melbourne Journal of International Law* 553.

pearl fishing unless a *modus vivendi* had been first agreed pending the final decision of the Court.[30]

Following a detailed study of law of the sea issues by the International Law Commission, the first Law of the Sea Conference was convened in 1958 and a second in 1960. Bailey was leader of Australia's delegation to those Conferences and Chair of the First Committee at the 1958 Conference, responsible for the territorial sea and contiguous zone. Bailey has outlined Australia's active role in the development of the 1958 Conventions, and particularly the definition of sedentary species in the Continental Shelf Convention.[31] Australia's approach to the law of the sea issues in the 1950s and 1960s was very much focused on Australia's particular national interests. Bailey identified these essentially as the economy and the safety and existence of its communications, having regard to Australia being an island state. He also recognised its stake in the interest of the states it was associated with, especially the United Kingdom and United States, and the control of the natural resources of the continental shelf.[32] He also identified a potential interest in Australia's ability to ensure the conservation of the fish stocks around the coast. Australia was well satisfied with the 1958 Conventions and ratified them in 1963.

There continued to be pressure to assert greater rights offshore. The Department provided legal advice as to possible measures to protect the Great Barrier Reef and to exclude foreign fishermen from the Gulf of Carpentaria. However, the government resisted asserting any additional jurisdiction over these areas.[33] It did, however, establish a 12 nautical mile fishing zone in 1967 and asserted a wide view of the extent of the continental shelf out to the edge of the continental margin.[34] Under Bailey's influence, Australia was not inclined to lead the way when it came to maritime jurisdiction issues but rather sought to focus on Australia's particular maritime interests and seek to protect them in a way that would not leave Australia exposed to international criticism by getting ahead of other states. In this, I consider he succeeded.

ii. Human Rights

One of the major new areas of international law that began to receive attention after the Second World War was human rights. Colonel Hodgson, the former Secretary to the Department of External Affairs, represented Australia in the drafting of the Declaration of Human Rights, adopted by the UN

[30] Declaration by Australia Recognizing as Compulsory the Jurisdiction of the International Court of Justice (6 February 1954) 186 UNTS 77.

[31] K Bailey, 'Australia and the Law of the Sea' (1960) 1 *Adelaide Law Review* 1, 10–11. See also K Bailey, 'Australia and the Geneva Conventions on the Law of the Sea' in DP O'Connell (ed), *International Law in Australia* (Sydney, Law Book Co, 1966).

[32] Bailey, 'Australia and the Geneva Conventions', above n 31, 231.

[33] Commonwealth, *Parliamentary Debates*, House of Representatives, 28 November 1968, 3436.

[34] Commonwealth, *Parliamentary Debates*, House of Representatives, 30 October 1970, 3107–09.

General Assembly presided over by Evatt as President in 1948. However, the Attorney-General's Department was heavily involved in Australia's participation in the subsequent work as the two international covenants on human rights were being negotiated. One of the few detailed historical studies into departmental involvement in international legal issues involving Australia looks directly at this issue. Annemarie Devereux in her book *Australia and the Birth of the International Bill of Human Rights 1946–1966*,[35] states that 'two public servants stand out in having exercised particular influence in shaping human rights policies: HFE Whitlam and Kenneth Bailey'.[36] Whitlam had earlier attended the Paris Peace Conference in 1946 and was responsible for putting forward Evatt's proposal for a European Court of Human Rights, an idea that was rejected at that time.[37] He was appointed as consultant on his retirement as Crown Solicitor and represented Australia at the 1950–54 sessions of the Commission on Human Rights, during the key drafting period.[38] In 1954, representation at the Commission was brought back into the fold of the then Department of External Affairs. However, as Devereux reveals there was little adjustment or development of policy as a result. The policy settled by Sir Percy Spender as External Affairs Minister in 1949 on election of the Government of Sir Robert Menzies, and implemented initially by Whitlam, remained largely in place, with little ministerial involvement throughout the 1950s and 1960s.

As a result, as Devereux notes, the input of departmental officers was important in shaping the detail of Australia's position. Devereux states that 'Dr Anstey Wynes, Leslie Lyons and Patrick Brazil … entered stage left or right to play a role in formulating or presenting Australian policies',[39] along with officers of External Affairs. Wynes was legal adviser in External Affairs from 1952 to 1959, Lyons was head of the Advisings branch in the Attorney-General's Department and Brazil was one of his officers, having joined the Department in 1953. Devereux argues 'the history of human rights policy making cannot be separated from the above individuals' personal philosophies, whether shaped by political affiliations or adherence to particular legal precepts'.[40] In her view, for instance, the legal conservatism of HFE Whitlam was 'a secondary factor at play in Australian policies from 1950 onwards'.[41]

This valuable study highlights the impact individual departmental officers can have on the way Australia's international law engagement occurs. However, one should not forget that behind particular legally cautious policies that may have been pursued by particular individuals, there was at the time also a

[35] Devereux, *Australia and the Birth of the International Bill of Rights*, above n 3.

[36] ibid 23.

[37] C Milner, 'Human Rights and International Law' in J Cotton and D Lee (eds), *Australia and the United Nations* (Barton, Department of Foreign Affairs and Trade, 2012).

[38] ibid 347.

[39] Devereux, *Australia and the Birth of the International Bill of Rights*, above n 3, 24.

[40] ibid 24.

[41] ibid 56.

Conservative government (Menzies Government from 1949 to 1966) and a fairly traditional legal profession in general.

Ironically, it was the election of the Whitlam Labor Government in 1972, led by the son of HFE Whitlam, that brought a new and more open approach by Australia to human rights. On 10 December 1972, five days after the Whitlam Government was sworn in, Australia signed the two international covenants – the International Covenant on Civil and Political Rights (ICCPR) and the International Covenant on Economic, Social and Cultural Rights (ICESCR). As Devereux has chronicled, the period from 1966 to 1972 involved much bureaucratic consideration of possible ratification at both federal and state level.[42] The Attorney-General's Department (through Pat Brazil) played a 'conciliatory role in assuaging concerns of other Departments', arguing that the proper course was somewhere in between a 'legalistic approach, that is that in every respect Australia's laws and practices should be in complete accordance with the provisions of the Covenants' and a more liberal approach, 'not worrying that every "t" was crossed and every "I" dotted'.[43] Brazil's pragmatic approach was strongly contested by the Department of Labour and National Service and any impetus to signature was halted by the negative reaction to that idea by William McMahon, the Minister for External Affairs, in June 1970.[44]

B. A Time of Growth: 1972–2000

The election of the Whitlam Government in December 1972 saw a significant increase in international law work for the Department. A closer look at the work of the Department in some particular areas of international law from 1972 to 2000 follows. The momentum throughout that period for interactions by Australia with international law generally continued, with an increased activism evident in periods of Labor governments.[45]

i. International Litigation

Between 1972 and 2000, the Department was involved in a large amount of international litigation, as well as issues that potentially could have involved such litigation.[46] The *Nuclear Tests* case against France was commenced in the ICJ in

[42] A Devereux, 'Australia's Journey to Ratification of the ICESCR and ICCPR' (2019) 36 *Australian Year Book of International Law* 163, 164–69.

[43] ibid 168.

[44] ibid 169.

[45] See J Crawford, 'International Law and Australian Federalism-Past, Present and Future' in B Opeskin and D Rothwell (eds), *International Law and Australian Federalism* (Melbourne, Melbourne University Press, 1977) 328–29.

[46] For a further discussion of Australia's involvement in ICJ litigation, see M Young, 'Australia and the International Court of Justice', ch 8 in this volume.

May 1973.[47] The Attorney-General, Senator Lionel Murphy took an active role, negotiating with French ministers and then appearing during proceedings. The case also heavily involved Solicitor-General Ellicott and his successor, Maurice Byers. Patrick Brazil was seconded full-time from his normal duties as head of the Advisings Division to work on the case and was appointed Agent. This involved challenging work coordinating the large Australian team of lawyers and scientists, including outside counsel of international standing. It also required deft handling of political sensitivities as well as embarrassments like the premature prediction by Prime Minister Whitlam of the likely result at a law dinner in Hobart the night before the decision. As well as Lauterpacht QC and Professor DP O'Connell, luminaries like Professor Roberto Ago and Professor Phillip Jessup were part of the team. Much of the work preparing the case was done overseas, particularly at the provisional measures stage, given the far less developed communications facilities that then existed. Francis Douglas (later KC at the Sydney bar) and myself, junior legal officers at the time, were also heavily involved in the case. This experience meant that when Australia found itself a defendant before the ICJ in the *Nauru Phosphates* case[48] in 1991 to 1992 and the *East Timor* case[49] in 1995, the Department was able to coordinate a team with input from Foreign Affairs and outside counsel. The Solicitor-General, Gavan Griffith was Agent in these cases and I, as head of OIL, was co-Agent. Major international litigation occurred again in 1999, when Australia launched proceedings against Japan under the dispute settlement provisions of the Law of the Sea Convention in relation to the Southern Bluefin Treaty. This is dealt with further in the chapter on the Department from 2000.[50]

As well as these cases, the Department was closely involved in a potential case with the United States over the cancellation by the Fraser Government of export permits for sand mining on Fraser Island.[51] Extensive discussions took place about a possible reference of the dispute to the ICJ but agreement could not be reached. Sir Clarrie Harders worked closely with Elihu Lauterpacht, the then Legal Adviser in Foreign Affairs, on this matter. Another dispute with the United States over the operations of the US carrier NorthWest Airlines led in 1993 to Australia triggering a request for arbitration under the bilateral Air Services Treaty. Australia appointed Patrick Brazil as one of the arbitrators.

[47] *Nuclear Tests (Australia v France)* (Interim Measures) [1973] ICJ Rep 99; *Nuclear Tests (Australia v France)* (Judgment) [1974] ICJ Rep 253.

[48] *Certain Phosphate Lands in Nauru (Nauru v Australia)* (Preliminary Objections) [1992] ICJ Rep 240.

[49] *East Timor (Portugal v Australia)* (Judgment) [1995] ICJ Rep 90.

[50] Campbell, above n 1.

[51] H Burmester, 'Australia and the International Court of Justice' (1996) 17 *Australian Year Book of International Law* 19, 24.

However, the matter was settled before arbitration occurred.[52] Bill Campbell was the main officer handling this matter.

ii. International Trade Law

A major area of international law where the Department was very active from the 1970s onwards was international trade law. Australia was a founding member of UNCITRAL, established by a UN General Assembly resolution in 1966, with its first members being elected in 1968. For many years, the Solicitor-General led Australia's delegation with extensive briefing from departmental officers. Australia joined the Hague Conference on Private International Law and the International Institute for the Unification of Private Law in 1973, as part of the Whitlam Government's desire to expand Australia's engagement with a broader range of international institutions to facilitate international business and other private law transactions across boundaries. This was the start of an eager embrace by many nations, including Australia, of a much more globally integrated world.

Australia's involvement in these organisations has seen adoption of model laws produced by UNCITRAL, for example, the International Commercial Arbitration Act 1974 (Cth) and the Cross-Border Insolvency Act 2008 (Cth). The 1980 Vienna Convention on the International Sale of Goods entered into force for Australia in 1989, after securing the passage of necessary laws by all the States and Territories. A number of Hague Conference Conventions have also been adopted, such as the Convention on International Child Abduction. However, federal complications resulting from the fact that many areas of private commercial law have been States' responsibilities, has often slowed Australian participation. The Department in the 1980s and 1990s worked closely with States and Territories, as well as bodies like the Law Council, to enable wider Australian participation in international commercial law treaties. As Bath has said, Australia's participation in the relevant international bodies has been active, but it has taken a 'cautious' approach in relation to adoption of much of the work of these bodies.[53] In the 1970s to 1990s, this was not for lack of enthusiasm within the Department, but rather reflected government unwillingness, particularly under the Fraser and Howard governments, to seek to implement treaties by Commonwealth legislation if they dealt with matters traditionally the preserve of state law. This was reflected, for instance, in the long delay to Australian ratification of the 1975 International Convention for the Settlement of Investment Disputes. This finally occurred in 1991, despite a draft bill being provided to the States as early as 1976. The ratification occurred with Western

[52] See J Baxter, 'Aviation and Space Law' (1994) 15 *Australian Year Book of International Law* 487, for key diplomatic documents.

[53] V Bath, 'Australia and International Commercial Law' in D Rothwell and E Crawford (eds), *International Law in Australia*, 3rd edn (Pyrmont, Law Book Co, 2017) 353.

Australia being excluded from the designated Australian constituent subdivisions covered by the treaty as Western Australian governments of various complexions continued to resist Australian participation.[54] This was not the only impediment to Australian ratification as the Treasury were not generally supportive of this treaty and this also delayed ratification.

To supplement the work in this area, the Department held annual International Trade Law seminars, commencing in 1974 and continuing until 1997. These seminars brought together private practitioners, academics and government lawyers and provided an opportunity to review the considerable work being done in relation to trade law. In 1984, the eleventh seminar was expanded to be an Asia-Pacific Regional Trade Law Seminar held in association with the Secretary of UNCITRAL and the Asian African Legal Consultative Committee. They ended primarily because of the increasing costs in the face of budget constraints.

Another trade law area where the Department was active was in the extra-territorial application of US anti-trust law. This involved Australia filing amicus briefs in US courts,[55] domestic blocking legislation in 1976 and 1979,[56] and treaties with the United States in 1979 and 1982.[57] This work was largely driven by Senator Peter Durack, Attorney-General in the Fraser Government from 1977 to 1983. In addition, bilateral investment treaties began to be negotiated from 1988, starting with China. Australia is now a party to over 20 such treaties, although, most recently, some have been overtaken by bilateral or multilateral free trade agreements.

The Department's contribution to international trade law was somewhat reduced in the latter part of the 1990s, largely due to financial constraints and changing government priorities. Ultimately, much of the ongoing international trade law work in the Department was handled by OIL. Pat Brazil as Secretary from 1983 to 1989 and Alan Rose, Secretary from 1989 to 1994, were enthusiastic in their support for international trade law endeavours. Other key officers in this area through the 1970s to 1990s included Trevor Bennett, as Head of the Business Law Division and later Deputy Secretary, John Greenwell, Keith Holland and Ian Govey.

[54] Commonwealth, *Parliamentary Debates*, House of Representatives, 28 September 1993, 1280, reproduced in 'International Economic Law' (1994) 15 *Australian Year Book of International Law* 507, 517.

[55] See, eg, Brief of Australia as Amicus Curiae in US Supreme Court in *State of West Virginia ex rel CSR Ltd v Hon A Andrew Macqueen, III, Judge of the Circuit Court of Kanawha County* (January 1994, No 21994).

[56] Foreign Proceedings (Restriction of Certain Evidence) Act 1976 (Cth); Foreign Antitrust Judgments (Restriction of Enforcement) Act 1979 (Cth).

[57] P O'Keefe, 'Australia and International Commercial Law' in KW Ryan (ed), *International Law in Australia*, 2nd edn (Sydney, Law Book Co, 1984) 339–43.

iii. Law of the Sea

The period from 1972 onwards saw the Department closely involved with other departments in law of the sea issues. The Department participated in the work leading to, and then during, the biannual sessions of the Third UN Conference on Law of the Sea. This Conference started in 1974 and continued until 1982 when the UN Convention on the Law of the Sea was adopted. Foreign Affairs led the Australian delegation, but the Department was represented from the beginning. Law of the sea was one of the areas identified in the 1975 division of responsibilities which was shared between the two departments. In reality, law of the sea issues involved a large number of departments as reflected in Australia's delegation to the Conference. For most of the period, the relevant departmental representative was Gerard Brennan, who had been appointed as Consultant to the Department in 1974, principally to work on law of the sea issues.

The Department was also closely involved in maritime boundary delimitation issues. The 1972–73 seabed boundary agreements with Indonesia had delegations led by the Solicitor-General, with Pat Brazil as a key delegation member. In relation to the Torres Strait Treaty, the sensitivities of Queensland meant that the Prime Minister and his Department were closely involved in the negotiations. The negotiations with Papua New Guinea were led by Malcolm Lyon of Foreign Affairs but the Department played a significant role, including determining the location of the 1879 boundary between Queensland and Papua. This enabled the Treaty, when signed in 1978, to recognise Papua New Guinea sovereignty over three small mudflats near the Papuan coast. There were claims at the time that this involved 'researching away' Australian sovereignty over the small mud flats. The relevant research done by Pat Brazil was published at the time that the Foreign Minister made a statement on the matter.[58] One feature of the Torres Strait Treaty is its creative approach to many of the unique boundary issues that arose from populated Australian islands close to the Papua New Guinea coast and the existence of traditional freedom of movement in the area.[59] The departmental representatives, along with many others involved in the negotiations, can justly claim to have made a major contribution to the shape of the final treaty.

The Department's involvement in boundary delimitation continued in the late 1980s with the negotiations for a Joint Development Zone with Indonesia in the Timor Gap. Again, the novel legal issues arising from joint control necessitated considerable legal work by the Department. The many domestic law ramifications of a joint zone were one of the motivations for the creation of a Special, and then Principal, Advisor (International Law) position in the Office of General Counsel in early 1989. This need for additional dedicated international

[58] H Burmester, 'The Torres Strait Treaty: Ocean Boundary Delimitation by Agreement' (1982) 76 *American Journal of International Law* 321, 325.

[59] ibid 321.

law resources in turn led to the small OIL being established at the end of that year, as outlined above.

The Department's key role in law of the sea issues continued throughout the 1990s. Bilateral maritime delimitation negotiations led by Foreign Affairs but involving Attorney-General's Department officers as the principal legal advisers, were held with France, the Solomon Islands, Indonesia and New Zealand. The Department also contributed at this time to workshops in the Pacific on maritime boundaries in an effort to encourage the Pacific Island states to pursue their own maritime delimitation negotiations.

I have elsewhere described Australia's approach at this time to jurisdictional claims under the law of the sea as 'orthodox' and 'not ahead of the field'.[60] It acted incrementally, only extending the territorial sea to 12 nautical miles in 1990, and only asserting an exclusive economic zone in 1994, when it also ratified the Law of the Sea Convention. Australia did, however, take an expansive view of the extent of its continental shelf and the rights associated with it, for example, power to control historic shipwrecks located on the continental shelf.

The Department also worked very closely with relevant departments responsible for fisheries in Australian waters. This led to bilateral fisheries agreements with Japan in 1967 and 1979, and negotiations for regional fisheries arrangements in the South Pacific.[61] The Department was particularly involved from 1999 to 2000 in the dispute with Japan over Southern Bluefin Tuna, which involved the first Annex VII arbitration under the Law of the Sea Convention accompanied by applications for provisional measures before the International Tribunal for Law of the Sea by both Australia and New Zealand. Bill Campbell was Agent for Australia in those cases.[62]

Another area of international law closely related to law of the sea where the Department was at the forefront was environmental law, particularly in relation to the marine environment. The Stockholm Conference on the Human Environment was held in 1972. When Senator Lionel Murphy was appointed Attorney-General at the end of 1972, he took a particular interest in international environmental law. The Department established an environmental group in the Advisings Division, with Ernst Willheim and Robert Muecke as key officers working on both domestic and international environmental law. The impetus at this time saw the Department providing legal input to other areas of government to implement the many new marine pollution Conventions that emerged at the end of the 1960s and early 1970s.

This involvement continued in later years in the International Maritime Organization (IMO) Legal Committee where the Department regularly represented Australia and was an active participant. The Committee developed new

[60] M Landale and H Burmester, 'Australia and Law of the Sea: Offshore Jurisdiction' in Ryan (ed), above n 57, 390–91.

[61] ibid 403.

[62] *Southern Bluefin Tuna (New Zealand v Japan; Australia v Japan)* (Provisional Measures) (1999) 117 ILR 148; *Southern Bluefin Tuna* (Jurisdiction and Admissibility) (2000) 119 ILR 508.

international rules on issues such as the regulation of ship sourced pollution, accidental discharges and liability for damage caused by hazardous and noxious substances carried in ships.[63] Members of the Office who attended these meetings included Ernst Willheim and Dr Rosalie Balkin, who went on to become Legal Adviser at the IMO.

VI. INTERNAL ENGAGEMENT: TRANSLATING INTERNATIONAL LAW INTO DOMESTIC LAW

The other key departmental role throughout has been the domestic interface of international law. This has required the Department to deal with federal–State sensitivities and the domestic implementation of international law obligations. The Department's role in this regard in key areas is now considered.

A. Law of the Sea

In Australia, issues of maritime jurisdiction are inextricably linked to the distribution of power within the federal system between the Commonwealth and the States. This led in the 1960s to significant work on a cooperative offshore petroleum scheme that would enable Australia to exploit the resources of the continental shelf. Sir Clarrie Harders, a future Secretary of the Department worked tirelessly on the issue. This led to the enactment of the Petroleum (Submerged Lands) Act 1967 (Cth).[64] There was, however, pressure to clarify that the Commonwealth rather than the States had jurisdiction over the whole offshore area beyond the low-water mark. An opinion by Attorney-General Tom Hughes and Solicitor-General Ellicott in January 1970 supported that view. Legislation was introduced in Parliament in 1970 but was not passed. It was left to the Whitlam Government to obtain the enactment of the Seas and Submerged Lands Act 1973 (Cth), asserting Commonwealth jurisdiction over the territorial sea and continental shelf.

This led to the High Court case *New South Wales v Commonwealth*, which confirmed Commonwealth jurisdiction beyond the low-water mark.[65] However, the Fraser Government elected in 1975 was prepared not to assert its full entitlements over the States. This led to detailed negotiations with the States over offshore jurisdiction. The Department, involving Brazil and Muecke as the

[63] H Burmester, 'Australia and the Law of the Sea: Protection and Preservation of the Marine Environment' in Ryan (ed), above n 57; S Palassis, 'Marine Pollution and Environmental Law' in R Baird and D Rothwell (eds), *Australian Coastal and Marine Law* (Sydney, Federation Press, 2011) 241–61.

[64] RD Lumb, 'The Offshore Petroleum Agreement and Legislation' (1968) 41 *Australian Law Journal* 453. For the views of Harders as to the changing law of the sea, see C Harders, 'The Sea-Bed' (1969) 3 *Federal Law Review* 202.

[65] *New South Wales v Commonwealth* (1975) 135 CLR 337.

main departmental officers, was intimately involved in the negotiations. They resulted, in 1979, in the Offshore Constitutional Settlement (OCS), which gave title to the seabed and jurisdictional rights over the water column of the then three nautical mile territorial sea to the States. This ensured the continuation of the status quo prior to the decision by the High Court. It also ensured that the Commonwealth could not in the future acquire the rights of the States to the seabed without paying compensation. Their rights were limited to three nautical miles even if the breadth of the territorial sea was extended. There were also detailed arrangements agreed as part of the OCS in relation to shipping, fisheries, crimes at sea, the Great Barrier Reef and the marine environment.[66] Many of the arrangements were complex and involved joint Commonwealth/State bodies. However, they are another example of creative legal work that protected Commonwealth international legal interests within a federal system.

Responsibility for the Seas and Submerged Lands Act 1973 (Cth) was transferred to the Department in 1990 and work was then accelerated to enable Australia to take advantage of the new maritime zones under the United Nations Law of the Sea Convention, which would enter into force in 1994. There were new proclamations in 1994 establishing an exclusive economic zone following the passing of the Maritime Legislation Amendment Act 1994 (Cth). This allowed Australia's maritime zones to conform with the 1982 Convention and enabled Australia to ratify the Convention that year.

One of the issues of critical interest to the States was the drawing of the territorial sea baselines. This meant detailed work with the States and relevant Commonwealth agencies leading to comprehensive baselines being first drawn in 1983. Much of the detailed negotiations with the States took place with State Solicitors-General. One issue of particular concern was the existence of historic bays and a joint report by Commonwealth and South Australian officials was prepared in 1986, with four bays in South Australia being proclaimed as historic bays in 1987.[67]

B. Human Rights

The election of the Whitlam Government with a strong commitment to human rights gave the potential ratification of the two Covenants a new focus. The Attorney-General, Senator Lionel Murphy, introduced the Human Rights Bill 1973, which created a 'political dust storm'.[68] Murphy sought to convince

[66] For a summary, see *Offshore Constitutional Settlement: A Milestone in Cooperative Federalism* (Canberra, Australian Government Publishing Service, 1980); RD Lumb, 'Australian Coastal Jurisdiction' in Ryan (ed), above n 57.

[67] Relevant documents are set out in H Reicher (ed), *Australian International Law: Cases and Materials* (Sydney, Law Book Company Information Services, 1995) 312–16.

[68] Devereux, 'Australia's Journey to Ratification of the ICESCR and ICCPR', above n 42, 173.

Whitlam that ratification should proceed without waiting for passage of the Bill. Whitlam did not agree[69] and the Bill was never enacted. The Department, ever pragmatic, prepared a paper arguing for ratification of the ICESCR, as this was aspirational in nature. This idea was endorsed by Foreign Affairs and their minister obtained the necessary approvals. The intention was to ratify the Covenant on 10 December 1975 and the necessary instruments were ready for this to occur. However, the Whitlam Government was sacked on 11 November 1975. Despite this, as Devereux relates, ratification went ahead during the caretaker period.[70]

The path to ratification of the ICCPR was lengthier, finally occurring in 1980. Devereux has carefully recorded the detailed negotiations between the Commonwealth and the States and the different approaches of federal departments.[71] The Attorney-General's Department was more cautious than Foreign Affairs, recognising that plans by the Attorney-General to establish some form of Human Rights Commission may warrant some pause in consideration of ratification. As well, under the Fraser Government, cooperative federalism meant the views of the States could not be ignored. This led Fraser to approve the appointment by Attorney-General Durack of Peter Bailey as an envoy to negotiate with the States. Ratification finally occurred in August 1980. Significant reservations and understandings accompanied ratification, including a controversial federal reservation.[72] These were largely withdrawn by the Hawke Government in 1984.[73] As Devereux notes, the bureaucratic desire to facilitate ratification may have led to an emphasis on the 'flexible' and 'progressive' nature of the obligations, at the expense of a focus on the need for further remedial action fully to implement the obligations.[74]

Ratification of the Covenants was the beginning of even greater involvement of the Department in international human rights issues. New international Conventions aimed at eliminating other forms of discrimination were concluded and implemented in legislation for which the Department became responsible.

The involvement of the Department in international human rights issues grew significantly with Australia's ratification of the First Optional Protocol to the ICCPR in 1991, allowing individual human rights complaints to the Human Rights Committee. The response to complaints was initially handled within the Human Rights Branch of the Civil Law Division, but from the mid-1990s, it was handled by OIL. The first individual communication involving Australia led the Human Rights Committee to declare that Tasmanian law which criminalised male homosexual conduct was inconsistent with rights protected by the ICCPR.

[69] ibid 173–74.

[70] ibid 175–76.

[71] ibid 175–78.

[72] International Covenant on Civil and Political Rights: Adopted by the General Assembly of the United Nations on 16 December 1966: Ratification (13 August 1980) 1197 UNTS 411. See also G Triggs, 'Australia's Ratification of the International Covenant on Civil and Political Rights: Endorsement or Repudiation' (1982) 31 *International & Comparative Law Quarterly* 278.

[73] See International Covenant on Civil and Political Rights (adopted 16 December 1966, entered into force for Australia 13 November 1980) ATS 1980 23.

[74] Devereux, 'Australia's Journey to Ratification of the ICESCR and ICCPR', above n 42, 190–91.

This led to Commonwealth legislation, namely the Human Rights (Sexual Conduct) Act 1994 (Cth), which overrode the Tasmanian law. Subsequent reactions by various Australian governments to decisions under the Optional Protocol were not so positive and there was, at times, evident resistance to implementation of Human Rights Committee recommendations, particularly in relation to migration decisions. Similarly, concluding observations by various of the treaty bodies after reviewing periodic reports by Australia have often not been welcomed. For instance, the report of the Committee on the Elimination of Racial Discrimination on Australia in 2000, expressing concern about some forms of racial discrimination, led to a joint statement by the Attorney-General and Foreign Minister rejecting the Committee's conclusions.[75]

C. Implementation of Treaties

Apart from implementation of the human rights Covenants, the 1980s and 1990s saw increased attention being given to the implications of Australian participation in treaties more generally. The significance of treaty ratification was brought to the fore by the *Tasmanian Dam* case, involving the World Heritage Convention.[76] The Convention had been ratified by the Whitlam Government.[77] In 1981, Fraser submitted the nomination of various Tasmanian national parks, including the Franklin/Lower Gordon, to the World Heritage Committee. Departmental officers became key participants in the battle at the World Heritage Committee to secure the listing of the Tasmanian parks over the objections of the new Tasmanian government. The Hawke Government elected in 1983 had promised Commonwealth legislation to prevent a dam being built within the parks. This directly led to the *Tasmanian Dam* case.

The case was a defining moment in Australian constitutional law involving the use of an international environmental treaty to preserve an area of world heritage against the wishes of a State. The Department's international lawyers, notably Geoffrey Dabb and Bill Campbell, provided input on issues such as treaty interpretation to the Commonwealth team working on the case. The decision of the High Court clarified the extent of the Commonwealth's external affairs power, the interpretation of treaties in Australian domestic law and the futility of federal clauses in treaties as a way to limit Commonwealth power. Similar issues arose concerning the Lemonthyme and Southern Forests listing which led to another court case.[78]

[75] See generally H Charlesworth and G Triggs, 'Australia and the International Protection of Human Rights' in D Rothwell and E Crawford (eds), *International Law in Australia*, 3rd edn (Pyrmont, Law Book Co, 2017) 131–36.

[76] *Commonwealth v Tasmania* (1983) 158 CLR 1.

[77] Convention for the Protection of the World Cultural and Natural Heritage (adopted 16 November 1972, entered into force 17 December 1975) 1037 UNTS 151.

[78] *Richardson v Forestry Commission* (1988) 164 CLR 261.

In the 1990s there were a number of cases in Australian courts dealing with incorporation of international law into domestic law and treaty implementation, such as the *War Crimes* case[79] and the *Teoh* case.[80] In *Nulyarimma v Thompson*, the Federal Court concluded that genocide as a crime under customary law was not part of Australian law in the absence of statute.[81] In the *War Crimes* case, the Office compiled the international law materials presented to the High Court and I appeared as one of the team of counsel and argued the international law issues.

In the *Teoh* case, I appeared as junior counsel and made submissions that Australia's adherence to a treaty not incorporated into Australian law could never give rise to a legitimate expectation. This submission was not well received by the Court.[82] The Court by majority instead held that ratification of a treaty was 'adequate foundation for a legitimate expectation, absent statutory or executive indications to the contrary, that administrative decision-makers will act in conformity with the Convention'.[83] The expectation was that the person affected was entitled to a hearing before the decision-maker departed from the Convention.[84] This decision was seen as having enormous implications, particularly for migration decisions, with treaties like the Convention on the Rights of the Child being invoked to challenge decisions. This prompted a joint statement by the Attorney-General and Foreign Minister of 10 May 1995, seeking to displace any legitimate expectations from arising as a result of joining a treaty. This was followed by a Bill being introduced into Parliament. This was not passed before the 1996 election. However, the new government (led by John Howard) made a similar statement on 25 February 1997 and introduced a similar Bill. It also was not passed.[85]

The case also brought to the fore wider concerns within Parliament and the community about the processes for Australian acceptance of treaty obligations. There had been procedures agreed between the Commonwealth and the States for consultation on treaties since 1982 and revised in 1983 and 1992.[86] The concern now was more with parliamentary scrutiny. A major report by the Senate Legal and Constitutional References Committee in November 1995 recommended a new parliamentary committee to scrutinise proposed treaty actions.[87] This resulted in the establishment of a Treaties Committee of both

[79] *Polyukhovich v Commonwealth* (1991) 172 CLR 501 (*War Crimes Case*).

[80] *Minister for Immigration and Ethnic Affairs v Teoh* (1995) 183 CLR 273 (*Teoh*).

[81] *Nulyarimma v Thompson* (1999) 165 ALR 621. See H Burmester and S Reye, 'The Place of Customary International Law in Australian Law: Unfinished Business' (2000) 21 *Australian Year Book of International Law* 39; *cf* D Guilfoyle, '*Nulyarimma v Thompson*: Is Genocide a Crime at Common Law in Australia?' (2001) 29 *Federal Law Review* 1.

[82] *Teoh*, above n 80, 291.

[83] ibid.

[84] See M Allars, 'International Law and Administrative Decisions' in B Opeskin and D Rothwell (eds), *International Law and Australian Federalism* (Melbourne, Melbourne University Press, 1977) 234–35.

[85] See, for the detail, ibid 232, 233–37; Senate Legal and Constitutional References Committee, *Trick or Treaty? Commonwealth Power to Make and Implement Treaties* (Report, November 1995) ch 6.

[86] For the text of the 1992 procedures, see Reicher, above n 67, 872–75.

[87] Senate Legal and Constitutional References Committee, above n 85.

Houses of Parliament in 1996. OIL officers were regularly required to appear before the Committee, along with officers from Foreign Affairs, to explain the domestic and international law ramifications of proposed treaty actions. The Office was also closely involved in the preparation of National Interest Analyses that were required to be tabled with every treaty Australia proposed to join. This became a major part of the work of the Office. A review conducted in 1999 concluded the new arrangements were working satisfactorily.[88]

VII. CONCLUSION

It is difficult to generalise, in a study like this, about work done by a government body over a period of 100 years. Nevertheless, what strikes me from my direct observation of the last 30 years of the twentieth century and my research into earlier periods, is the strong creativity of departmental lawyers in seeking positive, principled and workable solutions to new issues. This includes Garran working with Hughes to design 'C' class mandates, Bailey at the First Law of the Sea Conference, and Brazil working on the Offshore Constitutional Settlement or Torres Strait Treaty. The work of the Department on international law was, however, never done in isolation and often involved close collaboration with other areas of government, particularly Foreign Affairs. It was, of course, always constrained by the policies of the government of the day.

While some may point to legal conservatism in parts of the Department's international law contributions, this is not surprising. In part, it reflects the tenor of the governments of the time, but also the inevitable caution that government lawyers can be expected to display. Notwithstanding this, there was no unwillingness to embrace the opportunities and challenges when presented to protect and promote Australia's international law interests. The role of legal adviser to government, particularly in the area of international law, can be challenging. For instance, the resistance of various Australian governments to some of the views of international bodies in relation to Australia's human rights record, made the life of a departmental lawyer giving advice in that area difficult at times. But, as this study shows, being a departmental international lawyer can also involve a significant opportunity to help shape the contribution of Australia to new international legal developments.

Bailey described Garran's advice as 'never conceived in any negative, narrow or pedantic spirit' and as 'always put to constructive ends'.[89] Despite being a participant in the Department's work in the international law area for much of the latter period covered by this study, and hence not entirely objective, it seems to me apposite to apply the same generous description to the work of the Department's international lawyers throughout the twentieth century. Australia was well served in this regard during the period of this study.

[88] Commonwealth of Australia, *Review of the Treaty-Making Process* (Report, August 1999).
[89] K Bailey, 'Sir Robert Garran' (1957) 29 *Australian Quarterly* 9.

ATTORNEY-GENERAL'S DEPARTMENT AND INTERNATIONAL LAW TIMELINE (1900–2000)

1901	Department established. Robert Garran appointed Secretary.
1918–19	Garran accompanies Prime Minister Hughes (who was also Attorney-General) to London and Versailles Peace Conference.
1920–24	George Knowles attends League of Nation Assemblies, 1920, 1924. Secretary for Australia in British Empire delegation to Washington Conference on Limitation of Armaments 1921–22.
1930	Garran attends League of Nations. Australia represented at Codification of International Law Conference by UK delegates. Answers to Questionnaire reflected views of UK.
1932	Knowles appointed Secretary and Solicitor-General.
1937	Kenneth Bailey, then at Oxford, represents Australia at International Law Congress, Paris.
1941	Evatt appointed Attorney-General and Minister for External Affairs.
1943–45	Bailey appointed consultant to Evatt on constitutional and foreign affairs. Attends San Francisco conference in 1945.
1946	Bailey appointed Secretary and Solicitor-General. HFE Whitlam included in Australian delegation to Paris Peace Conference 1946.
1949	Menzies Government elected.
1950–54	HFE Whitlam, former Crown Solicitor, represents Australia at sessions of the Commission on Human Rights.
1950	Bailey raises with Department of External Affairs and Department of Commerce and Agriculture the ramifications of US declaration of rights over the continental shelf.
1953	Continental shelf proclamation.
1954	ICJ Optional clause declaration, including reservation about disputes over pearl fishing.
1957	Geneva Conventions Act 1957 (UK).
1958	Bailey leads Australian delegation to First UN Conference on Law of the Sea. Percy Spender elected to the ICJ.

1960 Bailey leads Australian delegation to Second UN Conference on Law of the Sea.

1964 Bailey retires. Anthony Mason appointed Solicitor-General.

1965–69 Clarrie Harders appointed Deputy Secretary; Patrick Brazil outposted from Department as Legal Adviser to Department of External Affairs. Attends Vienna Conference on the Law of Treaties.

1968 Australia elected to UNCITRAL.

1969 Bailey appointed Special Adviser to Attorney-General's Department and External Affairs.

1970 Clarrie Harders appointed Secretary. Bob Ellicott appointed Solicitor-General.

1972 Gough Whitlam elected as Prime Minister. Lionel Murphy appointed as Attorney-General.

Maritime boundary agreement with Indonesia covering Timor Sea, excluding Timor Gap.

1973 *Nuclear Tests* case commenced against France.

Seas and Submerged Lands Act 1973 (Cth).

Australia joins Hague Conference on International Law and UNIDROIT.

Human Rights Branch established.

1974 Third UN Conference on Law of the Sea commences. Gerard Brennan is departmental representative on delegation.

First International Trade Law Seminar held, then held annually until 1997.

1974–77 Frank Mahony, Deputy Secretary, leads Australian delegation to Diplomatic Conference on Additional Protocol to Geneva Conventions.

1975 *Seas and Submerged Lands* cases.

Division of responsibilities between Attorney-General and Foreign Affairs promulgated by Whitlam. Lauterpacht appointed as Legal Adviser to Foreign Affairs.

Racial Discrimination Act 1975 (Cth); Convention on the Elimination of All Forms of Racial Discrimination ratified. ICESCR ratified by Australia during caretaker period.

Fraser Government elected.

1977	Fraser confirms earlier division of responsibilities between Attorney-General's Department and Foreign Affairs. Peter Durack becomes Attorney-General. Frank Mahony, Deputy Secretary, leads Australian delegation to Conference on International Humanitarian Law, that adopts Additional Protocol I and II to the Geneva Conventions.
1978	Crimes (Foreign Incursions and Recruitment) Act 1978 (Cth). Torres Strait Treaty signed.
1979	Offshore Constitutional Settlement. Foreign Antitrust Judgments (Restriction of Enforcement) Act 1979 (Cth); *Westinghouse* case amicus brief. Clarrie Harders retires as Secretary; appointed as Legal Adviser to Foreign Affairs.
1980	ICCPR ratified.
1981	Gerard Brennan outposted from Attorney-General's Department to Department of Foreign Affairs and Trade as Legal Adviser. Marine Environmental Pollution legislation.
1982	Principles and Procedures for Commonwealth/State Consultation on Treaties.
1983	Hawke Government elected. Gareth Evans is Attorney-General. Patrick Brazil appointed as Secretary to Department. *Tasmanian Dams* case. Australia ratifies Convention on the Elimination of All Forms of Discrimination against Women.
1984	Gavan Griffith appointed Solicitor-General.
1985	Foreign States Immunities Act 1985 (Cth).
1987	Mutual Assistance in Criminal Matters Act 1987 (Cth).
1988	Extradition Act 1988 (Cth). Bilateral Investment Treaty with China.
1989	Nauru institutes proceedings against Australia in the ICJ in relation to phosphate mining. Joint Development Treaty with Indonesia re Timor Gap. Office of International Law (OIL) established. Burmester appointed head.
1990	Territorial Sea extended to 12 nautical miles.

1991	Portugal institutes proceedings against Australia over Timor Gap Treaty.
	Australia ratifies Convention on the Settlement of Investment Disputes between States and Nationals of Other States.
	Australia ratifies First optional Protocol to ICCPR.
	Polyukhovich (*War Crimes*) case.
1992	Abolition of OIL proposed by then Opposition.
	Biodiversity and Climate Change Conventions and Rio Conference.
	Kathy Leigh main legal adviser on Australian delegation.
1994	Australia ratifies UNCLOS.
1995	*Teoh* case; Joint statement by Evans and Lavarch.
	Burmester appointed Chief General Counsel. Bill Campbell appointed head of OIL.
1996	Howard Government elected.
	Joint Parliamentary Committee on Treaties.
	IMO Convention on Liability for Hazardous and Noxious Substances; Rosalie Balkin Australian delegation leader.
1997	International Transfer of Prisoners Act 1997 (Cth).
	Maritime Boundary Treaty with Indonesia.
1998	Rome Statute of the International Criminal Court adopted.
1999–2000	*Southern Bluefin Tuna* case against Japan in ITLOS and Annex VIII arbitral tribunal.
2000	UN Convention against Transnational Organized Crime adopted.

10

Australian Government Practice of International Law in the Twenty-First Century

BILL CAMPBELL

I. INTRODUCTION

THIS CHAPTER, WRITTEN by a former government international lawyer and counsel representing Australia before international courts and tribunals, examines Australian government practice of international law during the first two decades of the twenty-first century and likely trends into the future. It notes an increased Australian public awareness of international law and compares the practice of international law in the twenty-first century with Australian government practice in the latter part of the twentieth century. In so doing, it identifies a marked shift in focus with issues concerning the use of force, terrorism, people movement, global warming and free trade – and the connections between them – coming to the fore. It analyses also the burgeoning involvement of the Australian government in litigation concerning matters of international law in both domestic courts and international courts and tribunals, and the factors contributing to this trend. In the course of discussing these matters, issues of moment that arose in the course of the two decades are highlighted.[1]

II. GOVERNMENT INTERNATIONAL LAW PROVIDERS

It would be appropriate first to consider the current framework surrounding the provision of international law services to the Australian government. Under the

[1] For a discussion of earlier government practice of international law in the Attorney-General's Department, see H Burmester, 'International Law in the Attorney-General's Department: 1901–2000', ch 9 in this volume.

Legal Services Directions 2017 (LSD 2017) made pursuant to section 55ZF of the Judiciary Act 1903 (Cth) and, subject to exceptions outlined below, the provision of international law services to the government is restricted to three 'tied providers': the Attorney-General's Department (AGD); the Australian Government Solicitor (AGS); and the Department of Foreign Affairs and Trade (DFAT). All three tied providers may conduct international litigation and arbitrations on behalf of Australia; provide advice on Australia's or another country's obligations under international law; and provide advice on treaty negotiation and implementation.[2] Only the AGD and AGS are authorised to provide services in relation to 'domestic litigation involving a significant public international law issue' this being 'litigation where a court will or may decide whether Australia or another country has acted in conformity with its international law obligations'.[3]

The Attorney-General may approve the undertaking of tied international law work by another legal service provider subject to conditions that may include settlement of any advice in consultation with a tied provider.[4] The Attorney-General also may approve the performance of such work by the in-house legal area of a Commonwealth agency.[5] Briefing of counsel 'or other legal experts such as academics' on public international law work must be done through the AGD, AGS or DFAT.[6] The role of the Solicitor-General in providing international law services is preserved.[7]

The then Secretary of the AGD, Chris Moraitis, carried out a review of Commonwealth legal services which was released in 2016.[8] As part of that broad review Moraitis concluded that public international law services to government should remain tied to providers within government. He did consider whether there should be a single tied provider within government but concluded that the existing three service providers should be maintained.[9] This, in part, is because the Commonwealth Administrative Arrangements Order[10] allocates AGD responsibility for 'international law' and DFAT responsibility for 'treaties,

[2] Legal Services Directions 2017 (Cth) s 2.1, app A ss 2(a)–(d).

[3] ibid app A s 2(c). The same paragraph also provides: '[l]itigation involving legislation which implements a treaty will not be tied if it merely involves interpretation of that legislation or of the treaty for the purposes of applying that legislation and it does not raise the question whether Australia has complied with its international obligations'. Note 1 to s 2 provides that a 'treaty' includes international instruments of less than treaty status.

[4] ibid app A s 3B.

[5] ibid app A s 5(d). For example, such approval has been given to the Departments of Defence and Home Affairs in relation to defined areas of international law work.

[6] ibid app A s 4.

[7] ibid app A s 5(d).

[8] C Moraitis, *Secretary's Review of Commonwealth Legal Services* (Commonwealth of Australia, 2017). Mr Moraitis was a former DFAT Legal Adviser and thus well placed to consider the international law services aspects of the review.

[9] ibid 66.

[10] Commonwealth of Australia, 'Administrative Arrangements Order' (13 October 2022, effective from 14 October 2022): pmc.gov.au/sites/default/files/resource/download/aao-13-october-2022.pdf.

including trade agreements'. The review also suggested that a more formal consultation mechanism be put in place between the three providers.[11]

The principal area of international law practice within the AGD remains the Office of International Law (OIL), which was established in 1989, and now forms part of the International Law and Human Rights Division. The AGS is now part of the AGD and continues to provide international law services. The principal areas practising international law within DFAT are the Legal Division and the Office of Trade and Investment Law.

III. INCREASED PUBLIC AWARENESS OF INTERNATIONAL LAW

The first two decades of the twenty-first century have seen a pronounced increase in Australian public awareness of international law with a flow-on effect to the practice of international law within the Australian government. Three factors have led to this increased awareness. The first is globalisation and the ever-increasing span of international law, including its coverage of matters previously the principal domain of domestic law, for example in the field of the environment. The second factor is the day-to-day academic media commentary on the international law aspects of the issues of the day. Recent events subject to such commentary include the COVID-19 pandemic,[12] the actions of China in the South China Sea,[13] and the Trilateral Security Partnership between Australia, the United Kingdom and the United States (AUKUS).[14]

The third catalyst for increased public awareness of international law is the prominence of a number of issues arising during the period under discussion that engaged international law. Those issues include the maritime boundary dispute between Australia and Timor-Leste which spanned almost the whole of those two decades; Australia's military engagements in Iraq, Timor-Leste, Afghanistan and Syria as well as the Regional Assistance Mission to the Solomon Islands; irregular migration, otherwise known as 'stopping the boats'[15]

[11] Moraitis, above n 8, 66: '[t]he Review recommends that the Directions require all providers of public international law (whether tied provider or an entity providing advice under exemption) to notify OIL of all requests for advice provided in relation to public international law. In addition, arrangements should be clarified to promote better collaboration between providers. For example, allowing OIL to identify trends or overlap in work will ensure issues are handled consistently and duplication of effort is avoided. This would be supported by a formalised approach to collaboration between tied service providers (for example through regular meetings)'.

[12] eg, Australian National University, 'International Law and COVID-19': law.anu.edu.au/research/essay/covid-19-international-law.

[13] eg, Donald R Rothwell, 'Laying Down the Law in the South China Sea' (*East Asia Forum*, 30 July 2020): eastasiaforum.org/2020/07/30/laying-down-the-law-in-the-south-china-sea/.

[14] See, eg, Monique Cormier, 'The International Implications of AUKUS: A Poor Precedent for Non-Proliferation' (*ANZSIL Perspective*, December 2021): anzsilperspective.com/the-international-legal-implications-of-aukus-a-poor-precedent-for-non-proliferation/.

[15] 'Stopping the boats' is a euphemism adopted by Coalition governments for the interception of, and in some cases turning back, foreign vessels carrying persons whose entry into Australia would be unlawful under Australian law.

and offshore processing; and international litigation,[16] including the *Whaling in the Antarctic* case[17] and the *Documents* case[18] at the International Court of Justice (ICJ), as well as the tobacco plain packaging litigation before an arbitral tribunal,[19] a World Trade Organization (WTO) dispute settlement panel,[20] and the WTO Appellate Body.[21] Other recent examples include the COVID-19 pandemic, immunities of foreign dignitaries such as the then Foreign Minister of Myanmar, Aung San Suu Kyi,[22] the downing of Malaysian Airlines flight MH17, and the invasion of Ukraine by the Russian Federation. All these issues have been the subject of consideration, advice or other action by Australian government international lawyers.

IV. SIMILARITIES AND DIFFERENCES BETWEEN TWENTIETH AND TWENTY-FIRST CENTURY AUSTRALIAN GOVERNMENT PRACTICE OF INTERNATIONAL LAW

It is useful to consider the similarities and differences between the practice of international law in the federal government in the last two decades of the twentieth century as opposed to the first two decades or so of the twenty-first century – those four decades also being the sum of my experience as a government international lawyer.

A. Similarities

First, the primary role of a government adviser on international law remains that of assisting the government of the day to achieve its policies and goals within the limits of international law. Of course, those limits are subject to

[16] Australia's participation in international litigation in this period is covered in more detail below under the heading 'International Dispute Settlement'.

[17] *Whaling in the Antarctic (Australia v Japan: New Zealand Intervening)* (Judgment) [2014] ICJ Rep 226.

[18] *Questions Relating to the Seizure and Detention of Certain Documents and Data (Timor-Leste v Australia)* (Provisional Measures, Order of 3 March 2014) [2014] ICJ Rep 147 (*Documents* case).

[19] *Philip Morris Asia Limited v Commonwealth of Australia* (Award on Jurisdiction and Admissibility) (Permanent Court of Arbitration, Case No 2012-12, 17 December 2015) (*Philip Morris Asia Arbitration*).

[20] WTO, Australia: Certain Measures Concerning Trademarks, Geographical Indications and Other Plain Packaging Requirements Applicable to Tobacco Products and Packaging – Reports of the Panels (28 June 2018) WT/DS435/R; WT/DS441/R; WT/DS458/R; WT/DS467/R.

[21] ibid. WTO, Australia: Certain Measures Concerning Trademarks, Geographical Indications and Other Plain Packaging Requirements Applicable to Tobacco Products and Packaging – Reports of the Appellate Body (9 June 2020) WT/DS435/AB/R; WT/DS441/AB/R.

[22] The immunity of Aung San Suu Kyi under international law was canvassed before the High Court in *Taylor v A-G (Cth)* (2019) 268 CLR 224. The Court did not need to consider the issue as it found that the plaintiff could not bring a private criminal prosecution for the crime against humanity incorporated in s 268.11 of the Criminal Code Act 1995 (Cth).

continuous change as international law develops to meet new global challenges – and it is important that the legal advisers to the government keep abreast of those developments. What may be considered unlawful even at the start of the twenty-first century may as a result of a treaty or development of customary international law be lawful today. For example, many countries including Australia hold to the view that it is now lawful to use force against non-state actors in the territory of another state that does not consent to that use of force provided certain criteria, including the 'unwilling and unable principle', are met[23] – this being one of the so-called Bethlehem Principles.[24] In line with the advice it received from its international lawyers, the Australian government adhered to this view and then Attorney-General George Brandis published an opinion piece in the media to that effect.[25] While many do not accept such a principle exists in customary international law,[26] there was an undoubted need for international law to develop to stop non-state actors from hiding behind the territorial shield of the sovereign state from which they are launching attacks on other states.

Looking to the future, yet another area of development for consideration by Australia is humanitarian intervention, this being the legal basis relied upon by the United Kingdom (UK) in a 2018 statement concerning its armed intervention in Syria in response to the use of chlorine on civilian populations within Syria.[27] There is, as yet, no official Australian government position on the doctrine of humanitarian intervention, in marked contrast to its continuing support for the responsibility

[23] In terms of recent state practice, application of that criterion is reflected in the notifications to the UN Security Council by several countries, including Australia, under Art 51 of the Charter of the United Nations in relation to their actions against ISIL in Syria in the period 2014–15. See notifications to the President of the Security Council from Australia (9 September 2015, UN Doc S/2015/693); the United States (23 September 2014, UN Doc S/2014/695); and Canada (31 March 2015, UN Doc S/2015/221). Notifications of similar effect were made by other states including Turkey, Germany and Belgium. Earlier supporting state practice is catalogued in Elena Chachko and Ashley Deeks, 'Which States Support the "Unwilling or Unable" Test?' (*Lawfare*, 10 October 2016): www.lawfaremedia.org/article/which-states-support-unwilling-and-unable-test.

[24] 'Principles Relevant to the Scope of a State's Right of Self-Defense against an Imminent or Actual Armed Attack by Nonstate Actors' in D Bethlehem, 'Self-Defense Against an Imminent or Actual Armed Attack by Nonstate Actors' (2012) 106 *American Journal of International Law* 770, 775.

[25] George Brandis, 'It's a War of Self-Defence' *The Australian* (Surry Hills, 10 September 2015) 12. This followed earlier public adherence to that view expressed by the UK Attorney General, J Wright, 'The Modern Law of Self-Defence' (Speech at International Institute for Strategic Studies, 11 January 2017).

[26] See J Brunnée and SJ Toope, 'Self-Defence Against Non-State Actors: Are Powerful State Actors Willing But Unable to Change International Law?' (2018) 67 *International & Comparative Law Quarterly* 263, 267; Kevin Jon Heller, 'The Absence of Practice Supporting the "Unwilling or Unable" Test' (*Opinio Juris*, 17 February 2015): opiniojuris.org/2015/02/17/unable-unwilling-test-unstoppable-scholarly-imagination/. For earlier criticisms, see, eg, D Tladi, 'The Nonconsenting Innocent State: The Problem with Bethlehem's Principle 12' (2013) 107 *American Journal of International Law* 570.

[27] Prime Minister's Office, *Syria Action: UK Government Legal Position* (Policy Paper, 14 April 2018): www.gov.uk/government/publications/syria-action-uk-government-legal-position/syria-action-uk-government-legal-position.

to protect (R2P).[28] R2P, unlike humanitarian intervention, relies upon the adoption of a Chapter VII Security Council resolution to permit the use of force for humanitarian purposes. However, states cannot stand by and allow humanitarian crises such as genocide to unfold simply because of the use of the veto in the Security Council as the 2018 statement of the United Kingdom makes clear.[29]

Humanitarian intervention is an example of an issue that could, with the imprimatur of the government, be progressed proactively by its international law advisers and be the subject of a publicly expressed government position as was the case in relation to the support expressed in 2015 by the then Australian government for the unwilling or unable principle,[30] and its view on the scope of imminence as a precondition to an armed attack.[31] The absence of a public Australian government position on humanitarian intervention flows from a combination of factors: first, Australia's close association with the R2P principle; secondly, the perceived absence of a pressing need to take a position; and, in the past, lack of a consensus view among legal advisers to the government.

This example does raise a question about the extent to which international legal advisers to Australian governments can be part of the public debate on live questions of international law in addition to the responsible members of the government. Such participation by a legal adviser involves matters of timing, the forum involved and judgement. As to timing, it is far easier for legal advisers to involve themselves in public debate on a controversial legal issue if the government of the day has already taken a position on the issue. Even so, a legal adviser may feel it is inappropriate to do so, for example if they do not agree with the position taken by the government or their involvement in the debate would be counterproductive. These are matters of judgement. Participation will also depend on the forum. It is easier for a legal adviser to proffer views on live issues of international law faced by the then government in a limited academic forum as opposed to a public meeting. In either case, the application of Chatham House rules provides little or no comfort.[32] A good yardstick is if a legal adviser

[28] M Bliss, 'Responsibility to Protect (R2P)' (National Statement, 10 June 2015): www.dfat.gov.au/international-relations/international-organisations/un/unsc-2013-2014/national-statements/Pages/responsibility-to-protect-r2p.

[29] Many commentators are sceptical of the notion that humanitarian intervention forms part of existing customary international law. Some of those commentators do recognise the need to intervene to alleviate dire humanitarian circumstances such as those in Rwanda in 1994 but would prefer to characterise the force used in such an intervention as 'illegal but legitimate': see Marko Milanovic, 'Illegal But Legitimate?' (*EJIL:Talk!*, 10 April 2017): www.ejiltalk.org/illegal-but-legitimate/. Roberts, justifiably, is critical of the illegal but legitimate justification: Anthea Roberts, 'Syrian Strikes: A Singular Exception or a Pattern and a Precedent?' (*EJIL:Talk!*, 10 April 2017): www.ejiltalk.org/syrian-strikes-a-singular-exception-or-a-pattern-and-a-precedent/; A Roberts, 'Legality vs Legitimacy: Can Uses of Force Be Illegal But Justified?' in P Alston and E Macdonald (eds), *Human Rights, Intervention and the Use of Force* (Oxford, Oxford University Press, 2008).

[30] See above, n 25.

[31] George Brandis, 'The Right of Self-Defence Against Imminent Armed Attack in International Law' (*EJIL-Talk!*, 25 May 2017): www.ejiltalk.org/the-right-of-self-defence-against-imminent-armed-attack-in-international-law/.

[32] Participants are free to use the information received in a meeting, but neither the identity nor the affiliation of the speaker(s), nor that of any other participant, may be revealed.

is not willing to address an issue of international law before a parliamentary committee, they should not do so outside government circles.

Yet, another constant for government advisers on international law is that of reminding successive governments that they must have regard to, and abide by, two bodies of law – domestic law and international law – and in some cases the law of the third country. It is trite to say that although a particular action may be permitted under domestic law, it may not be permissible as a matter of international law – and vice versa. Both bodies of law need to be complied with. For example, while it may be permissible under domestic law (in the form of the Maritime Powers Act 2013 (Cth)) for Australia to return vessels (and those on board) that have unlawfully entered Australian waters to their country of departure,[33] this cannot be done unless Australia's obligations under international law are also met.[34] Since the reinstitution of the policy of vessel turn-back in 2013, Australia has refrained from returning certain persons on board vessels illegally entering Australian waters to the country of departure, where to do so would possibly place Australia in breach of its non-refoulement obligations – the non-return of West Papuans being a case in point.[35]

While it is possible to incorporate the relevant international law obligations into domestic law, thus ensuring compliance with both levels of law, there is a growing reluctance on the part of successive Australian governments to do so. This is primarily because governments wish to retain their role in determining questions of Australia's compliance with international law rather than ceding such questions to the courts, despite the increasing expertise of the courts in international law as evidenced by the decision of the Full Federal Court in *Ure v Commonwealth*.[36] Gone are the days of incorporating a provision in legislation such as section 65 of the Great Barrier Reef Marine Park Act 1975 (Cth), which states, in part: '[t]his Act has effect subject to the obligations of Australia under international law'. Indeed, provisions of opposite effect were inserted into

[33] Known colloquially as 'vessel turn-back'. For further perspectives on Australia's policy, see J Silverstein, 'Child Refugees, Child Rights: Sidestepping International Law in Australian Policy-Making', ch 12 in this volume.

[34] Those obligations include the initial interception of the relevant vessel being consistent with the United Nations Convention on the Law of the Sea (adopted 10 December 1982, entered into force 16 November 1994) 1833 UNTS 3, the consent or acquiescence to the return by both the flag state and the state to which it is being returned (usually the same state) and compliance with human rights obligations, including non-refoulement obligations. Rothwell and Stephens are reported as casting doubt over Australia's reliance on the doctrine of acquiescence to return vessels: ABC Fact Check, 'Is It Illegal to Turn Back Boats in International Waters to Indonesia?' (*ABC News*, 17 November 2014). The same view is expressed by the Andrew & Renata Kaldor Centre for International Refugee Law, 'Turning Back Boats' (Factsheet, April 2019). However, in the same ABC Fact Check, the former Attorney-General Philip Ruddock is reported as noting: 'legal advice was sought from the international division of the Attorney-General's Department that all steps taken were lawful'.

[35] 'Papuans Granted Temporary Visas' *ABC News* (23 March 2006). The West Papuans in question were granted asylum on the basis that they had a well-founded fear of persecution by reason of their pro-independence views.

[36] *Ure v Commonwealth* (2016) 236 FCR 458. See below n 95 and accompanying text.

the Maritime Powers Act 2013 (Cth) in 2014. These provide that the exercise of certain powers under the Act will not be invalid 'because of a failure to consider Australia's international obligations … or a defective consideration of Australia's international obligations or because the exercise of that power is inconsistent with Australia's international obligations'.[37] It would come as no surprise that international lawyers advising the government did not support those provisions not the least because they imply that a government may be prepared to exercise the relevant powers under the Act in a manner inconsistent with Australia's international obligations. Surprisingly, these provisions were not subject to the same degree of public and political criticism as the original provisions of the United Kingdom Internal Market Bill 2020 that would have enabled the disabling of international obligations by regulation.[38] As a result of that criticism, the offending UK provisions were removed[39] prior to the enactment of the Bill into law.[40]

An important aspect of assisting governments to achieve their goals remains the necessity to advise governments in a clear and timely way on urgent and/or developing issues or when actions they propose taking would place Australia in breach of its international obligations. In this respect, legal advisers to the Australian government have been proactive and have not waited to be asked if they considered it important for the government to have legal advice on an issue confronting it.[41]

Such issues may arise suddenly thus giving rise to a need for immediate advice. Within hours of the events in the United States of 11 September 2001, the Government of Prime Minister John Howard was provided with advice on the international law implications of those events both in terms of consequences and possible responses. Matters covered in the advice prepared in less than two hours included the application of international law to terrorist groups and Australia's obligations under the Australian New Zealand and United States Security Treaty (the ANZUS Treaty), particularly the obligation to provide assistance in the event of an armed attack on the United States.[42]

[37] Maritime Powers Act 2013 (Cth) ss 22A, 75A. Also, s 40(2) provides that one condition for the exercise of powers under that Act in the territorial, internal or archipelagic waters of another country is that a maritime officer or the Minister 'consider' the passage of the relevant vessel through those waters to be in accordance with the 1982 Convention. Section 40(3) provides that an exercise of power under s 40(2) 'is not invalid because of a defective consideration of the Convention'.

[38] eg, cl 45(3)(e) of the Bill provided: 'rights, powers, liabilities, obligations, restrictions, remedies and procedures that would otherwise apply in relation to aid, as a result of relevant international or domestic law, not to be recognised, available, enforced, allowed or followed'.

[39] Chris Morris, 'Brexit: Why Is the Internal Market Bill Controversial?' (*BBC News*, 9 December 2020): www.bbc.com/news/54088596.

[40] United Kingdom Internal Market Act 2020 (UK).

[41] Sir Michael Wood, former Legal Adviser to the UK Foreign and Commonwealth Office has described this essential element of practice as follows: '[c]ertainly it has always been the culture in the Foreign Office that the lawyers don't wait to be asked. They give advice if they see something that needs some legal input, often in telegrams, whatever, even in the newspapers. They send a minute. The Americans sometimes call that "aggressive" legal advising. But we don't wait to be asked': Evidence of Sir Michael Wood to the Chilcott Inquiry (6 January 2010) 7–8.

[42] Security Treaty between Australia, New Zealand and the United States of America [ANZUS] (adopted 1 September 1951, entered into force 29 April 1952) ATS 1952 2.

Another more recent instance of international law advisers responding to an urgent issue concerned the shooting down of Malaysian Airlines flight MH17 on 17 July 2014 over eastern Ukraine killing 298 passengers, 38 of whom were Australian nationals or permanent residents. Australian government officials met early in the morning of 18 July 2014 just hours after the attack to coordinate Australia's response,[43] a response that would require significant international law input. Lawyers from several agencies including the AGD, DFAT, the Australian Federal Police and the Department of Defence commenced the negotiation of seven separate international instruments to support the deployment of Australian personnel to Ukraine and the Netherlands. The purpose of that deployment was to assist in the recovery, identification and repatriation of victims; the establishment of an aircraft accident investigation; and the institution of a criminal investigation and the collection of evidence for use in a future prosecution.[44] The first instrument was signed on 24 July 2014 just seven days after the downing.[45] These seven instruments have continued to provide an underpinning to the ongoing investigations and criminal prosecutions.

The downing of Flight MH17 is also an example of a matter requiring initial urgent international law input transitioning into one requiring a longer-term international law contribution. After the initial urgent phase, Australia and the Netherlands informed Russia by third person note[46] that they held it accountable under international law for the downing of MH17 on the basis that Russia was responsible for the deployment of the Buk missile installation used to down the aircraft.[47] Trilateral consultations were held on that matter, which the Russian Federation brought to an abrupt end.[48] At an earlier point in time, the Dutch government had indicated, 'a possible next step is to present the case to an international court or organisation for their judgment'.[49] On 14 March 2022, Australia and the Netherlands commenced proceedings

[43] S Ierino, J Reid and A Sheehan, 'The International Law Framework Underpinning the Australian Government's Response to the Downing of MH17' (2015) 33 *Australian Year Book of International Law* 46.

[44] ibid.

[45] ibid 51: this recorded Ukraine's consent to Australia deploying its civilian and military personnel to Ukraine to assist in the search for, and the recovery of, remains as well as the conduct of the air accident and criminal investigations.

[46] Letter from the Minister of Foreign Affairs Stef Blok on the State Responsibility of Russia in the Matter of MH17 (31 May 2018): www.government.nl/documents/letters/2018/05/31/attachment-letter-to-parliament---copy-of-note-verbale.

[47] In this respect, Art 3*bis* of the Convention on International Civil Aviation obliges every state to refrain from resorting to the use of weapons against civilian aircraft: Convention on International Civil Aviation (adopted 7 December 1944, entered into force 4 April 1947) 15 UNTS 295 (Chicago Convention).

[48] 'Russia Withdraws from MH17 Talks with Netherlands and Australia' (*ABC News*, 15 October 2020): www.abc.net.au/news/2020-10-15/russia-withdraws-from-mh17-talks-with-australia-netherlands/12773036.

[49] Government of the Netherlands, 'MH17: The Netherlands and Australia Hold Russia Responsible' (25 May 2018): www.government.nl/latest/news/2018/05/25/mh17-the-netherlands-and-australia-hold-russia-responsible.

against the Russian Federation under Article 84 of the 1944 Convention on International Civil Aviation[50] alleging a breach of Article 3*bis* of the Convention which obliges Member States to 'refrain from resorting to the use of weapons against civil aircraft in flight'. The relevant dispute settlement body is the Council of the International Civil Aviation Organization (ICAO) consisting of 36 Member States.[51] An appeal lies from an ICAO Council decision on a dispute to the ICJ.[52]

An evolving issue also may be the catalyst for the provision of proactive international legal advice to the government. A somewhat controversial example is the Campbell and Moraitis advice of 12 March 2003 concluding that Australia had a legal basis under international law for the use of force in Iraq.[53] That advice was not requested by the Howard Government. It was prepared and given to that government in light of the rapidly developing events concerning Iraq. The advice was the subject of trenchant criticism based not only upon legal analysis of its substantive content but also, less convincingly, on its alleged brevity, the level at which it was given (in fact, the then most senior international lawyers in the AGD and DFAT) and other irrelevant points such as being titled 'Memorandum of Advice' as opposed to 'Legal Opinion'.[54] Such criticisms were made without knowledge of, among other matters, the actual process for developing the advice and by whom it was cleared before being given formally to the government.

A further catalyst for proactive advice is where a government-proposed course of action or position raises international law concerns. While it is open to governments to take a different view of Australia's international obligations from that of its legal advisers, it is very important that they be apprised of the views held

[50] Chicago Convention, above n 47.

[51] The Russian Federation filed preliminary objections challenging the jurisdiction of the ICAO Council to hear the dispute. Following an oral hearing before the ICAO Council on 17 March 2023, these objections were rejected in their entirety: P Wong, Minister for Foreign Affairs and M Dreyfus, Attorney-General (Cth), 'ICAO Council Decision on Jurisdiction in MH17 Legal Proceedings' (Joint Media Release, 18 March 2023).

[52] This appeal mechanism was the subject of a recent decision of the ICJ in *Appeal Relating to the Jurisdiction of the ICAO Council under Article 84 of the Convention on International Civil Aviation* (*Bahrain, Egypt, Saudi Arabia and United Arab Emirates v Qatar*) (Judgment) [2020] ICJ Rep 81.

[53] See 'Memorandum of Advice to the Commonwealth Government on the Use of Force against Iraq' (2003) 4 *Melbourne Journal of International Law* 178. This is one of the few examples of a legal advice to the government being tabled in the Commonwealth Parliament: Commonwealth, *Votes and Proceedings*, House of Representatives, 18 March 2003, 788 (John Howard, Prime Minister). The same part of the *Melbourne Journal of International Law* contains advices to the then Opposition Leader Simon Crean by George Williams and Devika Hovell (at 185) and by Grant Niemann (at 191). Both advices concluded that there was no legal basis for the use of force by Australia in Iraq.

[54] The following short example encapsulates the tone of such unconvincing procedural criticism: 'the Government has been content to table a mere "memorandum" of assertion, signed off at the departmental level of First Assistant Secretaries': 'This War Is Illegal: Howard's Last Top Law Man' *Sydney Morning Herald* (21 March 2003). See also Gabrielle Appleby, 'The Political Imperative for a Legal War' (*UNSW Newsroom*, 13 July 2016): newsroom.unsw.edu.au/news/business-law/political-imperative-legal-war.

by those advisers. A failure to provide such advice on the basis that it would not be welcomed by the government of the day would be inconsistent with the values of the Australian Public Service (APS) as defined in statute.[55] Similarly, a direction from the government aimed at stifling the provision of advice on matters of international law[56] would seem inconsistent with the ministerial standards adopted by the government in 2022.[57] Early input by government international lawyers into the policy and decision-making process can assist in avoiding such circumstances.

Yet, another constant has been the continuing contribution of Australia to the development of international law in both its substantive and procedural aspects. By way of example, Australia made significant contributions to the negotiation of the Arms Trade Treaty,[58] the Convention on Cluster Munitions,[59] the Paris Agreement,[60]

[55] Public Service Act 1999 (Cth) s 10(5): '[t]he APS is apolitical and provides the Government with advice that is frank, honest, timely and based on the best available evidence'.

[56] eg, the Legal Services Amendment (Solicitor-General Opinions) Direction 2016 (Cth) had the effect of preventing the Solicitor-General from providing legal advice, including on matters of international law, without the consent of the Attorney-General. Following criticism, the amendment was repealed in late 2016.

[57] The Code of Conduct for Ministers (Australian Government, June 2022) para 4.2 provides: '[m]inisters *must not encourage or induce other public officials, including public servants*, by their decisions, directions or conduct in office to breach the law, or *to fail to comply with the relevant code of ethical conduct applicable to them in their official capacity*' (emphasis added). Thus, there is a link between these Ministerial Standards and the APS Values: see above n 55.

[58] Arms Trade Treaty (adopted 2 April 2013, entered into force 24 December 2014) 3013 UNTS 269 – Australia was one of the seven co-authors of the original 2006 General Assembly Resolution calling for an arms trade treaty culminating in its adoption on 2 April 2013: J Bishop, 'Australia Ratifies the Arms Trade Treaty' (Media Release, 3 June 2014). The final text of the treaty was the product of a Final Arms Trade Treaty Conference chaired by Australia's then Ambassador to the UN in Geneva, Peter Woolcott.

[59] Convention on Cluster Munitions (adopted 30 May 2008, entered into force 1 August 2010) 2688 UNTS 39 – Australia played an active role in negotiating the Convention throughout the Oslo Process, including on the question of interoperability. At the time of the passage of the domestic implementing legislation in 2011, the then government noted that Australia 'has worked closely with international partners to achieve the strongest possible ban on these weapons': Senate Foreign Affairs, Defence and Trade Legislation Committee, *Criminal Code Amendment (Cluster Munitions Prohibition) Bill 2010 [Provisions]* (March 2011) para 1.12.

[60] Paris Agreement (adopted 12 December 2015, entered into force 4 November 2016) 3156 UNTS 79 – Australia was chair of the 'Umbrella Group' (Australia, Belarus, Canada, Iceland, Israel, Japan, New Zealand, Kazakhstan, Norway, the Russian Federation, Ukraine and the United States), one the major groupings of countries that played a role in the negotiation of the Paris Agreement in 2015, and the package of rules for its implementation at Katowice, Poland in 2018. The implementation of Australia's commitments under the Paris Agreement has been dogged by controversy particularly over its proposed use of 'carry-over' credits derived from over-meeting its commitments under the Kyoto Protocol to the United Nations Framework Convention on Climate Change (adopted 11 December 1997, entered into force 16 February 2005) 2303 UNTS 162. See, eg, James Fernyhough, 'Australia "Cheating" on Paris, Says Former UN Climate Chief' *Australian Financial Review* (9 March 2020). The government has not released any legal advice it may have on the issue: Mike Foley, 'Kyoto Carry-Over Credits "Baseless" in International Law, Experts Say' *Sydney Morning Herald* (4 March 2020). In December 2020, Prime Minister Morrison flagged the possibility that Australia would not seek to rely on carry-over credits: Bevan Shields and David Crowe, 'Australia Drops Plan to Use Kyoto Credits to Meet Paris Climate Target' *Sydney Morning Herald* (5 December 2020).

the Convention on Biodiversity Beyond National Jurisdiction[61] and international and regional fisheries treaties.[62]

Over the past two decades, Australia has negotiated five multilateral free trade agreements, four of which are in force:[63] the Comprehensive and Progressive Agreement for Trans-Pacific Partnership,[64] Agreement Establishing the ASEAN–Australia–New Zealand Free Trade Area,[65] Pacific Agreement on Closer Economic Relations Plus (PACER Plus)[66] and the Regional Comprehensive Economic Partnership (RCEP)[67] Since 2000, it also has negotiated 13 bilateral free trade agreements with important trading partners all of which have entered into force.[68] The prioritisation of free trade facilitation by recent Australian governments on a bipartisan basis has led to an increased allocation of international law resources to that task.

In 2004, Australia was the third country to make a submission to Commission on the Limits of the Continental Shelf (CLCS) seeking the Commission's recommendations on the outer limits of Australia's extended continental shelf (ECS) beyond 200 nautical miles from its territorial sea baseline.[69] On 9 April 2008, the CLCS recommended an Australian ECS of 2.65 million square kilometres

[61] 'Agreement under the United Nations Convention on the Law of the Sea on the conservation and sustainable use of marine biological diversity beyond national jurisdiction', UN GAOR 5th session (19 June 2023) UN Doc A/CONF.232/2023/4).

[62] eg, Agreement on Port State Measures to Prevent, Deter and Eliminate Illegal, Unreported and Unregulated Fishing (adopted 22 November 2009, entered into force 5 June 2016) 3161 UNTS; Convention on the Conservation and Management of High Seas Fishery Resources in the South Pacific Ocean (adopted 14 November 2009, entered into force 24 August 2012) 2899 UNTS 211.

[63] The Trans-Pacific Partnership (TPP) was agreed on 5 October 2015 but has not entered into force.

[64] Comprehensive and Progressive Agreement for Trans-Pacific Partnership (adopted 8 March 2019, entered into force 30 December 2018) 3346 UNTS.

[65] Agreement Establishing the ASEAN-Australia-New Zealand Free Trade Area (adopted 27 February 2009, entered into force 1 January 2010) 2672 UNTS 3; First Protocol to Amend the Agreement Establishing the ASEAN–Australia–New Zealand Free Trade Area (adopted 26 August 2014, entered into force 1 October 2015) ATS 2015 14; Transposition of Annex 2 (Product Specific Rules) of the Agreement Establishing the ASEAN–Australia–New Zealand Free Trade Area (entered into force 1 January 2019) ATS 2019 3.

[66] Pacific Agreement on Closer Economic Relations Plus (PACER Plus) (adopted 14 June 2017, entered into force 13 December 2020) ATS 2020 12.

[67] Regional Comprehensive Economic Partnership Agreement (adopted 15 November 2020, entered into force 1 January 2022) ATS 2022 1.

[68] Singapore, the United States, Thailand, Chile, Malaysia, South Korea, Japan, China, Hong Kong, Peru, Indonesia, India and the United Kingdom. The agreement with New Zealand entered into force on 1 January 1983: Australia–New Zealand Closer Economic Relations Trade Agreement (adopted 28 March 1983, entered into force 1 January 1983) 1329 UNTS 175 (CER). For further details, see DFAT, 'Free Trade Agreements in Force': www.dfat.gov.au/trade/agreements/in-force/Pages/free-trade-agreements-in-force.

[69] Australia, *United Nations Convention on the Law of the Sea: Submission to the Commission on the Limits of the Continental Shelf on the Outer Limits of Australia's Continental Shelf Extending beyond 200 Nautical Miles from the Territorial Sea Baseline* (Executive Summary, AUS-DOC-ES, 15 November 2004): www.un.org/Depts/los/clcs_new/submissions_files/aus04/Documents/aus_doc_es_web_delivery.pdf.

additional to its continental shelf within 200 nautical miles.[70] Australia's submission was ground-breaking in several respects, including in its provision of information on the outer limits of the ECS adjacent to the Australian Antarctic Territory (AAT). Australia felt obliged to submit information on that area because of the pending expiry of the then 10-year time limit on the making a submission to the CLCS.[71] However, Australia asked the CLCS not to consider the information on the area adjacent to the AAT 'for the time being' because of the sensitivities surrounding the assertion of a continental shelf adjacent to part of the Antarctic continent. The dialogue between the CLCS and Australia in the course of consideration of Australia's submission also had important ramifications for the Commission's subsequent practice, particularly on the interpretation and application of the key Article 76(6) of the 1982 Convention concerning submarine ridges.

Australia's contribution to the development of international law in the twenty-first century is not confined to government lawyers, as the contribution made by the late Professor James Crawford while on the International Law Commission (ILC) demonstrates. Of note were his contributions as final Rapporteur to the development of the ILC Articles on State Responsibility[72] and as final Chair of the Working Group developing the Draft Statute of the International Criminal Court.[73] Professor Crawford subsequently was elected to the ICJ in November 2014, with the bipartisan support of successive Australian governments over several years.[74] Other Australian international law academics have also played key roles in the development of international law, for example, in their contribution to the *Tallinn Manual 2.0 on the International Law Applicable to Cyber Operations*.[75]

[70] Commission on the Limits of the Continental Shelf, 'Statement by the Chairman of the Commission on the Limits of the Continental Shelf on the Progress of Work in the Commission' (CLCS/58, 25 April 2008). Much of that area has now been proclaimed in Australian law: Seas and Submerged Lands (Limits of Continental Shelf) Proclamation 2012 (Cth).

[71] The time limit was calculated from 16 November 1994, that being the date of entry into force of the 1982 Convention on the Law of the Sea.

[72] International Law Commission, *Draft Articles on Responsibility of States for Internationally Wrongful Acts* (Supplement No 10, A/56/10, November 2001) ch IV.E.1.

[73] International Law Commission, *Yearbook of the International Law Commission 1994* (United Nations, 1996) vol II. The ILC noted at para 89 of its report: '[the ILC] paid a special tribute to the Chairman of the Working Group at the present session, Mr James Crawford, for the outstanding contribution he made to the preparation of the draft statute by his tireless efforts and devoted work'.

[74] Following Professor Crawford's untimely passing, Professor Hilary Charlesworth, Melbourne Laureate Professor of Law at the University of Melbourne, was elected to the ICJ on 5 November 2021, and subsequently re-elected in 2023 for a full nine-year term.

[75] MN Schmitt (ed), *Tallinn Manual 2.0 on the International Law Applicable to Cyber Operations* (Cambridge, Cambridge University Press, 2017). The Australians involved included Professor Tim McCormack, Professor Rob McLaughlin, Professor Alison Duxbury, Dr Douglas Guilfoyle, Dr Sarah Heathcote, David Letts, Dr Bruce Oswald and Dr Dale Stephens.

B. Differences

So, what has been different in the practice of international law within the Australian government over the past two decades as opposed to the previous two decades? First, matters concerning the use of force and counter-terrorism have come to the fore in that period. Australia's involvement in armed conflicts and the use of force increased markedly over the last two decades thus giving rise to a concomitant increase in advice on both justifications for the use of force (*jus ad bellum*) and the law that applies to that use of force (*jus in bello*). Leaving aside the March 2003 legal advice to the government concerning the legal basis for the use of force in Iraq,[76] Australia's participation in the Iraq conflict engendered a plethora of international legal advice on weaponry, targeting, rules of engagement and related matters. This, in large part, was because that conflict involved the first major use of combat aircraft in an offensive role by Australia since the Vietnam conflict.

On the counter-terrorism side, the international law relating to cyber operations has undergone considerable development over the past decade as evidenced in the *Tallinn Manual* mentioned above. Australia's approach to the law on cyber operations is set out comprehensively in *Australia's International Cyber and Technical Engagement Strategy*.[77] Australia's position on the application of international law to state conduct in cyberspace is updated regularly and forms Annex B to the the current Strategy[78] This detailed position of Australia makes an important contribution to the developing customary international law concerning cyber operations.

A positive development over the past two decades has been the increasing engagement of Australia's international legal advisers with their counterparts in other countries. This engagement can be either formal or ad hoc. The formal includes bilateral meetings of legal advisers such as those with New Zealand, Canada and China led by DFAT, as well as multilateral meetings of legal advisers, such as the Council of Europe Committee of Legal Advisers on Public International Law known as CAHDI. United Nations (UN) Law Week, which coincides with meetings of the UN Sixth Committee, also provides an opportunity to meet with counterparts from other countries. These meetings are not confined to exchanges of information, important though they are. The legal advisers also play a role in the development and implementation of both

[76] See above, n 53.

[77] Commonwealth of Australia, *Australia's International Cyber and Technical Engagement Strategy* (2021) The first version of the strategy was released in October 2017.

[78] ibid 96. Annex B commences by stating: '[e]xisting international law … is applicable to State conduct in cyberspace … This includes, where applicable, the law regarding the use of force, international humanitarian law (IHL), international human rights law (IHRL), and the international law of state responsibility'. New Zealand has also released a document on international law and cyberspace: New Zealand Ministry of Foreign Affairs and Trade, 'The Application of International Law to State Activity in Cyberspace' (Media Statement, 1 December 2020).

treaty and customary international law. For example, the development of the Bethlehem Principles on the use of force against non-state actors was 'informed by detailed discussions over recent years with foreign ministry, defense ministry and military legal advisers from a number of states who have operational experience in these matters'.[79] Australia was one those states.

V. LITIGATION INVOLVING INTERNATIONAL LAW

Yet, another difference over the past two decades has been the marked increase in Australia's participation in international dispute settlement and in domestic litigation involving matters of international law.

A. International Dispute Settlement

The increase in Australia's involvement in international litigation is in part due to the creation of new international courts and tribunals in the latter part of the twentieth century with an ever-increasing jurisdiction. In this respect, one need only mention WTO dispute settlement,[80] the various forms of dispute settlement under the 1982 UN Convention on the Law of the Sea including the International Tribunal for the Law of the Sea (ITLOS),[81] Annex VII arbitration and Annex V conciliation, as well as other ad hoc arbitral tribunals established under various multilateral and bilateral agreements. Australia has been a pioneer in these new forms of dispute settlement, both as an applicant and respondent. Australia and New Zealand instituted the first Annex VII arbitration under the 1982 Convention being the *Southern Bluefin Tuna* cases,[82] which were heard in 2000 and it was the respondent in the first Annex V conciliation

[79] See Bethlehem, above n 24, 773. Brunée and Toope put it somewhat differently: '[o]ne might speculate that academic articles and policy briefs were consciously part of a process of norm entrepreneurship, building up claims around necessity and State practice to validate the unwilling or unable standard': see Brunée and Toope, above n 26, 283.

[80] Since 1995, and as of 5 July 2023, a total of 617 disputes have been brought to the WTO and over 350 rulings have been issued: World Trade Organization, 'Dispute Settlement': www.wto.org/english/tratop_e/dispu_e/dispu_e.htm. Of these, Australia has been the complainant in 11 cases, a respondent in 17 cases, and a third party in 120 cases: World Trade Organization, 'Disputes by Member': www.wto.org/english/tratop_e/dispu_e/dispu_by_country_e.htm. That is, as of 5 July 2023, Australia has been involved, one way or another, in just under a quarter of the total number of WTO dispute settlement cases.

[81] Australia made a provisional measures application in *Southern Bluefin Tuna (New Zealand v Japan; Australia v Japan)* (Provisional Measures) [1999] ITLOS Reports 280. It was respondent in *The Volga (Russian Federation v Australia)* (Prompt Release) [2002] ITLOS Reports 10, and has made submissions in two advisory opinion cases: *Request for Advisory Opinion Submitted by the Sub-Regional Fisheries Commission* (Advisory Opinion) [2015] ITLOS Reports 4; *Responsibilities and Obligations of States with Respect to Activities in the Area* (Advisory Opinion) [2011] ITLOS Reports 10.

[82] *Southern Bluefin Tuna (New Zealand-Japan, Australia-Japan)* (2000) 23 RIAA 1.

under the 1982 Convention, that being the *Timor Sea Conciliation* with Timor-Leste.[83]

Australia has achieved tangible benefits through its participation in international dispute settlement, both as an applicant and as a respondent. These benefits include:

- A negotiated arrangement on the management of Southern Bluefin Tuna that soon followed a finding against Australia and New Zealand on jurisdiction in the *Southern Bluefin Tuna* cases;[84]
- confirmation that Australia's pioneering tobacco plain packaging laws are completely consistent with Australia's obligations under international law;[85] and
- limitations on so-called scientific whaling as a result of the *Whaling in the Antarctic* case[86] instituted by Australia in the ICJ – perhaps being a major factor leading Japan to cease its whaling activities in the Southern Ocean.[87]

The cases to which Australia has been a party have also contributed to the development of principles of international law as well as the methodology of international courts and tribunals. For example:

- The contribution made by the *Southern Bluefin Tuna* provisional measures decision of ITLOS to the development of the precautionary principle in international law;[88]
- the duty of co-operation and the objective standard of review adopted by the ICJ in the *Whaling in the Antarctic* case as well as an acceptance of its role in disputes involving science;[89] and
- the ICJ's acceptance in the *Documents* case of the plausibility under international law of the right of confidentiality of, and non-interference in, a state's communication with its legal advisers.[90]

[83] *Report and Recommendations of the Compulsory Conciliation Commission between Timor-Leste and Australia on the Timor Sea* (Permanent Court of Arbitration, Case No 2016-10, 9 May 2018).

[84] See *Southern Bluefin Tuna* (2000), above n 82.

[85] See *Philip Morris Asia Arbitration*, above n 19.

[86] See *Whaling in the Antarctic*, above n 17.

[87] For further discussion of this case and other ICJ cases involving Australia, see M Young, 'Australia and the International Court of Justice', ch 8 in this volume.

[88] See *Southern Bluefin Tuna* [1999], above n 81, 296 [25]–[327]. See also DR Rothwell et al, *International Law: Cases and Materials with Australian Perspectives*, 3rd edn (Cambridge, Cambridge University Press, 2019) 603–05.

[89] See *Whaling in the Antarctic*, above n 17, 253–54, 297. Japan had argued unsuccessfully that the ICJ was not equipped to deal with matters of science.

[90] See *Documents* case, above n 18, 153.

In addition to the cases mentioned above,[91] Australia has participated in a number of advisory opinion cases before the ICJ[92] and ITLOS.[93] Australia also has for the first time intervened in ICJ proceedings under Article 63 of the Statute of the ICJ.[94]

B. Domestic Litigation

A growing element of the practice of international law within government is in the conduct of domestic litigation – including in constitutional cases. A lesser-known example is *Ure v Commonwealth*,[95] a case concerning the ownership of Elizabeth and Middleton Reefs, which lie to the north of Lord Howe Island. The legal question in that case was whether international law grants rights of private ownership to individuals over islands not yet claimed by any state. The plaintiff alleged that they enjoyed such rights of ownership in the two reefs and that the Commonwealth could not acquire those rights in the absence of the payment of just terms under section 51(xxxi) of the Australian Constitution.[96] The Full Federal Court conducted a skilful analysis of three of the sources of international law mentioned in Article 36(2) of the ICJ Statute – these being customary international law, general principles of international law and judicial decisions and the writing of publicists – and determined that no such rights of ownership existed under international law.

Another now common phenomenon is litigation at both the domestic and international level on the same issue, with input from government international lawyers at both levels. These actions may well be simultaneous and in circumstances where the international law rule concerning exhaustion of domestic remedies[97] does not seem to be in play, perhaps because of differing bases of

[91] See above, nn 17–21.

[92] *Legal Consequences of the Separation of the Chagos Archipelago from Mauritius in 1965* (Advisory Opinion) [2019] ICJ Rep 95; *Obligations of States in Respect of Climate Change* (Request for Advisory Opinion) General List No 187 [2023] ICJ 1.

[93] *Request for an Advisory Opinion submitted by the Sub-Regional Fisheries Commission* (Advisory Opinion) [2015] ITLOS Rep 4; *Request for an Advisory Opinion submitted by the Commission of Small Island States in respect of Climate Change and International Law* (Case No 31). For a discussion of Australia's approach to international litigation, see Young, ch 8 in this volume.

[94] *Allegations of Genocide under the Convention on the Prevention and Punishment of Genocide (Ukraine v Russian Federation)* (Admissibility of the Declarations of Intervention) General List No 182 [2023] ICJ 1.

[95] *Ure v Commonwealth*, above n 36. The High Court refused leave to appeal on 5 May 2016: *Ure v Commonwealth* [2016] HCASL 88. As noted above, this case demonstrated also the developing expertise of domestic courts in complex matters of international law.

[96] The plaintiff alleged that hydrocarbon reserves associated with the reefs had an estimated value of US$1.1 trillion: *Ure v Commonwealth*, above n 36, 460 [1].

[97] See J Collier and V Lowe, *The Settlement of Disputes in International Law: Institutions and Procedures* (Oxford, Oxford University Press, 1999) 195–98.

argument at each level.[98] Also, multiple proceedings at the international level may be involved.

A prominent example is the multiple legal challenges that were mounted against Australia's tobacco plain packaging laws.[99] These involved the *Philip Morris Asia Arbitration*[100] under the Hong Kong Australia Agreement for the Promotion and Protection of International Investment[101] commenced in November 2011; four WTO dispute settlement proceedings commenced in the period from 2012 to 2014 by the Dominican Republic, Cuba, Honduras and Indonesia;[102] and two constitutional challenges to the legislation in the High Court of Australia commenced in December 2011.[103] Such simultaneous proceedings stretch resources and raise issues of consistency of argument. For example, an argument helpful to achieving success in the arbitration could well be detrimental to the conduct of the WTO proceedings because of the differing legal obligations and interpretations at play in each forum. Achieving consistency required constant coordination between the teams defending each set of proceedings.[104] All of the legal challenges to the tobacco plain packaging laws, both domestic and international, ultimately failed. These pioneering Australian laws, as upheld by various courts, panels and tribunals, have stood as a model for similar laws in other countries.[105]

VI. CONCLUSION: THE FUTURE

The demand for the provision of international law services to Australian governments will steadily increase over the coming decades. This steady increase will not be confined to areas of current high demand, such as trade, the environment, the law of the sea,[106] human rights, humanitarian law, counter-terrorism

[98] eg, constitutional law at the domestic level and treaty-based arguments at the international level.

[99] Tobacco Plain Packaging Act 2011 (Cth).

[100] See *Philip Morris Asia Arbitration*, above n 19.

[101] Agreement between the Government of Australia and the Government of Hong Kong for the Promotion and Protection of Investments (adopted 15 September 1993, entered into force 15 October 1993) 1770 UNTS 386.

[102] See above, nn 20–21.

[103] *JT International SA v Commonwealth* (2012) 250 CLR 1.

[104] AGS had conduct of the defence in the constitutional cases; AGD and AGS for the defence of the Investor–State Dispute Settlement (ISDS) arbitration; and DFAT for the defence of the WTO proceedings.

[105] As of 21 October 2021, Australia, France, the United Kingdom, New Zealand, Norway, Ireland, Hungary, Thailand, Uruguay and Saudi Arabia implemented plain packaging laws, while Slovenia, Turkey, Belgium, Canada, Singapore, Israel, the Netherlands, Denmark, Myanmar, Burkina Faso, Romania, Georgia and Armenia had passed enabling laws: WHO Framework Convention on Tobacco Control and World Health Organization, *Tobacco Plain Packaging: Global Status 2021 Update* (Geneva, World Health Organization, 2022).

[106] Maritime delimitation may well be one area of decreased demand given the entry into force of the recently agreed boundary with Timor-Leste: Treaty between Australia and the Democratic Republic

and dispute settlement. It will occur also in areas of more recent international, national and public focus, including artificial intelligence and mass movements of people as well as in areas of renewed interest such as outer space.[107]

The fundamental approach to providing those international law services to government will likely remain the same, both in relation to the identity of the providers (principally the AGD and DFAT) and in its underlying ethos – an approach that has served governments well in the past. Continued close engagement of Australian legal advisers with their counterparts in other countries and their committed involvement to the ongoing development of international law will be essential to the maintenance of Australia's interests both domestically and internationally.

of Timor-Leste Establishing Their Maritime Boundaries in the Timor Sea (adopted 6 March 2018, entered into force 30 August 2019) ATS 2019 16.

[107] A recent development in relation to outer space has been Australia's signature on 13 October 2020 of the Artemis Accords: Principles for Cooperation in the Civil Exploration and the Use of the Moon, Mars, Comets and Asteroids for Peaceful Purposes: www.nasa.gov/specials/artemis-accords/img/Artemis-Accords-signed-13Oct2020.pdf. The Accords were developed under the auspices of the US National Aeronautics and Space Administration and are intended to provide a practical set of principles to guide space exploration cooperation among nations.

11

Ad Hoc and Arbitrary: International Criminal Law in Australian Courts

MONIQUE CORMIER*

I. INTRODUCTION

Australia has long been a staunch advocate of the modern international criminal justice project, having supported the establishment and operation of international war crimes tribunals since the end of the Second World War. Eminent Australian jurist, Sir William Webb, served as President of the International Military Tribunal for the Far East in Tokyo, while Australian military courts convened 300 trials of Japanese soldiers accused of war crimes between 1945 and 1951.[1] Australia supported the ad hoc, special and hybrid international criminal tribunals[2] and was an early and ardent champion of the International Criminal Court (ICC).[3] It is therefore somewhat ironic that Australia has developed a reputation as a 'haven' for war criminals, with an underwhelming record of domestic investigations and prosecutions for residents suspected of committing international crimes overseas.[4] Despite amending the

* I would like to thank Robert Brown for his excellent research assistance during the preparation of this chapter.

[1] These trials were held pursuant to the War Crimes Act 1945 (Cth), which was passed by both Houses of Parliament in a single day: National Archives of Australia, 'World War II War Crimes: Fact Sheet 61': www.naa.gov.au/sites/default/files/2020-05/fs-61-World-War-II-war-crimes.pdf. See also G Fitzpatrick, T McCormack and N Morris (eds), *Australia's War Crimes Trials 1945–51* (Leiden, Brill Nijhoff, 2016).

[2] Through financial support and other cooperation. See, eg, Department of Foreign Affairs and Trade (DFAT), *Annual Report 2010–2011* (DFAT, 2011) 106, 230; International War Crimes Tribunal Act 1995 (Cth); International Transfer of Prisoners Act 1997 (Cth).

[3] H Charlesworth et al, *No Country is an Island: Australia and International Law* (Sydney, UNSW Press, 2006) 72; A Byrnes, 'Australia and International Criminal Law' in DR Rothwell and E Crawford (eds), *International Law in Australia*, 3rd edn (Pyrmont, Lawbook Co, 2017) 215–18.

[4] David Humphries, 'How Australia Became a Haven for War Criminals' *Sydney Morning Herald* (10 April 2010) 11; G Boas and P Chifflet, 'Suspected War Criminals in Australia: Law and Policy' (2016) 40 *Melbourne University Law Review* 47, 85; M Aarons, *War Criminals Welcome: Australia, A Sanctuary for Fugitive War Criminals since 1945*, 2nd edn (Collingwood, Schwartz Publishing, 2020). Note that 'war crimes' and 'war criminals' are broad terms that typically encapsulate the commission of international crimes including war crimes, crimes against humanity, and genocide.

War Crimes Act 1945 (Cth) in 1989 for the express purpose of prosecuting the 'significant number' of accused Nazi war criminals living in Australia,[5] there were only three attempted prosecutions between 1989 and 1993.[6] There have been no further serious prosecution attempts for international crimes in the 30-plus years since, despite the introduction of the comprehensive International Criminal Court Act 2002 (Cth) in fulfilment of Australia's obligations as a State party to the Rome Statute.[7]

Given Australia's less-than-stellar track record of conducting investigations and prosecutions for international crimes, and its lack of a coherent 'war crimes policy',[8] it is perhaps surprising that international criminal law has nevertheless made its way into a wide variety of domestic court judgments. Australian courts have had to engage with international criminal law in multifaceted and unanticipated ways: in administrative law matters relating to refugee status; in cases about Australia's treatment of its Indigenous population; in decisions and appeals on extradition requests; and in matters of constitutional law, defamation and criminal procedure. The aim of this chapter, therefore, is to provide an overview of the different contexts in which international criminal law arises in Australian cases, and to assess how the courts have approached such international legal issues.

Section II of this chapter systematically reviews the diverse and largely ad hoc circumstances in which Australian courts have encountered allegations of international crimes.[9] It uses key cases to illustrate how international criminal law has been used in the varied proceedings and provides a brief evaluation of the different judicial approaches.

Section III builds on the discussions in section II by undertaking a more holistic assessment of how Australian courts have contributed to the broader

[5] War Crimes Amendment Act 1988 (Cth) s 3(a). A Special Investigations Unit under the auspices of the Attorney-General's Department was also established (in 1987) and tasked with investigating suspected war criminal immigrants to Australia: Attorney-General's Department (Cth), *Report of the Investigations of War Criminals in Australia* (Canberra, Australian Government Publishing Service, 1994).

[6] The three elderly accused were originally from Ukraine, living in South Australia. The only suspect actually tried was Ivan Polyukhovich, who was acquitted after a trial riddled with evidentiary and language difficulties. Charges against Heinrich Wagner were withdrawn due to his ill health, and there was insufficient evidence to try Mikolay Berezowsky. See Attorney-General's Department (Cth), above n 5; Boas and Chifflet, above n 4, 54; Damien Murphy, 'Cabinet Papers 1992–93: Hunting War Criminals Hits a Snag' *Sydney Morning Herald* (22 December 2016); Daniel Keane, 'Ivan Polyukhovich: How an Alleged Nazi War Criminal Was Acquitted by an Australian Court' (*ABC News*, 19 May 2018): www.abc.net.au/news/2018-05-20/nazi-war-criminals-in-australia-and-the-case-of-polyukhovich/9756454.

[7] The International Criminal Court Act 2002 (Cth) created new provisions for the domestic prosecution of war crimes, crimes against humanity and genocide in div 268 of the Criminal Code, reflecting the offences in the Rome Statute of the International Criminal Court (adopted 17 July 1998, entered into force 1 July 2002) 2187 UNTS 90 (Rome Statute). The Criminal Code is set out in a schedule to the Criminal Code Act 1995 (Cth).

[8] Boas and Chifflet, above n 4, 73.

[9] The chapter focuses on cases in Australian civilian courts, limited to matters that involve international crimes and international criminal law (as opposed to broader questions of public international law).

international criminal justice project through their domestic jurisprudence. While some judges and courts have undertaken serious consideration of relevant international criminal law, others have been hampered by formalism and a distrust of international law. The resulting body of case law suggests relatively arbitrary judicial attitudes towards the utility of international criminal law in Australian cases.

The chapter ends with some concluding remarks on the likelihood of Australian courts developing a more systematic and coherent approach to matters involving international crimes in the future.

II. AD HOC: INTERNATIONAL CRIMINAL LAW IN UNEXPECTED PROCEEDINGS

As mentioned above, the lack of prosecutions in Australia for international crimes has not precluded Australian courts from reviewing, applying, and – in some cases – developing international criminal law. International criminal law evolved to ensure that 'the most serious crimes of concern to the international community as a whole must not go unpunished'.[10] It is therefore curious to find international criminal law appearing in cases that are not criminal proceedings, and thus not concerned with punishment. In Australia, matters in which international criminal law issues arise are diverse in scope and often unexpected in substance. They are ad hoc in the sense that there is no systematic rationale behind the appearance of international criminal law in such cases. Courts consider it as and when is needed.

The purpose of this section is to provide an overview of how, and in what circumstances, Australian courts have considered and used international criminal law. It highlights particular cases to demonstrate the ad hoc nature of international criminal law's presence in matters ranging from administrative appeals and extradition disputes, to constitutional challenges, defamation proceedings and cases relating to Australia's treatment of Aboriginal peoples.

A. Administrative Processes and Refugee Law

Consideration and application of international criminal law has occurred with surprising frequency in the Australian administrative law system, due to the role of the administrative tribunals and courts in determining refugee status.[11] Under Article 1F(a) of the 1951 Refugee Convention, a person can be denied refugee

[10] Rome Statute, above n 7, preamble.

[11] See generally A Duxbury, 'Excluding the Undesirable: Interpreting Article 1F(a) of the Refugee Convention in Australia' in DA Blumenthal and TLH McCormack (eds), *The Legacy of Nuremberg: Civilising Influence or Institutionalised Vengeance?* (Leiden, Brill Nijhoff, 2008).

status where 'there are serious reasons for considering that [he or she has] committed a crime against peace, a war crime or a crime against humanity'.[12] In Australia, the responsibility for making decisions on protection visas falls to the minister in charge of the immigration portfolio, or to his or her delegates.[13] The Article 1F exclusion clause is replicated in section 36(2C)(a)(i) of the Migration Act 1958 (Cth), meaning that the minister may refuse to issue a protection visa to an asylum seeker if there are serious reasons for considering that he or she has committed 'a crime against peace, a war crime or a crime against humanity'.[14] A decision of the minister or delegate to refuse or cancel a protection visa on the Article 1F exclusion grounds is reviewable by the general division of the Australian Administrative Tribunal (AAT).[15] Decisions of the AAT may in turn be appealed to the Federal Court of Australia. This means that the AAT and Federal Court have had to consider and apply international criminal law in the context of administrative decision-making.

Neither Article 1F(A) of the Refugee Convention nor section 36(2C) of the Migration Act define 'a crime against peace, a war crime or a crime against humanity', instead leaving it to decision-makers to refer to the definitions 'in the international instruments drawn up to make provision in respect of such crimes'.[16] This has led to some detailed consideration of the appropriate choice of international instrument and the relative merits of the different definitions of crimes available in those instruments. In various decisions,[17] the AAT and Federal Court have reviewed international instruments ranging from the post-Second

[12] Convention Relating to the Status of Refugees (adopted 28 July 1951, entered into force 22 April 1954) 189 UNTS 150 (Refugee Convention). See also M Zagor, 'Persecutor or Persecuted: Exclusion under Article 1F(A) and (B) of the Refugees Convention' (2000) 23 *University of New South Wales Law Journal* 164.

[13] Migration Act 1958 (Cth) s 29. At the time of writing, the Minister for Home Affairs is the government official responsible for immigration. The immigration minister's title and portfolio has changed numerous times over the years.

[14] See also, ibid s 5H(2)(a).

[15] ibid s 500(1)(c).

[16] This phrase is found in Article 1F(a) of the Refugee Convention. The exclusion clauses in ss 5H(2)(a) and 36(2)(a) of the Migration Act 1958 (Cth) were amended in 2014 to read 'the person has committed a crime against peace, a war crime or a crime against humanity, *as defined by international instruments prescribed by the regulations*' (emphasis added). Regulation 2.03B of the Migration Regulations 1994 (Cth) now prescribe 12 international instruments which may be used to define the exclusionary crimes. See 'Chapter 7: Exclusion and Cessation' in Administrative Appeals Tribunal, Migration and Refugee Division Legal Services, *A Guide to Refugee Law in Australia* (Commonwealth of Australia, 2021): www.aat.gov.au/guide-to-refugee-law-in-australia.

[17] See, eg, *W97/16 and Minister for Immigration and Multicultural Affairs* (1998) 51 ALD 432; *SRNN and Department of Immigration and Multicultural Affairs* [2000] AATA 983; *SAH and Minister for Immigration and Multicultural and Indigenous Affairs* [2002] AATA 263; *SAL and Minister for Immigration and Multicultural and Indigenous Affairs* [2002] AATA 1164; *SRHHH and Minister for Immigration and Multicultural and Indigenous Affairs* [2005] AATA 1020; *SRYYY v Minister for Immigration and Multicultural and Indigenous Affairs* (2005) 147 FCR 1; *SZCWP v Minister for Immigration and Multicultural and Indigenous Affairs* [2006] FCAFC 9; *WBV and Minister for Immigration and Citizenship* [2007] AATA 2046; *MZYVM v Minister for Immigration and Citizenship* [2013] FCA 79; *MRWF and Minister for Immigration and Border Protection* (AAT No 2014/1704, 19 May 2017).

World War London Agreement and Nuremberg Charter, to the Rome Statute and the ICC's Elements of Crimes.[18] The importance of correctly interpreting and applying the elements of war crimes and crimes against humanity has also been emphasised.[19]

In the 2005 case of *SRYYY v Minister for Immigration and Multicultural and Indigenous Affairs*,[20] for example, the Federal Court considered whether the AAT had erred in excluding an applicant for a protection visa who had admitted to committing violent acts against civilians while in the Sri Lankan army. In a detailed analysis of the elements of crimes against humanity and war crimes as defined in the Rome Statute, the Court found that the AAT had failed to appreciate that 'there is a fundamental difference between the requisite elements of these two offences'[21] and had therefore 'applied the wrong legal test'.[22] More interesting was the Court's conclusion that the AAT had erred in not considering whether the Rome Statute's defence of superior orders was available to the appellant. Such a defence would absolve him of criminal responsibility for war crimes, and therefore negate any serious reasons for considering he had committed a crime.[23]

The decision has been described as 'a thorough and sophisticated analysis of the way in which art 1F of the Refugee Convention should be interpreted'.[24] The detailed consideration and application of international criminal law by

[18] Agreement for the Prosecution and Punishment of the Major War Criminals of the European Axis, (adopted 8 August 1945, entered into force 8 August 1945) 8 UNTS 279 (London Agreement and Nuremberg Charter); Rome Statute, above n 7; International Criminal Court, 'Elements of Crimes' (reproduced from the Official Records of the Assembly of States Parties to the Rome Statute of the International Criminal Court, First Session, New York, 3–10 September 2002): www.icc-cpi.int/Publications/Elements-of-Crimes.pdf. Other considered instruments include the Statute of the International Criminal Tribunal for the former Yugoslavia, annexed to UNSC Res 827 (25 May 1993) UN Doc S/RES/827 (1993); Statute of the International Criminal Tribunal for Rwanda, annexed to UNSC Res 955 (8 November 1994) UN Doc S/RES/955 (1994); Geneva Convention for the Amelioration of the Condition of the Wounded and Sick in Armed Forces in the Field (adopted 12 August 1949, entered into force 21 October 1950) 75 UNTS 31 (Geneva Convention I); Geneva Convention for the Amelioration of the Condition of Wounded, Sick and Shipwrecked Members of Armed Forces at Sea (adopted 12 August 1949, entered into force 21 October 1950) 75 UNTS 85 (Geneva Convention II); Geneva Convention Relative to the Treatment of Prisoners of War (adopted 12 August 1945, entered into force 21 October 1950) 75 UNTS 135 (Geneva Convention III); Geneva Convention Relative to the Protection of Civilian Persons in Time of War (adopted 12 August 1949, entered into force 21 October 1950) 75 UNTS 287 (Geneva Convention IV) (collectively, the Geneva Conventions).

[19] See, eg, *SRNN*, above n 17; *SHCB v MIMIA* (2003) 133 FCR 561; *SRYYY*, above n 17; *SZCWP*, above n 17; *SZITR v Minister for Immigration and Multicultural Affairs* (2006) FCA 1759. The AAT or Federal Court have not had to consider the meaning of 'a crime against peace'.

[20] *SRYYY*, above n 17.

[21] ibid 32.

[22] ibid 33.

[23] ibid 35–36.

[24] P Johnston and C Harris, 'SKYYY v Minister for Immigration and Multicultural and Indigenous Affairs: War Crimes and the Refugee Convention' (2007) 8 *Melbourne Journal of International Law* 104, 120.

the Federal Court is to be applauded,[25] although it does raise the question of whether there is an expectation that members of the AAT should be able to engage in a similarly advanced analysis of this specialist area of law.[26]

B. Extradition Disputes

It should also be noted that in evaluating whether the exclusion clause applies to prevent a person from receiving a protection visa, these Australian administrative law tribunals and civil law courts are, in effect, undertaking a criminal assessment. AAT members and Federal Court judges are analysing international criminal law to apply it to a set of facts and come to a conclusion about whether they think there are serious reasons for considering that the applicant has committed a war crime, a crime against humanity or a crime against peace. Yet, the standard of proof in such matters has been held to be 'clear and convincing evidence' rather than 'beyond a reasonable doubt',[27] and any decision to refuse a protection visa is an administrative outcome rather than a criminal punishment. The fact that the AAT is not a court exercising judicial power within the meaning of Australia's Constitution raises further questions about the propriety of the AAT effectively making pronouncements on a person's criminal responsibility, a function usually reserved to the judiciary.[28] Nevertheless, given that the tribunal provides written reasons for its decisions, these administrative reviews and appeals make up the lion's share of Australia's judicial contribution to international criminal law.

Mark Aarons writes that 'successive governments have knowingly allowed hundreds (perhaps many more) of men responsible for the cruel imprisonment, torture, rape and mass execution of tens of thousands of innocent civilians to make Australia home'.[29] In light of Australia's poor record of investigating and prosecuting such crimes, as well as the sheer number of alleged offenders allowed to migrate to Australia, it is not surprising that there have been requests for extradition of some suspected war criminals. More surprising is how few of these requests have been successful.

[25] The AAT has determined that it is bound by Federal Court decisions: 'there can be no question that this Tribunal is bound to follow relevant judicial pronouncements': *JSP Partners Pty Ltd and Tax Agents' Board of Victoria* [2008] AATA 131.

[26] Johnston and Harris, above n 24, 121. The AAT has created guides for its members that cover substantive issues of law over which the AAT has jurisdiction. One such guide is *A Guide to Refugee Law in Australia*, above n 16, ch 7 of which contains an overview of how crimes against peace, war crimes and crimes against humanity have been interpreted in international law. It also refers to previous AAT cases that have dealt with Art 1F and relevant Federal Court decisions.

[27] *SRYYY*, above n 17, 27.

[28] For an overview of the relationship and tensions between administrative merits review and judicial decision making, see P Cane, 'Merits Review and Judicial Review: The AAT as Trojan Horse' (2000) 28 *Federal Law Review* 213.

[29] Aarons, above n 4, 21.

In Australia, extradition is governed by the Extradition Act 1988 (Cth) which allows certain 'extradition countries'[30] to request that Australia facilitates the arrest and surrender of persons in Australia who are accused or convicted of an 'extradition offence'.[31] Assessment of whether the requested person is eligible for extradition is made by a magistrate, and the Attorney-General is responsible for deciding whether an eligible person is to be surrendered.[32] A person deemed eligible for extradition may seek review of this decision by the Federal Court or a State or Territory Supreme Court.[33]

While Australia has received a handful of requests since the end of the Second World War for the extradition of accused Nazis and suspected war criminals from the former Yugoslavia, the majority of these have been refused[34] or were otherwise not able to be fulfilled.[35] There have been only two cases in which persons deemed eligible for extradition to face prosecution for war crimes have launched legal challenges to the magistrate's decision: Dragan Vasiljkovic and Charles Zentai. Both matters involved high-profile, protracted litigation over many years, and both raised some interesting international criminal law issues.[36] Of the two matters, the final *Zentai* decision was the most consequential, and the most controversial.[37]

In 2005, Hungary sought extradition of Zentai for an alleged war crime of killing a young Jewish man in November 1944. Zentai spent seven years and countless legal proceedings challenging his extradition,[38] culminating in the High Court's verdict that he should not be extradited.[39] The majority's decision

[30] An 'extradition country' is one with which Australia has an extradition agreement via bilateral or multilateral treaties or other extradition schemes. See Attorney-General's Department, 'International Crime Cooperation Arrangements': www.ag.gov.au/international-relations/international-crime-cooperation-arrangements.

[31] An 'extradition offence' is an offence against the law of the requesting country 'for which the maximum penalty is death or imprisonment, or other deprivation of liberty, for a period of not less than 12 months': Extradition Act 1988 (Cth) s 5.

[32] ibid ss 19, 22.

[33] ibid s 21.

[34] See ACC Menzies, *Review of Material Relating to the Entry of Suspected War Criminals into Australia* (Canberra, Australian Government Publishing Service, 1987) attachment D; Boas and Chifflet, above n 4, 68–73.

[35] eg, Latvia requested extradition of Konrad Kaljes for Nazi war crimes, but he died in 2001 during his appeals process: Patrick Barkham, 'Konrad Kalejs' *Guardian* (12 November 2001). In 2019, Serbian Zoran Tadic was wanted by Croatia for war crimes in the Yugoslav Wars, but fled Australia before any extradition request could be actioned: Jacquelin Magnay and Paul Maley, 'Accused War Criminal Flees to Serbia' *Weekend Australian* (Canberra, 2 March 2019) 1.

[36] See, eg, *Vasiljkovic v Minister for Justice and Customs* (2006) 234 ALR 643.

[37] *Minister for Home Affairs v Zentai* (2012) 246 CLR 213 (*Zentai* (High Court)).

[38] For an overview of the lengthy procedural history, see M O'Brien, 'Minister for Home Affairs of the Commonwealth v Zentai' (2013) 20 *Australian International Law Journal* 189, 190.

[39] Zentai's extradition proceedings had reached a point in which he had been deemed eligible for extradition and the Minister had made the decision to extradite him to Hungary. Zentai appealed this decision to the Federal Court and was successful: *Zentai v O'Connor [No 3]* (2010) 187 FCR 495. The Minister appealed to the Full Court of the Federal Court which upheld the ruling against extradition: *O'Connor v Zentai* (2011) 195 FCR 515. The Minister's further appeal to the High Court was then unsuccessful: *Zentai* (High Court), above n 37.

hinged on the fact that 'war crimes' were not introduced into Hungarian law as criminal offences until 1945, and that Article 2.5(a) of the Australia–Hungary Extradition Treaty required that the accused conduct was 'an offence in the Requesting State at the time of the acts or omissions constituting the offence'.[40] Despite the existence of the ordinary crime of murder in Hungarian law in 1944, the majority of the High Court held that the specific offence with which Zentai was charged (namely the war crime of unlawful execution) must have been an offence in Hungary at the time of its commission.[41]

While much of the High Court's reasoning in *Zentai* was an exercise in statutory interpretation, there were some half-hearted attempts to engage with principles and practice of international criminal law. For example, in considering the prohibition on retroactivity in Article 2.5(a) of the Extradition Treaty, French CJ briefly contemplated the fact that the International Covenant on Civil and Political Rights allows for retroactive trial and punishment if the act in question 'was criminal according to the general principles of law recognized by the community of nations' at the time it was committed.[42] His Honour nevertheless declined to apply this qualification to Zentai's alleged conduct on the basis that the Australia–Hungary Extradition Treaty 'is one of general application to a range of offences without distinction between those which might be regarded as crimes against international law and those which might not'.[43]

The High Court's decision in *Zentai* was criticised for its 'highly textual approach' to the interpretation of the Extradition Treaty,[44] with the protracted proceedings also viewed as an indictment of Australia's extradition procedures.[45] Over the course of 19 judicial decisions relating to extradition, there was never even a prima facie consideration of Zentai's guilt or innocence.[46] In 2017, Zentai died in Perth at age 96, never having answered the case against him.[47]

[40] Treaty on Extradition between Australia and the Republic of Hungary (adopted 25 October 1995, entered into force 25 April 1997) ATS 1997 13.

[41] War crimes are serious violations of the laws of war applicable during armed conflict. See, eg, Geneva Conventions, above n 18; Rome Statute, above n 7, Art 8.

[42] *Zentai* (High Court), above n 37, 226 (French CJ); International Covenant on Civil and Political Rights (adopted 16 December 1966, entered into force 23 March 1976) 999 UNTS 171, Art 15.

[43] *Zentai* (High Court), above n 37, 226 (French CJ), 236 (Gummow, Crennan, Kiefel and Bell JJ).

[44] H Cullen and B Burgess, 'Extradition from A to Z: Assange, Zentai and the Challenge of Interpreting International Obligations' (2015) 39 *University of Western Australia Law Review* 208, 228.

[45] M Stubbs, 'Zentai and the Troubles of Extradition' (2013) 39 *Monash University Law Review* 894, 897–98.

[46] A consequence of Australia's 'no evidence' model of extradition, which does not require the state seeking extradition to provide any evidence to support the allegations of criminal conduct. See ibid 897; G Griffith and C Harris, 'Recent Developments in the Law of Extradition' (2005) 6 *Melbourne Journal of International Law* 33, 53.

[47] Joshua Levi, 'Zentai Dies at 96' *Australian Jewish News* (7 January 2018).

C. Australia's Treatment of Aboriginal Peoples

In 1999, two cases relating to Australian government policies affecting traditional Aboriginal lands were heard together in the Federal Court.[48] The appellants in *Nulyarimma v Thompson* claimed that the government's 'Ten Point Plan' on native title and subsequent Native Title Amendment Act 1998 (Cth) constituted acts of genocide.[49] The applicant in *Buzzacott v Hill* also alleged that genocide had occurred as a result of the failure of the Australian government to seek world heritage listing for the lands of the Arabunna people.[50] At the time of both claims, Australia was a party to the Genocide Convention,[51] but had not enacted implementing legislation. In the combined *Nulyarimma v Thompson*, the Federal Court therefore had to consider the question of whether genocide could be prosecuted in Australian courts in the absence of legislation making genocide a crime in Australian law.

Nulyarimma was not the first case before an Australian court to deal with the question of whether the Australian government had perpetrated genocide against the Aboriginal population. Two years earlier in *Kruger v Commonwealth*,[52] the High Court was tasked with assessing the constitutionality of the Aboriginals Ordinance 1918 (NT), which authorised the removal of Aboriginal children from their families and their placement in 'institutions or reserves' between 1925 and 1949.[53] In its consideration of whether this law authorised genocide, the High Court held that because the Ordinance predated Australia's ratification of the Genocide Convention by more than 30 years, and because the Convention had not yet been implemented in domestic legislation, the crime of genocide was not part of Australian law.[54] Even if it was, the Aboriginals Ordinance did not evince the specific intent 'to destroy, in whole or in part, a national, ethnical, racial or religious group'.[55]

In contrast to the High Court's cursory discussion of genocide in *Kruger*, a significant portion of the Federal Court's judgment in *Nulyarimma* was focused on deconstructing the history and law of the crime of genocide. It considered whether the non-derogable obligation to prosecute the crime of genocide under

[48] *Nulyarimma v Thompson* (1999) 96 FCR 153.

[49] The 'Ten Point Plan' was the Australian government's response to the High Court decision in *Wik Peoples v Queensland* (1996) 187 CLR 1, in which the Court found that Aboriginal native title rights to land were not necessarily extinguished by the grant of pastoral leases. The appellants claimed that the Ten Point Plan (enacted into law through the Native Title Amendment Act 1998 (Cth)) 'resulted in the unjustifiable extinguishment of native title in certain circumstances … [and] that that extinguishment gave rise to the crime of genocide': ibid 207.

[50] ibid 158.

[51] Convention on the Prevention and Punishment of the Crime of Genocide (adopted 9 December 1948, entered into force 12 January 1951) 78 UNTS 277 (Genocide Convention).

[52] *Kruger v Commonwealth* (1997) 190 CLR 1.

[53] ibid 2.

[54] ibid 70 (Dawson J), 159 (Gummow J).

[55] ibid 70–71 (Dawson J), 89 (Toohey J), 108 (Gaudron J).

customary law and its justiciability under universal jurisdiction meant that the crime of genocide could be 'received' into domestic law.[56] While Merkel J held that it could be considered a 'universal crime under international and municipal law', His Honour concluded that the conduct in question did not amount to genocide.[57] Like the High Court in *Kruger*, Wilcox and Whitlam JJ found that the crime of genocide was not cognisable in Australian courts without implementing legislation.[58]

It is noteworthy that all three judges in *Nulyarimma* accepted that genocide is a *jus cogens* crime of universal jurisdiction. As Douglas Guilfoyle observes, '[g]iven the difficulties that often surround proof of the existence of a customary rule and its content this alone is significant'.[59] But, the conclusion by both the High Court and Federal Court that genocide could not be recognised as a crime in Australia was controversial, to say the least.[60] The introduction of the International Criminal Court Act 2002 (Cth) remedied this lacuna by incorporating the crime of genocide into the Criminal Code.[61] This offence is not, however, retroactive,[62] which leaves a significant impunity gap for accusations of historical genocide in Australia.

D. A Constitutional Challenge to the War Crimes Act

As has already been seen, the High Court has weighed in on several cases involving accusations of international crimes. While these and other cases occasionally raise questions of constitutional law,[63] the High Court's best-known foray into international criminal law was the 1991 constitutional challenge of *Polyukhovich v Commonwealth*.[64] Ivan Polyukhovich, an Australian citizen living in South Australia, was accused of committing war crimes in Ukraine between 1942 and 1943. He was charged pursuant to the amended War Crimes Act 1945 (Cth), which provided for the prosecution of Australian citizens or residents who committed war crimes outside Australia during the Second World War. Polyukhovich challenged the constitutionality of the War Crimes Act 1945 (Cth), the validity of which the High Court upheld in a 4:3 decision. *Polyukhovich* is divided into seven separate judgments, each of which at least

[56] See, eg, *Nulyarimma*, above n 48, 189–91 (Merkel J).
[57] ibid 215 (Merkel J).
[58] ibid 161 (Wilcox J), 173 (Whitlam J).
[59] D Guilfoyle, '*Nulyarimma v Thompson*: Is Genocide a Crime at Common Law in Australia?' (2001) 29 *Federal Law Review* 1, 24.
[60] S Joseph, '*Kruger v Commonwealth*: Constitutional Rights and the Stolen Generations' (1998) 24 *Monash University Law Review* 486, 494–95; M Flynn, 'Genocide: It's a Crime Everywhere, but Not in Australia' (2000) 29 *Western Australian Law Review* 59; Guilfoyle, above n 59.
[61] Criminal Code Act 1995 (Cth) sch 1 div 268 subdiv B (Criminal Code).
[62] International Criminal Court Act 2002 (Cth) sch 1 Art 24.
[63] See, eg, *Kruger*, above n 52; *R v Tang* (2008) 237 CLR 1.
[64] *Polyukhovich v Commonwealth* (1991) 172 CLR 501.

touches on matters of international law in relation to the external affairs power of the Australian Constitution.[65]

The judgments of Brennan and Toohey JJ are particularly notable for their detailed consideration of international criminal law. Brennan J, for example, explored whether there is a rule of customary international law that obliges states to prosecute suspected war criminals for extraterritorial offences.[66] His Honour concluded that there was not sufficient evidence of widespread state practice and *opinio juris* to support such an obligation, but that the external affairs power of the Constitution could be enlivened by the existence of a matter of international concern, whether or not it was accompanied by an obligation.[67] Toohey J undertook a comprehensive analysis of what is meant by war crimes and crimes against humanity in international law.[68] Both judges examined the justiciability of international crimes via universal jurisdiction.[69] Brennan J ultimately held that the War Crimes Act was invalid on the basis that the war crimes offence in that statute 'does not correspond with the international law definition of international crimes existing before 8 May 1945'.[70] Toohey J, on the other hand, was part of the majority in finding that the Act was valid. His Honour acknowledged that the definition of a war crime in the Act is described 'in terms which do not of themselves attract notions of international law', but that the Act as a whole 'is in accord with what international law understands as war crimes and crimes against humanity at the relevant time'.[71]

The outcome of *Polyukhovich* in affirming the validity of the War Crimes Act allowed for Australia's one and only civilian war crimes trial to go ahead. In 1993, Ivan Polyukhovich was found not guilty by a South Australian Supreme Court jury in a trial that could not overcome the evidentiary challenges posed by time and distance.[72] It is ironic, therefore, that the constitutional challenge to the War Crimes Act contributed more to the development of international criminal law in Australia than the sole prosecution under the Act.

E. Defamation

In 2018, former Special Forces soldier Ben Roberts-Smith brought defamation proceedings against several Australian media outlets and journalists. Roberts-Smith, a well-known public figure and Australia's most decorated veteran, alleged that the respondents had severely damaged his reputation by

[65] Australian Constitution, s 51(xxix).
[66] *Polyukhovich*, above n 64, 559–60 (Brennan J).
[67] ibid 560–61.
[68] ibid 664–77.
[69] ibid 562–69 (Brennan J), 658–63 (Toohey J).
[70] ibid 576 (Brennan J).
[71] ibid 682 (Toohey J).
[72] Keane, above n 6.

publishing articles containing imputations that Roberts-Smith committed war crimes while deployed in Afghanistan. In *Roberts-Smith v Fairfax Media Publications Pty Ltd [No 41]*[73] the Federal Court sat for 110 days over 13 months in 2021 and 2022. The media dubbed it 'the trial of the century' and a 'proxy war crimes trial' given its high-profile nature and the high stakes involved.[74] In Besanko J's 726-page decision, His Honour found that the respondents had proven on the balance of probabilities that the majority of the imputations were 'substantially true'.[75] This included the imputations that Roberts-Smith had committed, or was complicit in, four murders of Afghan men who were *hors de combat*.

Given the civil nature of the proceedings, it is to be expected that most of the judgment deals with the criminal allegations in factual terms rather than by reference to the legal elements that would need to be proven beyond reasonable doubt in a criminal trial. Yet some of the findings are made with specific references to the Criminal Code. For example, in relation to one particular incident, Besanko J considered the meaning of various modes of criminal liability before concluding that Roberts-Smith either jointly committed the war crime of murder 'within ss 11.2A and 268.70 of the Criminal Code' or that he was complicit in the murder 'within ss 11.2 and 268.70 of the Criminal Code'.[76] Despite the considerable body of jurisprudence from international courts on the interpretation of joint commission and complicity, Besanko J did not stray from the Australian common law in determining the meaning of these terms.[77] Neither was there any discussion of why or how the killing constituted a war crime under section 268.70 of the Criminal Code which requires that 'the perpetrator's conduct takes place in the context of, and is associated with, an armed conflict that is not an international armed conflict'.

There is an interesting tension in the judgment between the civil procedure involved in the case and the criminal conduct. On the one hand, it was not a criminal trial and the court was tasked with determining, on the balance of probabilities, whether the allegations are substantially true as a defence against reputational damage. On the other hand, Besanko J's finding that the allegations are substantially true was, in effect, a finding that Roberts-Smith probably committed war crimes 'within' the Criminal Code. But the question of whether a Division 268 war crime has been committed under the Criminal Code is not simply a question of fact; it is legally complex and requires consideration of various physical, mental and contextual elements, modes of liability and possible defences. Undoubtedly Besanko J's analysis was sufficient for the purposes

[73] *Roberts-Smith v Fairfax Media Publications Pty Ltd [No 41]* [2023] FCA 555.

[74] Ben Doherty, 'Ben Roberts-Smith: The Explosive Allegations of War Crimes at the Heart of the Defamation Case' *Guardian* (1 June 2023).

[75] There were 14 defamatory imputations in total, not all of which were related to war crimes.

[76] *Roberts-Smith*, above n 73, [940]–[942].

[77] ibid [218].

of defamation, but it is difficult to reconcile the conclusion that Roberts-Smith committed war crimes within the meaning of the Criminal Code with such negligible consideration of the specific elements that make up an international crime.

F. Criminal Appeals and Procedure

i. The Offence of Slavery in Australian and International Law

On occasion, Australian courts have had the opportunity to consider international criminal law in a domestic criminal context. Unlike the other cases discussed above, the 2008 High Court decision in *R v Tang*[78] was originally a criminal case, the respondent having been tried and convicted in the Victorian County Court of various slavery offences under Division 270 of the Criminal Code.[79] Slavery as a stand-alone offence is not typically considered to be an 'international crime' in the same category as war crimes, crimes against humanity and genocide.[80] Slavery is nevertheless one of the oldest *jus cogens* crimes under customary international law,[81] codified in the 1926 International Convention to Suppress the Slave Trade and Slavery.[82] The respondent in *Tang* was the owner of a licensed brothel in Melbourne, and convicted of slavery offences in relation to five Thai nationals who were illegally brought to Australia to be sex workers in the brothel. The respondent was the first person to be convicted of slavery offences in Australia.[83]

One of the issues on appeal was whether the definition of slavery in the Criminal Code was limited to 'chattel slavery', namely 'the legal capacity of an owner to treat a slave as an article of possession'.[84] Writing for the majority, Gleeson CJ undertook a detailed analysis of the definition of slavery in international law, concluding that because there was never any legal capacity to own a person in Australia, the Criminal Code slavery offence could not be limited to chattel slavery.[85] In order to distinguish slavery from exploitative or harsh labour conditions, His Honour found that it is then a matter of considering 'the nature and extent of the powers exercised over a complainant'.[86] Where

[78] *Tang*, above n 63.

[79] Tang successfully appealed her conviction in the Court of Appeal of the Supreme Court of Victoria. The Crown was then granted special leave to appeal to the High Court.

[80] Acts of slavery may constitute a crime against humanity if 'committed as part of a widespread or systematic attack against any civilian population': Rome Statute, above n 7, Art 7(1)(g). See also Criminal Code, above n 61, s 268.10, which makes 'enslavement' a crime against humanity.

[81] MC Bassiouni, 'International Crimes: *Jus Cogens* and *Obligatio Erga Omnes*' (1996) 59 *Law & Contemporary Problems* 63, 68.

[82] International Convention to Suppress the Slave Trade and Slavery (adopted 25 September 1926, entered into force 9 March 1927) 60 LNTS 253 (Slavery Convention).

[83] *Tang*, above n 63, 27.

[84] ibid 18.

[85] ibid 20 (Gleeson CJ).

[86] ibid 24 (Gleeson CJ).

a person is exercising powers of effective or de facto ownership over another person, that may be sufficient for the purposes of section 270.3 of the Criminal Code.[87] Tang's conviction was upheld, and the judgment was lauded as bringing 'much depth of understanding to the parameters of what constitutes "slavery" both in the Australian context, but also in international law'.[88]

ii. Commencement of Prosecution for International Crimes in Australian Courts

In the nearly two decades since the enactment of the Rome Statute crimes into Australian law, there have been two high-profile citizen attempts to initiate universal jurisdiction proceedings in Australian courts against foreign leaders for international crimes. In 2011, then President of Sri Lanka, Mahinda Rajapaksa, was scheduled to travel to Australia for the Commonwealth Heads of Government Meeting when an Australian citizen filed charges against him in the Melbourne Magistrates' Court, alleging Rajapaksa's commission of war crimes and crimes against humanity during the Sri Lankan civil war.[89] Under the Criminal Code, any Division 268 proceedings concerning genocide, crimes against humanity, war crimes and crimes against the administration of justice of the ICC 'must not be commenced without the Attorney-General's written consent'.[90] Within a day of the charges being filed, the Attorney-General exercised his discretion to quash the proceedings.[91] While there is no requirement that the Attorney-General provides reasons for any decision to refuse consent, a spokesperson claimed that it was because the prosecution of Rajapaksa would be a breach of head of state immunity laws.[92]

While the attempted prosecution of Rajapaksa did not see the inside of a court room, in 2018 another private Australian citizen lodged a charge-sheet in the Melbourne Magistrates' Court against Aung San Suu Kyi, the Foreign Minister of Myanmar. Aung San Suu Kyi was visiting Australia at the time, and the charge-sheet alleged that she had committed a crime against humanity in relation to the Rohingya ethnic minority in Myanmar.[93] Predictably, the

[87] ibid 20 (Gleeson CJ).

[88] J Allain, '*R v Tang*: Clarifying the Definition of "Slavery" in International Law' (2009) 10 *Melbourne Journal of International Law* 246, 246.

[89] Michael Gordon, 'Sri Lankan President Accused in Australian Court' *The Age* (Melbourne, 25 October 2011).

[90] Criminal Code, above n 61, s 268.121(1).

[91] Aja Styles and Michael Gordon, 'Sri Lankan PM Will Not Answer War Crimes Claims' *Sydney Morning Herald* (26 October 2011).

[92] ibid. See generally A Hood and M Cormier, 'Prosecuting International Crimes in Australia: The Cases of the Sri Lankan President' (2012) 13 *Melbourne Journal of International Law* 235.

[93] Ben Doherty, 'Aung San Suu Kyi: Lawyers Seek Prosecution for Crimes against Humanity' *Guardian* (27 March 2018.

Attorney-General refused to grant consent for the prosecution to go ahead on the grounds of Aung San Suu Kyi's immunity. Not satisfied with this outcome, the citizen commenced a special case in the original jurisdiction of the High Court seeking to quash the decision of the Attorney-General. The case of *Taylor v Attorney-General (Cth)* gave the High Court the opportunity to consider the legislative requirement for the Attorney-General to consent to the prosecution of international crimes in Australia.[94] The plaintiff raised several questions of law, including whether the Attorney-General's decision is subject to judicial review and, if so, whether the Attorney-General erred in refusing consent on the basis of immunity. The majority of the High Court held that it was 'unnecessary to answer' the question of judicial review, and that any question of error on the basis of immunity 'does not arise'.[95] The Court instead focused on the very narrow issue of how to interpret the clause: 'proceedings for an offence under this Division must not be commenced without the Attorney-General's written consent'. The majority held that only the Attorney-General – not private citizens – can initiate prosecutions against genocide, crimes against humanity, war crimes and crimes against the administration of justice of the ICC.[96] Therefore, in the attempt to prosecute Aung San Suu Kyi, the Attorney-General did not have any option other than refusing consent.[97]

It was a disappointing outcome for a case that had the potential for some robust analysis of the requirements for the Attorney-General's consent and for the High Court to consider the finer points of personal immunity for senior officials accused of committing international crimes. There are legitimate legal and policy reasons to ensure foreign leaders are immune from court proceedings in Australia.[98] Yet, the High Court has significantly narrowed the possible pathways to prosecution for international crimes in Australia by disallowing citizen-initiated charges, meaning that the potential for citizens to initiate prosecutions against lower-level perpetrators is now off the table.[99]

[94] *Taylor v A-G (Cth)* (2019) 93 ALJR 1044.

[95] ibid 1055–56.

[96] ibid 1055. Such proceedings can only be 'prosecuted in the name of the Attorney-General' in accordance with the Criminal Code, above n 61, s 268.121(2).

[97] *Taylor*, above n 94, 1055.

[98] s 36(1) of the Foreign States Immunities Act 1985 (Cth) extends the Diplomatic Privileges and Immunities Act 1967 (Cth) to heads of state, which in turn implements the Vienna Convention on Diplomatic Relations into Australian law. Under this Convention, diplomatic agents are inviolable and immune from the jurisdiction of the host state: Vienna Convention on Diplomatic Relations (adopted 18 April 1961, entered into force 24 April 1964) 500 UNTS 95, Arts 29, 31. The rationale for conferring immunities on foreign leaders is to facilitate stable international relations and enable international diplomacy. See generally, Hood and Cormier, above n 92.

[99] See Rawan Arraf, 'High Court of Australia Closes Door on Private Prosecutions in Taylor v Attorney-General' (*Opinio Juris*, 14 February 2020): opiniojuris.org/2020/02/14/high-court-of-australia-closes-door-on-private-prosecutions-in-taylor-v-attorney-general/. For a general discussion and comparative analysis on private prosecutions, see JD Mujuzi, 'The Right to Institute a Private Prosecution: A Comparative Analysis' (2015) 4 *International Human Rights Law Review* 222.

G. Conclusion to Section II

The above overview of the key cases in which Australian courts have encountered allegations of international crimes illustrates the rather ad hoc nature of the judiciary's encounters with international criminal law. It also begins to give a sense of the rather arbitrary approach that Australian courts have taken with respect to any substantive engagement with international criminal law, which is the focus of the final section of this chapter.

III. ARBITRARY: USEFUL CONTRIBUTIONS AND MISSED OPPORTUNITIES

Despite a clear lack of investigations and prosecutions for international crimes in Australia, Australian courts have nevertheless engaged with questions, principles and themes pertaining to international criminal law as they arose in various proceedings. How, then, should Australia's limited judicial contribution to the international criminal justice project be assessed? It is difficult to discern a coherent narrative from the cases reviewed in section II. There are some decisions in which judges embraced the intricacies of international criminal law and applied them as far as practicable to the matter at hand. Others merely acknowledged international law in passing or took a purposely conservative approach to its utility. The discrepancy between such cases may, in some instances, be explained by procedural limitations on judicial review or appeal. More likely is that the lack of proper engagement with international criminal law is a symptom of the lingering reluctance of some Australian judges to see international law as anything other than an encroachment on Australian sovereignty.[100]

Of the cases discussed in section II, *Polyukhovich v Commonwealth*[101] and *Nulyarimma v Thompson*[102] are arguably Australia's main judicial contributions to international criminal law state practice. *Polyukhovich*, for example, was cited on several occasions by the International Criminal Tribunal for the former Yugoslavia as support for the notion that a crime against humanity under customary international law does not require a policy or plan.[103] *Polyukhovich* has also been cited as an example of allowing the retroactive application of war crimes legislation where the conduct in question was considered criminal by treaty or customary international law at the time of commission.[104] *Nulyarimma* is held up as evidence of how some jurisdictions do not accept that

[100] See generally, H Charlesworth et al, 'Deep Anxieties: Australia and the International Legal Order' (2003) 25 *Sydney Law Review* 423.

[101] *Polyukhovich*, above n 64.

[102] *Nulyarimma*, above n 48.

[103] *Prosecutor v Kunarac, Kovac and Vukovic* (Appeals Chamber Judgement) IT-96-23-A (12 June 2002) n 114; *Prosecutor v Kronjelac* (Judgment) IT-97-25-T (15 March 2002) n 197; *Prosecutor v Đorđević* (Appeals Chamber Judgement) IT-05-87/1-A (27 January 2014) 21.

[104] See, eg, *R v Finta* [1994] 1 SCR 701 (La Forest J) [24]; R Cryer, D Robinson and S Vasiliev, *An Introduction to International Criminal Law and Procedure*, 4th edn (Cambridge, Cambridge University Press, 2019) 71.

customary international law is capable of directly creating offences in domestic law.[105] Lord Mance of the UK Supreme Court praised the Federal Court for its consideration of 'the precise basis on and extent to which customary international law may become part of domestic law'.[106] Conversely, *Nulyarimma* has been criticised in Australia for lacking 'intellectual rigour' in its analysis of the relationship between customary international law and domestic law[107] and has been described as 'morally repugnant [for suggesting] that genocide is not a crime in Australia'.[108]

Other Australian cases that have achieved some traction internationally include Article 1F exclusion clause decisions such as *SRYYY v Minister for Immigration and Multicultural and Indigenous Affairs*.[109] In a rare acknowledgement of an Australian case by the US Supreme Court, *SRYYY* was cited in *Negusie v Holder* by Stevens J and Breyer J in support of the proposition that any exclusion under Article 1F of the Refugee Convention must be for 'culpable conduct' with consideration being given to any mitigating factors.[110] Foreign commentators have also noted Australia's contribution to international criminal law in the refugee context, with the Federal Court's detailed analysis in *SRYYY* parsed and critiqued in legal scholarship.[111]

The High Court's analysis of the offence of slavery in *R v Tang* has attracted particular praise from scholars, with Jean Allain writing that 'the High Court should be commended for providing the most far-reaching and cogent examination to date of the definition of "slavery" as established in international law'.[112] The Court's broader definition of slavery has been compared favourably to the narrow interpretation applied by the European Court of Human Rights in *Siliadin v France*[113] and described as 'a valuable contribution to understanding slavery under international law'.[114] The comprehensive and progressive legal

[105] See, eg, A Cassese et al, *International Criminal Law: Cases and Commentary* (Oxford University Press, 2011) 235–36; A Cassese (ed), *The Oxford Companion to International Criminal Justice* (New York, Oxford University Press, 2009) 628, 859.

[106] *Keyu v Secretary of State for Foreign and Commonwealth Affairs* [2015] UKSC 69, 111 (Lord Mance).

[107] Guilfoyle, above n 59, 24–33; Flynn, above n 60, 64–75; B Saul, 'The International Crime of Genocide in Australian Law' (2000) 22 *Sydney Law Review* 527, 532–34; Charlesworth et al, 'Deep Anxieties', above n 100, 455–57.

[108] Guilfoyle, above n 59, 36.

[109] *SRYYY*, above n 17.

[110] *Negusie v Holder*, 555 US 511, 536–37 (2009).

[111] See, eg, J Rikhof, 'War Criminals Not Welcome: How Common Law Countries Approach the Phenomenon of International Crimes in the Immigration and Refugee Context' (2009) 21 *International Journal of Refugee Law* 453, 470–72; SS Juss, 'Complicity, Exclusion and the "Unworthy" in Refugee Law' (2012) 31 *Refugee Survey Quarterly* 1, 33–35; Z Egelman, 'Punishment and Protection, Two Sides of the Same Sword: The Problem of International Criminal Law under the Refugee Convention' (2018) 59 *Harvard International Law Journal* 461, 480–81, 490–92.

[112] Allain, above n 88, 257.

[113] *Siliadin v France* (App no 73316/01) ECHR 2005-VII 333. See, eg, ibid 246–47; S Tully, 'Sex, Slavery and the High Court of Australia: The Contribution of R v Tang to International Jurisprudence Case Comment' (2010) 10 *International Criminal Law Review* 403, 415–16; I Kolodizner, 'R v Tang: Developing an Australian Anti-Slavery Jurisprudence' (2009) 31 *Sydney Law Review* 487, 496, fn 49.

[114] Tully, above n 113, 423.

analysis in *Tang* is an example of what Australian courts might have to offer in relation to the development of international criminal law and its application to prosecution of international crimes. As mentioned earlier, the offence of slavery is not, however, an international crime in the same category as war crimes, crimes against humanity and genocide.[115] Prosecuting a private individual for an offence committed in Australia, against a small group of victims, is nowhere near as politically sensitive as convening a criminal trial against foreign state agents for mass atrocities committed overseas.

Indeed, political sensitivities seemed to be at the forefront of the High Court's collective mind in *Taylor v Attorney-General (Cth)*, when the majority claimed in a passing remark that allowing the initiation of a private prosecution for international crimes would 'have the real potential to embarrass Australia internationally'.[116] While concerns about international embarrassment should arguably be left to the diplomats, the majority's apprehension about Australia's international reputation was not reflected in the rest of the judgment. Instead, it focused on a narrow interpretation of the object and purpose of the International Criminal Court Act 2002 (Cth), emphasising Australia's 'international rights' in relation to complementarity.[117] The Court viewed the enabling legislation as primarily ensuring that Australia would retain primacy to exercise its jurisdiction over crimes under the Rome Statute.[118] While this is undoubtedly one of the main purposes of the legislation, the Court ignored other, broader, purposes of implementing Statute crimes into Australian law. The Second Reading Speech for the International Criminal Court Bill 2002 (Cth), which was used by the High Court majority to support its narrow interpretation, reveals a wider appreciation for the aims of international criminal justice.[119] The Attorney-General at the time, Darryl Williams, spoke about the importance of ending impunity for international crimes, the role of the ICC in enhancing international peace and security and its potential deterrent effect on perpetrators.[120] He further declared that 'it is the primary duty of every state to exercise its national criminal jurisdiction over these crimes'.[121] It is hard to see how the High Court's decision to constrain the commencement of prosecutions at the procedural level will contribute to such aims.

Similarly uninspiring was Besanko J's avoidance of almost anything relating to international criminal law in the *Roberts-Smith* defamation proceedings,

[115] Crimes such as slavery are usually 'committed *against* States. They do not involve States as such or, if they involve State agents, these agents typically act for private gain': Cassese et al, above n 105, 114 (emphasis in original).

[116] *Taylor*, above n 94, 1055 (Kiefel CJ, Bell, Gageler and Keane JJ).

[117] ibid 1050.

[118] ibid.

[119] Commonwealth, *Parliamentary Debates*, House of Representatives, 25 June 2002, 4318–23 (Daryl Williams), cited in ibid.

[120] *Parliamentary Debates*, ibid 4318–19.

[121] ibid 4320.

despite the fact that allegations of war crimes were the very subject of the dispute. There was another missed opportunity in the High Court's refusal to engage in any consideration of the broader purpose of extradition in the case of Charles Zentai.[122] Using the principles of treaty interpretation outlined in the Vienna Convention on the Law of Treaties,[123] the High Court contemplated the context, object and purpose of the Australia–Hungary Extradition Treaty.[124] The minister had argued that extradition treaties should be afforded 'a broad and generous construction so far as the text permits, to facilitate the purpose of bringing justice'.[125] The High Court majority rejected this in favour of the far more prosaic conclusion that the purpose of the Treaty is 'to give effect to the reciprocal obligations to extradite persons for extraditable offences'.[126] The Court saw no apparent need to consider whether such a literal interpretation of the purpose of extradition would result in Zentai's impunity. It is unclear why the majority did not adopt a broader interpretation of extradition's purpose akin to that of Gleeson CJ in *Vasiljkovic* six years earlier.[127] Gleeson CJ wrote that extradition allows 'an adjudication to be made in a foreign place, according to foreign law, in circumstances where Australia had no intention itself of bringing the person to trial for the conduct of which the person is accused'.[128] This reflects the *aut dedere aut judicare* principle, and aligns with Australia's obligations under international law to either extradite or prosecute persons accused of committing international crimes. In *Zentai*, the High Court determined that the applicant would not be extradited to Hungary to stand trial for a war crime, yet Australia clearly 'had no intention itself' of prosecuting Charles Zentai for the accused conduct.

The High Court's interpretation of the Australia–Hungary Extradition Treaty in *Zentai* was denounced as 'highly technical and selective', and as '[prioritising] domestic legal sensibilities over international obligations'.[129] This type of accusation is not new. Australian courts have attracted criticism in the past for harbouring 'the perception of international law as a source of un-Australian, chaotic and fanciful norms'.[130] Their apparent reluctance to consider and apply international law principles and, in particular, the inconsistent and arbitrary

[122] *Zentai* (High Court), above n 37.

[123] Vienna Convention on the Law of Treaties (adopted 23 May 1969, entered into force 27 January 1980) 1155 UNTS 331, Arts 31–32.

[124] *Zentai* (High Court), above n 37, 222–23 (French CJ).

[125] ibid 214.

[126] ibid 238–39 (Gummow, Crennan, Kiefel and Bell JJ).

[127] One possible answer can be found in the High Court's broader evolution away from considering contextual factors in its judgments, towards a preference for strict legalism. This, Desmond Manderson writes, has resulted in a 'textual straitjacket and contextual blindness': D Manderson, 'The Big Picture: Imagining the Constitution' (2021) 49 *Federal Law Review* 303, 309.

[128] *Vasiljkovic*, above n 36, [34].

[129] Cullen and Burgess, above n 44, 232.

[130] Charlesworth et al, 'Deep Anxieties', above n 100, 424.

approach courts have taken to the relationship between international law and domestic law, has disappointed Australian scholars of international law.[131]

It appears that 'inconsistent and arbitrary' is also the most apt characterisation of the way Australian courts have dealt with international criminal law. Such inconsistency is likely the result of differing views held by different judges about the importance of sovereignty and the relationship between international and domestic law. It may go some way towards explaining why some judges, in cases such as *Zentai* and *Taylor*, have taken a cautious, overtly technical approach to the legal issues that all but ignore the underlying allegation that an international crime was committed. Yet, other judges, in cases like *Polyukhovich* and *SRYYY*, have embraced the principles and precedents found in international criminal law and, in doing so, provided a particular Australian contribution to this evolving body of global law.

IV. CONCLUDING REMARKS

Individual judicial predilections towards the role of sovereignty and the relationship between international and domestic law almost certainly play a role in the seemingly arbitrary levels of engagement with international criminal law by various Australian courts. The absence of a more predictable and systematic approach to matters involving international crimes and international criminal law might also be explained by the ad hoc nature of the types of cases that come before Australian courts. There is very little in the way of a connective thread to join the cases discussed in this chapter, beyond the fact that they all involve one or more accusations of international crimes. With the exception of *R v Tang*, the cases are not concerned with questions of guilt or innocence, punishment or broader criminal justice issues. It is therefore not surprising that courts preoccupied with matters ranging from refugee status, extradition requests, defamation, constitutional validity and criminal procedure have taken different views of the relevance of international criminal law. In this regard, the absence of Australian civilian court judgments dedicated to developing and applying international criminal law in the context of domestic prosecutions for international crimes is keenly felt. Without a track record of prosecuting persons accused of international crimes, the analysis and evolution of international criminal law will always be on the outer margins of Australian jurisprudence.

The ad hoc and arbitrary approach to international criminal law by Australian courts could more broadly be said to reflect the uneven, transactional attitude of successive Australian governments to the international criminal justice project. When required for Australia's diplomatic standing, Australia touts 'emphatic

[131] ibid 446–58; P Mathew, 'International Law and the Protection of Human Rights in Australia: Recent Trends' (1995) 17 *Sydney Law Review* 177, 195.

support for international criminal justice'[132] on the world stage. When domestic politics are at stake, war crimes investigations are abandoned[133] and international crimes allegations downplayed.[134] Australia's well-documented reluctance towards investigating and prosecuting international crimes may, however, be reaching a turning point. At the time of writing, there appears to be genuine political will to pursue investigations into allegations of war crimes committed by Australian soldiers in Afghanistan.[135] In March 2023, a former Special Forces soldier became the first person to be charged with committing an international crime under the 2002 laws. The accused soldier was arrested and charged with one count of murder as a war crime under section 268.70 of the Criminal Code.[136] Whether there will be more charges and arrests is by no means certain, but by taking seriously its international responsibility to investigate and prosecute international crimes, Australian courts will hopefully have the opportunity to develop a more coherent and consistent approach to international criminal law in the future.

[132] Statement by Ms Julia O'Brien, First Secretary, Permanent Mission of Australia to the United Nations, 'The Role of International Criminal Justice and Reconciliation', DFAT: www.dfat.gov.au/international-relations/international-organisations/un/unsc-2013-2014/national-statements/Pages/the-role-of-international-criminal-justice-and-reconciliation.

[133] Janine MacDonald, 'War Crimes Unit Closed after Five Years, No Results' *The Age* (Melbourne, 4 January 2000) 2.

[134] Paul Daley, 'Australia Has Never Been Good at Acknowledging Its Troops Have Been Guilty of Acts of Inhumanity' *Guardian* (5 September 2020).

[135] Inspector-General of the Australian Defence Force, 'Afghanistan Inquiry Report' (Report, 10 November 2020): afghanistaninquiry.defence.gov.au.

[136] Australian Federal Police, 'Former Australian Soldier Charged with War Crime' (Media Release, 20 March 2023): www.afp.gov.au/news-centre/media-release/former-australian-soldier-charged-war-crime.

Part III

Australians and International Law

12

Child Refugees, Child Rights: Sidestepping International Law in Australian Policy-Making

JORDANA SILVERSTEIN

I. INTRODUCTION

Oliver White, a senior policy officer at UNICEF Australia, informed me in an oral history interview I conducted with him in April 2018, that the Australian migration policy framework is shaped by, variously, a 'growing anti-migrant sentiment, and increased xenophobia and racism and protectionism', as well as a desire to 'secure the border [and] prevent people arriving irregularly. And, in that instance, these special protections that exist for children, under international law, in practice are just completely disregarded'. He continued, that when it comes to the treatment of people seeking asylum and making their own way to Australia by boat,

> children are detained, they're turned back, they're refouled, they're sent to Nauru, where they're poorly treated, and exposed to violence and sexual abuse ... But one of your questions was around have children been considered differently to adults when forming refugee policy? And they should be, but I don't think they have been in this instance ... You've got the Government that is very much aware of its obligations and is progressively taking steps to ignore or remove those obligations from legislation, or to try to sidestep them.[1]

This conception of this disregarding is the focus of this chapter, in which we will come to understand the ways that principles of international law surrounding child refugees and asylum seekers are situated within ideas of child refugee policy-making in Australia. I am interested here in thinking through international law as a set of instantiated practices and ideas, as produced by people working within the human rights frameworks and institutions in Australia, in order to explore politicians and human rights practitioners' understandings of the place

[1] Interview with Oliver White (Sydney, 18 April 2018).

of some key international law principles and human rights ideas relating to child refugees and asylum seekers in twenty-first-century Australia. In order to do so, I will explore the work of a variety of human rights bodies, instruments and ideas, as articulated in oral history interviews I conducted in 2018 and 2019. Through an examination of these interviews, and of the words of these human rights actors, we can gain insight into how they comprehend ideas of international law and human rights to be variously deployed, or avoided, in Australian child refugee policy-making. Through their words we can see some of the ways in which the relationship between the international and domestic is imagined within ideas of Australian politics and political practice, and the ways it is refracted through ideas and practices of maintaining the racialised border. That is, we will come to understand that people working within human rights institutions in Australia understand the international – and international law – to be predominantly deliberately avoided by policy-makers as they are conceptualising and crafting child refugee policy. As has been documented by other legal scholars with regard to a range of human rights instruments in Australia,[2] this is a common attitude held by policy-makers and politicians, wherein the instruments are more likely to be pushed to the side, avoided, rather than attended to. This process occurs despite, as we shall see, the emotional weight given to considerations of children and their concerns in political discourses. Although care is professed, mechanisms which discursively perform that care (even if that discourse is not accompanied by material practice) are often disavowed.

There is an international and domestic legal framework within which the policy-makers explored in this chapter operate. The Refugee Convention of 1951,[3] its 1967 Protocol,[4] and the Convention on the Rights of the Child of 1989 (CRC)[5] are the key relevant international law mechanisms which shape the policy work undertaken. Domestically, the key relevant pieces of legislation are the Migration Act 1958 (Cth), first introduced in 1958 and heavily amended since then, and the Immigration (Guardianship of Children) Act 1946 (Cth), which has likewise been amended but retains its key principle of making the Immigration Minister guardian of child migrants and refugees who travel across the border and into Australia without a guardian.[6]

In this chapter I will examine interviews I conducted with a variety of people: Oliver White; Gillian Triggs, the former President of the Australian Human Rights

[2] See, eg, M Chiam, 'International Human Rights Treaties and Institutions in the Protection of Human Rights in Australia' in M Groves, J Boughey and D Meagher (eds), *The Legal Protection of Rights in Australia* (London, Bloomsbury Publishing, 2019); D Ghezelbash, *Refuge Lost: Asylum Law in an Interdependent World* (Cambridge, Cambridge University Press, 2018).

[3] Convention Relating to the Status of Refugees (adopted 28 July 1951, entered into force 22 April 1954) 189 UNTS 137.

[4] Protocol Relating to the Status of Refugees (adopted 31 January 1967, entered into force 4 October 1967) 606 UNTS 267.

[5] Convention on the Rights of the Child (adopted 20 November 1989, entered into force 2 September 1990) 1577 UNTS 3 (CRC).

[6] Immigration (Guardianship of Children) Act 1946 (Cth) s 6.

Commission (AHRC); Lucy Morgan, a Specialist Adviser in Immigration in the Human Rights Scrutiny Team at the Australian Human Rights Commission; and Elizabeth Elliott, a Distinguished Professor in Paediatrics and Child Health at the University of Sydney, who worked on the AHRC's 2014 Inquiry into Children in Detention. Alongside this I will examine the words of politicians and other policy-makers who expressly reiterate that domestic legislative and political approaches to controlling the borders, and controlling child refugees, have no room for international law and its human rights concerns. Through the examination of the discourses and narratives which they produce, we can further understand the ways that the place of refugee and asylum-seeking children is conceptualised by the Australian polity and society as being outside the domestic, and is thus a foreign concern.

Following Sara Ahmed's work, in this chapter I am thinking about and through 'orientations', in order to ponder her question at the beginning of *Queer Phenomenology*: 'what difference does it make "what" we are oriented toward?'[7] I will think this through in relation to how policy-makers and human rights institutions and workers are variously oriented towards international law, Australian politicians, Australian history and child refugees. Ahmed explains that 'orientation is a matter of how we reside in space … of how we inhabit spaces as well as "who" or "what" we inhabit spaces with'.[8] Moreover,

> orientations involve different ways of registering the proximity of objects and others. Orientations shape not only how we inhabit space, but how we apprehend this world of shared inhabitance, as well as 'who' or 'what' we direct our energy and attention toward.[9]

Orientations, thus, are a question of familiarity, of how we engage with the familiar and the unfamiliar, and how we make things familiar or unfamiliar.[10] Thinking with these ideas, I will consider principles of international law as items which people are oriented towards or away from, and will consider the effects, and affects, of that orientation. What can we learn by understanding policy-makers' work, ideas and words in this way? I will answer this with particular reference to the ways that some policy-makers consider refugee children – both as individual people and as a category of person – and the ways that modes of policy-making become a set of descriptions of orientation and familiarity.

Thus, I am looking at the ways in which interviewees discussed refugee and asylum-seeking children, or the political management of those children, in order to think about the different orientations which exist towards these children, and towards governments. These orientations are shaped by histories of colonisation, imperialism and white Australia. Through these interviews we can gain a

[7] S Ahmed, *Queer Phenomenology: Orientations, Objects, Others* (Durham, NC, Duke University Press, 2006) 1.

[8] ibid.

[9] ibid 3.

[10] ibid 7.

sense of the feelings about children, politicians and international law that the interviewees carry, which orient both the interviewees and the work they carry out.

II. METHODOLOGY

I conducted these oral history interviews in locations of the interviewees' choosing, either in their offices or homes. The interviews were wide-ranging, as I asked questions and maintained conversation about the work they and their organisations have done, their own personal history with relation to their jobs, and the ways that they think about their work. As numerous scholars have shown, oral history interviews have a certain texture, as they create a dynamic between interviewer and interviewee in the room in which they take place.[11] The responses, answers or testimonies provided through oral history interviews need consciously to be understood as works of memory. They testify to how interviewees remember and reflect at the time of the interview upon their past lives and work, rather than an objective truth about 'what happened' (a truth, indeed, which is never accessible or in existence). In this way, they weave past and present together. Having undertaken the interviews, transcripts were produced and verified by the interviewee, and the interviews were then analysed using discourse analysis techniques. I undertake a close reading of them, looking for ways to understand the words and ideas which my interviewees spoke. The readings and conclusions which I reach might therefore not accord with how the interviewees understand themselves and their work (although of course it might). I read and analyse these interviews in order to place them within a longer Australian and international history of attention to international law when considering the human rights of child refugees.

While each interview reflects the force of the interviewees thoughts alone, rather than testifying to an objective truth of a situation, by assembling this archive of interviews – alongside the words of policy-makers from their time in Parliament – we can attain a collective sense of how international human rights bodies and instruments have been considered by governments and policy-makers across recent decades. This, however, is not a totalising history, but rather a discursive snapshot.

[11] See, eg, E Faye, 'Psychoanalysis and the Barred Subject of Feminist History' (1995) 10 *Australian Feminist Studies* 77; R Reynolds, 'Trauma and the Relational Dynamics of Life-History Interviewing' (2012) 43 *Australian Historical Studies* 78; V Yow, '"Do I Like Them Too Much?": Effects of the Oral History Interview on the Interviewer and Vice-Versa' (1997) 24 *Oral History Review* 55; K Holmes, 'Does It Matter If She Cried? Recording Emotion and the Australian Generations Oral History Project' (2017) 44 *Oral History Review* 56.

III. UNDERSTANDINGS OF THE CHILD

Despite the fact that approximately half of the world's refugees are children,[12] 'the Refugee Convention is complicated in its application to children [as] it was designed with the adult male as the archetypical refugee'.[13] This has implications for the way in which it is applied within Australia, particularly given the reticence expressed by some policy-makers towards international law and its place within domestic policy and law, as I will explore below.

The figure of the 'child refugee' has played a large role in Australian political discourse and the figure of the child in general carries substantial emotional weight.[14] This is compounded by the CRC which, as is articulated by Kirsten Sandberg, 'is based on the idea that it is useful to view children as a group'.[15] While we can question whether it is truly useful to view children as a group – and recognise that containing them in a group is historically contingent – it is important to think about what work this grouping does.[16] For instance, scholars such as John Tobin, Jacqueline Bhabha and numerous others have explained that imagining children as inherently and purely vulnerable is both fundamental to the way in which the CRC understands children and 'carries the risk that they will be defined by their vulnerabilities'.[17] Children are, of course, much more than vulnerability and inadequacy.

[12] See, eg, UNICEF, 'Uprooted: The Growing Crisis for Refugee and Migrant Children' (Report, September 2016): www.unicef.org/publications/index_92710.html.

[13] M Crock and H Martin, 'Finding Refuge in Australia: How Law and Policies Affect the Entitlements of Children Entering as Refugees and Humanitarian Migrants' in M Crock (ed), *Creating New Futures: Settling Children and Youth from Refugee Backgrounds* (Annandale, The Federation Press, 2015) 50.

[14] For an expansion of this view see, for instance, J Silverstein, *Cruel Care: A History of Children At Our Borders* (Clayton, Monash University Publishing, 2023); J Silverstein, '"Because We All Love Our Country": Refugee and Asylum-Seeking Children, Australian Policy-Makers, and the Building of National Sentiment' (2019) 65 *Australian Journal of Politics & History* 532. For explorations of the emotionality of children see, eg, B Baird, 'Child Politics, Feminist Analyses' (2008) 23 *Australian Feminist Studies* 291; J Damousi, 'The Campaign for Japanese-Australian Children to Enter Australia, 1957–1968: A History of Post-War Humanitarianism' (2018) 64 *Australian Journal of Politics & History* 211; M Tomsic, 'The Politics of Picture Books: Stories of Displaced Children in Twenty-First-Century Australia' (2018) 15 *History Australia* 339; J Faulkner, 'Ghosts of Eugenics' Past: "Childhood" as a Target for Whitening Race in the United States and Canada' (2019) *Critical Race and Whiteness Studies Journal: First Glimpse* 2: acrawsa.org.au/2019/06/21/first-glimpse-journal-article-2/; M Ticktin, 'A World Without Innocence' (2017) 44 *American Ethnologist* 577; R Sheldon, *The Child to Come: Life after the Human Catastrophe* (Minneapolis, MN, University of Minnesota Press, 2016).

[15] K Sandberg, 'The Convention on the Rights of the Child and the Vulnerability of Children' (2015) 84 *Nordic Journal of International Law* 223.

[16] The field of the history of childhood is vast. For a foundational history of childhood, see, eg, P Ariès, *Centuries of Childhood: A Social History of Family Life* (New York, Knopf, 1962). For a foundational history of child refugees see, eg, T Zahra, *The Lost Children: Reconstructing Europe's Families after World War II* (Cambridge, MA, Harvard University Press, 2011).

[17] J Tobin, 'Understanding Children's Rights: A Vision Beyond Vulnerability' (2015) 84 *Nordic Journal of International Law* 155.

When the CRC is applied in the domestic Australian context, it is evident that it is often sidelined. Kim Rubenstein and Jacqueline Field noted in 2015 that 'Australia's current law is insufficient to protect these [refugee] children's best interests and acknowledge their individual circumstances, as required by the UN Convention on the Rights of the Child'.[18] Moreover, as Mary Crock and Hannah Martin have shown, people who fit into the category of child refugees do not face one set of circumstances in their interaction with Australian policy, procedure or law. In 2015 they wrote that

> there has never been a time of greater disparity in the rights, entitlements and prospects of child refugees in Australia. Depending on how, when and where a child arrives, their rights can vary from almost the full rights of a citizen to virtual nothingness.[19]

Given this complex interplay between international law and domestic policy and law, I will now explore how the interviewees – all of whom work within this tense relationship – described the group of people we could call 'refugee or asylum-seeking children', and consider the role of an orientation towards international law norms in producing these ideas.

When I interviewed Elizabeth Elliott, Distinguished Professor in Paediatrics and Child Health at the University of Sydney, who had served as an expert adviser during the AHRC's Inquiry into Children in Detention in 2014, she described some stories of children she met in the detention centre on Christmas Island and Nauru who were depressed, suicidal, self-harming and who had witnessed great trauma and experienced family separation. She told me of 'one man [who] said to me – with three sons, two of whom were very depressed – you know, I didn't bring my family to Australia – children to Australia to teach them how to commit suicide'.[20] From her perspective,

> children are vulnerable in their developmental stages. And then … there's detention without cause, lack of good living conditions, lack of access to health care and lack of access to education. 'Punitive' was the word I was thinking of, a punitive approach. So adding a layer of trauma to other layers of trauma. And the overriding sentiment was just hopelessness.[21]

She told me about a quote from a 16-year-old boy that she featured in the report into Wickham Point Detention Centre, where he had said '[t]he Prime Minister of Australia says he is saving our lives but at the same time he is killing us'.[22] In Elliott's analysis, it was a case of 'out of sight, out of mind' influencing

[18] K Rubenstein and J Field, 'Citizens in their Own Right: Achieving Adequate Recognition of Children in Australia's Immigration and Citizenship Framework' in M Crock (ed), *Creating New Futures: Settling Children and Youth from Refugee Backgrounds* (Annandale, The Federation Press, 2015) 243.

[19] Crock and Martin, 'Finding Refuge in Australia', above n 13, 49.

[20] Interview with Elizabeth Elliott (Sydney, 27 November 2018).

[21] ibid.

[22] E Elliott and H Gunasekera, 'The Health and Well-Being of Children in Immigration Detention: Report to the Australian Human Rights Commission Monitoring Visit to Wickham Point Detention

governmental decisions. She believed that the government was preoccupied by the 'security' concerns of the post-9/11 world, that they actively equated 'all asylum seekers with terrorists' and that 'politically it was good [for them] that they kept them out and kept them out of sight'.[23] This policy was, in her view, led by governments who ignored their human rights obligations, and as such was analogous to the treatment of 'remote Aboriginal communities'.[24] Indeed, as Elliott stated, 'denying children, even very sick children, access to health is definitely against their human rights'.[25]

When I asked if she thought that 'it's useful thinking of the child as particularly vulnerable, or as a separate category to adults', Lucy Morgan from the AHRC began by considering the place of adults, stating that she

> think[s] it is important whenever doing advocacy in human rights that it's clear that adults are rights holders as well, and even though the obligations towards adults may not be the same as children, they still exist. But, at the same time, and particularly looking at immigration context, the way you would treat adults is not an appropriate way to treat children.

This is because, as she said,

> special allowances do have to be made for their particular status as children, particularly if they arrive unaccompanied. So, although saying children have particular vulnerabilities, that's not to negate the fact that the adults have rights as well, but it's also to, I think, point out that there are additional obligations you have towards a child because of their unique status.[26]

The precise quality of that 'unique status' was left unelaborated, but this idea of children as vulnerable, it seems, was imagined by Morgan as being shared by government. She told me:

> I don't actually think that there's any particular interest from any government I've seen in putting children into detention, because there's not really much good that comes of it, even from the government's perspective … I think it's just within Australia's legislation, the grounds for a detention are fairly broad … And, so the corollary of that is children end up in detention. But I don't think there's a particular motivation for that to happen. It's more just a consequence of the way our law is written.[27]

However, the political record suggests the contrary. At a hearing of the AHRC's 2014 Inquiry into Children in Detention, Greg Lake – a former department official on Christmas Island, responsible for 'preparing the criteria by which

Centre, Darwin, NT' (Report, 16–18 October 2015) 19: www.humanrights.gov.au/our-work/asylum-seekers-and-refugees/publications/health-and-well-being-children-immigration.

[23] Interview with Elizabeth Elliott, above n 20.

[24] ibid.

[25] ibid.

[26] Interview with Lucy Morgan (Sydney, 18 April 2018).

[27] ibid.

people would be selected to go offshore'[28] – testified regarding a conversation in 2012 between him and the office of Chris Bowen, the Australian Labor Party's Minister for Immigration and Citizenship. Lake stated that he was told by the office that his 'responsibility according to this phone call was to select the children that looked the youngest' to send them to detention on Manus Island, when the centre there was being reopened.[29] Lake explained that through this phone call from Bowen's office, he understood that the government 'wanted to send a deterrent message … [so] it was important to send some children'. Madeline Gleeson has noted that 'one of the criteria used for Manus was that children had to be at least seven years old, since doctors had advised that it was not possible to vaccinate children younger than this against the diseases there'.[30] That is, the government was looking for the youngest looking children, who were over seven years old. Thus, children were being deliberately sent to the most punitive form of detention. This followed Bowen's earlier position on the detention of child refugees – a position similarly held by other immigration ministers, from both sides of Parliament – wherein he worked to amend the Migration Act 1958 (Cth) and the Immigration (Guardianship of Children) Act 1946 (Cth) in 2011 in order 'to remedy the current, patently unworkable, situation precluding the involuntary transfer of unaccompanied minors to other countries'.[31] Bowen stated in Parliament that it was important to change this situation as

> a blanket inability of the government of the day to transfer unaccompanied minors to a designated country provides an invitation to people smugglers to send boatloads of children to Australia. No government can stand for the gaming of the system and risking of children's lives in this way.[32]

This is one example of domestic law being amended in order to deliberately evade the protections suggested by both international law, for example, that 'in all actions concerning children … the best interests of the child shall be a primary consideration',[33] and Australian human rights bodies.

Morgan's view also contrasts with Gillian Triggs' understanding of politicians. Triggs told me that she does not 'really understand politicians … They operate ideologically in terms of party. So trying to understand them and understand why they persisted with these cruel policies for so long is almost beyond

[28] M Gleeson, *Offshore: Behind the Wire on Manus and Nauru* (Sydney, NewSouth Publishing, 2016) 46.

[29] This testimony by Greg Lake to the AHRC 2012 Inquiry into Children in Detention is cited in ibid 47. Lake provides similar testimony in a 2016 interview with journalist Michael Green. See Behind the Wire and the Wheeler Centre, 'The Messenger #5: A Safer Place' (*Wheeler Centre*, 13 March 2017): www.wheelercentre.com/broadcasts/podcasts/the-messenger/5-a-safer-place.

[30] Gleeson, above n 28, 46–47.

[31] Commonwealth, *Parliamentary Debates*, House of Representatives, 21 September 2011, 10945 (C Bowen).

[32] ibid.

[33] CRC, above n 5, Art 3(1).

comprehension'.[34] For Triggs then, politicians are oriented primarily towards themselves and each other and the class of people and institutions which make up formal politics and government. This, in her view, plays an important role in determining how notions of 'best interests of the child' are treated, how they sit within the hierarchy of policy and political concerns. Indeed, the examples above point to some of the deep problems with the materialisation of the concept of 'best interests of the child': in the Australian refugee context, it relies on faith in a superior authority wielding power by making decisions for another group about what is in their 'best interests', and being prepared to follow the sentiments signified by the appropriate human rights conventions. Moreover, it relies on faith in a decision-making power which is informed by a belief that forms of white knowledge, insight and care are pre-eminent and correct.[35] I will return to this below.

For Triggs, who headed the AHRC's Inquiry and subsequent report, 'The Forgotten Children', the existence of the International Covenant on Civil and Political Rights, as well as the CRC, were of direct use in prosecuting the AHRC's case in the media for the rights of the children in detention, even if they did not see the same success with government politicians. Triggs explained that, when carrying out the Inquiry:

> We brought the media with us all the time. We made that decision. But the media really got the point about the children and it helped me as a lawyer to say that one of the great scandals is that Australia signed up to that treaty but never implemented it in Australian law, and so that's a huge impediment to actually going to a court … in relation to children in particular, apart from very specific bits of legislation that deal with child welfare and so on. So we felt that by putting a focus on our international obligations, which is our mandate at the Human Rights Commission in any event, we were able to focus on those provisions but also have the benefit of the jurisprudence of the committee on children.

When asked whether it was a strategic decision to focus on children she explained that 'it was a legal decision … [as] Australia's bound by those obligations'. But,

> focusing on the children had a strategic advantage as well because we felt that *that would move people more*, that you can hold adults more morally responsible or ethically responsible for their actions but you couldn't do that to children, and it's common across every major legal system that you do not detain children other than for very, very specific reasons and for the shortest possible time.[36]

Children here are seen as less responsible, more innocent and vulnerable, with an orientation towards their affective – or emotional – hold as being of political use in prosecuting a human rights argument.

[34] Interview with Professor Gillian Triggs (Melbourne, 28 March 2018).

[35] This is connected to Aileen Moreton-Robinson's conception of Australia as a 'white possession'. See, for instance, A Moreton-Robinson, *The White Possessive: Property, Power, and Indigenous Sovereignty* (Minneapolis, MN, University of Minnesota Press, 2015).

[36] Interview with Professor Gillian Triggs, above n 34 (emphasis added).

For Oliver White, and from the perspective of UNICEF (which was established globally in 1946 and set up headquarters in Australia in 1966),[37] children are understood as both 'vulnerable' and as possessing particular 'strengths', 'capacities', 'contributions' and insights. 'UNICEF's top-line messaging', he told me,

> would be that these children are vulnerable because they are first and foremost children, and we recognise that children have particular vulnerabilities … And, so we need to make sure that those children are protected essentially, so that they can develop to healthy thriving adults. And then in terms of a migrant refugee child that there's this double kind of vulnerability … And I think another key message that UNICEF has around children and adolescents in particular is the contribution they have to make. States have an obligation to listen to children around Article 12,[38] and to take those views into consideration, but our experience is that children and adolescents in particular have got a lot of very valuable things to say about their own lived experience.

But while states may have that obligation under international law, treaties and conventions, in practice they are often pushed to the side and other considerations are brought to the fore.

IV. 'BEST INTERESTS OF THE CHILD'

Wayne Gibbons – a former senior public servant in the Immigration Department in the 1990s, who was, among other professional roles, 'regarded as a key architect of the Government's hardline response to the boat-people', of mandatory detention[39] – stated in an interview in 2017 that he believed international human rights law was inappropriately applied in Australia. With the use of administrative law,

> we started to have judges – and there were a few who were very activist on the immigration front – reach into various international agreements like the Convention on Refugees and try to import those principles into Australian law, notwithstanding they're only treaties and they're not part of our domestic law.[40]

We see in this a narrative wherein lawyers or international human rights bodies intervening on behalf of people making asylum claims are understood as being a disruption to the proper functioning of the sovereign state and its national borders. International law, and human rights instruments and institutions, hold no place in domestic law for some policy-makers. This is part of the making of

[37] UNICEF Australia, 'About Us': www.unicef.org.au/about-us.

[38] Note that Art 12 of the CRC, above n 5, provides that 'States Parties shall assure to the child who if capable of forming his or her own views the right to express those views freely in all matters affecting the child, the views of the child being given due weight in accordance with the age and maturity of the child'.

[39] Margo Kingston, 'Boat-People Hardliner to Leave Immigration' *Canberra Times* (9 June 1993) 3.

[40] Interview with Wayne Gibbons (Canberra, 14 November 2017).

the Australian border as a physical boundary, a set of practices, and within it an imagined community.

In the 2018 interview I conducted with Gillian Triggs, we discussed the ways in which ideas of 'best interests of the child' played out during her tenure. Focusing on section 6 of the Immigration (Guardianship of Children) Act 1946 (Cth) which provides that the Minister for Immigration is the guardian of unaccompanied migrant, refugee and asylum-seeker children, we discussed how various advocates and politicians have lobbied, over the last 20 years, for this to be changed. This is one measure for unaccompanied children which forms part of 'the current Australian legislative framework of guardianship of unaccompanied asylum-seeker children [which] neither addresses their particular vulnerabilities nor affords their particular rights and protections'.[41] As I narrated in *Cruel Care: A History of Children at Our Borders*, Triggs' account of her conversations with Scott Morrison, when he was Minister for Immigration and Border Protection, underscored Morrison's understanding of himself as ultimate controller and arbiter, the incarnation, in a sense, of white-settler colonial law, disdainful of key international law norms.[42] Triggs recounted a related experience with a colleague of Morrison's in the Liberal Party, Peter Dutton. In her encounters with Dutton, she asserted, there was

> [n]o debate, no discussion, no engagement, nothing. He just did what he knew he was bound to do, which is listen to me. He's the [Immigration] Minister in charge of the Department. He had to listen to me, but that was it, nothing. No response at all on any substantive matter that I raised.[43]

Both Morrison and Dutton, in Triggs' narration, were disdainful of key international law norms.

Triggs, in her meetings with ministers, was in a sense the embodiment of international law and human rights instruments in Australia. These meetings provide a snapshot of how governments understand, perform and constitute the interaction between international law norms and government policies around refugee children. They serve as an illustration of the way that Triggs understood how the category of the asylum-seeking or refugee child is articulated in and by government policy. That is, these moments demonstrate the ways that human rights norms surrounding child refugees and asylum seekers are understood to be secondary to imagined concerns around the Australian border, society

[41] I Bennett, 'Political Barriers to Reform: Analysing Australia's Legitimation of the Guardianship Framework' (Honours Thesis, University of Technology Sydney, 2020) 1.

[42] Jordana Silverstein, *Cruel Care: A History of Children at Our Borders* (Clayton, Monash University Press, 2023) 126.

[43] Interview with Professor Gillian Triggs, above n 34, also cited in Silverstein, *Cruel Care*, ibid, 191. I requested an interview with Peter Dutton, however received a reply from his office telling me 'Thank you for your request for the Minister to participate in an interview. Unfortunately due to his current programme he is unable to take part': Statement from the Office of the Hon Peter Dutton MP (Personal Communication, 13 June 2018).

and polity, and to the politician as embodying an overriding authority. We can also see this border instantiated in the realm of children's rights in responses I have received to interview requests. When I contacted Megan Mitchell, the then National Children's Commissioner at the AHRC, I was informed by her assistant that Mitchell understood herself to 'not [be] a suitable candidate for your project as it is not something within in her scope of work'.[44] She instead recommended that I speak with the Human Rights Commissioner or the Race Discrimination Commissioner. Child refugees and asylum seekers were defined as outside the remit of the Children's Commissioner's work; there is a border being established between citizen and non-citizen children. But in Triggs' rendition, there was a performance by Dutton and Morrison of their orientations with regard to the conception of the 'best interests of the child', as they actively worked to decentre – or to use Ahmed's phrasing, to defamiliarise – this concept within Australian policy and law. All of these examples function to constitute and limit the realm of Australian concerns.

This de-centring was echoed by Oliver White, who stated that

> the fact that the Australian Government has been detaining children, the fact that you've got the Minister of Immigration that is the guardian, but also the jailor, and the fact that we don't really have any proper mechanisms for the Government to consider the best interests of children when it's making decisions around where it sends children or how it responds shows a pretty strong sort of disregard ... Governments seem to try to get away with what they can.[45]

It is also demonstrated in the work of people providing advice to government. Paris Aristotle, the Director of 'Foundation House: The Victorian Foundation for Survivors of Torture', was appointed in 2012 by Prime Minister Julia Gillard to form an 'expert panel' together with former Defence Force Chief Angus Houston and former Head of the Department of Foreign Affairs and Trade, Michael L'Estrange, to provide advice on how to respond to asylum seekers making their way to Australia by boat. Or, as the *ABC* framed it, '[t]he expert panel was set up by the Government in an attempt to find a way to stop asylum seekers risking their lives at sea'.[46] When Aristotle spoke to the Parliamentary Joint Committee on Human Rights about the report produced by the 'Expert Panel', which led to the reopening of immigration detention facilities in Manus Island and Nauru, he and the other authors were asked for their perspective on how their recommendations sat alongside international human rights conventions. All three emphasised that they saw no contradiction between the two, with Aristotle arguing that '[i]t is a very difficult question, because there are

[44] Email from Laura MacColl, Executive & Research Assistant to the National Children's Commissioner, Australian Human Rights Commission (Personal Communication, 9 March 2018).

[45] Interview with Oliver White, above n 1.

[46] Naomi Woodley, 'Expert Panel to Deliver Asylum Policy Findings' *ABC News* (13 August 2012): www.abc.net.au/news/2012-08-13/expert-panel-to-deliver-asylum-policy-findings/4194116.

different views about what is compliance with international obligations and what is not'.[47] He continued to narrate that he was

> not sure what it means about our international conventions. After we released the report I had friends who said, 'Oh, but, Paris, this breaches this. It's not consistent with the Convention on the Rights of the Child'. I was left wondering why I needed to wait for a child to get here, to go through the trauma of a boat journey – perhaps to die – before my interests in engaging that convention occurred. We felt that it was far better to create the conditions and the circumstances that would protect children. On one of the boats that went down that Angus referred to, there was a 13-year-old boy in the water for 18 hours. He watched his uncle, his father and his brother all drown. People were taken by sharks during that exercise. No-one can tell me that that is in the best interests of a child. In my work I see the drawings that children do in detention centres of being on boats and being circled by sharks. We know the traumatic consequences of that. We do not want to stop any of them being protected or fleeing persecution and obtaining the protection they deserve. We want to make it better, safer and fairer for as many of them as possible, and I am hoping people can get on board with that objective and that goal.[48]

In Aristotle's narration of the factors at play we see a weighing up of concerns, with him instilling the idea that domestic conceptions of what is most important are pre-eminent. Using language centred around care, and personal anecdotes about what he has seen, Aristotle enabled himself to claim expert knowledge about what was 'best' for these children. From a cursory understanding of the policy of turning back the boats, however, it is clear that it breaches international law prohibitions against refoulement.[49] Moreover, Aristotle's formulation here uses a false binary around what can be considered the 'best interests of the child' and works to hide, or erase, the conditions from which the children are fleeing. In his articulation of his care for their potential traumas or death faced on the boats or in the detention centres, he seems to refuse engagement with the harms, violence, traumas and potential death which causes people to get onto a boat.

The use of children's affective discursive power to support one's argument against the use of international law instruments is a tactic deployed across the political spectrum. For instance, in October 2015, in response to calls from the Australian Medical Association 'to heed concerns at Melbourne's Royal Children's hospital about discharging asylum seeker children back into detention', Dutton was reported as having asserted that while he 'understood' the 'concerns', 'the Defence and Border Force staff on our vessels who were

[47] Commonwealth, *Parliamentary Debates*, Parliamentary Joint Committee on Human Rights, 17 December 2012, 15 (P Aristotle): parlinfo.aph.gov.au.

[48] ibid 16.

[49] Violeta Moreno-Lax, 'The Interdiction of Asylum Seekers at Sea: Law and (Mal)practice in Europe and Australia' (Policy Brief 4, Kaldor Centre for International Refugee Law, May 2017): www.kaldorcentre.unsw.edu.au/sites/default/files/Policy_Brief_4_Interdiction_of_asylum_seekers_at_sea.pdf.

pulling dead kids out of the water don't want the boats to restart'.[50] And in his June 2015 parliamentary speech on the Migration Amendment (Regional Processing Arrangements) Bill – a Bill which aided in the establishment of the offshore detention regime, most particularly by enabling payments to be made to facilitate it happening – the Leader of the Opposition, Bill Shorten, asserted that the Opposition would support the

> legislation because it is our policy. Our policy is based on fundamental principles. How do we best ensure safety at sea? How do we stop people smugglers preying on the desperation of the persecuted, the vulnerable and the dispossessed? How do we make sure that genuine refugees get that second chance and that those who are not genuine are sent home? How do we ensure that Australian Navy and Customs officials never ever again face the grim task of pulling bodies from the water off Christmas Island? I am sure that I speak for all of us in this place when I say that the devastating loss of life – the drownings, the perishing of vulnerable people, of children – is something that we cannot in good conscience ever accept. It is human tragedy we must do everything in our power to prevent. Labor stands resolutely to make sure that the dangerous sea voyage from Java to Christmas Island remains closed.

Vulnerability. Children. Desperation. Danger. These are the key watchwords. And Labor was positioned by Shorten as a party which cared and which could operationalise control in the service of protection.[51]

These policy-makers represent the realm and regime of the domestic sphere, making decisions as they do from within that epistemology. As such, when they assert their ability to make a claim to what is in a child's 'best interests' – and particularly when they do so to reaffirm the sovereign, securitised and exclusionary national border – they affirm the pre-eminence of the domestic over the international. But to return to Morgan, from her perspective,

> it's not necessarily an issue with a particular Minister, one or the other, it's more just that the framework does not allow for the Minister to play that guardianship role effectively, because it wasn't designed for this group of children.

The problem, as she saw it, was that the guardian framework was designed for children brought to Australia during the Second World War, and thus its history means that

> it was just a framework that wasn't built for the group of children to which it now most often applies … And, for that reason … we end up with these conflicts, where the Minister is playing dual roles that don't allow them to fully consider the best interests of the child as the primary consideration.

[50] Helen Davidson, 'Hospital Doctors Protest to Demand Release of Children from Detention' *Guardian* (11 October 2015).

[51] Commonwealth, *Parliamentary Debates*, House of Representatives, 24 June 2015, 7491 (B Shorten).

While this concern about the legislation and its historical roots is widely shared by scholars, politicians and policy-makers, we can note that Morgan's response presumes a fundamental positive interest emanating from the government: an understanding that the government is oriented towards humanitarianism.[52] How does this fit in with how legal scholars have understood Australia's relationship with international law?

V. THE INTERNATIONAL IN THE DOMESTIC

Australia's policies towards child refugees accord with a history of Australian 'anxiety' about the role of international law in the domestic realm, as articulated by Hilary Charlesworth, Madelaine Chiam, Devika Hovell and George Williams.[53] 'There is a fear', they write, 'that international law undermines Australian sovereignty or the capacity to govern ourselves as we choose'.[54] This is 'akin to a form of legal xenophobia' they explain, with a fear of something which comes from outside the national sphere.[55] It is thus unsurprising that one realm in which this is expressed is in the treatment of refugees and asylum seekers. As numerous legal scholars have shown, there is a broader problem in relation to the way that Australia views its human rights obligations: human rights mechanisms, conventions and laws are pushed to the side within Australian policy thinking.[56] Thus while the outlined anxiety and fear attains a particular form through child refugee policy in recent decades, it rests on a much longer settler-colonial history of the genocidal repression and exclusion of those produced as racial others, and the modern opposition to adopting and implementing human rights tools. The founding invasion and dispossession continues

[52] On the history of the Immigration (Guardianship of Children) Act 1946 (Cth), see J Silverstein, '"I Am Responsible": Histories of the Intersection of the Guardianship of Unaccompanied Child Refugees and the Australian Border' (2016) 22 *Cultural Studies Review* 65; J Silverstein, '"The Beneficent and Legal Godfather": A History of the Guardianship of Unaccompanied Immigrant and Refugee Children in Australia, 1946–1975' (2017) 22 *History of the Family* 446.

[53] H Charlesworth et al, 'Deep Anxieties: Australia and the International Legal Order' (2003) 25 *Sydney Law Review* 423.

[54] ibid 424.

[55] ibid.

[56] Chiam, above n 2, 230, 246. For legal discussions around the problems of human rights obligations see, eg, H Charlesworth, *Writing in Rights: Australia and the Protection of Human Rights* (Sydney, UNSW Press, 2002); H Charlesworth and G Triggs, 'Australia and the International Protection of Human Rights' in DR Rothwell and E Crawford (eds), *International Law in Australia*, 3rd edn (Melbourne, Thomson Reuters, 2017); S Joseph and M Castan, *The International Covenant on Civil and Political Rights: Cases, Materials, and Commentary*, 3rd edn (Oxford, Oxford University Press, 2013); J Whyte, 'Human Rights and the Collateral Damage of Neoliberalism' (2017) 20 *Theory and Event* 137; B Golder, 'Beyond Redemption? Problematising the Critique of Human Rights in Contemporary International Legal Thought' (2014) 2 *London Review of International Law* 77.

into the present through mechanisms and regimes such as the treatment of child refugees and asylum seekers.[57]

Jane McAdam points out that Australia's treatment of asylum seekers by differentiating them by their mode of arrival – whether pre-approved and arriving by plane or without prior authorisation and arriving by boat – ignores international law principles which do not make this distinction: 'a person either has a well-founded fear of persecution, or does not'.[58] In addition, McAdam makes clear that the treatment of refugees and asylum seekers by Australian government policy over the twenty-first century 'breach[es] Australia's international human rights obligations in some way', as 'they undermine the humanitarian object and purpose of the Refugee Convention, but they also violate concrete legal obligations'.[59] And as Alice Edwards noted in her 2003 examination of Australia's Temporary Protection Visa regime, 'Australia's current temporary refugee protection regime has many questionable aspects, including Australia's commitment to its treaty obligations'.[60]

Sara Dehm has also argued that 'international law's principal subject, the modern territorial state, [is] premised upon the logic of the border'.[61] Additionally, '[m]odern international law allocates lawful authority over space and people primarily through its principal subject, the state'.[62] This is a circumstance, Dehm further demonstrates, that is produced through a logic of necropolitics, producing death for those who interact with it.[63] Dehm writes, following Achille Mbembe, that 'necropolitics … is a modern form of power that has come to govern through death'.[64] Thus we must pay attention to the notion that the harm created by the sovereign border is not antithetical to international law but rather is produced in part by it. Moreover, following Dehm's lead, we can understand that the sidelining of certain international law principles outlined above is not a mistake or error but rather is part of a colonial process of reinforcing exclusion through the exertion of Australian sovereignty. This sovereign ability to control, to determine 'who will come to this country and the manner in which they will come' – to rephrase former Prime Minister

[57] This is a product of what Patrick Wolfe analysed as being a situation wherein 'invasion is a structure, not an event'. See P Wolfe, 'Nation and MiscegeNation: Discursive Continuity in the Post-Mabo Era' (1994) 36 *Social Analysis: The International Journal of Anthropology*, 93–152.

[58] J McAdam, 'Editorial: Australia and Asylum Seekers' (2013) 25 *International Journal of Refugee Law* 437.

[59] ibid 443.

[60] A Edwards, 'Tampering with Refugee Protection: The Case of Australia' (2003) 15 *International Journal of Refugee Law* 210.

[61] S Dehm, 'International Law at the Border: Refugee Deaths, the Necropolitical State and Sovereign Accountability' in S Chalmers and S Pahuja (eds), *Routledge Handbook of International Law and the Humanities* (London, Routledge, 2021) 3.

[62] ibid 8.

[63] ibid 2.

[64] ibid 3.

John Howard's infamous injunction[65] – has a long history. As Tracey Banivanua Mar showed through a history of transnational, or international, organisations and laws, a series of controls were placed on Indigenous Peoples and Pacific Peoples' movement around Australia and the Pacific from the beginnings of colonisation.[66] Additionally, mechanisms such as the White Australia Policy (with all its attendant legislation) aided in controlling the racial make-up of Australia.[67] This history provides the backdrop to more recent decisions by policy-makers, witnessed and narrated here by Australia-based human rights institutions, workers and authorities, to prioritise maintaining the harsh border.

VI. CONCLUSION

My intention in this chapter has been to outline the ways in which international law is thought about, rather than to argue that international law needs to necessarily be considered more within the realm of the domestic. As we look around the world, at the ways that states, institutions and organisations internationally treat child refugees and asylum seekers, it is evident that governments, international law and global institutions are incapable of ending the violence refugees and asylum seekers face. There is something fundamentally amiss that is not remedied by simply implementing international human rights and international law approaches into the domestic, for these approaches would only reinforce some of the problems, as Dehm – quoted above – shows. It is useful however to have our attention drawn to the languages through which discussions about international law occur, to see the ways that it is understood, spoken about and drawn into conversations in Australia, in order to understand the layers of the global incapacity.

Sara Ahmed explains that orientation can be seen in 'how "proximity" and "distance" come to be lived by being associated with specific bodies as well as places'. This is a racial process, she argues: looking at

> orientations might allow us to reinvestigate the 'alignments' between body, place, nation, and world that allow racial lines to be given. The 'matter' of race is very much about embodied reality; seeing oneself or being seen as white or black or mixed does affect what one 'can do', or even where one can go, which can be redescribed in terms of what is and is not within reach.[68]

[65] J Howard, 'Liberal–National Coalition' (Campaign Launch Speech in Sydney, New South Wales, 28 October 2001).

[66] T Banivanua Mar, *Decolonisation and the Pacific: Indigenous Globalisation and the Ends of Empire* (Cambridge, Cambridge University Press, 2016).

[67] K Snoek, 'Marginalised Subjects, Meaningless Naturalizations: The Tiers of Australian Citizenship' (PhD Thesis, University of Melbourne, 2019).

[68] Ahmed, above n 7, 112.

When policy-makers orient themselves away from international law therefore, they are doing so as part of a racialised process. They are reinforcing the whiteness of themselves and the Australian governing state, and its ability – its jurisdiction – to decide on the fates of (non-white) others. As Patrick Wolfe wrote, race 'is made in the targeting'.[69] Thus by examining the words of those who work within the human rights frameworks in Australia, who attempt to bring these discourses, narratives and understandings of refugee and asylum-seeking children to the Australian political sphere, we can gain a sense of the racialised orientations which exist within Australian political thinking.

This exploration of the intersection between human rights bodies, child refugee policy and policy-makers' understandings of international law, demonstrates that Australian domestic policy is 'oriented' away from international law. This is the sense of orientation offered by Ahmed, wherein being oriented away from international law signifies being oriented away from human rights discourses and practices. Instead, governments are oriented towards a form of border control which both relies on sentimentalised ideas of children and evades responsibility for working alongside those children for their freedom and justice. The signifiers of international law, that is, remain subservient to the signifiers of a closed-off and xenophobic country.

[69] P Wolfe, 'Settler Colonialism and the Elimination of the Native' (2006) 8 *Journal of Genocide Research* 388.

13

'This is Our Conference': Elizabeth Reid, Second Wave Feminism and Australia's Performance of International Law in the 1970s

JON PICCINI

I. INTRODUCTION

THE WORLD CONFERENCE for International Women's Year (IWY), held at short notice and amidst inadequate facilities in Mexico City over June and July 1975, was far from a global celebration of women. While a recent book dubs the year as a whole 'the greatest consciousness raising event in history', its associated conference was dominated by autocratic leaders, whose heads of delegation – often the spouses of said autocrats – delivered a profusion of unsurprisingly glowing accounts of their nation's elimination of the 'woman problem'.[1] Princess Ashraf Pahlavi of Iran, chairperson of the conference's Consultative Committee and prominent articulator of the dominant statist reading of both women's and human rights, stands as an exemplar of the gathering's capture by perhaps less than sincere articulators of global sisterhood.[2] In such a context, Australia's delegation leader could not have struck a more different tone.

Philosopher, women's liberationist and recently appointed Adviser to the Prime Minister on Women, Elizabeth Reid, used her time at the official plenary

[1] J Olcott, *International Women's Year: The Greatest Conciseness Raising Event in History* (Oxford, Oxford University Press, 2017). For other literature on IWY, see J Olcott, 'Cold War Conflicts and Cheap Cabaret: Sexual Politics at the 1975 United Nations International Women's Year Conference' (2010) 22 *Gender & History* 733; K Ghodsee, 'Revisiting the United Nations Decade for Women: Brief Reflections on Feminism, Capitalism and Cold War Politics in the Early Years of the International Women's Movement' (2010) 33 *Women's Studies International Forum* 3.

[2] See R Burke, 'Competing for the Last Utopia? The NIEO, Human Rights, and the World Conference for the International Women's Year, Mexico City, June 1975' (2015) 6 *Humanity* 47.

to condemn the year's inadequate agenda, summarised in the official slogan of 'Development, Equality and Peace'.[3] Equality was a 'limited and possibly harmful goal' which might only 'normalise' rather than eliminate oppression, while the search for world peace would 'remain unattainable … until such time as violence against women is recognised and understood, and ceases'.[4] Reid's most concerted words were left for the topic of development, a central one for a United Nations (UN) in the midst of its Second Development Decade, and where discussions of Third World uplift and a New International Economic Order (NIEO) were prominent. The quest for 'productivity and efficiency at any cost', the Australian warned, rendered discussions of women only 'vague exhortations, insincere rhetoric and token gestures'.[5] In such a scenario, Reid's closing remark that 'this is our conference' registers more as protest than statement of fact.

This chapter tells the story of how Reid became, if only briefly, a central figure in Australia's performance and negotiation of international law. A political appointee – Reid was the first person to hold an official position as adviser on women to a head of government anywhere in the world – the Australian straddled multiple identities. First, she was head of the delegation of a sovereign state at a gathering where matters of international law were to be formulated, and was as such accountable to its geopolitical needs, particularly a cautious opposition to Third World demands at the United Nations. Secondly, Reid was at the conference to represent Australian women and in particular a powerful women's liberation movement, within which many shades of opinion existed on Reid's position and the Mexico conference. It was the tension between these two roles, I argue, that defined her experience at the IWY conference. While Helen McCarthy makes it clear that the deeply suspicious approach of Britain's Foreign Office to IWY clashed with the more hopeful, women-centred approach of non-governmental organisation (NGO) delegates, Reid complicates this dichotomy in the Australian example.[6]

I begin this chapter by contextualising Reid's speech against a long history of Australian engagement with international law. It was the election of Gough Whitlam's modernising and progressive government in December 1972 that saw Reid gain such a prominent profile. The 22 years of neglect, if not outright disdain, that conservative governments had directed towards the United Nations

[3] On the Australian domestic context of Reid's appointment and debates within the feminist movement, see J Piccini, '"Women Are a Colonised Sex': Elizabeth Reid, Human Rights and International Women's Year 1975' (2018) 49 *Australian Historical Studies* 307; M Arrow, *The Seventies: The Personal, the Political and the Making of Modern Australia* (Sydney, NewSouth Publishing, 2019) ch 4.

[4] 'Statement by the Leader of the Australian delegation: Ms Elizabeth Reid' (21 June 1975), Papers of Elizabeth Reid (National Library of Australia, MS 9262, Series 14, Box 42, Folder 84).

[5] ibid.

[6] H McCarthy, 'The Diplomatic History of Global Women's Rights: The British Foreign Office and International Women's Year, 1975' (2015) 50 *Journal of Contemporary History* 833.

and its human rights programme inspired Whitlam to re-establish Australia's name as a multilateral power. Reid is also placed within a tradition of Australian women's internationalism, and the past work of women in the diplomatic arena. Next, I explore the more immediate context of Reid's intervention, namely rival notions of rights as articulated during IWY. Whitlam's equalitarian version stuck closely to the ideas articulated in the Universal Declaration of Human Rights (UDHR), on which Australian diplomats worked between 1947 and 1948, while the dominant reading at the United Nations was based on a developmentalist ethos that emerged during the 1960s. Reid's women's liberation movement looked critically on both perspectives, rejecting the notion of complementary gender roles which underlay human rights thought and viewing the veneration of development as instrumentalising women.

Lastly, I look at how these three imaginings came together in Mexico City. Transcripts of speeches and records relating to the Australian delegation reveal how Reid navigated the conference's conflicting agendas and convoluted vocabulary. In so doing, Reid furthered the slow process of 'feminising' international law, enacting a form of 'minor jurisprudence' – legal thinking which breaks with existing canons and prioritises marginalised voices.[7] In so doing, she simultaneously exposed the implicit bias and agendas that underlay the conference's instrumentalist understanding of women rights, and served the geopolitical interests of her own nation. As well as a case study of one woman's role in Australian international law, this chapter offers new insights on received wisdom regarding Whitlam's multilateralism, the rise of human rights, and women's agency in international affairs. I ask: how multilateral was Whitlam's foreign policy when push came to shove? What role did women's liberationists play in the ascendence of the 'human' to the centre of international politics in the late 1970s? And finally, how much do Cold War polarities continue to inform our views of women's internationalism?

II. THE APPOINTMENT: WHITLAM, MIDDLE POWER DIPLOMACY AND THE LEGACY OF WOMEN'S INTERNATIONALISM

Elizabeth Reid – Canberra-based philosopher, former public servant and member of the city's women's movement – was out of place in Australia's political elite, let alone its international diplomatic circuit. The recently divorced mother-of-one, who worked as a senior tutor at the Australian National University (ANU) and had travelled widely abroad, met reporters for a kerbside interview on the day of her appointment in April 1973 with daughter Kathryn in her lap. Reid fended off questions on controversial topics ranging from abortion and the

[7] C Tomlins, 'Law As … IV: Minor Jurisprudence in Historical Key. An Introduction' (2017) 21 *Law Text Culture* 1, 2.

legalisation of access to marijuana.[8] This was only the first of many instances in which Reid would be pilloried and interrogated by a widely sexist media, whom she would in turn try to utilise to 'find common ground with women outside the women's movement'.[9] The idea of young staffer Peter Wilenski, Whitlam was supportive of Reid's office – for which she was selected from over 400 applicants. He provided significant resources to fund Reid's activities, including a 13-month 'listening tour' around Australia.[10] Reid's outsider status in Canberra – a 'New South Wales educated, Oxford Don' who was 'tall, lithe, with light brown hair and the facts at her fingertips', as one newspaper put it – was part of Whitlam's agenda to set a very different tone at home and abroad.[11]

A middle-class lawyer representing the outer suburban Sydney district of Werriwa, Whitlam had led the Australian Labor Party to electoral victory in December 1972. As well as putting an end to 23 years of conservative rule, he also represented a reforming tendency within the Australian Labor Party, turning what had been a party of male blue-collar workers towards professionals and social movements.[12] Whitlam appears in existing histories of Australian international law alongside another former Labor leader, Herbert Vere Evatt, as a signal contributor. His election marked a 'renaissance of interest in global human rights standards', as Hilary Charlesworth and Gillian Triggs put it, with over 100 treaties, conventions and other documents signed, ratified or adopted in a little under three years.[13] Diplomatic recognition was extended to East Germany, mainland China and North Korea, an official end was declared to Australian participation in the Vietnam War, and forceful protests were made over Nixon's Christmas bombing campaign in 1972. These moves were part of a clear piece of diplomatic theatre. As Whitlam put it, they marked 'a more independent Australian stance in international affairs' whereby the nation 'will enjoy a growing standard as a distinctive, tolerant, co-operative and well-regarded nation … in the world at large'.[14]

Such a public performance reflects what Carl Ungerer describes as the two key styles of Australian middle power diplomacy. Whitlam's Labor represented an 'activist and independent' policy, focused on multilateral institutions, while alliances with 'great and powerful friends', first Great Britain and later the United States (US), were the mainstay of conservative coalition governments of

[8] *Sydney Morning Herald* (9 April 1973) 1.

[9] Arrow, above n 3, 93.

[10] ibid 94.

[11] *Canberra Times* (9 April 1973) 1.

[12] On Whitlam's rise to power and time in government, see J Hocking, *Gough Whitlam: A Moment in History* (Carlton, Melbourne University Press, 2009); J Hocking, *Gough Whitlam: His Time* (Carlton, Melbourne University Press, 2014).

[13] H Charlesworth and G Triggs, 'Australia and the International Protection of Human Rights' in DR Rothwell and Emily Crawford (eds), *International Law in Australia*, 3rd edn (Sydney, Thomson Reuters Australia, 2017).

[14] Quoted in DJ Murphy, 'Problems in Australian Foreign Policy, January to June 1973' (1973) 19 *Australian Journal of Politics & History* 331, 340.

the Liberal and Country parties.[15] The basis of Labor's reputation for multilateralism, and the model that Whitlam chose to follow, was the Curtin and Chifley governments of the 1940s – and in particular their External Affairs Minister and Attorney-General, Evatt.[16] Coming into government only months before the Japanese attack on Pearl Harbor, John Curtin and his government were early if cautious supporters of transforming the wartime UN alliance into a post-war institution, which might replace the defunct League of Nations. Curtin and Evatt no doubt saw the performance of Prime Minister William 'Billy' Hughes at the Paris Peace Conference in 1919 as an object lesson on how not to work in multilateral institutions. At the behest of the United States and Britain, Hughes had demanded the harshest terms on defeated Germany and loudly opposed Japan's calls for a racial equality clause, weakening the fledgling organisation and arguably laying the foundations for the next conflict.[17] Now, an organisation to guarantee peace, as well as a post-war world of plenty, had to be first priority – and by 1943 Evatt supported placing the wartime UN alliance on a permanent basis.

For Evatt, who left his position as the youngest ever appointee to the High Court to run for office in 1940, the domestic and international were connected. Wary of the League's failures, and cautious about the powers of a proposed Security Council in the new organisation, Evatt was instrumental in transforming what was envisaged as a largely formalistic General Assembly into one with wide powers of discussion and sanction. He grandiosely christened it a 'forum in which the conscience of the peoples of the world should have its most potent expression'.[18] While Evatt became 'the more or less acknowledged leader of the small powers', he simultaneously worked to strengthen domestic jurisdiction provisions that ensured the General Assembly or Security Council could only act on matters relating directly to the maintenance of peace. 'Internal matters such as the migration policy of a state', Evatt reported to Parliament, 'will not fall within the scope of the organisation'.[19] Such a contradictory attitude is equally evident in Evatt's response to the beginnings of decolonisation: he favoured a

[15] C Ungerer, 'The "Middle Power" Concept in Australian Foreign Policy' (2007) 53 *Australian Journal of Politics & History* 538, 543.

[16] On the existence of a distinct Labor style in foreign policy, see D Lee and C Waters (eds), *Evatt to Evans: The Labor Tradition in Australian Foreign Policy* (Sydney, Allen & Unwin, 1997).

[17] On Hughes' role at Versailles, see WJ Hudson, *Billy Hughes in Paris: The Birth of Australian Diplomacy* (West Melbourne, Thomas Nelson Australia and the Australian Institute of International Affairs, 1978); A Duxbury, 'Participation in the "Gilded Ball": Australia and the Council of the League of Nations', ch 2 in this volume. On the consequences, see A Patience, *Australian Foreign Policy in Asia: Middle Power or Awkward Partner?* (Oxford, Routledge, 2018) ch 5.

[18] Quoted in N Meaney, 'Dr HV Evatt and the United Nations: The Problem of Collective Security and Liberal Internationalism' in J Cotton and D Lee (eds), *Australia and the United Nations* (Canberra, Department of Foreign Affairs and Trade, 2012).

[19] Commonwealth, *Parliamentary Debates*, House of Representatives, 30 August 1945, 5030.

compromise position with the Dutch regarding Indonesian independence, only to be overruled by Chifley, and vocally supported the creation of an Israeli state.[20]

As much as Whitlam adopted Evatt's multilateralist policy, he was also reacting against what was perceived as the retreat from multilateralism evident in governments of the Menzies era (1949–72). The deepening Cold War saw a turn towards regional security pacts, such as the South East Asia Treaty Organisation, as well as a close relationship with both the United Kingdom, and the United States through the Security Treaty between Australia, New Zealand and the United States of America (ANZUS).[21] While Australia developed close ties with newly independent anti-communist nations in Asia, this was part of a broader strategic orientation towards ensuring America's continued footprint in the region.[22] Governments of this era openly doubted the utility of the United Nations as an international forum, particularly as the issue of racism and colonialism came to dominate debate in the General Assembly. Australia's representatives were 'amongst the most rigid in their opposition' to demands for national independence for colonies, eager as they were to 'defer the decolonisation of those European empires in their region … which stood between them and the unknowns of Asian nationalism and communism'.[23] Vulnerable to attack on immigration and Indigenous policy, not to mention the territories of Papua and New Guinea, Australia's Attorney-General Paul Hasluck fondly reminisced in 1968 of 'a time where there had been no racial issue in any United Nations debate'.[24]

Whitlam's election was indeed a breath of fresh air in this context. The 'twin covenants' on human rights – treaties which made the promises of the UDHR binding on nations – were signed within a matter of days, ending decades of obstruction and obfuscation. Long seen as 'soft' on the issue of racial discrimination in southern Africa, Australia broke ranks with the United States in February 1973 by voting for a resolution condemning white-minority led Rhodesia, while also rejoining the UN Decolonisation Committee and ratifying the International Covention on the Elimination of All Forms of Racial Discrimination.[25] The United Nations was again placed at the centre of Australia's policy, but like Evatt, Whitlam was not single minded in his

[20] D Fettling, 'JB Chifley and the Indonesian Revolution, 1945–1949' (2013) 59 *Australian Journal of Politics & History* 517; P Mendes, 'The Australian Left's Support for the Creation of the State of Israel, 1947–48' (2009) 97 *Labour History* 137. For a fuller account of Evatt at the San Francisco Conference, see A Pert, 'Australia and the United Nations', ch 6 in this volume.

[21] For an overview of Australian foreign policy during these years of conservative dominance, see F Bongiorno, 'The Price of Nostalgia: Menzies, the "Liberal" Tradition and Australian Foreign Policy' (2005) 51 *Australian Journal of Politics & History* 400.

[22] D Halvorson, 'From Cold War Solidarity to Transactional Engagement: Reinterpreting Australia's Relations with East Asia, 1950–1974' (2016) 18 *Journal of Cold War Studies* 130.

[23] D Lowe, 'Australia at the United Nations in the 1950s: The Paradox of Empire' (1997) 51 *Australian Journal of International Affairs* 171.

[24] *Canberra Times* (9 September 1968) 3.

[25] Murphy, above n 14. See also R Burke and J Piccini, 'Australia at the United Nations' in B Brooklyn, BT Jones and R Strating (eds), *Australia on the World Stage: History, Politics and International Relations* (London, Routledge, 2022).

multilateralism, ensuring that Australia's interests were front and centre. This is perhaps clearest in the biggest blot on Whitlam's foreign policy performance, East Timor, the Indonesian annexation of which he 'green lit' and subsequently defended.[26] Reid's appointment and widely publicised role in the government's programme of activities of IWY sat within this broader context of developing Australia's authority as a progressive power in international affairs, both facilitating and restricting her diplomatic role.

Reid's position and subsequent role as international dignitary also placed her somewhat uncomfortably within a long tradition of Australian women's internationalism. The national enfranchisement of white women in 1902 reflected the early Federation's reputation as a 'social laboratory', an achievement which saw activist Vida Goldstein secure a personal audience with US President Theodore Roosevelt as part of a six-month lecture tour across North America.[27] Jessie Street, socialist and long-time feminist organiser, continued this tradition into the post-war era, attending the League of Nations during the 1930s and becoming the only woman on Australia's delegation to the UN's founding conference in San Francisco.[28] She played an outsized role in the creation of the Committee on the Status of Women (CSW), within the Economic and Social Council, and was elected inaugural deputy chairperson. Street also argued for gender equality provisions in the Charter of the United Nations (UN Charter) that put her at odds with her own government's wishes to protect Australia's male breadwinner basic wage model.[29] Denied a second term on the CSW in 1948, Street continued her activism in a non-governmental capacity.

The trajectory of Street's career notwithstanding, Australian women continued to make their voices heard in different organs of the United Nations, and the wider diplomatic community, during the post-war period. Persia Campbell, an Australian born economist who moved to the United States in her early thirties, sought to universalise the Australian 'welfarist model' to the rest of the world. Her work as the US representative to the Food and Agricultural Organization (1949–52), and non-government representation via the International Federation of University Women and like organisations well into the 1970s, proved influential.[30] Reid's albeit brief role as international representative saw her join yet another elite club, that of Australian women who forced their way into

[26] See AH Henry, 'Gough Whitlam and the Politics of Universal Human Rights' (2019) 24 *International Journal of Human Rights* 796. See also C Fernandes, 'Australia, Timor-Leste and International Law', ch 5 in this volume.

[27] C Wright, '"A Splendid Object Lesson": A Transnational Perspective on the Birth of the Australian Nation' (2014) 26 *Journal of Women's History* 12, 12–13.

[28] L Coltheart, 'Citizens of the World: Jessie Street and International Feminism' (2005) 31 *Hecate* 182.

[29] C Ward, 'Jessie Street: Activism without Discrimination' in S Berger and S Scalmer (eds), *The Transnational Activist: Transformations and Comparisons from the Anglo-World since the Nineteenth Century* (London, Palgrave Macmillan, 2018).

[30] A Rees, 'Lessons from Australia: Persia Campbell and the International Afterlives of Federation-Era Welfarism' (2017) 48 *Australian Historical Studies* 519.

the diplomatic corps in the post-war years. Ruth Dobson, whose remarkable perseverance saw her serve in numerous temporary advisory roles to Australian delegations at the United Nations during the 1950s and 1960s, would become the first female career diplomat to be appointed to an ambassadorship in 1974.[31] Penelope Wensley, whose career in the Australian Public Service began only months after the notorious 'marriage bar' was lifted in 1966, began her post as First Secretary to the Australian Embassy in Mexico City in 1975.[32]

Reid's appointment also prompted deep division within sections of the women's movement in Australia which, like those across the Western world, was divided on the best way to achieve change. While Whitlam, in announcing her appointment, reported Reid's membership of both the Women's Electoral Lobby – a liberal reform group aimed at incremental change – and the Women's Liberation Group, which advocated a more revolutionary, systemic approach, she found it difficult to represent these quite distinct agendas.[33] For some radicals, Reid had become a tool of the male status quo. Hobart's Women's Liberation newspaper *Liberaction* depicted her grovelling to Whitlam, 'please sir, can I have some more?', while Sydney's *MeJane* announced that they would never accept a women's representative chosen by men.[34] Some reformers, on the other hand, judged that Reid seemed to be taking a step too far. Rather than questioning the desirability of equality, and the nature of complementary gender roles, the Tasmanian Committee for IWY hoped only for the achievement of 'equality of opportunity in responsible partnership' with men.[35] As Michelle Arrow puts it, the gargantuan nature of Reid's role as Women's Adviser, not to mention the running of IWY, was 'almost impossible'.[36] Such a polarisation of views was equally evident in the discussion of IWY in Australia and abroad – as the Year's many contradictory meanings became apparent.

III. THE YEAR: IWY AND THE MULTIPLE MEANINGS OF HUMAN RIGHTS

The decision to designate 1975 – the 30-year anniversary of the UN Charter's signing – IWY emerged from the slow process of creating international law

[31] S Marchant, 'Dobson, Ruth Violet (1918–1989)' (2007) 17 *Australian Dictionary of Biography* (MUP): adb.anu.edu.au/biography/dobson-ruth-violet-12424.

[32] 'India: A Roller Coaster' (*Hindu Business Line*, 29 October 2004): www.thehindubusinessline.com/todays-paper/tp-life/article29157665.ece. On the marriage bar, see L Colley, 'For Better or for Worse: Fifty Years Since the Removal of the Marriage Bar in the Australian Public Service' (2018) 64 *Australian Journal of Politics & History* 227.

[33] 'Appointment to the Prime Minister's Staff' (Press Statement No 73, 8 April 1973): pmtranscripts.pmc.gov.au/release/transcript-2888.

[34] *Liberaction* (Hobart, March 1975) 1; *Sydney Morning Herald* (9 April 1973) 1.

[35] J Dulfer-Hyams, 'Tasmanian State Committee International Women's Year: IWY Assessment and Consolidation Report' (August 1975), Papers of Elizabeth Reid (National Library of Australia, MS 9262, Series 14, Box 31, Folder 7a).

[36] Arrow, above n 3, 93.

regarding gender discrimination. In 1967, 20 years after the CSW's founding, the Declaration on the Elimination of Discrimination against Women (DEDAW), a consolidation and expansion of three prior Conventions on the Political Rights of Women (1954), the Nationality of Married Women (1957–58) and Consent to Marriage (1962–64), was unanimously passed by the General Assembly.[37] The CSW appealed to the General Assembly in 1972 to designate an IWY, hoping to use this as momentum towards a binding convention on women's rights.[38] First proposed at a bureau meeting of the communist-dominated Women's International Democratic Federation (WIDF) in East Berlin in 1971, in February 1972 Romania's representative took a proposal to the CSW for a year that recognised 'the important activities of the women's organisations … which for thirty years has fought consistently in all fields for women's rights'.[39] It received General Assembly endorsement in December 1972.

In Australia, IWY was greeted as part of the post-war push for formalised human rights norms. This was clear in Whitlam's speech for International Women's Day in 1974, where IWY was presented as a way 'to encourage equality of opportunity for women and improve their status throughout the world'.[40] 'It is a fundamental objective of the Government', he declared, 'to ensure respect for civil liberties and human rights and for that reason the Government is committed to the promotion of equal rights for women'.[41] In presenting funding for the year to Cabinet, Whitlam was even clearer about the connection between IWY, human rights and Australia's international reputation:

> International Women's Year … presents us with an opportunity to focus on women in our society, to consolidate improvements already achieved, and to enable Australia to become once again a pacesetter for the rest of the world in advancing basic human rights.[42]

Human rights, and the United Nations in general, was a family concern for Whitlam. In a speech delivered on Human Rights Day (10 December) 1973, he castigated the 'poor record' of his predecessors and outlined the Australian Labor Party's success in clearing the way for Australia's signature or ratification of numerous declaration and covenants, finishing by quoting his father,

[37] On the development of DEDAW and CEDAW, see S Zwingel, *Translating International Women's Rights: The CEDAW Convention in Context* (Basingstoke, Palgrave Macmillan, 2016).

[38] RM Popa, 'Translating Equality between Women and Men across Cold War Divides: Women Activists from Hungary and Romania and the Creation of International Women's Year' in S Penn and J Massino, *Gender Politics and Everyday Life in State Socialist Eastern and Central Europe* (New York, Palgrave Macmillan, 2009).

[39] Quoted in L Milner, '"The Most Important Event in IWY": Freda Brown and the World Congress for International Women's Year' (2020) 17 *History Australia* 172, 178.

[40] 'International Women's Day' (Press Statement No 197, 7 March 1974): pmtranscripts.pmc.gov.au/release/transcript-3181.

[41] ibid.

[42] 'FOR CABINET: International Women's Year' (13 June 1975) in 'International Women's Year 1975' (National Archives of Australia, NAA, Series A5931, Control Symbol CL1171, Item ID 5142275).

Fred Whitlam. Crown Solicitor from 1936 to 1949, Whitlam Snr contributed to the drafting of the UDHR and served as an Australian representative on the Commission on Human Rights. For Whitlam Snr, as it had for Evatt, human rights meant material progress and standard of living, Australia's responsibility to 'share in the task of securing higher standards and better living conditions, not alone for her people, but for people in other countries of the world'. The UN Charter's promise 'to promote social progress and better standards of life', Whitlam Snr insisted, was as vital as the UDHR's broader promises of individual freedom.[43] It is then unsurprising that, in a speech delivered to the 10-member National Advisory Committee that was appointed with Reid as chair to run Australia's IWY activities, Whitlam described 1975 as 'a year for all nations to make a concerted effort towards ensuring women enjoy the basic dignity of human rights, that they are integrated into society and that there is a recognition of their contribution to society'.[44]

Such rhetoric of integration and contribution was more explicit in Whitlam's Cabinet submission, where the activities of IWY were justified on the basis that '[i]f we are to properly utilise our human resources, ensure basic human rights and improve the quality of our lives we must release the energy and develop the talents of all of our population'.[45] This equation of human rights with standards of living and the mobilisation of a population appear foreign today, but was in keeping with the key meaning of human rights during the 1940s: a 'vision of a postwar collective life … in which personal freedoms would fit with more widely circulating promises for some sort of social democracy' and 'the persistent framework of nation-states that would provide that better life'.[46] This state-based reading of rights arguably reached its zenith in the mid-1970s, when nations of the Global South prepared a set of demands that would realise the promise Fred Whitlam set out, summed up in the expansive agenda of the NIEO, formalised in the Charter on the Economic Rights and Duties of States.[47] This document proposed resource sovereignty – including the right of states to nationalise foreign-owned industry – as well as trade liberalisation and North–South technology transfers as a solution to the intractable nature of underdevelopment and neocolonialism.[48]

[43] 'Speech by the Prime Minister, Mr EG Whitlam QC, MP, for the United Nations Association Human Rights Day' (Speech at Australia National University, Canberra, 10 December 1973): pmtranscripts.pmc.gov.au/release/transcript-3098.

[44] 'Speech by the Prime Minister: International Women's Year' (Speech at the Inaugural Meeting of the National Advisory Committee, Canberra, 11 September 1974): pmtranscripts.pmc.gov.au/release/transcript-3385.

[45] 'FOR CABINET', above n 42.

[46] S Moyn, *The Last Utopia: Human Rights in History* (Cambridge, Belknap Press, 2010) 44.

[47] On the NIEO, see, in particular, the articles collected in a special issue of (2015) 6 *Humanity: An Interdisciplinary Journal of Human Rights, Humanitarianism and Development*; and S Moyn, *Not Enough: Human Rights in an Unequal World* (Cambridge, Belknap Press, 2018) ch 4.

[48] UNGA Res 29/3281 'Charter of the Economic Rights and Duties of States' (12 December 1974) UN Doc A/RES/29/3281.

Thus, while Whitlam's ideal of human rights partially dovetailed with those who championed a 'right to development' at the United Nations, his government shared the dismay of other Western leaders over the new 'structural approach' to rights which sought 'to identify and seek to remove structural obstacles that lie at the root of many an injustice as [well as] to deal with their symptoms in the form of particular violations'.[49] This view meant that women's particular predicament were but symptomatic of bigger, structural, economic forces: and this was where the IWY discussion should be focused. As Mexican Attorney-General and conference chairperson Ojeda Paullada put it, the Mexico City conference would not be 'a forum for enumerating the political and social problems that women face', but '[o]n the contrary … must approve a series of international documents of fundamental political value'.[50] Women were to be sidelined at their own conference by seemingly bigger issues.

While contestation between collective and individual approaches to human rights animated much interstate disputation during IWY, the women's movement itself rarely employed the term at all. A taken-for-granted formulation at 1995's Fourth World Congress on Women, that 'women's rights are human rights' had not entered the vocabulary in 1975, owing largely to the relative obscurity of human rights outside international law and diplomacy. It would not be until later in the 1970s that Jimmy Carter's presidency and Amnesty International's winning of the Nobel Peace Prize, among other events, would catapult human rights to the forefront of popular discussion.[51] The emerging women's liberation movement also rejected the rights and equality focus of activists like Street in the 1940s, who had seen the possibilities of human rights for women's issues. As Susan Castley, a research officer within Reid's office, remarked in a report prepared for Australia's IWY delegation: '[e]quality is not the answer so long as our society remains sexist. Equality would mean women becoming more like men. What is needed is for people to become more like human beings'.[52] It was the deeper, social and cultural oppressions signified by 'sexism', rather than a lack of opportunity for women to adopt male roles and responsibilities, which would be the centrepiece of Reid's intervention at Mexico City.

First coined in the United States in the late 1960s, the term 'sexism' was soon widely used across North America to describe, as one populariser put it, someone 'who proclaims or justifies or assumes the supremacy of one sex over

[49] Phillip Alston quoted in J Dehm, 'Righting Inequality: Human Rights Responses to Economic Inequality in the United Nations' (2019) 10 *Humanity: An International Journal of Human Rights, Humanitarianism, and Development* 443, 449.

[50] Burke, 'Competing for the Last Utopia?, above n 2.

[51] Moyn, *The Last Utopia*, above n 46.

[52] S Castley, 'Sexism: Introductory Remarks' in *Women in Australian Society: Analyses and Situations* (Canberra, Australian National Advisory Committee for International Women's Year, 1975) 8.

the other'.[53] In Australia, the term quickly gained traction in the mid-1970s, via prominent books like Anne Summers' *Damned Whores and God's Police* (1975), which likened the term to racism or indeed the process of colonisation that her book's subtitle referenced, as 'a means of categorising people and assigning their social function'.[54] Inculcated from the time that a person is defined as a male or female based on their physical attributes alone, sexism 'divides up all the qualities a human being has, or potentially has, and says that women should have and be valued for half of these qualities'.[55] It was this aspect of ideology that was constraining the advancement of the women's movement, for 'society is, in its present sexist form, divided up in such a way as to make sure that women have little access to the kinds of institutions in our society that determine what kind of society we will have'.[56] The presence of a few women in bureaucracies, governments or trade unions does not change the fact that 'all of these institutions, because they are mostly run by men, are run for men'.[57] The IWY Conference proved a remarkable space, then, for the thrashing out of these diverse, contradictory imaginaries of a new world.

IV. THE CONFERENCE: THE COMPROMISES OF REPRESENTATION AT MEXICO CITY

The World Conference for the IWY almost never took place. Only in late 1974, as the United States became aware of the need to counter a Soviet-backed conference in East Berlin, did the Western bloc insist that a modest budget be made available for a UN gathering in Bogota, Colombia, a location that was quickly switched to Mexico City owing to civil unrest.[58] Elizabeth Reid, attending the United Nations in New York as early moves towards organising the World Conference got under way in October 1974, judged preparations to be 'in a chaotic last minute mess'.[59] Partly owing to this confusion, Reid wrote to Whitlam that Australia could yet make 'an informed and valuable contribution' as part of an Iranian-suggested Special Consultative Committee that would draft the conference's Plan of Action.[60] Such plans had emerged from previous

[53] FR Shapiro, 'Historical Notes on the Vocabulary of the Women's Movement' (1985) 60 *American Speech* 3, 7.
[54] A Summers, *Damned Whores and God's Police: The Colonisation of Women in Australia* (Melbourne, Penguin Books, 1975) 22.
[55] Castley, 'Sexism', above n 52, 7.
[56] ibid 8.
[57] ibid.
[58] 'Elizabeth Reid to Gough Whitlam: World Conference: Mexico 23 June–24 July 1975' (24 November 1974) in 'International Women's Year – United Nations Conference – Mexico City' (National Archives of Australia, NAA, Series A1209, Control Symbol 1975/577, Item ID 8870406).
[59] ibid.
[60] ibid.

'thematic' conferences, on the human environment in Stockholm (1972) and population in Bucharest (1974). Reid stated that

> given our stances at the United Nations and at national level if we were prepared to put a lot of hard work into this proposal it would be the most valuable contribution Australia could make at an international level during the year.[61]

Reid subsequently secured a position on the Committee, which met in February to March 1975. The Department of Foreign Affairs (DFA) instructed Australia's representatives in New York to offer her 'as much support as possible', particularly as the draft Plan of Action might require 'substantial revision and/or amendment'.[62]

This focus on a non-binding, effectively aspirational, document like the Plan of Action demonstrates Savitri Taylor and Klaus Neumann's contention that Australian diplomats and lawyers were 'not confident that "soft law" would be treated as entirely non-binding'.[63] The status of UN resolutions and declarations was deeply contested at the time, with non-aligned and socialist nations believing that the General Assembly and associated bodies could 'create … new legal principles to regulate international relations'.[64] When the Draft Plan was released in February 1975, Australia's UN representatives considered it 'too long', containing 'specific and detailed' proposals on a significant range of issues based largely on development and population priorities, but found little that was politically problematic. The need to 'ward off attempts to dilute these recommendations' was paramount, it was felt, 'rather than coming forward with proposals to strengthen them'.[65] Reid, on the other hand, saw much to critique in the draft document and used her position on the Consultative Committee to challenge the prevailing, instrumentalist agenda. This was clearly evident in the wording of the Plan itself, the purpose of which was to 'stimulate national and international action to solve the problems of under-development and of the socio-economic structure which places women in an inferior position'.[66] Issues of particular concern to women – from family planning to funding for small scale agriculture – took a back seat.

A forum held in conjunction with the Committee meeting on the topic of 'Women and Men: The Next 25 Years' afforded Reid an opportunity to publicly

[61] ibid.

[62] 'International Women's Year: Consultative Committee Meeting' (15 February 1975) in 'International Women's Year – United Nations Conference – Mexico City' (National Archives of Australia, NAA, Series A1209, Control Symbol 1975/577, Item ID 8870406).

[63] S Taylor and K Neumann, 'Australia and the 1967 Declaration on Territorial Asylum: A Case Study of the Making of International Refugee and Human Rights Law' (2018) 30 *International Journal of Refugee Law* 8, 11.

[64] AC Castles, 'Legal Status of UN Resolutions' (1967) 3 *Adelaide Law Review* 68, 78.

[65] 'IWY Consultative Committee: Draft Plan of Action' (20 February 1975) in 'International Women's Year – United Nations Conference – Mexico City' (National Archives of Australia, NAA, Series A1209, Control Symbol 1975/577, Item ID 8870406).

[66] *Report of the World Conference of the International Women's Year, Mexico City*, 19 June–2 July 1975 (New York, United Nations, 1976) 11.

insist that the Mexico conference should aim for nothing less than 'a new definition of development'.[67] Preparing to depart from Canberra, Reid requested that DFA representatives at the United Nations make available to her a copy of Danish economist and long-time UN staffer Ester Boserup's *Woman's Role in Economic Development* (1970), a foundational text in what would become the field of 'Women in Development'.[68] Boserup argued that that 'Western-led development reduced the status of and opportunities for women' in the Third World, particularly via the diminution of traditional roles in domestic and agricultural production.[69] It is perhaps surprising, given the seemingly anti-Western tone of her work, that US embassies worldwide were furnished with a digest version of the book prior to the Mexico conference.[70] However, Reid's speech at this preparatory forum provides an answer: Boserup's ideas were seen as a way to challenge NIEO proponents who sought to tie the betterment of women to a nation's level of overall development. 'Development cannot and must no longer be measured in terms of Gross National Products and economic growth rates' Reid insisted, citing Boserup almost word for word. It had 'a human face, not a harsh, pragmatic, economic one', and the necessity of development should not be used to 'claim that improving the lives of women is a luxury which a particular country at a particular time may not be able to afford'.[71]

Reid's speech also highlighted some of the rhetorical dexterity she would demonstrate in Mexico City, redeploying terms vital to the 1970s UN lexicon and putting them to feminist ends. In claiming that 'women are the oldest colonial and under developed group in the world', the Australian at once appealed to the language of anti-colonialism, formalised in the 1960's Declaration on the Granting of Independence to Colonial Countries and Peoples, and sought to stake a claim for women as international legal subjects.[72] In stating that development discourse 'so often goes hand in hand with Westernisation', for example, Reid claimed that 'this is a further form of colonialism from which women in particular are forced to suffer – cultural colonialism'. By claiming the colonial status of women everywhere – east and west, north and south – Reid joined with Western representatives, such as progressive US Congressperson Bella Agzub, in seeking to unite women across deeply demarcated Cold War boundaries. Agzub's

[67] 'Inward Cablegram' (11 March 1975), Papers of Elizabeth Reid (National Library of Australia, MS 9262, Series 2, Box 1, Folder 7).

[68] 'International Women's Year: Consultative Committee Meeting' (21 February 1975) in 'International Women's Year – United Nations Conference – Mexico City' (National Archives of Australia, NAA, Series A1209, Control Symbol 1975/577, Item ID 8870406); E Boserup, *Woman's Role in Economic Development* (London, George Allen & Unwin, 1970).

[69] BL Turner II and M Fischer-Kowalskic, 'Ester Boserup: An Interdisciplinary Visionary Relevant for Sustainability' (2010) 107 *Proceedings of the National Academy of Sciences of the United States of America* 21963, 21964.

[70] ibid 21964.

[71] 'Inward Cablegram', above n 67.

[72] ibid; UNGA Res 1514 'Declaration on the Granting of Independence to Colonial Countries and Peoples' (14 December 1960) UN Doc A/RES/1514(XV).

attempt to 'bridge the gap between women from different worlds by reiterating the exploitation of domestic and foreign minority women by multinationals' rather than focusing on the stark material differences between worlds, for example, arguably played into the hands of her own government, of whom she was at least rhetorically very critical.[73] Scholars have long written off women's rights campaigners of the Second and Third Worlds as being mere tools of authoritarian states, but Reid's role in New York and then Mexico City shows such complicities were equally common in the First. Reid's experience, however, also demonstrates how space for agency always exists within these roles, as recent scholarship on the socialist world has highlighted.[74]

Returning from New York, Reid expressed her disappointment with the state of the Draft Plan, particularly its 'insensitivities to the problems of women in the developing world'.[75] Reid had protested in New York that IWY's 'primary concern' needed to be 'the vast majority of women, who are not here and will not be at Mexico City ... whose voices will never be heard by the decision makers in their countries', a broadside directed at the autocrats who would dominate the gathering. The concern of Australian diplomats shifted soon after Reid's return however, to the potential use of the 'Caracas Declaration', a document prepared by the Economic Commission for Latin America that reflected the imperatives of the NIEO, as the basis for a conference statement. The problem of these political issues, or what the US State Department called 'unrelated encumbrances' in a meeting with Australian diplomats in Washington DC, came more into focus as the conference drew closer.[76] While keen to publicise Australia's independence from the Anglo–US order as part of a pivot towards multilateralism, the influence of Australia's 'great and powerful friends' remained. A lengthy booklet was prepared for Australia's delegation, wherein it was remarked that despite 'helpful but inadequate' attempts to redraft the Plan of Action at March's Consultative Committee, it would be important to 'head off moves ... to inject extraneous political and economic issues' in Mexico.[77] It was necessary for Reid and her fellow delegates to simultaneously bear the 'heavy responsibility to the Australian community, and especially of course, to Australian women', while making sure to 'promote Australia's concerns and interests'.[78] The Australians were diplomats first, activists second.

[73] S Masaya, 'Bella Agzub's Dilemma: The Cold War, Women's Politics and the Arab-Israeli Conflict in the 1970s' (2018) 30 *Journal of Women's History* 112, 124.

[74] The key text in this recent outpouring of scholarship is F de Haan, 'Continuing Cold War Paradigms in Western Historiography of Transnational Women's Organisations: The Case of the Women's International Democratic Federation (WIDF)' (2010) 19 *Women's History Review* 547.

[75] 'Minutes of Meeting' (11 April 1975), Papers of Elizabeth Reid (National Library of Australia, MS 9262, Series 14, Box 32, Folder 15).

[76] 'International Women's Year: Mexico Conference' (24 May 1975) in 'International Women's Year – United Nations Conference – Mexico City' (National Archives of Australia, NAA, A1209, Control Symbol 1975/577, Item ID 8870406).

[77] 'Overall Approach of the Australian Delegation', Papers of Elizabeth Reid (National Library of Australia, MS 9262, Series 14, Box 41, Folder 72).

[78] ibid.

Australia dispatched 10 representatives to Mexico City, a mixture of 'femocrats' such as Susan Castley, Susan Ryan, Sarah Dowse and Margaret Whitlam – Gough Whitlam's wife and prominent campaigner – as well as several male bureaucrats more familiar with UN procedure.[79] A further 10 activists were appointed to the NGO 'Tribune', an initiative that had begun at the 1974 population conference, that effectively created a shadow conference of development groups, activists and aid organisations. The Tribune's discussions were far freer flowing and radical than those at the conference proper, but the two gathering's geographic isolation – at least 30 minutes' drive across the busy Central American capital – served to discourage much cross-pollination.[80] This was only one of the challenges which plagued the gathering. The DFA warned that 'it cannot be assumed that the conference will be a successful one', indeed with 'considerably less' preparatory work having been undertaken than had occasioned the population conference, and the existence of 'severe budgetary and staffing restraints … the odds are rather the other way'. There were not enough translators or secretarial support available, while food poisoning was particularly widespread, affecting 'some of every delegation all of the time'.[81] Such difficulties notwithstanding, Reid was still able to play a larger-than-life role in the gathering, described in one American report as 'one of the most outspoken feminists at the official UN conference', alongside Western feminist dignitaries like Germaine Greer and Betty Friedan.[82] She was quoted in the conference's semi-official newspaper, *Xilonen*, as leading 'the first official attacks on the draft World Plan of Action', arguing that it presented women as 'instruments to achieve "desirable" national goals' instead of 'people in their own right'.[83]

This emphasis on the shared personhood of women was suggested by the DFA as a way of defusing political tensions at the gathering. Delegates were instructed to 'focus attention on the unifying objectives and themes in a realistic and practical way', particularly through 'promot[ing] fundamental human rights in terms of women's dignity, their right to have a major say in determining their own part in the development process'.[84] Reid's speech at the third plenary, on 22 June 1975, demonstrated a turn away from her more confrontational approach in New York. 'Sexism' was introduced as a universalist critique of male power, which also undermined the demands of developing nations to a greater slice of the global economic pie. Sexism was a term 'we must cease being afraid to use', Reid claimed, as it 'cuts across social and cultural differences

[79] On 'femocrats', see H Eisenstein, *Inside Agitators: Australian Femocrats and the State* (Sydney, Allen & Unwin, 1996).

[80] Burke, 'Competing for the Last Utopia?', above n 2, 51.

[81] 'Overall Approach of the Australian Delegation', above n 77.

[82] H Papanek, 'The Work of Women: Postscript from Mexico City' (1975) 1 *Signs: The Journal of Women in Culture and Society* 215, 217.

[83] 'Australia Wants Changes to the Plan' *Xilonen* (Mexico City, 24 June 1975).

[84] 'Overall Approach of the Australian Delegation', above n 77.

within and between countries'.[85] This new terminology was carefully articulated within the existing language of law: '[t]he basis of racism, racial discrimination, alien domination and the taking of territory by force is similar to the basis of the violence against women which we call sexism'.[86] Nor was Reid dismissive of Third World concerns, agreeing that 'the demand for a new international economic order is far from a peripheral issue to the debate at this conference'.[87]

Rather than directly attack the Third World position, Reid tactically mobilised critiques of the Australian development model to undermine expansive claims for economic equality. 'Economic development has not brought with it unqualified advantages for Australian women', she insisted, instead it denied them economic independence – a reference to the male breadwinner model – and made them subservient to the same 'dehumanising' patterns of work as men.[88] What was needed instead were 'culturally appropriate concepts of development', which reflected the traditional, independent and often central role of women in many agricultural societies. If the Australian experience was an 'object lesson' for some, it should be a salutary shock to others. Western development models and concomitant growth in standards of living might not only prove impossible for the Third World, but also undesirable. While far from Reid's instructions to avoid undue politicisation and highlight unifying objectives – a demonstration of her agency even within this heavily scripted and staged international forum – the recourse to ideas of sexism and colonialism ended up serving both agendas well. And while Reid's speech appears to have registered little to no impact on proceedings in 1975, a move by Australia and New Zealand to include a paragraph about sexism in the Plan of Action arising from 1980's Second World Conference in Copenhagen sparked what Kristen Ghodsee terms 'intense debate', with the term eventually relegated to a footnote.[89]

How can the threads of Reid's contribution in Mexico City be untangled? Her interventions at both the Consultative Committee and the World Conference proper certainly speak to categorisation as a form of minor jurisprudence, which aims to 'cut holes in the fabric of law' to reveal its implicit biases and agendas.[90] Equally, it could be read as an immanent critique, drawing on the language of power to reveal its own flaws and elisions, and in so doing extend its meanings and possibilities.[91] It is also impossible to ignore the fact that while Reid clearly inhabited a minor or excluded role, as a woman, non-lawyer and non-politician,

[85] 'Statement by the leader of the Australian Delegation: Ms Elizabeth Reid' (21 June 1975), Papers of Elizabeth Reid (National Library of Australia, MS 9262, Series 14, Box 42, Folder 84).

[86] ibid.

[87] ibid.

[88] ibid.

[89] Ghodsee, 'Revisiting the United Nations Decade for Women', above n 1, 7.

[90] P Goodrich, 'How Strange the Change from Major to Minor' (2017) 21 *Law Text Culture* 30.

[91] For a recent example of this, see MH Petrova, 'Weapons Prohibitions through Immanent Critique: NGOs as Emancipatory and (De)securitising Actors in Security Governance' (2018) 44 *Review of International Studies* 619.

her critiques of Third World notions of development served not only the women of the Global South whom Reid aimed to represent, but the geopolitical interests of her nation. However, attempts to understand Reid's role as either inducting a new actor into the halls of international law, or as a front for big-power politics, are equally insufficient. Indeed, these roles were mutually enabling and restricting. As Genevieve Renard Painter points out, 'major jurisprudence provides the background conditions against which potentially transformative speech is evaluated' – the minor and the major are always already entangled.[92] Reid, for her part, expressed significant discomfort at being a First World feminist abroad. From the outset, she had refused claims to speak for 'all women' –'[h]ow can I, I am white and middle class' – and reflected upon her return to Australia of the gap between 'women from the Third World [who] tend to discuss the physical conditions of their lives', and those from the West who were 'pre-occupied by social attitudes and relationships'.[93] A sign of Reid's disillusionment with the First World feminism she took to Mexico is apparent in her decision to leave Whitlam's service in October 1975, travelling to Iran to head the UN-affiliated Asia and Pacific Centre for Women and Development.[94]

V. CONCLUSION

The case study of Elizabeth Reid as an individual within the Australian history of international law allows several key observations. First, it brings into question the Whitlam Government's seemingly dramatic shift from a bilateral, particularly American, focus for Australian foreign policy, to one that prioritised multilateralism and eschewed the quest for domination. Reid's performance of middle power diplomacy during IWY, attempting to serve as a bridge between the interests of developed and developing powers and peoples, also shows how this posture concealed the Whitlam Government's ongoing commitment to the American alliance. The DFA's orders to forestall the inclusion of 'political' content in conference documents shows not only continuities with the previous conservative government's stand-offish approach to international organisations, but that Australia's position clearly lay with the developed, Western world. Indeed, a key observation of the Harries Committee Report into Australian relationships with the Third World, published in 1979, was that such an approach

[92] GR Painter, 'Law as Minor Jurisprudence: Is it a Mistake?' (2017) 21 *Law Text Culture* 276, 290.

[93] *Sydney Morning Herald* (9 April 1973) 1; Australian National Advisory Committee, International Women's Year, *International Women's Year Conference, Mexico City 1975* (Canberra, Government Printer, 1975).

[94] On this move, see R Burke, '"My Work Does Not Wait for Revolutions": Elizabeth Reid and the Possibilities of State Feminism in Iran' in J Damousi and J Smart (eds), *Contesting Australian History: Essays in Honour of Marilyn Lake* (Melbourne, Monash University Publishing, 2019).

was unbelievable and should be avoided – it was clear to other nations where Australia stood.[95]

A close engagement with Australian priorities and women's movement agendas also provides a fascinating window into the state of human rights politics in the few years before their 'revolution'. The Whitlam Government's commitment to human rights law, from the signing of key covenants to the attempt to pass Australia's first Bill of Rights, is well known.[96] Both Whitlam and the non-aligned states, whose numerical strength and solidarity made them dominant powers of the UN's Third Committee, understood, if to different degrees, that human rights meant the development of national capacity and improvements to standards of living. Such rhetoric was, however, a relatively barren terrain for the newly ascendant second-wave feminist movement, which rejected as outdated the language of human rights and equality. Even so, frequent refrains from Reid and other members of Australia's delegation to either personhood or the 'human' qualities of women, not to mention the mobilisation of sexism as a universalist challenge to particularistic Third World demands, points towards the Western women's movement's importance to the (re)emergence of human rights as a politics of individual violation.[97]

Finally, Reid's case problematises easy assumptions about women's roles in international law and politics during the Cold War. Her position as a First World feminist in the employ of and directly responsible for the interests of a government, helpfully complicates the binary that has framed histories of women's organisations in the post-war era: of agential, 'proactive' women in the First World and oppressed, 'reactive' women in the Second (and indeed, Third).[98] Much as representatives of socialist states or non-aligned nations were restricted by the undemocratic nature of their governments, requiring careful balancing of women's interests with those of the party or regime, Reid needed both to satisfy a government cautious of unduly radical international legal principles and challenge women's instrumentalisation in service of political and economic ends. Her use of the term 'sexism' and colonialism, then, highlight her agency and willingness to resist the edicts of a government adamant to avoid difficult political topics and champion amorphous 'human rights' in their place. Agency and structure were a spectrum, not a polarity, during IWY.

[95] *Australia and the Third World: Report of the Committee on Australia's Relations with the Third World* (Canberra, Australian Government Publishing Service, 1979).

[96] See H Burmester, 'International Law in the Attorney-General's Department: 1901–2000', ch 9 in this volume.

[97] On how this vision of individual women's rights defeated a Soviet-inspired version, focused on social and economic rights, see C Donhert, 'Women's Rights in Cold War Europe: Disentangling Feminist Histories' (2013) 8 (Supp) *Past & Present* 178.

[98] See N Funk, 'A Very Tangled Knot: Official State Socialist Women's Organizations, Women's Agency and Feminism in Eastern European State Socialism' (2014) 21 *European Journal of Women's Studies* 344; K Ghodsee, 'Untangling the Knot: A Response to Nanette Funk' (2015) 22 *European Journal of Women's Studies* 248, for the different positions in this debate.

14

The First Australian and New Zealand Society of International Law, 1933–38

MADELAINE CHIAM*

I. INTRODUCTION

THE AUSTRALIAN AND New Zealand Society of International Law (ANZSIL) celebrated 30 years of existence in 2022. To commemorate this milestone, the organisers of the Annual ANZSIL conference gathered all but one of the past and present ANZSIL presidents to reflect on the Society's first 30 years.[1] In his reflections, Philip Alston noted that the founders of the modern ANZSIL had been aware of an earlier incarnation of a society with this name and had sought to align themselves with it. In her opening remarks at the conference, the 2022 President, Karen Scott, drew parallels between the ANZSIL of 2022 and the earlier ANZSIL, established in 1933. Reflecting on the events of 2022, Scott commented that she felt 'quite bleak when ruminating on … the irrelevance of international law this year', and she imagined 'many scholars, lawyers and practitioners would have felt similarly in 1933'.[2]

The first ANZSIL is something of an enigma in the history of international law in Australia. After a high-profile 'arrival' in 1933, including a widely reported first meeting, and the release of Proceedings of this meeting in 1935, the Society held only one further meeting in 1938, before quietly fading away. And yet, as Scott's 2022 remarks suggest, the first ANZSIL remains significant

* Thanks to Stephanie Falconer for her research assistance for this chapter. Thanks also to Alison Duxbury, and to the participants at the following three events for their feedback on earlier versions of this chapter: the 2018 ANZSIL Conference; Adil Hasan Khan's 2018 Workshop on 'The Office of the Southern Jurist Diplomat'; and the 2022 La Trobe International and Comparative Law Research Group 'Work-in-Progress' workshop.

[1] Australian and New Zealand Society of International Law, '29th Annual ANZSIL Conference: International Law and Global Inter-Connectedness' (Conference Programme, 2022).

[2] K Scott, 'Opening Remarks' (29th Annual ANZSIL Conference: International Law and Global Inter-Connectedness, Canberra, 30 June 2022).

for the history of international law in Australia and New Zealand. In this chapter, I give an account of the 1930s' ANZSIL: its creation, membership, interests and eventual demise. This account is a micro-history of a local international law society that aims, through an exploration of the hopes and concerns of the membership, to contribute to a greater understanding of the place of international law in the social and political world of Australia. The story of ANZSIL also provides insights into the international legal issues that were of concern within the Dominions of the British Empire and into how international law was regarded by elite members of those societies. These details contribute to a fuller picture of the ways that international law worked in domestic societies during the 1930s, when faith in the League of Nations was in decline.

The primary source for this chapter is the volume of proceedings of the first ANZSIL meeting (held in 1933) that were published in 1935, a volume that can still be found in many Australian law libraries. I also examined the papers of some of the men who were involved with the Society, which has allowed a fuller understanding of the Society than that provided by the volume alone. My account is confined to Australian experiences of ANZSIL as, despite its name, there appears to have been little contribution from New Zealanders to the 1930s ANZSIL. The chapter proceeds as follows: first, it provides the legal and political contexts for the establishment of the first ANZSIL, including the roles of the two other internationally oriented societies that existed at the time – the League of Nations Union and the Australian Institute for International Affairs. The chapter then describes the events around ANZSIL's creation, some of the key members of the Society and the issues that concerned ANZSIL's members. The chapter concludes with an account of the reception and demise of the Society.

II. AUSTRALIA AND THE WORLD IN 1933

A. The Legal and Political Context of 1933 Australia

Australia in 1933 was in a state of economic malaise and political weariness where, for those who were internationally inclined, the initial hopes for peace through the League of Nations were fading and concerns were growing about German and Japanese military expansion.[3] In the first three months of 1933 alone, Adolf Hitler was appointed Chancellor of Germany; Japan withdrew from the League of Nations following the League's condemnation of Japan's invasion of Manchuria;[4] and the League's World Disarmament Conference

[3] See, eg, P Jankowski, *All Against All: The Long Winter of 1933 and the Origins of the Second World War* (London, Profile Books, 2020).

[4] Stewart Brown, 'Japan Stuns World, Withdraws from League' *United Press International* (24 February 1933): www.upi.com/Archives/1933/02/24/Japan-stuns-world-withdraws-from-league/

floundered.[5] Economically, 1933 was the peak of the Depression and Australia's unemployment rate was among the highest in the world.[6] Australia was still formally a Dominion of the British Empire in 1933 and its responses to world events were shaped by its ongoing lack of international legal personality.[7] The Balfour Declaration of 1926 and the Statute of Westminster 1931 had declared the British Dominions to be autonomous communities, with legislative powers independent of the Empire,[8] but Australia had not immediately taken advantage of the greater independence offered by these legal forms. Indeed, the Australian Parliament had requested that an amendment be inserted into the Statute of Westminster stating that the Statute could not be adopted by Australian governments until the Parliament of Australia had consented to its adoption.[9] This had been the suggestion of John Latham, one of Australia's leading lawyers and politicians who in 1933 was federal Attorney-General and Minister for External Affairs, but at the time of drafting the Statute of Westminster was Leader of the Opposition.[10] The Australian Parliament did not pass the necessary implementing legislation until 1942.[11] Australia's reluctance in relation to the Statute of Westminster meant that Australia had the ability to act as an independent nation, but was choosing not to. This created a modified international legal personality, the powers and boundaries of which were subject to much debate. In 1933, there remained considerable legal and political ambiguity around Australia's ability to conduct international relations.

The ambiguity over Australia's international legal personality manifested in a number of ways. The federal government's power over 'external affairs',

2231840119817/. For a contemporary account of the events leading to Japan's withdrawal, see 'Editorial Comment' (1933) 96 *World Affairs* 3, 4–5.

[5] See, eg, CJ Kitching, *Britain and the Geneva Disarmament Conference: A Study in International History* (Basingstoke, Palgrave Macmillan, 2003).

[6] M Peel and C Twomey, *A History of Australia* (Basingstoke, Palgrave Macmillan, 2011) 185. See also RG Gregory and NT Butlin (eds), *Recovery from the Depression: Australia and the World Economy in the 1930s* (Cambridge, Cambridge University Press, 1988).

[7] For a general discussion of the history and status of Australia as a Dominion, see, eg, K Roberts-Wray, *Commonwealth and Colonial Law* (London, Stevens & Sons, 1966); MHM Kidwai, 'International Personality and the British Dominions: Evolution and Accomplishment' (1975) 9 *University of Queensland Law Journal* 76; DP O'Connell, 'The Evolution of Australia's International Personality' in DP O'Connell (ed), *International Law in Australia* (Sydney, Law Book Co, 1966); L Zines, 'The Growth of Australian Nationhood and Its Effect on the Powers of the Commonwealth' in L Zines (ed), *Commentaries on the Australian Constitution: A Tribute to Geoffrey Sawer* (Sydney, Butterworths, 1977). See also F Bongiorno, 'The Rise and Fall of "a Hyphenated Condition": Australia, the British Empire and the Commonwealth', ch 3 in this volume.

[8] Inter-Imperial Relations Committee, *Imperial Conference 1926* (Report No E(IR/26), 1926) 2 (Balfour Declaration); Statute of Westminster 1931 (22 & 23 Geo 5 c 4).

[9] D Lee, 'States Rights and Australia's Adoption of the Statute of Westminster, 1931–1942' (2016) 13 *History Australia* 258, 261.

[10] S Macintyre, 'Latham, Sir John Greig (1877–1964)' in B Nairn and G Serle (eds), *Australian Dictionary of Biography: Volume 10 1891–1939* (Carlton, Melbourne University Press, 1986). See also a list of members in the Lyons Ministry: Department of Parliamentary Services, 'Ministers in the Lyons Ministry from 06.01.1932 to 07.11.1938': handbook.aph.gov.au/Ministry/17.

[11] Lee, above n 9; Bongiorno, ch 3 in this volume.

for example, was interpreted in a restricted fashion.[12] This power was initially understood to refer only to relations with Britain and other members of the Empire and was not viewed as a general grant for Australia to exercise independent foreign relations power, which remained exclusively a matter for the Imperial government.[13] By 1933, however, Australia and the other Dominions had exercised some powers of an independent state, including being a signatory to the Treaty of Versailles, holding independent membership of the League of Nations, and becoming party to some other treaties.[14] Indeed, in 1933, Australia assumed the presidency of the Council of the League of Nations.[15] At the same time, Australia in 1933 did not exercise its own diplomatic relations, relying instead largely on 'Imperial' (ie, British) foreign policy and diplomacy to lead Australia's positions.[16] Australian governments did not consider that they could exercise autonomous decisions in matters of war and peace, up to and including 1939 when Britain declared war on Germany. At that time, Australia's then Prime Minister Robert Menzies famously declared 'Great Britain has declared war upon [Germany] and … as a result, Australia is also at war'.[17]

Australia's international relations and policies in the 1930s were a product of deeply racially inflected approaches to the world.[18] Australian governments' commitment to a 'White Australia' had been demonstrated to international audiences in 1919, through Prime Minister Billy Hughes' trenchant opposition to the racial equality clause in the League of Nations Covenant.[19] Australia had also been granted joint mandatory powers, with New Zealand and Great Britain, under the League of Nations Mandate System over Nauru and New Guinea.[20] Antony Anghie has argued that Australia's decades-long rule over Nauru and New Guinea was an 'Australian Empire', while Cait Storr has discussed how these relations created a form of sub-imperialism.[21] Australian

[12] See generally H Charlesworth et al, 'Deep Anxieties: Australia and the International Legal Order' (2003) 25 *Sydney Law Review* 423.

[13] See ibid. See also A Twomey, 'Federal Parliament's Changing Role in Treaty Making and External Affairs' (Research Paper 15 1999–2000, Parliament of Australia, 7 March 2000).

[14] ibid.

[15] A Duxbury, 'Participation in the "Gilded Ball": Australia and the Council of the League of Nations', ch 2 in this volume.

[16] See, eg, EM Andrews, 'Patterns in Australian Foreign Policy' (1972) 26 *Australian Outlook* 31.

[17] R Menzies, 'Declaration of War' (Speech, 3 September 1939): aso.gov.au/titles/radio/menzies-speech-declaration-war/.

[18] See, eg, C Byrne, 'Australia's Pursuit of Place in the World' in JM Lewis and A Tiernan (eds), *The Oxford Handbook of Australian Politics* (Oxford, Oxford University Press, 2021). For a discussion of Australia's race-based policies as part of a wider racist internationalism, see H Reynolds and M Lake, *Drawing the Global Colour Line: White Men's Countries and the Question of Racial Equality* (Carlton, Melbourne University Press, 2008).

[19] See Reynolds and Lake, ibid 265–72; Duxbury, ch 2 in this volume.

[20] M Chisholm, '"Treat-Them-Gently-at-All-Costs-and-Please-the-United Nations": The UN Trusteeship Council and Capital Punishment and Clemency in Papua and New Guinea, 1954–65', ch 4 in this volume.

[21] A Anghie, 'Race, Self-Determination and Australian Empire' (2018) 19 *Melbourne Journal of International Law* 423; C Storr, *International Status in the Shadow of Empire: Nauru and the Histories of International Law* (Cambridge, Cambridge University Press, 2020).

attempts at establishing better relations in Asia in the 1930s, largely for trade purposes, were received sceptically, with Chinese and Japanese representatives in particular querying Australia's restrictive immigration policies.[22] Migrants who attempted to enter Australia in 1933 remained subject to the notorious dictation test under which they could be excluded or deported if they failed to write 50 words in a European language determined by an immigration official.[23]

One view of Australia's position in the world in 1933 was captured by PD Phillips, a lawyer and teacher, who became a vice-president of the Australian League of Nations Union (LNU) and was involved with the first ANZSIL conference.[24] In the editorial of the LNU's 1933–34 Annual Report, Phillips gave voice to the weariness and concern of this period of the interwar years, where he wrote:

> Four years of economic depression and political disturbance have left their mark deep on contemporary civilisation. The buoyancy of trade and the stability of domestic conditions apparent in many countries during the later nineteen twenties suggested not merely the recovery but restoration of pre-war conditions, so that the war itself, appalling indeed in its wastage of human life, seemed likely to become in memory and history not more than a temporary interruption … of the normal social development and progress of mankind … To-day, the war and its sequel appear to have a different signature.[25]

B. International Law and International Societies in 1933 Australia

The shifting boundaries of Australia's relations with the world meant that Australians in 1933 were acutely aware of how vulnerable their security and prosperity were to international events. This awareness gave considerable purchase to societies committed to education and discussion of international affairs. There were two internationally oriented societies with a strong presence in 1933 Australia: the Australian Institute of International Affairs (AIIA) and the LNU. The pool of Australian international experts in the 1930s meant that the AIIA and the LNU had many shared members from the political class. Any new society devoted to international matters, such as the proposed ANZSIL, needed a mandate that was distinct from the existing societies while also having an appeal to both the elites and, potentially, non-expert audiences.

[22] T Kendall, *Within China's Orbit? China through the eyes of the Australian Parliament* (Canberra, Department of Parliamentary Services, Parliament of Australia, 2008).

[23] See, eg, M Williams, *Australia's Dictation Test: The Test it was a Crime to Fail* (Leiden, Brill, 2021).

[24] See LW Maher, 'Phillips, Sir Philip David (1897–1970)' in J Ritchie (ed), *Australian Dictionary of Biography: Volume 15 1940–1980* (Carlton, Melbourne University Press, 2000); Minutes of Third Meeting of the Provisional Executive of the Australian and New Zealand Society of International Law, Box 1009/63/97.

[25] Australian League of Nations Union, Victorian Branch, *Annual Report* (Report, 1933–34) 1.

The AIIA was modelled on the Royal Institute for International Affairs (RIIA) (or Chatham House) and was established to promote peace. The AIIA (consistently with its model the RIIA) saw its role as providing a forum for social and political elites to access 'superior, independent expertise and analysis through discussions and publications'.[26] Still in existence today, the AIIA's mission has developed into one centred on public membership and engagement. This shift is apparent in the description of the AIIA's original mission of 'the objective, scientific study of international affairs'[27] to its current aim 'to help Australians know more, understand more, and engage more in international affairs'.[28] The AIIA had been established first with state-based branches, but these were centralised to create a federated AIIA in 1933, making 1933 also a significant year for this society.[29] John Latham had participated in drafting the Constitution of the original Royal Institute and he was involved in establishing the Victorian branch of the society.[30] Following the creation of the federated AIIA in 1933, the first AIIA national president was appointed: Archibald Hamilton Charteris, a Scot who had taken the new position of Challis Chair of International Law and Jurisprudence at the University of Sydney in 1920, and who had helped to establish the New South Wales branch of the AIIA in 1924.[31] Charteris was an energetic and charming figure who contributed considerably to Australian understanding of international affairs via his regular columns in the *Sydney Morning Herald* and his broadcasts on radio programmes on the Australian Broadcasting Corporation.[32] Along with Latham and other political elites, Charteris formed part of a 'close network of established intellectuals with some social and political influence'.[33]

The LNU's object was to also promote peace and to do so in line with the purposes of the League of Nations itself. To this end, the LNU had a strong focus on disarmament and a significant part of its work involved promoting the case for disarmament within Australia.[34] The LNU also had a focus on educating the Australian population, which led to it conducting peace education campaigns in schools and participating, with other peace groups, in the 'International Peace Campaign' from 1936.[35] The membership of the LNU was a largely upper/middle-class constituency of Australians, including a significant

[26] D Stone, 'A Think Tank in Evolution or Decline? The Australian Institute of International Affairs in Comparative Perspective' (1996) 50 *Australian Journal of International Affairs* 117, 118.

[27] ibid.

[28] Australian Institute of International Affairs, 'About Us': www.internationalaffairs.org.au/about-us/about-the-aiia/.

[29] Stone, above n 26.

[30] Macintyre, above n 10.

[31] JG Starke, 'Charteris, Archibald Hamilton (1874–1940)' in B Nairn and G Serle (eds), *Australian Dictionary of Biography: Volume 7 1891–1939* (Carlton, Melbourne University Press, 1979).

[32] D Hassall, 'Professor AH Charteris and the Study of International Law in Australia' (1997) 18 *Australian Year Book of International Law* 175.

[33] Stone, above n 26, 119.

[34] See, eg, Australian League of Nations Union, above n 25.

[35] H Summy, 'Countering War: The Role of the League of Nations Union' (2014) 33 *Social Alternatives* 15. See also, Australian League of Nations Union, above n 25.

number of women. This was a group whose commitment to peace and to the League had been galvanised by the First World War.[36] There were LNU branches in each State of Australia and John Latham was the first president of the Victorian branch of the LNU, established in 1921.[37] For the LNU, 1933 was also a significant year as it was in that year that the State branches of the LNU (except Tasmania) met in Melbourne for the first conference of the LNU.[38]

Education about international affairs also occurred through Australian universities. As a field of study, the subject 'Public International Law' had mixed status in the few Australian law schools that existed in 1933. The subject was restored to the curriculum of the Melbourne Law School in 1933, having been taught as part of a subject called 'Modern Political Institutions' for the previous 20 years.[39] 'Public International Law' (PIL) had never left the curriculum of the Sydney Law School, where it was a compulsory subject until 1959, and was taught by the succession of holders of the Challis Chair in International Law and Jurisprudence, including Charteris and (from 1942) Julius Stone.[40] In contrast, Adelaide Law School stopped teaching PIL in 1906 and it did not return to the curriculum until the 1950s. Notwithstanding the Law School's attitude to the subject, Adelaide Law School did have as its Chair of Law the 'most prolific publicist of the inter-war period in Australia', Coleman Phillipson.[41] The first Law School in Queensland, the TC Beirne School of Law, was not established until 1936.[42] When it was established, one of its earliest staff members was Thomas Penberthy Fry, an intrepid Queenslander with a diploma from the Hague Academy of International Law, a Bachelor of Civil Law degree from Oxford and a Doctorate in Juridical Science from Harvard.[43] Fry had returned to Australia in 1931, where he first joined the Queensland bar.[44] Fry was also instrumental in the establishment of the first ANZSIL.

III. AN 'INTERNATIONAL LAW' SOCIETY

The Constitution of the first ANZSIL describes its object as follows: '[t]he object of the Society is to foster the study of public and private international law, and in particular the study of those topics which affect or are likely to affect Australia or New Zealand'.[45] In the context of Australia's growing, if

[36] Summy, above n 35.
[37] Macintyre, above n 10.
[38] Australian League of Nations Union, above n 25, 4.
[39] IA Shearer, 'The Teaching of International Law in Australian Law Schools' (1983) 9 *Adelaide Law Review* 61, 70.
[40] ibid 70.
[41] ibid 72.
[42] University of Queensland, 'History': law.uq.edu.au/about/history.
[43] WN Harrison, 'Thomas Penberthy Fry' (1952) 2 *University of Queensland Law Journal* 86.
[44] ibid.
[45] The Australian and New Zealand Society of International Law, *Proceedings* (Carlton, Melbourne University Press, 1935) vol 1, xiii.

still ambiguous, status in international relations, creating a society with this object made sense. Indeed, the Introduction to the Proceedings identified two factors that underpinned the need for a society focused on international legal issues: the 'increase … in the national status of [the Dominions of Australia and New Zealand] since the Great War';[46] and 'the extensive economic interests of the two countries in the field of international trade'.[47] In the view of the authors of the Introduction, limitations on Australia's ability to address these two developments had become particularly acute during and after the First World War, with both courts and governments 'handicapped' by the dearth of 'men trained in international law'.[48]

Notwithstanding this aim, in the parallel contexts of weariness about international affairs and the already existing international societies, the decision to establish a new society committed to international law is perplexing. The AIIA and the LNU by this time had overlapping aims and members and the creation of a third international society would stretch the capacities of Australia's small group of elites interested in international affairs even further. For the authors of the Introduction, ANZSIL could still be distinguished from the other two societies through its *legal* nature. 'The Society', the Introduction stated, 'is a legal Society'.[49] And, in case there was any doubt, the Introduction continued: '[the Society] does not intend to study international affairs as such, nor encroach in any way on the field occupied by the Australian Institute of International Affairs, the Australian League of Nations Union, and similar organizations'.[50] The legal focus of the Society was built into its membership structure, with the Constitution requiring that the elected officers of ANZSIL consist of representatives of 'the Judiciary, the Law Schools, the Legal and Diplomatic Departments of Governments, and Practising Members of the Legal Profession'.[51]

The consequence of this focus on membership from the legal profession and associated groups is evident in the initial membership and leadership of ANZSIL. The Society was formally established at a meeting at the Sydney Law School on 21 February 1933, where the Constitution was adopted and the first ANZSIL Executive Council was elected.[52] Two law academics were elected to the key leadership positions: Archibald Charteris was elected President of ANZSIL and Thomas Fry was made Honorary Secretary. These positions were supported by a host of elected vice-presidents, who were all key members of the Australian legal fraternity. Some of the most familiar names include: John Latham, then federal Attorney-General; HV Evatt and Owen Dixon, then

[46] ibid xxiii.
[47] ibid xiii.
[48] ibid.
[49] ibid.
[50] ibid xiv.
[51] ibid xxiii.
[52] There had been two earlier meetings that laid the groundwork for this formal establishment, see ibid xiv.

judges on the Australian High Court; Victor Le Gay Brereton, Judge Advocate General of the Australian military forces; Sir John Peden, the Dean of Sydney Law School; and Professor Kenneth Bailey, Dean of Melbourne Law School. The other most notable figure in the ANZSIL membership, elected a Councillor of the first ANZSIL, was Robert Menzies, then Attorney-General of Victoria and later Australia's longest-serving and arguably most influential Prime Minister. From New Zealand, the Proceedings claimed eight members, with Professor RM Algie of Auckland University College the only New Zealand-based member appointed to any formal role (Councillor).[53]

ANZSIL was then conceived and established as a society of the elite men of the Australian and, to a much lesser extent, New Zealand legal scenes. While international law was not yet an established professional pathway in these Dominions – either in academia or in government – creating a society with a collection of elite members was geared towards the development of this professional class. ANZSIL would also serve as a vehicle through which expertise in international law could be shared. Owen Dixon pressed for this form of knowledge dissemination in his opening speech to the ANZSIL Conference, where he said:

> [O]ne of the most important things which this Society can do for those who are not engaged in, and cannot pursue the study of international law, … is to make accessible … the ever-growing mass of information to keep pace with which is quite beyond the capacity of persons who must do practical daily work in the law.[54]

But if the primary aim of ANZSIL was to create a society focused on international legal issues, the legal profession in Australia, and in particular those with an interest in international law, was not large enough to sustain the Society in the longer term. Ordinary membership of the Society was thus open to non-legal professionals or, as the Introduction describes them, 'laymen who are interested in international law so far as it assists them to a better understanding of international affairs'.[55] At the time of the first meeting of ANZSIL, the Society had 100 members, around 30 of whom attended the inaugural conference.[56] The size of the Australian legal profession also meant that cross-overs in membership between ANZSIL, the AIIA and the LNU were impossible to avoid. Many members of ANZSIL were also members of one or both of the AIIA and the LNU. Latham, who had been involved with the AIIA in the United Kingdom, was a leader of the LNU in Victoria and a vice-president of ANZSIL. Fry, honorary secretary of ANZSIL (and its driving force), had established the Queensland chapter of the AIIA. Perhaps most strikingly, Charteris, the first President of

[53] ibid xiv.
[54] ibid xix.
[55] ibid xiv.
[56] The Conference was held 17–21 August 1933 in the Sydney University Senate Room, on Thursday–Saturday evening, with a session on Saturday morning: ibid xiv–xv.

ANZSIL, was unable to attend the Society's first conference as he was attending the Toronto Conference on British Commonwealth Relations, as the leader of the AIIA.[57]

In acknowledging the interest of non-lawyers in international law and embracing a purpose to foster understanding of international law among both lawyers and non-lawyers, ANZSIL shared to some degree the originating purpose of the American Society of International Law (ASIL). The dissemination of international law – and a conception of international law as a means to achieve international justice – had been at the core of the establishment of the ASIL. The opening article in ASIL's journal, published in 1907, is by Elihu Root, then the US Secretary of State, and is titled, 'The Need of Popular Understanding of International Law'.[58] In the article, Root argued that a condition of peace between nations was 'general public knowledge of international rights and duties' because

> [t]he more clearly the people of a country understand their own international rights the less likely they are to take extreme … views of their rights and the less likely they are to be ready to fight for something to which they are not really entitled.[59]

Root's argument, grounded as it was in the desire to prevent war, does not map neatly on to ANZSIL's aims because Australia's Dominion status (and its failure to pass the Statute of Westminster) meant that it still did not have independent power to declare war and peace. However, the principle that Root proposed – that the more that people understand international law the more they may understand their own nation's rights and interests – was shared by ANZSIL's founders. ANZSIL sought both to develop a class of lawyers with international legal expertise in order that there were more people qualified to advise on Australia's interests; and to secure wider public support for those interests by educating members of the public in international law matters. These twin aims were captured by Sir William Cullen, Chancellor of the University of Sydney, whose speech at the first conference includes the following exhortation:

> There is no subject of law which I know, that is more profoundly interesting. It aims at reason and justice, to do that which is fair between nation and nation, and between the nationals of different nations …
>
> So I would exhort every teacher and student of law to make a point, in the interest not only of his own study of a fascinating subject, but in the interests of his own country and nation, not to neglect the study of international law.[60]

The extent to which the creation of ANZSIL was influenced by ASIL is difficult to discern from ANZSIL's papers, which do not refer to ASIL explicitly. It is clear

[57] ibid xviii.

[58] E Root, 'The Need of Popular Understanding of International Law' (1907) 1 *American Journal of International Law* 1, 2.

[59] ibid 2.

[60] *Proceedings*, above n 45, xxi–xxii.

that there was interaction between the members of each society and that, at the very least, they were aware of each other. There was, for example, an announcement in the 1934 edition of the *American Journal of International Law* about the establishment of ANZSIL, including a description of the first conference and an invitation to ASIL members to join.[61] In addition, the elite men of the ANZSIL were a well-travelled class who would have been aware of ASIL and the nearly 30 years of work that it had undertaken prior to the founding date of ANZSIL (1933).

In considering the relationships between ANZSIL and the ASIL, the figure of Thomas Fry is important. In the establishment phase of ANZSIL, it was Fry who signed the letters inviting the many men to take on roles within ANZSIL. As Honorary Secretary, it was Fry who received the correspondence about ANZSIL and it was to his Brisbane address that interested members were to send their applications for membership of ANZSIL. Fry is noted in the Introduction to the Proceedings as the organiser of the initial meetings concerning ANZSIL and Dixon described Fry as 'very largely responsible' for the formation of ANZSIL, noting that 'we all owe him a great debt'.[62] In an obituary written about Fry in the *University of Queensland Law Journal*, he was remembered as a man with 'boundless energy'.[63] Fry then seems to have brought his experiences with international law in Europe and the United States to Australia, and with his 'boundless energy', he convinced the major legal figures in Australia at the time to support a third society focused on international affairs, but this time specifically dedicated to international law.

IV. ISSUES OF INTEREST TO THE FIRST ANZSIL

What then were the international legal issues of concern to the members of ANZSIL? As the Society's objects indicate, ANZSIL's focus was on those matters of particular interest to Australia and New Zealand, which remained Dominions with ambiguous international legal personality. It is no surprise that the issues raised at the first conference and published in the Proceedings are issues that arise from the status of the Dominions in international law. From 1933 to 1935, the question of Australia's international legal personality could not be separated from any consideration of Australia's relationship with international law. The Proceedings include chapters by some of the men who were the most active participants in the first ANZSIL: W Harrison Moore, John Latham, HV Evatt, Kenneth Bailey, Archibald Charteris and Thomas Fry. The issues canvassed in the chapters include the positions of the Dominions in foreign affairs and as

[61] 'The Australian and New Zealand Society of International Law' (1934) 28 *American Journal of International Law* 138, 138–39.

[62] *Proceedings*, above n 45, xiv, xix.

[63] Harrison, above n 43, 86.

League of Nations Mandatory Powers, the status of consuls in Australia, the basis of international obligations within Australia under treaty and custom, and the treatment of prisoners of war.

All the chapters raise questions about the capacities of Australia to act in international affairs and the proper status of Australian actions under international law. Australia's capacities were bound up in the complexities raised by Dominion law and the actions of the other Dominions. In his chapter 'Separate Action by the British Dominions in Foreign Affairs', for example, Moore canvassed Australia's foreign relations via an examination of the complex machinations of Dominion relations with the Soviet Union, which manifested in conflicting positions between the Dominions.[64] This 'tangle', Moore wrote, was one 'in which the political has to be distinguished from the legal, and the legal may be on different planes, international or municipal'.[65] Kenneth Bailey made similar observations in his chapter on 'Australia and the International Labor Conventions' where he noted that the changing status of the Dominions had been 'so recent and so rapid' that even 'well-informed persons' were still expressing the view that the Dominions had no international legal personality.[66] Both chapters contain detailed doctrinal analysis of examples and materials that underscored the rapid shifts in Australia's international legal status, shifts which Moore cited as a 'special reason for the institution of a Society of International Law'.[67]

Also notable are the topics that were not included in the Proceedings nor raised at the conference itself. The papers delivered at the conference and in the Proceedings did not include any detailed analysis of the major international events of the time, in particular those relating to war and peace. There is no record of discussions at the ANZSIL Conference of the World Disarmament Conference or of the tensions within the League in relation to Japan and Germany. In one sense, this silence is a predictable response to Australia's status as a Dominion, where the Imperial Parliament retained the right to speak as 'one voice' for the Empire on war and peace. The general reluctance in relation to war and peace may also, however, have stemmed from the dominance of both the LNU and the AIIA in the field. Extensive consideration of the issues of war and peace within ANZSIL would not have been consistent with its stated aim of not encroaching on the areas occupied by the LNU and the AIIA.

ANZSIL's reluctance to discuss issues of war and peace or the League makes the chapter by John Latham in the Proceedings particularly intriguing. Titled 'Some Recent International Problems', Latham's chapter offers 'some observations upon certain new problems in international relations' arising specifically

[64] WH Moore, 'Separate Action by the British Dominions in Foreign Affairs' in The Australian and New Zealand Society of International Law, *Proceedings* (Carlton, Melbourne University Press, 1935).

[65] ibid 1.

[66] KH Bailey, 'Australia and the International Labour Conventions' in The Australian and New Zealand Society of International Law, *Proceedings* (Carlton, Melbourne University Press, 1935) 102.

[67] Moore, above n 64, 1.

from the international system created by the League.[68] I noted earlier how Latham was involved in all of the internationally oriented societies in Australia and he described himself in the chapter as an 'active supporter' of the League.[69] Sensitive then to ANZSIL's aims not to impinge on the work of the LNU or the AIIA, Latham's chapter charts a careful path between critique of the League's work 'from the point of view of general principle', while refraining from commenting on any particular situation.[70] Latham's chapter makes a number of arguments, including that economic sanctions are 'really an act of war'; an analysis of the complications in identifying an aggressor in a war; and his proposition that the abolition of the status of neutrality was inconsistent with the peaceful purposes of the League.[71] Latham's overall aim was to exhort support for a League of Nations founded, 'not upon technical rules, but upon a realistic view of international justice'.[72] In 1933, when Latham delivered this paper at the ANZSIL Conference, he was the Minister for External Affairs. By 1935, when the Proceedings were published, Latham had retired from politics and been appointed Chief Justice of the Australian High Court. Latham's audience, both at the conference and for the Proceedings, would also have been aware of Latham's credentials to speak about the League, including as a member of the Australian delegation to the Disarmament Conference.[73] Latham's status would have given a unique salience to the arguments in his chapter. The overall dispirited tone of the chapter and its inclusion in the Proceedings hints at the concerns that the members of ANZSIL might have shared, but that they could point to only obliquely in the formal records of the Society.

V. RECEPTION AND DEMISE

The creation of ANZSIL and occasion of its first conference were widely reported in the Australian press, with articles on these events included in newspapers in most of the Australian States.[74] These articles generally contained straightforward reporting of the purposes and membership of ANZSIL, with a small number also including descriptions of some of the papers presented

[68] JG Latham, 'Some Recent International Problems' in The Australian and New Zealand Society of International Law, *Proceedings* (Carlton, Melbourne University Press, 1935) 18.

[69] ibid 18.

[70] ibid.

[71] ibid 19–25. Quote from ibid 21.

[72] ibid 26.

[73] Macintyre, above n 10.

[74] See, eg, 'International Law: Society's First Conference' *Telegraph* (Brisbane, 12 August 1933) 11; 'International Law Australasian Conference. Mandatory Powers' *West Australian* (Perth, 22 August 1933) 7; 'Foreign Affairs: International Law Society: First Conference Opens' *Newcastle Morning Herald and Miners' Advocate* (New South Wales, 18 August 1933) 6; 'International Law: Conference in Sydney' *Sydney Morning Herald* (New South Wales, 16 August 1933) 12; 'International Law Conference at Sydney' *The Mercury* (Hobart, 15 July 1933) 3.

at the conference.[75] After they were published in 1935, the Proceedings also received attention from the Australian press, with reviews of the Proceedings again in most of the key daily newspapers.[76] The reviews were generally positive and many identified Australia's developing international status as a key factor underpinning the need for a society such as ANZSIL. *The Argus*, for example, wrote of the 'vastly increased importance which public international law has attained for the Governments and citizens of the Dominions', and the review in *The Advocate* noted how 'timely' the Proceedings were 'not only to lawyers, but to many thoughtful minds outside their ranks'.[77]

The ANZSIL Proceedings were also reviewed in international legal circles. Arnold McNair reviewed the volume in the *Journal of Comparative Legislation and International Law*, and there are reviews in the *Cambridge Law Journal* and a Canadian journal called *Pacific Affairs*, which point to the shared interests of Canadians with their Dominion counterparts.[78] All of the reviews welcomed the establishment of the Society and expressed excitement about future editions of the Proceedings. McNair, for example, wrote that the Proceedings deserved 'a very hearty welcome' and the review in the *Cambridge Law Journal* congratulated the Society 'on its first enterprise and on a valuable contribution to the special literature on International Law'.[79] McNair noted the commitment to educating the public about international law in his review, remarking approvingly that the Proceedings were 'evidence of the determination of a group of leading men in these two Dominions to ensure that their new international status ... shall be backed by an instructed public opinion'.[80] Charles Martin in the *Pacific Affairs* review also highlighted the public education aspects of the Proceedings, describing them as offering 'splendid instruction for the layman and the overseas internationalist, in the foreign affairs of the Antipodes as they embrace the field of law'.[81]

Despite this celebrated start and its ambitions, ANZSIL held only two conferences before disappearing from public records. The first conference, in

[75] See, eg, 'Labour Conventions: Australia's Position' *Sydney Morning Herald* (New South Wales, 21 August 1933) 10; 'Control of New Guinea: Australia's Authority: Mr Justice Evatt's Contention' *Telegraph* (Brisbane, 21 August 1933) 7; 'International Law Australasian Conference: Mandatory Powers' *West Australian* (Perth, 22 August 1933) 7.

[76] See, eg, 'Rights and Wrongs' *Telegraph* (Brisbane, 7 December 1935) 14; 'Our Foreign Relations' *West Australian* (Perth, 23 November 1935) 4; 'International Law' *Argus* (Melbourne, 9 November 1935) 7; 'International Law: Australian Problems' *Sydney Morning Herald* (New South Wales, 2 December 1935) 10.

[77] 'International Law' *The Argus* (Melbourne, 9 November 1935) 7; 'Australia and International Law' *The Advocate* (Melbourne, 16 January 1936) 3.

[78] AD McNair, 'Book Review: Australian and New Zealand Society of International Law' (1936) 18 *Journal of Comparative Legislation and International Law* 323, 323; BEK, 'Book Review: The Australian and New Zealand Society of International Law: Proceedings, Vol 1' (1938) 6(3) *Cambridge Law Journal* 484; CE Martin, 'Book Review: Proceedings of the Australian and New Zealand Society of International Law: Vol 1' (1936) 9 *Pacific Affairs* 621.

[79] McNair, above n 78, 323; BEK, above n 78, 484.

[80] McNair, above n 78, 323.

[81] Martin, above n 78, 622.

Sydney in August 1933, was the event from which the Proceedings and most of the records of ANZSIL's activities arise. The second conference was held in May 1938 at the University of Melbourne and attendees included Charteris, Latham and Dixon.[82] There appear to be no published proceedings from this meeting, though its occurrence was reported through newspaper reports of the speech delivered at the conference dinner by Sir Isaac Isaacs, former High Court Justice and recently retired Governor-General of Australia. May 1938 was a time of high tension in Europe[83] and Sir Isaac's message to ANZSIL was a sombre one. He railed in the speech against the 'casting aside' of 'some of the most important guiding principles inherent in international law'.[84] In Sir Isaac's view, the treaty and customary obligations not to resort to war, which were the 'foundation of international law', had been broken by some nations and 'unless the foundations could be restored the superstructure could not stand'.[85] In correspondence with his daughter Marjorie a few days after the conference, Sir Isaac described himself as having made a speech at the 'dinner of the International Law Society, when I had to tell them that there is at the present time no such thing as public international law'.[86]

While Sir Isaac might have been premature in proclaiming the demise of international law, his despairing speech did mark the final event of a Society that had been so enthusiastically established five years earlier. ANZSIL ended, it seems, through no formal process, but rather through a loss of momentum from its membership. When contemplating the end of ANZSIL, Thomas Fry again becomes important. If Fry was the driver of the first ANZSIL then he may also have been one of reasons that it did not continue. The same obituary that described Fry as having 'boundless energy' also described him as 'not always well-received' and as having 'trod on many toes, with the result that professional opinion in Queensland has done him less than justice'.[87] As integral as Fry was to drawing together the elite of the Australian legal profession to create the first ANZSIL, the drive that made him successful also seems to have generated a prickly side to his character. If this is so, it seems likely that Fry did not have the personality to keep those same elite men together on a long-term basis around a society for international law.

It is unfair to make the short life of ANZSIL the responsibility of a possibly difficult man, however. There were many other factors that would have made the continuation of an international law society difficult after 1938. Perhaps most obvious is the timing of its ending, with its second conference held only months before the start of the Second World War and at a time when, as Sir Isaac's speech

[82] 'League Ideals: Plea by Sir Isaac Isaacs: International Law' *The Age* (Melbourne, 30 May 1938) 10.

[83] See, eg, GL Weinberg, 'The May Crisis: 1938' (1957) 29 *Journal of Modern History* 213.

[84] 'League Ideals', above n 82.

[85] ibid.

[86] 'Letter Sir Isaac Isaacs to Marjorie' (2 June 1938, Box MS27555/1/411, National Library of Australia).

[87] Harrison, above n 43, 88.

indicates, international law was regarded as diminished, at best. Comparison with ASIL is instructive here too. In Benjamin Allen Coates' account of the establishment and success of ASIL, two things are central to ASIL's success.[88] First the energy and drive of James Brown Scott, who was singlehandedly responsible for putting together so much of the material in the first years of ASIL. Second, and perhaps more significantly, ASIL received significant funding from the Carnegie Endowment for International Peace, which enabled Scott to devote time to ASIL, to travel and to continue to produce ASIL publications. ANZSIL may have had the 'boundless energy' of Fry, but it did not have an endowment, and certainly not the kind of endowment that supported ASIL.

VI. CONCLUSION

Although the first ANZSIL did not achieve the long existence that its creators hoped for, its brief existence was an important one. The Proceedings are a valuable record of both the people engaged in international legal work in interwar Australia and of their thinking. In drawing on the ANZSIL Proceedings to write this chapter, I have used the Proceedings in exactly the way that the editors wanted people to. In the opening paragraph in the Introduction to the Proceedings, the editors state that they

> thought it may be useful to place on record, in this, the first volume of the Proceedings, a good deal of information concerning the Society itself, its inauguration and its initial activities …. [Allowing] readers [to form] a general picture of what this new Society is, and what it hopes to do.[89]

More fundamentally, the fact that an international law society was created in interwar Australia illustrates how important international law was seen to be, at least briefly, in the 1930s. The existence of the first ANZSIL takes on even more significance when compared with the modern ANZSIL, which was only established in 1992. The modern ANZSIL had been preceded by a group of scholars and government officials who met annually via events called the 'International Law Weekend', but these had only begun in the 1970s and the participants in these events remained relatively elite. It was not until the 'New World Order' of the 1990s that a completely public-facing international law society was again created in Australia. As the modern ANZSIL commemorated its 30 years of existence in 2022, it seems important to bring the first ANZSIL back into the story of international law in Australia and to acknowledge the contribution of the Proceedings as a record of a particular moment in Australian legal history.

[88] BA Coates, *Legalist Empire: International Law and American Foreign Relations in the Early Twentieth Century* (New York, Oxford University Press, 2016).

[89] *Proceedings*, above n 45, xiii.

Index

Abbott, Tony (Prime Minister), 119
Aboriginal peoples, treatment of, 239–40 (case law)
Aboriginals Ordinance (1918) (NT), 239
Abyssinia crisis, 35–9
advisory opinions (ICJ), Australia's reticence over, 177
Agreed Memorandum on the Commonwealth Secretariat (1965), 52
Albanese, Anthony (Prime Minister), 122
Albanese Government (2022–), 122–3, 124
American Society of International Law (ASIL), 302
  ANZSIL, influence on, 302–3
Amery, Leo (British politician), on Dominions, 56–7
Annex VII arbitration under 1982 Convention (*Southern Bluefin Tuna case*): Australia and New Zealand institute, 226–7
Arms Trade Treaty, Australia's contribution to, 120, 221
Asia-Pacific Economic Cooperation (APEC) (1989), 55
asylum seeker children:, 267–8
asylum seekers, differentiated by mode of arrival, 270
Attorney-General's Department (AGD) (the Department), 181
  international law, importance for, 183
  international law timeline and, (1900–2000), 206–9
  international trade law, involvement in, 196–7
  Law of the Sea and, 198–200
  maritime boundary delimitation issues and, 198–9
  payment for services of, 185
  pre-WWII, 182, 187
Australia:
  Arms Trade Treaty, contribution to, 120, 221
  compulsory conciliation, rejection of, 93–4
  East Timor, failure to respect obligations to, 85–6 (case law)
  East Timor, invasion of, 75–7
  East Timor's desire for self-determination, reaction to, 82–3
  geographical isolation of, effect of, 8
  international legal personality of, 295 –6
  League of Nations, membership of, 21–2, 39–40
  post-WWI, national aspects of, 44–5
  UK, relationship with (WWII), 99–101
Australia, the United Kingdom and the United States partnership (AUKUS) (2021), 42, 54
***Australia v France* (1973)**, 166–8
***Australia v Japan: New Zealand intervening* (2014)**, 168–9, 214, 226
Australian:
  conservative governments 1949–72, 105–7
  courts, prosecution for international crimes in, 244–5
  Government Solicitor (AGS), 185, 212
  immigration policies, 297
  Institute of International Affairs (AIIA), 297–8, 300
  League of Nations Union (LNU), 297, 298–9, 300
  legal status, establishment of, 47–8
  women's internationalism, 279
Australian and New Zealand Society of International Law (ANZSIL), 294–5, 299–300
  ASIL's influence on, 302–3
  inaugural meeting of, 300
  proceedings, publication of, 305–6
Australian colonialism, 60–2, 65
  capital punishment and, 64, 67
Australian nationalism, 48–49
Australian New Zealand and United States Security Treaty (ANZUS Treaty), 51, 218
Australian Secret Intelligence Service (ASIS), 91

Bailey, Sir Kenneth:
  career of, 190–2
  Secretary to AGD, as (1946–64), 186, 190
  Special Adviser, as (1969–72), 186

Balfour Declaration (1926), 47, 51, 295
Barwick, Sir Garfield (ICJ judge), 167
Bishop, Julie (Minister for Foreign Affairs), 121
Body, Alfred, 186, 187
Boserup, Ester:
Reid's support of, 286–7
'Women in Development', on, 286–7
Brennan, Gerard, 187–198
'British Commonwealth':
increased use of term, 45
Menzies on, 51
1940's development of, 50
British Empire (nineteenth century), concept of, 44
Bruce, SM:
Council of League of Nations, involvement with, 24–5
League of Nations, Australia's contribution to, on, 40
Bruce Report 1939, 25, 31, 40
***Buzzacott v Hill* (1999)**, 239

Cambodia peace plan (1992), 112
CANZUK, 42
capital punishment:
Papua New Guinea, in, 62–4
Carleton, Chris, 88, 89
Casey, Richard (Australian liaison officer), 23–4, 106
Centre for Strategic and International Studies (CSIS), 79–80
***Certain Phosphate Lands in Nauru* case:**, 169–70
***Chagos* case (2017)**, 177–8, 180
Charlesworth, Professor Hilary (ICJ Judge), 164–5
Chifley, Ben, 49, 50, 61, 277–8
child refugees' human rights norms, government ministers' views on, 265–6
children:
asylum seeker *see* asylum seeker children
detention, in, AHRC 2014 Inquiry, 260–1
Manus Island, going to, 261–2
protection of under international law, 255
refugee, protection of, 260
***Chile v Bolivia* (2002)**, 164–5
climate change:
Rudd's support, 118–19
states' obligations on, advisory opinions on, 178
Closer Economic Relations (CER) Agreement (1983), 55
Cobo Study (1983), 135, 136, 137
Collaery, Bernard (ASIS), 91, 92, 94, 95
Commission on the Limits of the Continental Shelf (CLCS), Australia's submission to, 222–3
'Committee of Thirteen', 36–7
Committee on the Elimination of Racial Discrimination (CERD), 115, 127
self-determination of Indigenous People, on, 146–7
Committee on the Status of Women (CSW), 279
Commonwealth, 42–3
decline in usefulness, 53–4
'New Commonwealth' (1950s and 1960s), 52
Commonwealth legal services, 2016 review, 212–13
***Commonwealth v Tasmania* (1983)**, 203
compulsory conciliation (UNCLOS, Article 298), 93–5
Australia's rejection of, 93–4
continental shelf:
exploitation of resources, 200
resources, Bailey's work on, 191–2
Convention Against Torture:
Australia's involvement in, 113
2002 Optional Protocol (OPCAT), Australia's accession to, 118, 121
Convention on Biodiversity Beyond National Jurisdiction (2023), Australia's contribution to, 222
Convention on Cluster Munitions, Australia's contribution to, 221
Convention on International Civil Aviation 1944, Article 84, 220
Convention on the Elimination of All Forms of Discrimination against Women (CEDAW), 115
1999 Optional Protocol to, Australia's accession to, 118
Convention on the Rights of the Child (CRC), 256, 259–60, 263, 267
***Cooperating for Peace* (Evans)**, 113
Council of League of Nations:
barriers to trade, consideration of by, 30–1
Bruce's involvement with, 24–5
Dominions' representation on, 22–3, 23–4
economic and financial matters, Australia's consideration of, 29–30

Council of the International Civil Aviation Organization (ICAO), 220
Crawford, James (ICJ Judge), 157, 163
cyber operations law, Australia's approach to, 224

Daes, Erica-Irene on Permanent Forum on Indigenous Issues, 150
Deakin, Alfred, Attorney-General, 188–9
Declaration on the Elimination of Discrimination against Women (DEDAW), 281
Declaration on the Rights of Indigenous Peoples:
  Article 42, General Comment on, 150
  General Assembly's endorsement of, 143–4
Declaration Recognizing as Compulsory the Jurisdiction of the International Court of Justice (2002 Declaration), 159–60
  optional clause declaration by Australia, 160–1
'Declarations Recognizing the Jurisdiction of the Court as Compulsory' (UK) (2017), expansion of, 161
decolonisation and Portugal, 77–8
Deer, Kenneth, on Permanent Forum on Indigenous Issues, 149–50
defamation, 241–3
  Roberts-Smith's action for, 241–3 (case law)
Department of Defence, 183
Department of External Affairs, post-WWII, 183
Department of Foreign Affairs (DFA), 285, 286, 288, 290
Department of Foreign Affairs and Trade (DFAT) (Australia), 83, 89–90, 160, 212
development, definition of (Reid), 285–6
Dixon, Chief Justice Owen, 52
'domestic jurisdiction' provision, Evatt's work on, 104–5
domestic law:
  international law incorporated into, 204–5
Dominion nationalism, 48–9
Dominions:
  Council of League of Nations, representation on, 22–3, 23–4
Dumbarton Oaks draft, 101

East Timor, 78
  conflict, Australia's contribution to peace-keeping force (1999 and 2006), 115–16
  independence of, 80
  Indonesia and, 75–7, 79–80, 80, 83–4
  petroleum exploration permits close to, 78–9
  self-determination and, 81–3
  United Nations Decolonisation Committee and, 81–2
***East Timor (Portugal v Australia)* (1995),** 85–91, 171–2, 195
Economic and Social Council (ECOSOC), 105, 106
  Indigenous Populations, study of discrimination against (1971), 134
Evans, Gareth, Minister for Foreign Affairs, 111–13
Evatt, Herbert Vere, 46
  career and appointments of, 105
  'domestic jurisdiction provision', on, 104–5
  General Assembly and Security Council, on, 277
  General Assembly powers, work on, 103–4
  multilateralist policy of, 277–8
  UN Conference on International Organisations (1945), work on, 101–2
  veto power, work on, 102–3
  White Australia policy, protection of, 104
Expert Mechanism of the Rights of Indigenous People (EMRIP), 151
  recommendations, acceptance of, 153
Expert Panel to Deliver Asylum Policy Findings (Expert Panel) (Aristotle) (2012), 266–7
Extradition Act 1988, 237
extradition disputes, 236–8

Five Eyes intelligence arrangements, 54
'Forgotten Children, The' (AHRC inquiry and report), 263
Fraser Coalition Government (1975–83):
  South Africa and Southern Rhodesia, work on, 109–10
free-trade agreements, Australia's negotiation of, 222
French nuclear tests (1973), 166–8 (case law)
Fry, Thomas, 307

Garran, Sir Robert, 20, 185, 187, 188–90, 205
General Assembly:
Declaration on the Rights of Indigenous Peoples, endorsement of, 143–4
Evatt on, 103–4, 277
genocide, 239–40 (case law)
Australian law, not part of, 204 (case law)
Gillard, Julia (Australian Prime Minister), 119
Great Barrier Reef Marine Park Act 1975, 217

Hansan, Pauline, 114
Harders, Sir Clarrie, 186
Harries Committee Report into Australian relationships with the Third World (1979), 290–1
Hasluck, Paul, 66
Hawke Labor Government (1983–91), 110–13
Howard Government (1996–2007), 113–16
Hughes, William, Prime Minister, 44–5
Article 16 (League of Nations Covenant), opinion on, 21
League of Nations, on, 17–18, 20
mandated territories, critique of, 21
Paris Peace Conference aims, 19
Woodrow Wilson's proposals, 19–20
human rights, 201–2
Australia's participation in, 192–4
Commonwealth legislation on, 203
treaty bodies, 114–15
Whitlam's views on, 281–2
women's rights and, 283
Human Rights Bill 1973, 201–2
Human Rights Council, establishment of, 143
humanitarian intervention, 215–16

Immigration (Guardianship of Children) Act 1946 Section 6, 265
Indigenous Peoples:
definition of, 144
equality and self-determination, development of, 130
identifying characteristics of, 136
right to self-determination, 146
states at international level, engagement with, 133
UN, participation in, 154
UN Voluntary Fund for, 136–7
Working Group, access to, 136
Indonesia:
Australia's support for, 83–4
invasion of East Timor (1975), 83–4
international:
crimes, prosecution of in Australian Courts, 244–5
criminal justice, Australia's judicial contribution to, 246–50
dispute settlement, Australia's involvement in, 225–7
International Convention for the Settlement of Investment Disputes (1975), Australian ratification of, 196–7
International Convention on the Elimination of All Forms of Racial Discrimination, 278
International Court of Justice (ICJ):
advisory jurisdiction, Australian support of, 175–6
Australian judges, appointment of, 161–5
International Covenant on Civil and Political Rights (ICCPR), Australia's participation in, 113, 194
ratification of, 202
International Covenant on Economic, Social and Cultural Rights (ICESCR), 133, 194
ratification of, 202
International Criminal Court Act 2002, 230, 240
International Force – East Timor (INTERFET), 88
International Labour Organization (ILO), 145
international law:
domestic law, incorporation into, 204–5
domestic realm, in, 269–70
government advisors' awareness of, 217–18
protection of children under, 255
public awareness of, 213–14
International Law Commission (ILC), Crawford's guidance of, 163
international legal advisors:
engagement with foreign counterparts, 224–5
public debate, participation in, 216–17
International Maritime Organization (IMO), the Department's involvement in, 199–200
International Tribunal for the Law of the Sea (ITLOS), 225
International Women's Year (IWY) (1975):
equality and, 283
justification of activities, 282

NGO Tribune, Australian representation at, 288
Reid's summary of, 273–4
Iraq, use of force in, 220
Isaacs, Sir Isaac, speech on international law (1938), 307

Joint Standing Committee on Treaties (JSCOT), 160, 184

Keating Labor Government (1991–96), 110–13
Knowles, Sir George, 185, 190
***Kruger v Commonwealth* (1997),** 239–40
Kyoto Protocol, Australia's ratification of, 117

Latham, John (LNU president), 48, 295, 298, 299, 300–4
League of Nations, support for, 305
Lauterpacht, Sir Elihu, 173, 176
Law of the Sea, 200–1
Bailey's work on, 191–2
Brennan on, 187
Conference 1958, 192
Convention (UNCLOS), 89–90
International Tribunal for (ITLOS), 225
AGD involvement with, 198–200
League of Nations, 26, 131
Australia's membership of, 21–2, 39–40
Australia's participation in, Bruce's and McDougall's contributions to, 40
committees of, 26
First Nations Americans and, 131
Hughes on, 20, 17–18
Mandates, 60
Legal Consequences of the Separation of the Chagos Archipelago from Mauritius in 1965 (Chagos), 177
Legal Services Directions 2017 (LSD) (2017), 212
Liberal-National Coalition (2013), 119
***Libya–Malta* case (1985),** 88–9
Locarno Pact:
breach of, 33–5
London Declaration (1949), 50
Lowe, Vaughan, 88, 89

Mahony, Frank (Deputy Secretary 1977), Geneva Convention Protocols, work on, 187
Malaysian Airlines flight MH17, 120
Australian governments' response to, 219
trilateral consultations with Russia, 219–20
Malezer, Les, biographical and career details, 125–9
Manus Island, 261–2
maritime boundary delimitation issues, the Department's involvement with, 198–9
Maritime Boundary Treaty 2019, 94
Maritime Legislation Amendment Act 1994, 201
Maritime Powers Act 2013, 217, 218
McDougall, Frank:
League of Nations, contribution to, 40
Menzies, Robert, 47, 48, 50, 105, 296, 301
British Commonwealth, on, 51
Migration Amendment (Regional Processing Arrangements) Bill (2015), 268
***Minister for Home Affairs v Zentai* (2012),** 237–8, 249–50
***Minister for Immigration and Ethnic Affairs v Teoh* (1995),** 204–5
Moore, Professor Harrison, 24, 190, 303, 304
Morgan, Lucy (AHRC), interview with, 261, 262, 268, 269
Morrison, Scott (Australian Prime Minister), 122
multilateralism, views on, 122

National Congress of Australia's First Peoples (2010–16), 128
national governments, Indigenous Peoples' relationship with, 133
Native Title Amendment Act 1998, 239
Nauru and New Guinea, Australian rule over, 296
***Nauru Phosphates* case (1991–2),** 195
New International Economic Order (NIEO), 282
***New South Wales v Commonwealth* (1975),** 200
***New Zealand v France* (1995),** 167–8
***Nuclear Tests* case (1973),** 194–5
nuclear weapons, advisory opinions on, Australia's participation in, 177
***Nulyarimma v Thompson* (1999),** 239–40, 246–7

Office of International Law (OIL, the Office), 182, 213
abolition of proposed, 185
creation of (1989), 184
Officer, Keith, 24, 27, 28, 29, 30
optional clause declaration, 159
Australia (2002), by, 160–1

Papua New Guinea (PNG), capital punishment and clemency in, 62–4
Paris Peace Conference, Prime Minister Hughes' aims, 19
Parker v The Queen (1963), 52
Permanent Court of International Justice (PCIJ), 159
Permanent Forum on Indigenous Issues (2002), 129, 148–50
  Daes, Deer and Robinson on, 149–50
  members of, 148–9
petroleum exploration permits, close to Portuguese Timor, 78–9
Petroleum (Submerged Lands) Act 1967, 200
Philip Morris Asia Arbitration (2015), 228
Polyukhovich v Commonwealth (1991), 240–1, 246–7
'popular consultation' (Timorese referendum), 87–8
Portugal:
  decolonisation and, 77–8, 79

Quinlan, Gary (Australian ambassador), 119–20

R v Aro of Rupamanda (1957), 68–70
R v Gaumbu (1957), 68–70
R v Tang (2008), 243–4, 247–8
Refugee Convention (1951), Article 1F (a), 233–5
Reid, Elizabeth, 275–6, 279–80
  Boserup, supports, 286–7
  definition of 'development', 285–6
  IWY (1975), on, 273–4
  World Conference of the IWY, on, 284–5
responsibility to protect (R2P), 215–16
Revolutionary Front for an Independent East Timor (FRETILIN), 80–1, 82
Roberts-Smith v Fairfax Media Publications Pty Ltd (no 41)(2023), 242–3, 248–9
royal prerogative of mercy, 63–4
Rudd, Kevin:
  climate change, support for, 118–19
  Kyoto Protocol, ratification of, 117
  multilateralism, support for, 117
Rudd Government 2007–13, 117–19

Scott, James Brown (ASIL), 308
seabed boundary delimitation, 79, 84, 89, 95
Seabed Treaty 1972, 78–9
Seas and Submerged Lands Act 1973, 200, 201
Security Council:
  Australia elected to (1985–6), 111
  Australia's bid for seat on (2013–14), 117–18
  Evatt on, 277
Security Treaty between Australia, New Zealand and the United States of America (ANZUS), 51, 218, 278
self-determination:
  Australian government policy on, 87–8
  East Timor and, 81–2, 171–2
  Indigenous Peoples', 141–2, 146
  Portugal on, ICJ verdict on, 86–7
self-government in Australia, 46
settler-colonial state, Australia as, 7–8
slavery, offence of, in Australia and international law, 243–4 (case law)
Solicitors-General:
  appointees, of, 186–1
Special Rapporteur on the Rights of Indigenous People, 147–8
Spender, Sir Percy, 106, 107, 162–3
SRYYY v Minister for Immigration and Multicultural and Indigenous Affairs (2005), 235–6, 247
Statute of Westminster 1931, 47–8
Street, Jessie, 279, 283
Sub-Commission on the Prevention of Discrimination and Protection of Minorities (the Sub-Commission), 134–5
Suez Crisis (1956), effect on Australia, 51–2
Suharto, President, 79–81, 87, 183

Taylor v Attorney-General (2019), 245, 248
Telefomin killings:
  background to, 64
  clemency for, 64–7
  official reaction to, 64–5
  UNTC, after, 65
The Gambia v Myanmar (2022), 164
Third United Nations Conference on the Law of the Sea, biannual sessions of (1974–82), 198
Timor Gap, 79
Timor Gap Treaty 1989, 84–5, 88, 92
Timor-Leste, *see* 'East Timor'
Timor-Leste v Australia (2016), 92
Timor-Leste v Australia (*Documents* case) (2014), 172–4, 226
Timor Sea Treaty (2002), 90, 92
Tjan, Harry, 79–80
Treaty on Certain Maritime Arrangements in the Timor Sea (CMATS), 91

Treaty on the Prohibition of Nuclear Weapons, Australia's attitude to, 123
Triggs, Gillian, interview with, 262–3

United Kingdom (UK):
  Commonwealth reservation (2004), 159, 161
  relationship with Australia (WWII), 99–101
United Nations (UN):
  Australia and, 107, 112–13, 114–15
  Fraser Coalition Government downgrades, 109, 110
  Organisation, Australia and New Zealand on (1944), 101
  Whitlam's views on, 281–2, 283
United Nations Association of Australia (UNAA), 120
United Nations Conference on Disarmament, 110–11
United Nations Conference on Indigenous Peoples (WCIP) (2014), 151–3
United Nations Conference on International Organisations (1945), Evatt's work on, 101–2
United Nations Declaration on the Rights of Indigenous Peoples, Australia's vote against, 115
United Nations Decolonisation Committee, 278
  East Timor and, 81–2
United Nations Member States not supportive of indigenous peoples' rights over land, 138
United Nations Security Council advisory opinions, Australia's rejection of, 176–7
United Nations Transitional Administration of East Timor (UNTAET) 1999, 88
United Nations Transitional Authority in Cambodia (UNTAC), 112
United Nations Trustee Council (UNTC), 59, 62
  petitioning, 71–3
  territories replace League of Nations Mandates, 60
United Nations Voluntary Fund for Indigenous Peoples (1985), 136–7
United States anti-trust law, AGD's activity in territorial application of, 197
Ure v Commonwealth (2016), 217, 227
Usamando, execution of (1954), 67–8

Vondel case (1902), 188

war crimes:
  committed outside Australia by Australian citizens, 240–1 (case law)
  decision-makers' definitions of, 234–5
  extradition for, 237
War Crimes Act 1945, 232
  constitutional challenge to, 240–1
Western Sahara, advisory opinion on legal status, 176–7
Whaling in the Antarctic case (2014), 168–9, 214, 226
White, Oliver (UNICEF Australia officer), 255
  children, on, 264, 266
White Australia policy, 114
  Evatt protects, 104
Whitlam, E Gough, 107–8
  foreign policy of, 278–9
  human rights, views on, 281–2, 283
  international affairs, effect on, 276–7
  United Nations, views on, 281–2, 283
Whitlam, HFE, 193
Whitlam Labor Government 1972–5, 107–9
  principal policy changes under, 108–9
women:
  political rights of, conventions on, 281
  rights of and human rights, 283
  'Women in Development', Reid on, 286–7
Wong, Penny (Foreign Minister), 122–3, 124
Working Group of the Commission on the Draft Declaration on the Rights of Indigenous People (1995), 140–1
  Chairman's Text, 142
Working Group on Indigenous Populations (WGIP, the Working Group) (1982), 136, 137–40
  aims of, 137
World Conference for the International Women's Year, Reid on, 284–5
World Council of Indigenous People (WCIP), 132–4, 152–3
World Heritage Convention (1975), 203

www.ingramcontent.com/pod-product-compliance
Ingram Content Group UK Ltd.
Pitfield, Milton Keynes, MK11 3LW, UK
UKHW020239290926
15470UKWH00002B/627